T0289976

PRAISE FOR
MANAGING FUZZY PROJECTS IN 3D

This excellent book provides a road map for implementing strategy. Full of examples and practical insights, it is essential reading for anyone dealing with complex problems, multiple stakeholders, and the pressures of imminent deadlines.

—Anita McGahan, PhD (Harvard)
former President of the Academy of Management;
current Professor of Strategic Management at the
Rotman School of Management and at
Munk School of Global Affairs & Public Policy

Lavagnon Ika and Jan Saint-Macary provide in their new book a fresh look at projects. By adopting a multidisciplinary approach, they address three separate interrelated approaches to a project's complexity: the triple constraint of time, cost, and quality; the multiple expectations of diverse stakeholders and parties associated; and the psychological intangible needs of the different groups involved inside and outside the project. Indeed, the multidisciplinary approach is a timely matter, whose time has come, and indeed, has long been missing. I welcome the introduction of this book to the market, and highly recommend it.

—Aaron J. Shenhar, PhD
coauthor of the first Harvard Business School bestseller
on project management *Reinventing Project Management*
and Professor of Projects, Innovation, and Leadership

In pursuit of useful answers to tough policy questions, this book explores sundry ways of achieving simplicity on the other side of complexity. It belongs on the shelf of all project thinkers and practitioners.

—Robert Picciotto
former Vice President Corporate Planning and Budgeting,
World Bank

An innovative and much needed systematic approach to assessing the cultural dimension of international development organizations in light of achieving the Sustainable Development Goals!

—Marie-Hélène Adrien, PhD
Senior Consultant in Evaluation, Universalia Management Group

An insightful book to help you think through and manage people and political dimensions throughout the life of complex projects.

—Reynold Douyon
IT Project Manager and Consultant

In *Managing Fuzzy Projects in 3D*, we shift from the traditional view that projects are rational endeavors guided by equations, formulas, and mathematical methods to a more holistic view that includes psychological, political, and human dimensions. This humanistic view brings new approaches to how we work and lead projects. Professors Lavagnon Ika and Jan Saint-Macary highlight in their work the aspects of integration, adaptive approach, and ability to react as the critical competencies of those leading and working on projects. This understanding and behavior ensures that benefits are obtained for the organization, internal stakeholders, and, at the end, society in general.

—Ricardo Viana Vargas, PhD
former President, Project Management Institute; former Director of Infrastructure and Project Management, United Nations

MANAGING FUZZY PROJECTS IN 3D

MANAGING FUZZY PROJECTS IN 3D

A Proven, Multi-Faceted Blueprint for Overseeing Complex Projects

LAVAGNON IKA
JAN SAINT-MACARY

New York Chicago San Francisco Athens London Madrid
Mexico City Milan New Delhi Singapore Sydney Toronto

1 2 3 4 5 6 7 8 9 LCR 27 26 25 24 23

ISBN 978-1-264-27834-3
MHID 1-264-27834-9

e-ISBN 978-1-264-27835-0
e-MHID 1-264-27835-7

Library of Congress Cataloging-in-Publication Data

Names: Ika, Lavagnon A., author. | Saint-Macary, Jan, author.
Title: Managing fuzzy projects in 3D : a proven, multi-faceted blueprint for overseeing complex projects / Lavagnon A. Ika and Jan Saint-Macary.
Description: New York : McGraw Hill Education, [2023] | Includes bibliographical references and index.
Identifiers: LCCN 2022034702 (print) | LCCN 2022034703 (ebook) | ISBN 9781264278343 (hardback) | ISBN 9781264278350 (ebook)
Subjects: LCSH: Project management.
Classification: LCC HD69.P75 .I45245 2023 (print) | LCC HD69.P75 (ebook) | DDC 658.4/04—dc23/eng/20220721
LC record available at https://lccn.loc.gov/2022034702
LC ebook record available at https://lccn.loc.gov/2022034703

CONTENTS

ACKNOWLEDGMENTS

This book has been a voyage of discovery in the complex world of projects and project management. It could not have been done without the support of many people, especially as it spanned over a decade.

It is grounded in the research I have done over the last 20 years. But, research is rarely a solo adventure. I am indebted to my coauthors: Jeff Pinto, Peter Love, Jonas Söderlund, Damian Hodgson, Graham Winch, Lauchlan Munro, Simon Feeny, Jack Meredith, and Ofer Zwikael, to name but a few.

I was inspired by the work of great scholars such as Albert Hirschman, Gerd Gigerenzer, Peter Morris, Aaron Shenhar, Rodney Turner, Ralf Müller, Michael Porter, Henry Mintzberg, Ann Langley, Daniel Kahneman, Bent Flyvbjerg, Terry Williams, and Andy Davies. Other colleagues were inspiring, as role models who played a key role in my growing as a project management researcher, notably in the early years in my career. Sincere thanks to Mario Bourgault, Christophe Bredillet, Martina Huemann, and Janice Thomas.

The accidental project management researcher I have become will forever be grateful to the project management community and certainly to numerous colleagues whose names cannot be mentioned here for lack of space. They know who they are! Indeed, the discipline of project management has over the years opened plenty of opportunities for me and this book is no exception.

I also thank my teachers in Benin, where I was born and raised, for planting in me the seeds of curiosity and excellence. The Telfer School of Management at the University of Ottawa offered me a supportive environment. As this book extends over 10 years, it started at the Université du Québec, where I crossed the paths of professors such as Sébastien Azondékon, who steered me toward a master's in project management, Jacques Bernard Gauthier and Pierre Cossette, who helped solidify my methodological background, and my coauthor and friend Jan Saint-Macary. Not to mention Amadou Diallo and Denis Thuillier, who generously supervised my PhD. The thousands of students who have crossed my roads and challenged my teaching over the years have contributed to the clarity of the ideas in this book. A special thanks to those with whom I coauthored papers such as Vasyl Lytvynov, Jennifer Donnelly, Pascal Kacou, and Alassane Bandé.

Many thanks to the dozens of interviewees and the hundreds of practitioners who have contributed to my research by responding to surveys or sharing important project documents on case studies.

I am indebted to the Telfer School of Management who has funded the Major Projects Observatory and to SSHRC and FQRSC who have funded my research over the years.

This book has been deliberately written for practitioners. I would like to thank Jan for pushing me gently but assuredly to render my insights for project management practice down-to-earth and accessible to everybody. I believe that theory should meet practice and rigor should meet relevance to help solve some of the world-scale challenges through projects.

Jan and I are indebted to Judith Newlin at McGraw Hill and the whole McGraw Hill team who provided top-notch support even when things were not as quick as promised on our front.

Finally, I will ever be grateful to the star of my life, my beloved Étoile (literally "Star" in English) for her unconditional love. Without her friendship and support throughout the last 25 years, this book would not have been completed.

Thanks to my lovely kids, Ulysse and Mélyne—two of my most successful projects; my belated dad, Séverin, who always believed in education and taught me the love of books; and my beloved mum, Joséphine, who has always been present for me. Not to mention all my brothers and sisters whose love fills me with joy.

Lavagnon Ika

Like in any fuzzy project, the roots of this book are many, and elusive even to its authors. Though they were just "mom and dad" to me, my father, a civil engineer, worked on projects, and my mother, a teacher and principal, managed a small school. I am indebted to them for planting the seeds of the main idea in this book, namely the importance of the human factor in all organized endeavors.

I learned a lot from Pierre Brunet, teacher and guide throughout my doctoral studies; from Henry Mintzberg who was always frank and generous; and from hundreds of graduate students I taught or supervised, and whose varied experiences and viewpoints enriched my own. Thanks also to my university colleagues (and nonetheless friends) from varied disciplines, and to Lavagnon Ika, friend, colleague, and coauthor with whom I exchanged ideas and gained novel insights.

On walks of 10,000 steps or more, I benefited greatly from my discussions with Eddy Cavé, a writer of many books, and Ralph Denizé, a project manager on the international scene. Their support and our weekly Zoom discussions with a larger group of friends kept me motivated and writing throughout an endless COVID-19 winter. Our heated exchanges made me see things from a variety of angles, in 3D and more. Together, we discussed (and solved) many world problems, at least on paper. I owe a special thanks to Colleen Cooney, who read the many iterations of this book and gave generously of her time and talent, often with short deadlines. Even though all these people, and many others, enabled me to bring this book to fruition, they are not responsible for its content.

On a strictly personal note, I would like to thank Rebecca, my wife, my best friend, and manager in her own right, who helped me clarify my thinking from start to finish. I dedicate my efforts to our children, Kiana and Tasha, enlightened young citizens who should have a say in the projects, big and small, that are shaping their world.

Jan Saint-Macary

FOREWORD

Having significant experience, over the years, as a corporate consultant and trainer (in addition to my university position), I have consistently found a disturbing trend toward reductionism when it comes to working with organizations and proposing "simple" solutions to complicated problems. We all see examples of this same phenomenon, simply by scrolling through internet sites. "Seven tips for managing this," "Conflict resolution made easy," "Five ways to know if you are getting the most from that. . . ." The list of promised solutions goes on and on. The problem, of course, is that these elegant solutions rarely—if ever—provide the value promised at the outset. Reducing challenging problems to a series of simplistic bromides or programmatic steps sounds good, in theory, but it invariably puts the burden right back on the frustrated manager, who, after reading these seemingly intuitive articles is bound to come away with a mistaken impression that if everything is so simple, why are they still not "getting it"?

Real projects are messy, involve multiple pressure points, and require project managers to listen to, acknowledge, and balance competing sets of demands and expectations from numerous stakeholders, all while keeping the project on track and maintaining positive momentum. Finding the way forward while pursuing value for the organization puts project managers in a challenging and highly visible position. In short, there is nowhere to hide bad results or miscues, no placating disgruntled customers or increasingly intrusive senior managers loudly wondering how the project is going. In this situation, precisely what project managers do *not* need is another set of simple "how-to" advisories. They need real answers to real questions that are posing immediate or long-term threats. "Simple" is not the solution; "complexity" is what they seek. Not complexity in the form of unnecessary complications, confusing jargon, and "prof-speak," or abstract theorizing, but a complexity that pulls us away from seductively easy solutions to difficult problems. They need a complexity that identifies the challenges projects pose in real life, and one that offers thorough solutions. In short, the "fuzziness" that defines so many modern projects can only be addressed by recognizing its challenges and addressing them head-on.

Project-based work occupies a unique setting within organizations, as this book points out. Project managers sit at the junction of strategic management activities, concerned with leading teams through turbulent, external challenges to identify and gain commercial success, global leadership, or other important benefits that the firm values. At the same time, projects directly affect the internal activities of organizations, proposed and managed to improve operations, reduce inefficiencies, and give the firm a competitive advantage over its rivals. In modern organizations, no idea is too big and no challenge is too difficult to conquer. Consider, for example, the current efforts by Meta Corporation to develop "metaverse" technology, offering a virtual reality internet. Initially budgeted at US$10 billion, Meta's commitment to the ultimate in disruptive technology demonstrates a clear example of massive, complex project development to create and dominate a new market in which technological "reality" is being realized and reshaped on a recurring weekly basis. Alternatively, American automakers General Motors and Ford are spending billions on new tooling and manufacturing processes to support their transition to e-vehicles, using project management for car and component design and production. Projects like Operation Warp Speed, to rapidly develop vaccines for global pandemics like COVID-19, or initiatives to reduce emissions to net-zero compliance are other examples of the heights that can be reached through projects.

The promise of successful projects lies in direct proportion to the challenges they offer. Simple, "neat" projects may have more standard solutions and means for managing them because they are more narrowly defined, or perhaps only intended to be developed internally, with specific goals and simple expectations. But what happens when organizations aim at greater things? Big dreams require big, messy (or "fuzzy") projects to find solutions when the opportunities themselves are difficult to clearly name. In my example, US$10 billion invested in something as nebulous and evolving as a new "metaverse" suggests that funding this project is just the start; goals and development parameters are bound to be highly fluid and shaped as the project progresses, as one breakthrough seeds new projects or one blind alley cancels others. The challenges we expect today will be largely unpredictable within a year. Key stakeholders will also come and go. Great things may come from great ventures, but the end stage is rarely in sight at the beginning of the journey. Our desire to manage fuzzy projects can result in much, but it will come at a cost of reorienting the way we think about project management at its most basic level.

I was particularly taken with the "constructive complexity" offered in this book. The goal here is not to be either too simplified in analyzing modern project management, nor to confuse the reader by creating a dense, jargon-packed analysis that merely confuses. Rather, Ika and Saint-Macary find that critical middle ground of offering a clear-eyed view of the practice of modern project management, while bringing to bear decades of useful scholarship and practical advice. As a result, the book blends current, state-of-the-art theory with real-world practice, not talking down to its reader but also not opting for easy solutions or unhelpful reductionism. Complex projects require a complex treatment, but that never has to come at the cost of clarity.

There can be no "one-size-fits-all" approach to managing projects because, as Drs. Ika and Saint-Macary point out, projects are not just sets of activities aimed to accomplish a unique goal, they are—themselves—uniquely different from each other and therefore, require practitioners managing them and scholars studying them to acknowledge this inherent "fuzziness." One of the real advantages of this book is the blending of rational, psychosocial, and political perspectives. Rational project management involves the steps needed to run a project, the challenges of organizing, scheduling, and controlling a project from start to finish. While it may make a number of logical assumptions, rational approaches are how project management is taught in school or through corporate training. It provides the necessary skills to set a project up and oversee its development. But, of course, rational approaches are never enough in themselves. They are seductive in letting us think that they offer an objective, unsentimental method for running projects; beliefs that are not only untrue, but seriously damaging for the likelihood of project success. In fact, it is only when we blend (as this book does) rational approaches with both psychosocial (human behavior) and political (power, influence, and hierarchy) that we can get the full picture. As I mentioned, this is *constructive complexity*; it provides the three-dimensional view that project managers desperately need to succeed. Managing just one or even two of these dimensions will simply offer a flat, abraded understanding of project challenges. It is only when all three dimensions come fully into view that we can hope for the "clarity" to be found in fuzzy projects.

Ika and Saint-Macary bring together their woven threads of theory and practice by introducing perhaps their most useful feature: a toolbox for addressing "fuzzy" projects, including critical questions to ask at the outset, methods for reorienting and offering midcourse reality checks on project progress, and a cautionary treatment of the embedded biases that each of us brings to decision-making and the manner with which we approach complex problems. Their ideas are amply illustrated through numerous current (and even ancient!) examples of project successes and failures, and the flawed decision-making that either doomed them from the outset or contributed to a resulting "death spiral" during development. They introduce the adaptive toolbox for decision-making under uncertainty by making use of carefully constructed heuristics, intuition, and rules of thumb, and all with the goal of fighting complexity; not through ever more complicated thought processes, but through finding the practical simplicity that the former chief economist of the Bank of England, Andrew Haldane, argued is key to addressing modern uncertainties. Ika and Saint-Macary's adaptive toolbox is a wonderful example of them practicing what they preach—creating a model for practitioners of pragmatic and profound simplicity as a response to the fuzziness of modern complexity in projects.

This book, *Managing Fuzzy Projects in 3D,* is among the first to combine a unique (and uniquely satisfying) set of features. Using a fictional protagonist (Nancy Smart) and facing a series of challenges in managing a fuzzy project, we are taken through a variety of critical decisions and key players who can impact her project's performance. Understanding the project *mandate,* we first become aware of the specific objectives of her project. Then, we learn about her interactions with project *principals,* the clients or sponsors who authorized the project at the outset. Finally, Nancy is confronted with a variety of challenges related to *agents,* project team members responsible for implementing the project. What becomes immediately clear is that successful projects may all begin with a clear mandate, but they don't end there. Through the combinations of challenges (rational, psychosocial, and political) and the need to engage with key steps and players (mandate, principals, and agents), it quickly becomes clear just how complicated successful project management is. Put another way, I defy anyone to read this book and then willingly return to simplistic, reductionist approaches to managing projects. Complexity doesn't need to be complicated; it just needs to be authentic. A clear, scholarly authenticity rings out clearly throughout this book.

Professors Lavagnon Ika and Jan Saint-Macary bring years of work experience as well as top-notch scholarly credentials to this book. Grounded by their own years of industry involvement in multinational settings, they offer a book with the broadest possible application and have found the "sweet spot" when it comes to taking the current state of theory and practice in projects and combining them with useful insights that are immediately recognizable (and usable) for professionals. The book is seeded from cover to cover with stories, illustrations, and cautionary tales of projects and project managers—both successful and unsuccessful. Ika and Saint-Macary are superb storytellers and also embody the current generation of project management scholars who have taken the developments from earlier decades of research and practice in project management and learned not only the important lessons, but also the critical additional questions. The strength of this book is its blending of classical and current scholarship on project management within the modern context of where projects are now—that is, what the modern corporation faces in bringing projects to successful conclusion. Not content to leave us with a theoretical treatment, Ika and Saint-Macary conclude these chapters with a series of practical lessons or tips for practice. Project managers can come away from this book with a head full of ideas and a pocketful of practical guidance for getting things done. I began reading *Managing Fuzzy Projects in 3D* with professional interest. I soon found myself reading it with a quickened sense of enthusiasm. The combination of deep scholarship, practical wisdom, and clear writing style is captivating and makes this book such a valuable addition to our discipline.

Jeffrey K. Pinto, PhD
Samuel A. and Elizabeth Lee Black Chair in Management of Technology
Penn State University

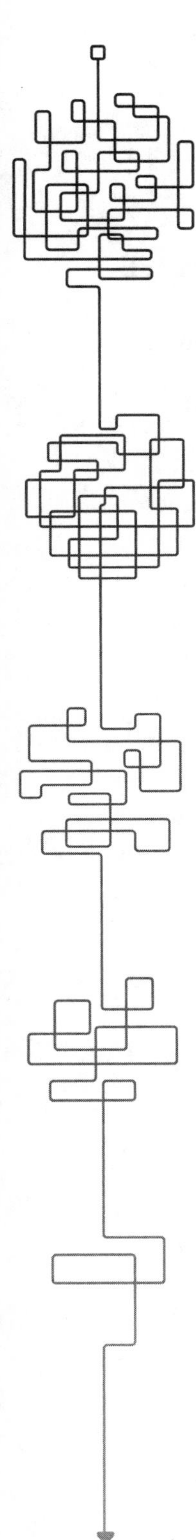

CHAPTER 1

INTRODUCTION (WHY THIS BOOK)

Nothing is permanent, except change.
—Heraclitus

You are a newly appointed project manager, and your responsibility is to execute a project methodically, within the time, cost, and quality constraints specified in your mandate. Your task will be complex, but your mandate will keep you focused. If only it were that simple!

Every project starts with an idea that turns into a commitment to move forward and get something done. But since each project is unique by definition, some are more challenging to implement than others. Traditional "neat" projects have goals that are clear-cut, measurable, and stable. But, some projects may also have elusive goals or stakeholders with differing expectations. We refer to the latter as "fuzzy projects." While you may know initially the formal clients, unknown yet influential individuals or groups (the stakeholders) could influence the project at any given stage. Furthermore, you may not have complete control over your team, nor will you always have the full and unified support of upper management. The resources and responsibilities specified in the mandate will probably be changed by your bosses or clients, or even by the team members carrying out the mandate. These potential sources of change can significantly alter the project's initial objective or implementation.

Although project management has gained popularity over the past 40 years (Garel, 2013), this field is poorly understood by organizations and its practitioners (Nieto-Rodriguez, 2021). Instead of a well-defined traditional project, you may have to deal with a fuzzy project that will evolve in unexpected ways depending on the internal environment (e.g., immediate organizational environment) or broader external environment, which includes other organizations.

You are not alone. Meet Nancy Smart, a project manager recently hired at ExPlus. After her initial briefings, she suspects that this new project, also the company's first, will be politically and socially more complex than expected. In this book, we follow Nancy as she navigates managing a fuzzy project. Her thinking and questions at various stages help introduce the ideas being addressed in each chapter. Her case study also serves to ground the 3D Project Management theory, and hopefully, inspires you to think about your own projects in fresh ways. Together, Nancy and you will learn to recognize fuzzy projects, assess the limits of traditional project management tools, and use more appropriate methods to understand and manage the essential dimensions of any project.

NANCY SMART AND THE FX PROJECT

Please step into the office (temporary, of course) of Nancy Smart.

Nancy is settling into the newly created but vaguely defined position of *project manager*. Before joining ExPlus, she had managed projects in a variety of organizations in the private and public sectors. Her first project was to set up a physical fitness training program in a medium-size company. For the next 12 years, she managed construction projects and the launch of products mainly in retail and information technology.

Nancy is part of a new breed of project managers since she is not an engineer, financial expert, or programmer. At her job interview, Nancy acknowledged her lack of experience in the financial field. This was not an issue for ExPlus, as they are interested in her project management training and experience; they need a project manager, not a financial expert. So she feels confident and ready to meet the new challenges of this job.

ExPlus is not wasting time getting Nancy up to speed. She has already been welcomed by middle and senior managers, and met the department heads who will work with her on the FX project. Her immediate boss, the VP of Insurance and Bonding, gave her an in-depth briefing on the project background and the specific mandate (see Box 1.1).

BOX 1.1

The ExPlus Organization's FX Project & Mandate

ExPlus is a (fictitious) financial services company that provides support to US companies involved in the export of services, as well as agricultural and manufactured products. Founded in 1990, ExPlus raises and manages its own capital. It works closely with banks, sureties, and insurance companies throughout the United States, some of which have representation on its board of directors.

Over the past 20 years, ExPlus has gradually focused on managing its treasury activities and on financing large companies, even though small and medium-size enterprises (SMEs) represent 90 percent of its clientele, in numbers but not in volume. A growing number of ExPlus managers and employees feel that these major financing and cash management activities are much more prestigious than services aimed at SMEs.

Despite these concerns, the ExPlus board approved a new strategy to refocus and better serve SMEs. With this strategic move, ExPlus would allow SMEs to have full access to their credit lines by providing a guarantee to their respective bankers. Currently, up to 20 percent of the credit line of an SME can be earmarked as collateral for foreign exchange risk. This new financial product will give SMEs more access to working capital and they will face less uncertainty. It will also be a boon for both ExPlus and the banks.

So, what is Nancy Smart's *mandate*? Within 18 months, she has to set up the exchange rate guarantee program for SME exporters. With ExPlus as guarantor and their line of credit freed up, SMEs will have access to more working capital and face less uncertainty.

Though she generally feels good about the project, this morning Nancy is feeling apprehensive. At 38, she has enough project management experience to sense that this project is a real "hot potato."

The first red flags went up when some company executives made these concerning comments upon meeting her:

- *So, you are the "smart one" everyone's been raving about.*
- *We are doing project management here, now? Let's see how that goes.*
- *Project management? Another fad. The flavor of the month, I guess!*

The unexpected wariness and skepticism about her project management role is making Nancy uncomfortable and has alerted her to some potential internal politics.

These reactions prompted Nancy to do some digging. She observed that ExPlus operates halfway between a professional bureaucracy and a machine bureaucracy, which is very far from the project-based structure that is being set up for the FX initiative. Furthermore, she heard that ExPlus had some bad experiences with past projects (these endeavors were never officially labeled nor run as "projects"). Since senior management has a lot riding on the FX initiative, they are keen to use project-based management to ensure successful implementation and completion. However, some internal stakeholders are wary of using project management practices and would prefer to do things the "old way."

The stakes are high, and Nancy is feeling the pressure. As she goes over her notes, Nancy tries in vain to read between the lines to grasp what her boss implied or did not say about the political and social realities of the project. She knows that a manager cannot anticipate everything, but it is frustrating that she cannot see the pitfalls she will inevitably face in a few weeks. Where is "Waldo" hiding in this fuzzy project?

As we will see, many internal or external factors can hinder the best designed and methodically executed projects: the project's context or nature may be unstable; the principals can change their minds during execution; stakeholders may interfere and new ones can emerge; project team members might also act in unexpected ways. These circumstances are signs of a fuzzy project, and the traditional rational project management approach cannot handle the unique challenges.

PROJECT MANAGEMENT MUST KEEP UP

Project management is no longer limited to industrial activities as it is increasingly used in the service sector. It has become the predominant management type in modern sectors where goods and services have a short life cycle, projects are very diverse and complex, and several organizations must collaborate to undertake these projects jointly. In this evolving context, project managers must leave the beaten track and explore a type of management adapted to twenty-first-century realities.

Managing Fuzzy Projects in 3D offers a practical method for dealing with fuzzy projects. We view the project from the traditional, rational dimension but also from the political and psychological dimensions that are often neglected.

Managing in a Climate of Change

During the 2020 COVID-19 pandemic, modern consumers were just getting comfortable shopping by phone or over the internet when suppliers began testing more sophisticated services such as pizzas delivered by driverless cars and drones. In the future, people who want to shop by car will trust their driverless car to take them to a store with no cashiers in sight. These examples illustrate that innovations constantly offer new possibilities. Welcome these technological changes, and step fully into the twenty-first century.

The innovations that transform our daily lives are popularized by organizations around us. They initiate and accelerate major change through research and development. As soon as a new, state-of-the-art product or service is successful, the race is on to surpass it, often by the same organization, fearing that their competitors may overtake them. In this global marketplace, it only takes one organization to make a major shift in products or ways of doing things, and other organizations will be affected through a ripple effect. The shocks and aftershocks are felt *within* organizations (systems and processes) and *outside* them (interactions between organizations and their customers).

The creation of such products and services, like smartphones, for instance, occurs in a context in which the necessary operations—*the value creation chain*—are increasingly divided up and spread over several continents (Krugman, 1995). This value chain includes services from accounting to research & development, as well as physical products. It is not uncommon for dozens or even hundreds of organizations to produce the components for a single product or service. Such is the case with Carrefour, a French retail corporation that has suppliers in Europe, Asia, and South America. Similarly, Apple works with more than 500 suppliers located mainly in China and Japan, but also in South Korea, Taiwan, Malaysia, the United States, and Europe. Apple's products must then converge to 16 final assembly plants.

Yet, in the turmoil of transformations that they both undergo and fuel, organizations need to foster calmer internal environments to carry out their operations. These inner enclaves are needed to reduce production costs and ensure a continuous supply of quality products and services. Organizations must simultaneously manage the daily routine and the discontinuity of changes. They also must balance operational efficiency (the constant honing of their internal functioning) and strategic effectiveness (the harmonization of the entire organization with its external environment). See Box 1.2.

BOX 1.2

A Few Words on Efficiency and Effectiveness

In management, *effectiveness* is measured by the results achieved. The better the results, the more effective the system: distance traveled, sales volume, number of patients treated or satisfied customers, and so on. *Efficiency*, on the other hand, takes into account the resources used to achieve these results: the number of liters per 100 km, the time or person-hours it takes to treat patients or dig wells, the amount of money invested to increase customer satisfaction or sales.

Efficiency can be expressed in terms of the ratio of results achieved to resources used, such as sales per square meter, miles per gallon, or liters consumed per 100 km. Thus, if tripling the resources used (such as the amount invested) only doubles the results achieved (patients treated), operations have become more effective but less efficient in terms of the resources deployed.

Figure 1.1 illustrates four possible scenarios. Those that are at both extremes are easy to assess. Since scenario I is both effective and efficient, while IV is neither, we can readily accept I and reject IV. In the short and medium terms, the more complex scenarios managers will face are II and III. Scenario III (inefficient but effective) is the lesser of two evils since efficiency can often be achieved over time. We should keep in mind that these scenarios reflect situations at a given point in time.

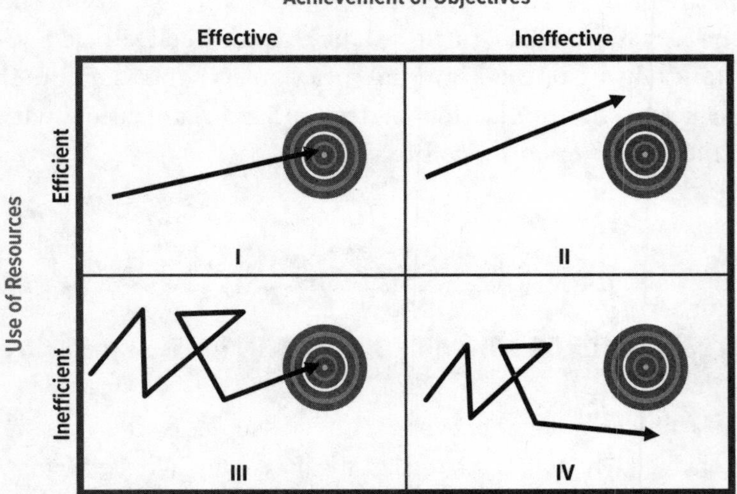

FIGURE 1.1 Combinations of efficiency and effectiveness

When an organization deploys a new strategy, it must first try to be effective and later try to become more efficient. To be effective, it must offer a set of products and services that meet the requirements of the external environment and its internal capacity. Through the learning curve and economies of scale, it can then strive to become efficient by reducing the costs associated with its new strategy.

Project management finds its relevance in this dual reality that organizations face, constantly balancing stability and change. As they deal with these shifts, managers learn from the successes and failures of their projects, big or small. But what exactly does managing a project entail? And why should a multidimensional approach be used to carry it out? Aren't things complicated enough? To answer these questions, we need to look further into the contexts in which organizations conceive and carry out projects.

Innovation for Success

Globalization, change, uncertainty, complexity, and competition are unavoidable realities facing organizations today. Each day, they must navigate a Darwinian environment marked by abrupt and significant change. To succeed and survive, they must adapt and innovate quickly and effectively.

Modern organizations operating in market-driven economies are engaged in what Schumpeter (1942) called "creative destruction." Changing production methods, different raw materials, new goods and services, and the emergence of new markets create breakthroughs that lead to the demise of outdated activities and give rise to their replacements.

In addition to technological innovations that result in new ways of doing things, organizations must deal with the economic and sociological changes that create new ways of living and change customer preferences and behaviors. Under the impetus of the capitalist initiative, no organization is immune to the storms that continually influence supply and demand. For example, during the COVID-19 pandemic, organizations in the transportation, tourism, and food service sectors (such as Debenhams, Hertz, Intu, Laura Ashley, JCPenney, Virgin Australia) had to file for bankruptcy. Other organizations in the health, emergency, manufacturing, and food supply sectors were stretched to their limits. Still others, such as American Airlines, United Airlines, Delta Air Lines, Lufthansa, Air Canada, British Airways, Airbus, General Electric, Rolls-Royce, and TUI, only managed to cope by making drastic staff cuts. Nearly all organizations were impacted, even those that at first were not in the eye of the storm. The relative calm turned out to be temporary. Indeed, through a domino effect many well-known companies were adversely affected, like Compaq, Kodak, Nortel, Texaco, the Royal Bank of Scotland, Woolworth, Sears, and Toys “R” Us.

Historically, other well-known firms managed to recover from changes in their environments, but only by making radical changes to their internal operations and with regard to their respective environments. While they faltered at first, they managed to recover: IBM in 1992; the American television channel CBS around 1995; Apple in 1997; Lego in 1998; GM, Chrysler, and Starbucks in the 2008 financial crisis; Best Buy in 2010; Netflix in 2011. Other companies have flourished amid the COVID-19 pandemic: Alphabet, Amazon, Nvidia, Zoom, Home Depot, and Walmart.

All organizations face the constant challenge of anticipating change and adapting adequately, smoothly, and within their means. Change may be erratic, as setbacks can follow remarkable periods of growth. Sometimes events may pull the organization in opposite directions. The COVID-19 pandemic dramatically curtailed Uber’s ride-sharing activities while boosting its food delivery services. Signals are hard to interpret; for example, an economic downturn may eliminate weaker competitors. The pruning that ensues may lead to an increased market share for the surviving organizations, giving them a false sense of success and security.

The subtle art of survival in the face of creative destruction highlights the dilemma facing organizations. They must either improve their current products, services, operations, or processes—or they must develop new ones. Projects build the future, but when and how should organizations undertake projects to induce or respond to changes?

We can learn important lessons as we look back at the survival of some organizations. Success has peaks and valleys. With sales of 15 million units, the Model T car secured more than 50 percent of the US market for Ford among 100 domestic competitors. Ford dominated that market in the 1920s, only to undergo an equally remarkable fall at the end of that decade. Faced with the more attractive cars offered by General Motors (GM), Ford sales plummeted. The company had to stop producing its famous Model T in May 1927. It restructured and completely retooled its assembly lines to manufacture the new Model A. To make such a radical change, the company had to cease production for six months at the world's largest plant at the time and lay off 6,000 workers.

Fifty years later, in the late 1980s, Ford repeated its feat with the Taurus, which became the bestselling car in the United States. It was yet another resounding commercial success, with more than two million vehicles sold.

Oddly, success can lead to failure. As Miller (1990) explains using the "Icarus Paradox":[1] *success can breed overconfidence* and can lead to dogmatism and complacency, when managers cling obsessively to strategies that worked well in the past. Reluctant to deviate from a set strategic direction, they become *builders* who want relentless growth, *artists* so enamored with innovation that they ignore what their customers want, utopian *pioneers* who want to constantly clear new land, or *salespeople* so consumed by the lure of profit they want to sell anything to anyone. In 1995, facing intense competition from Japanese manufacturers, Ford tried to hit another home run with a revamped Ford Taurus.

Unfortunately, it did not meet expectations, and it never regained the same popularity with consumers.

In adapting to changes in consumer tastes and preferences, some organizations offer product enhancements incrementally, such as software that consumers can acquire over time, or loyalty programs and subscriptions that provide a continuous revenue stream. Others actually plan to make their products and services obsolete as part of a strategy to limit competition.

An organization's success depends on its ability to manage and deliver change using projects. Indeed, projects can make and break an organization's strategy. Such was the case for the Airbus A380, where delivery delays caused cost overruns and huge penalties forced the parent company to restructure. Like Ford, Airbus avoided bankruptcy and survived. However, this did not save the superjumbo jet from business failure and Airbus retired the A380—a plane that some suggest should never have been built.

In contrast, a significant number of "dot.com" companies could not survive, vanishing in the turmoil of the mid-to-late 1990s. In the 2008 recession, the US and other governments bailed out their large companies and major banks that had seemed invulnerable. Without these rescue operations, many would have closed their doors. Only 14 percent of the companies on the original Fortune 500 list of largest companies (drawn up in 1955) still exist today. Similarly, *Forbes* now estimates that more than 70 percent of Fortune 1000 companies will disappear over the next few decades.

Yet many organizations survive changes and even thrive afterward. Several American, European, and Asian automobile manufacturers are over 100 years old. In 2008, the Bank of Korea surveyed more than 5,500 companies worldwide with over 200 years of continuous operations. Surprisingly, more than half of them were Japanese, and 90 percent had fewer than 300 employees. In some cases, the national environment and small size seem to be important factors in their longevity.

While there is plenty of research and speculation about why organizations fail, there is some consensus about one way they tend to succeed: they adapt and transform over time. In particular, they do a good job managing their relationship with the environment, and reorganize their internal operations when necessary. Each key area of activity—*internal, external, and mixed*—has given rise to a particular management type. In general, each organization adopts a unique, more or less well-balanced mix of these different, yet complementary and synergistic, management types.

THREE TYPES OF MANAGEMENT

Different types of management exist because organizations must simultaneously carry out activities of a very different nature, scope, and pace throughout their life cycle. Some activities are limited to small subunits or divisions, while others are organization-wide. Certain activities are continuous and with no apparent end, while others are temporary and are undertaken for a fixed duration known in advance. Management types deal with the organization's internal environment (units, divisions, or functions), the external environment (customers, suppliers, and regulators), or both jointly.

The two best-known types relate to ongoing organizational activities: *operations management* which focuses on the organization's internal environment, and *strategic management* which aims to harmonize the internal and external environments. We will, however, focus on a third type: *project management*, which often considers both the internal and external environments. What distinguishes project management from other management types is its temporality because its activities are of a predetermined duration.

Each management type takes a specific perspective on the organization, a unique paradigm with its own traditions and methods that rely on proven techniques and tools. However, none of these management types is an end in itself, and all three are essential to ensure the day-to-day management of the organization and its long-lasting success.

In this chapter, we view project management, "the art and science of converting vision into reality" (Turner, 1996), as overlapping the more traditional management types of strategy and operations. To that end, we highlight some general but fundamental considerations valid for organizations of all sizes and purposes, whether governmental, commercial, or not-for-profit.

Operations Management

Firmly rooted in daily routine, operations management is responsible for optimizing the organization's internal activities, which are essential for survival, especially in the short term. It includes the management of purchasing, sales, and physical, financial, and human resources. It covers production and manufacturing operations, as well as the supply chain including logistical support provided by the accounting and IT departments (see Figures 1.2 and 1.3).

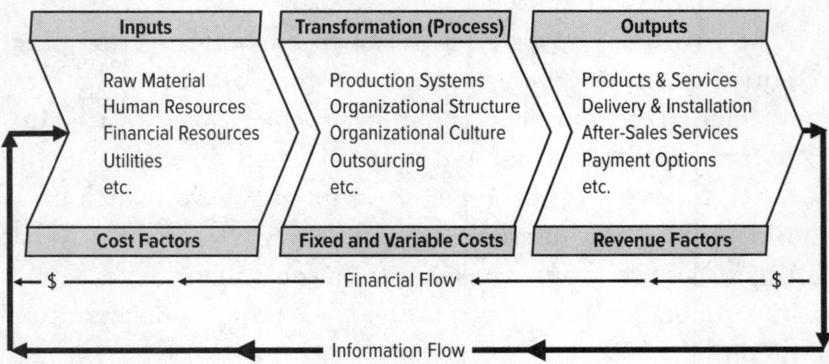

FIGURE 1.2 Operations management—factors and processes

Operations management aims to transform the inputs (materials, financial resources, labor, etc.) from the organization's external environment into outputs (the goods and services provided to clients in the external environment). Inputs, therefore, represent the resources that the organization must acquire from its environment, while outputs are the goods and services that generate revenues (or donations for not-for-profit organizations). In the case of for-profit organizations, they must pay for virtually all inputs (interest must be paid for loans, for instance), while they receive money for outputs (products, services, warranties, after-sales services). By extension, we can use this analogy and apply it to not-for-profit organizations, and to any subunit or division within any organization, since they all need to obtain resources (their inputs) and provide goods and services (their outputs).

In this value chain, the operations managers of each unit or division respond to requests from internal customers (other units, divisions, and departments), external customers, and within their own unit or division.

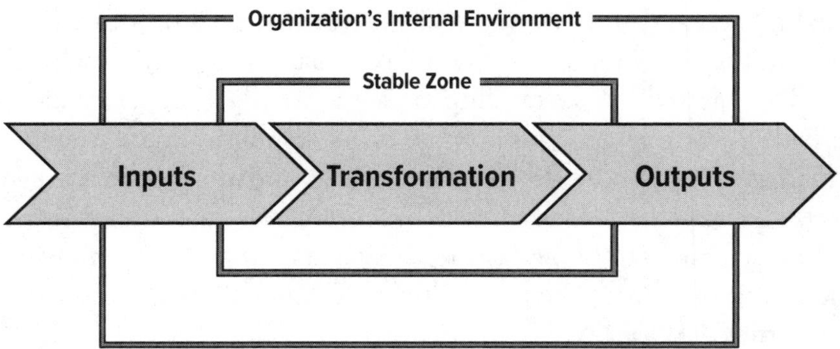

FIGURE 1.3 The operations management transformation process

To manage these operations efficiently, the arrangement and coordination of these activities must be fine-tuned. Therefore, managers must create and maintain a relatively stable internal environment by anticipating change, mitigating potential disruptions, and making necessary corrections in a measured manner. The adaptation mechanism mirrors the homeostatic process observed in higher animals who can maintain their body temperature despite external fluctuations. The vital organs keep functioning through the coordinated response of other parts of the body, maintaining a steady internal temperature despite radical changes in the environment.

Since operations management focuses primarily on the optimal use of resources, it aims for efficiency or, as Peter Drucker (1966) says, "the art of doing things right." It applies proven analytical and quantitative methods that improve processes and reduce uncertainty, and if not uncertainty, its effects.

Strategic Management

With a long-term perspective, strategic management is concerned with the overall direction of the entire organization. Strategic managers must strive to ensure that the organization is on the right track and in harmony with its external environment. As a result, they use monitoring and follow-up tools to acquire a global and integrated understanding of a constantly evolving reality. Given the scope and importance of its responsibilities, strategic management is not tied to any one unit and must take a long-term perspective characterized by complexity and uncertainty. It must ensure the long-lasting existence of the organization by focusing on effectiveness, or "doing the right things," according to Drucker (1966).

In an environment where change is gradual or predictable, these two types of management—operations and strategic—may suffice. However, this is not always the case, as the changes required are sometimes rapid and unforeseen. The case of Blackberry, the smartphone manufacturer and former darling of Nasdaq, is particularly illuminating. When challenged by Apple's iPhone,

Blackberry had no choice but to embark on a major restructuring in 2013. It cut thousands of jobs and significantly reduced its operating costs.

These two traditional types of management are complementary. Typically, *strategic changes*—global and radical—fall under the purview of the CEO and the board of directors, while *operations management* is the responsibility of middle and senior management. The fact that these types are hierarchically on unequal footing facilitates their coordination.

Focusing on strategy with little concern for day-to-day operations and concrete action sets the organization adrift, locked in the world of ideas. Conversely, if the sole concern is operations management, the organization becomes excellent at doing something that customers no longer need. Operational excellence should not be conflated with strategic effectiveness.

If each organizational unit focuses on its own internal efficiency, the organization becomes balkanized—divided into smaller and separate parts. Given these conflicting demands, a difficult balance must be maintained to ensure that the organization remains operationally efficient and yet strategically effective in a changing environment. This tricky balancing act explains the emergence of a third type of management, tasked with making changes periodically to ensure success in the short term and survival in the long term.

Project Management New and Improved

Project management has gained popularity and made inroads into new areas, so let's take a fresh look at it. Practiced for centuries, but only formally recognized since the end of World War II (Morris, 2013), project management reconciles effectiveness-focused strategic management with efficiency-focused operations management (Slevin and Pinto, 1987). Although it is the youngest and least known by the general public, it is increasingly used in contexts marked by constant change. Halfway between operations and strategic management, this hybrid management type differs in that its activities are essentially temporary. It responds to the need to change either internal operations or the organization's products and services. As a result, it can reconcile two distinct objectives: (1) *efficiency*, the realm of operations management, which requires continuity; and (2) *effectiveness*, the realm of strategic management, which ensures longevity.

Unlike the other two types, project management activities tend to be defined in terms of duration and scope. This third management type is the main focus of *Managing Fuzzy Projects in 3D*.

TABLE 1.1 The Three Management Types: Project Management Operates Between Strategic and Operations Management

	Management Types		
Characteristics	**STRATEGIC MANAGEMENT**	**PROJECT MANAGEMENT**	**OPERATIONS MANAGEMENT**
Responsibility	Ensure longevity by harmonizing the organization with its external environment	Carry out specific initiatives within the framework of Time, Cost, Quality (TCQ)	Efficiently produce the organization's goods and services
Focus	Overall guidance and management under uncertainty	Innovation and change management	Production and efficiency of systems
Mission	Harmonize the organization with its environment	Make the necessary changes	Produce goods and services
Goal	Anticipate and decide accordingly	Find the best ways to carry out required changes	Produce and market
Role	Orient: Overall orientation and management under uncertainty	Innovate: Innovation and change management	Execute: Production of goods and services

(*continued*)

TABLE 1.1 *(continued)*

	Management Types		
Characteristics	**STRATEGIC MANAGEMENT**	**PROJECT MANAGEMENT**	**OPERATIONS MANAGEMENT**
Scope	Wide: Includes internal and external environments, plus the whole organization	Circumscribed: Internal processes and external groups + organizational units involved in initiative	Narrow: Limited to the task and internal processes + units or divisions of the organization
Operating Mode	Foresight and anticipating	Problem-solving and implementing solutions	Coordinating and fine-tuning
Time Horizon	Undefined. Long-term objectives. → Stability	Predetermined. Nonrecurring objectives. → Temporality	Ongoing. Recurring, short-term objectives. → Regularity
Key Success Factors	Effectiveness	Effectiveness and efficiency	Efficiency
Motto	Doing the right things	Making things better	Doing things right

OUR CONTRIBUTION TO PROJECT MANAGEMENT

In writing this book, we reviewed failed projects to understand why they performed poorly and studied successful projects to identify what contributed to their success. This retrospective analysis has taught us important lessons. First, it underscores that managers need to question the narrow approach advocated by traditional project management: in other words, stick to the project plan dutifully and stay focused. Second, a project's success cannot be measured by efficiency alone, as it must also consider effectiveness, including realizing benefits and meeting stakeholder expectations.

Although traditional project management aims to be rigorous and efficient, many practitioners and authors actually criticize it for being ineffective, counterproductive, and even at times nonsensical (see, for example, Shenhar & Dvir, 2007; Morris, 2013; Nieto-Rodriguez, 2021). Some projects are completed but do not yield the results that their sponsors expected. Others meet the time, cost, and quality constraints, but fail to benefit the community, and may even harm its larger social and natural environment, leaving many stakeholders disappointed.

Projects that are well managed according to traditional precepts can fail miserably. Too often, the reductionist project management approach has led to situations where "the operation was a success, but the patient died." Such was the case with the Chad-Cameroon oil pipeline led by ExxonMobil at the turn of the twenty-first century. Completed on time, it did not produce the expected results in terms of international development or meet the needs and expectations of its beneficiaries: the poor. More recently, Google Glass, literally "the internet in your eyes," was a "well-executed" product development project, but it failed to meet business case expectations and was canceled just after two years.

How can such project management failures be avoided? First, we need to identify at the outset the type of project we are dealing with, or what it may turn out to be. This book distinguishes "neat" projects from "fuzzy" projects. Neat projects focus on *efficiency*, aiming for clear, measurable, and stable mandates; their principals and agents (team members) often form relatively stable, homogeneous groups. Conversely, fuzzy projects focus on *effectiveness* and have intangible mandates that are subject to change over time; principals may have divergent interests or even change their minds, and the project may be entrusted to agents (team members) who are very autonomous and have their own and even differing views on the project. To deal with the sheer level of complexity and uncertainty that fuzzy projects entail and increase their chances of success (see Maylor, Turner, & Murray-Webster, 2013), we need to go beyond the confines of the rational approach, which tends to work well for neat projects, and also consider the political and psychosocial dimensions of project management.

Second, we need to assess the ancillary role given to all projects—be they seen as neat or fuzzy—as they are routinely viewed as mere instruments for deploying organizational strategy. The role projects play in strategy formulation or execution should not be an afterthought. Many projects, especially those that are fuzzy, must be integrated into the strategic thinking process early on. In this way, the project becomes an instrument of strategy in its own right. Therefore, the project needs to be situated among other projects, programs, or portfolios of the target organization, and its conception must include strategy, finance, policy, and even politics in the broad sense of the term (Morris, 2013).

Based on these considerations and recent advances in project management, our goal is to "reconcile" this specific management type with the operations and strategic management approaches from which it has been separated, and at times seems opposed to in the excessive quest for efficiency. In short, give the project its rightful place within the organization's larger context.

A BOOK FOR MANAGERS AND STAKEHOLDERS

In a well-known essay, the English philosopher Isaiah Berlin (1953) expanded upon an old fable about hedgehogs and foxes to draw a contrast between those who view the world through a single lens (hedgehogs), and others who draw on a wide variety of experiences (foxes). This allegory can be used to describe two broad types of project managers: those who see and do everything through a central idea (hedgehogs) and those who see things from multiple angles and can take different courses of action (foxes).

Specialists can efficiently carry neat projects to term using a clear set of rules and objectives for which they are thoroughly trained. Generalists have a much broader vision of the world:

they know their limits and call upon specialists from other fields as needed, bringing in the expertise needed for a fuzzy project to be successful.

Project managers of the generalist type need to be skilled in several areas. They must effectively plan and carry out the mandate—the specific objective of the project—manage the political aspects, and navigate between the parties' opposing interests. They must also consider the project's strategic, political, and psychosocial ramifications. With this multipronged approach, they can better balance the demands of time, cost, and quality, and reconcile the need for efficiency and effectiveness with the expectations of stakeholders. They do all this in a context where several principals (coalitions or stakeholder groups) and agents (members of the implementing team or agency) are involved.

Unfortunately, the standard incentive mechanisms put forward by organizations can discourage project managers from acting like a fox, because performance assessments and their potential rewards influence the project manager's behavior. As they say in business circles: What is measured gets done.

This book challenges the traditional project management approach, which holds the narrow view that almost all projects are "neat" (or easily made so). Practitioners and researchers generally view organizations, along with the projects they undertake, as rational, objective entities free from major political, social, and cultural tensions. In this vision of a conflict-free organizational world, some practitioners mistakenly assume that the project alone is an appropriate and sufficient level of analysis. They overlook the project's subsets (such as team members) or the broader organizational system of which the project is a part. While this rational view may be appropriate in neat circumstances, it can be naïve and misleading for fuzzy projects that include stakeholders with different backgrounds and conflicting interests or expectations.

Once we go beyond the simple considerations of time, cost, and quality, and adopt a three-dimensional (3D) perspective (the mandate, principals, and agents), it becomes clear that planning the project on a purely "rational" basis will not ensure its success. Some projects are broader and more complex than the formal mandate suggests, and successful completion involves more than just fulfilling the terms of reference or just the mandate. Indeed, it is about making the project a success for the principals, agents, and other key stakeholders. This sociopolitical view of success also applies to the delivery of fuzzy projects that seek to tackle world-scale challenges such as global poverty reduction, COVID-19 vaccine development, or climate change adaptation, which generally involve multiple project managers and stakeholders.

This book takes project management into new territory unshackled by the mental constraints of "the golden triangle" that dominate the traditional approach. We take into account the political role of the principals and the psychosocial characteristics of agents, in order to better equip practitioners to face the complex realities of fuzzy projects and thus avoid the pitfalls of the traditional way of managing rather neat projects. The book is timely. For example, *A Guide to the Project Management Body Of Knowledge (PMBOK® Guide)*, published by theProject Management Institute (PMI, 2021), the largest organization of its kind, has moved from a process-based approach to a principle-based approach, where creating and delivering value, engaging with stakeholders, navigating complexity and uncertainty, leading in and adapting to changing contexts are critical for success. The multidimensional method is only part of what makes this approach novel and valuable. It is not prescriptive, as it avoids the "cookbook approach." Instead, it is descriptive and grounded, inviting managers to draw their own conclusions based on the project's internal and external contexts. It highlights the need for project management practitioners and top managers to do a broader and more in-depth analysis of the project using a triple lens: the *rational* (mandate-centered perspective), *political* (principal-centered perspective), and *psychosocial* (agent-centered perspective). This approach has significant advantages for both the project manager and the project's ultimate success (Saint-Macary & Ika, 2015).

The project manager is not just a fox but a chameleon. In order to deliver benefits and meet stakeholder expectations, the project manager, like a fox, needs to adopt a broader perspective. To become an adaptive leader, like the chameleon, the project manager must strive to understand context including stakeholders, both internal and external. In a true ecologically rational manner, the project manager can count on an "adaptive toolbox" that will help navigate the rational, political, and psychosocial dimensions of managing fuzzy projects. In this instance, true leadership means deliberately and intuitively understanding what tool will work for a given situation and what dimension(s) will match the management requirements of the situation (Gigerenzer, 2014).

OUR METHODOLOGY

Managing Fuzzy Projects in 3D offers a more nuanced reading of the project than the traditional approach. Step by step, we consider the critical parts of a project: the scope, needs and objectives (expressed and unstated), deliverables, constraints and risks, stakeholders, planning, and implementation.

Using a *rational* lens, we explore the limits of the mandate-based approach, which mainly focuses on the project's specific objective and deliverables. Through a *political* lens, we reveal how principals with divergent or unstable interests can use the project as an instrument, and we examine the practical consequences of those tensions. Finally, we view the agents (project team members) through a *psychosocial* lens because they often prove to be more than just compliant, disciplined implementers when given enough latitude.

To help practitioners better understand the content of the book, we contrast, notably in Chapter 9, the three different perspectives—*rational, political, and psychosocial*—by their characteristics, advantages, disadvantages, and relevance to project management. The three perspectives are complementary; each one sheds light on factors overlooked by the others, and together they give a clearer view of the project, with fewer gray areas. While this triangulation work means more time, energy, and thought by the project manager and principals, it will prevent pitfalls and improve the project's management.

We use these perspectives sequentially in Chapters 6, 7, and 8 to examine three fundamental elements of project management: the *mandate*, which spells out the specific objective and parameters of the project; the *principals*, who are the sponsors or the clients who authorized it; and the *agents*, who are the project managers and team members charged with implementing the project. These elements are critical in all projects, be they large or small, neat or fuzzy.

According to traditional project management training manuals, the formal mandate's terms of reference should include all of the activities required to execute a project. These terms are given by the principals and then entrusted to the agents. Therefore, the mandate, principal(s), and agent(s) are essential and privileged sources of information for understanding and evaluating the entire project. The mandate is often found in the project charter or the project management plan. These two documents are referenced in practical guides, such as the *PMBOK®*.

While every project begins with a mandate, the principals or agents often have the final say on how it is implemented. In this context, these three elements—the mandate, principals, and agents—are needed to define the project more fully. Let us consider three cases where one of the three elements is more influential than the other two.

Many projects can be understood, managed, and evaluated almost exclusively by referring to the mandate. The mandate can unambiguously lay out exactly what the principal (the sponsor, owner, or client of the project) expects from the agent (the project manager). A simple example of a project of the first type is a home renovation where interlocking pavers will replace an asphalt driveway.

To understand, monitor, and evaluate a clearly laid-out home project, an external observer needs to focus mainly on the *mandate* (the work order, in this case), with no need to interact with either the principal (the owner) and even the agent (the contractor) after establishing their qualifications. Moreover, the contractor could even subcontract the work as the mandate can be clearly and fully expressed in a written work order. In this scenario, the time, cost, and quality constraints outlined in the purchase order would be sufficient to understand, carry out, and evaluate the project.

Other projects, however, should focus more on the *principal*. Using another home renovation example, the so-called principal may turn out to be a couple or even an entire family, including in-laws (the group is presumed to act as one). The principal can be so involved at every stage that the actual mandate only becomes clear to the agent contractor at the end of the project. The homeowners may only know what they want as the work progresses, changing their minds multiple times, undoing and redoing what they had previously asked for.

In this second case, an external observer could not fully understand the project using the terms in the original purchase order. Learning about the principal would help the manager to monitor and evaluate the project's progress. In the home renovation example, understanding the project and evaluating it would be even more complicated if the couple had different visions and expectations. Large-scale or major projects can also be principal focused. A well-known case is the expansion of the wall on the US-Mexico border initiated under the Trump presidency, but whose funding was the responsibility of a politically divided US Congress.

In addition to projects of the first and second types, there are those that cannot be planned in advance for practical reasons, including a high level of uncertainty or information asymmetry between principals and agents. Consequently, project implementation rests more heavily on the *agents*. Examples of projects of the third type are military interventions, bold product and service innovations, breakthrough scientific or innovation projects, or team sports events. They can also be as mundane as residential renovation projects where agents play a leading role due to their expertise and the latitude they need to exercise. Such is the case of a gardening project done by an experienced landscaper or a home makeover by interior designers. In both cases, the agents provide extensive advice to the homeowners.

In this third example, the work order (mandate) could not be as explicit as in the projects of other types. Take the example of a soccer game. To monitor and evaluate progress, an external observer would have to pay attention to the coaches and athletes. Regardless of the initial plan, as soon as the game starts (project), the project's outcome essentially rests with the players on the field (agents). There may have been an initial game plan, but as boxing champion Mike Tyson noted, "Everybody has a *plan* until they get punched in the face."

CONCLUSION

The basic purpose of an organization is to provide certain goods or services in a particular environment. To that end, its key activities fall into two broad categories: producing and ensuring its own survival. The first set of activities are operational and carried out internally. The others are strategic, aimed at ensuring an adequate fit between its internal and external environments. However, the organization's internal production system and its strategic relationship with the external environment change periodically. These changes vary in scope and speed, and may be initiated internally or triggered by external forces, in a given sector or worldwide, as were the 2008 recession and COVID-19 pandemic. In responding to these changes, organizations typically carry out projects that must be implemented efficiently and effectively. They are deemed successful when they are implemented within time, cost, and quality constraints, and also meet business case and stakeholder expectations.

Many internal or external factors can derail the best designed and methodically executed projects. When faced with unforeseen circumstances, the traditional, rational project management perspective should be broadened. By considering the context of the project, and assessing it on three dimensions and not just one, managers are in a position to assess the project's uncertainties and risks and achieve better results.

Five takeaways are proffered for project managers and sponsors:

1. Organizations are torn between the need for fitness (operational efficiency) and the need to maintain a good fit with their external environment (strategic effectiveness).
2. Globalization, change, uncertainty, complexity, and competition are part of a Darwinian environment of survival of the fittest. Hence the importance of projects and project management. Project management straddles operations management and strategic management, and it reconciles the dual need for efficiency and effectiveness.
3. Traditional project management tends to focus on management processes rather than project outcomes. It often delivers efficiency (meeting time, cost, and quality constraints) at the expense of effectiveness (the business case's expected benefits or the impacts of the deliverable on the organization, stakeholders, and society). Given existing incentive mechanisms, the project manager tends to use a strictly rational approach, often failing to meet stakeholder expectations, and thus its strategic and societal goals.

4. Any project can be characterized by its mandate, principals, and agents. The *Managing Fuzzy Projects in 3D* approach ensures that the project's specific objective contributes to the strategic benefits (mandate), fulfills the expectations of the principals (top management and clients), and satisfies the interests of the agents (project team members).
5. Traditional management may work well for neat projects, but it is unsuitable for fuzzy projects with unclear or shifting objectives, and stakeholders who have divergent interests and change their minds. The three perspectives (rational, political, and psychosocial) on which *Managing Fuzzy Projects in 3D* is based are complementary, but also synergistic. Together, they offer a comprehensive way of making sense of the project. Thus, they will enable project managers to implement the project mandate as tasked, meet the expectations of internal and external stakeholders, and contribute to the organization's larger environment.

REFERENCES

Berlin, I. (1953). *The hedgehog and the fox: An essay on Tolstoy's view on history*. Princeton University Press.

Drucker, P. (1966). *The effective executive*. Harper.

Garel, G. (2013). A history of project management models: From pre-models to the standard models. *International Journal of Project Management, 31*(5), 663–669.

Gigerenzer, G. (2014). *Risk savvy: How to make good decisions*. Penguin Books.

Krugman, P. (1995). Growing world trade: Causes and consequences. *Brookings Papers on Economic Activity, 26* (1), 327–377.

Maylor, H., Turner, N., & Murray-Webster, N. (2013). How hard can it be? Actively managing complexity in technology projects. *Research Technology Management, 56*(4), 45–51.

Miller, D. (1990). *The Icarus paradox.* Harper Business.

Morris, P. W. G. (2013). *Reconstructing project management.* John Wiley & Sons.

Nieto-Rodriguez, A. (2021). *Project management handbook. How to launch, lead, and sponsor successful projects.* Harvard Business Review Press.

PMI (2021). *A guide to the project management body of knowledge (PMBOK®* guide) and *the standard for project management.* Project Management Institute.

Saint-Macary, J., & Ika, L. A. (2015). Atypical perspectives on project management: moving beyond the rational, to the political and the psychosocial. *International Journal of Project Management and Organization, 7*(3), 236–250.

Schumpeter, J. A. (1942). The process of creative destruction. In *Capitalism, socialism and democracy*, Chapter 7. Harper.

Shenhar, A., & Dvir, D. (2007). *Reinventing project management.* Harvard Business School Press.

Slevin, D. P., & Pinto, J. K. (1987). Balancing strategy and tactics in project implementation. *Sloan Management Review, 29*(1), 33–41.

Turner, J. R. (1996). Editorial: International project management association global qualification, certification and accreditation. *International Journal of Project Management, 14,* 1–6.

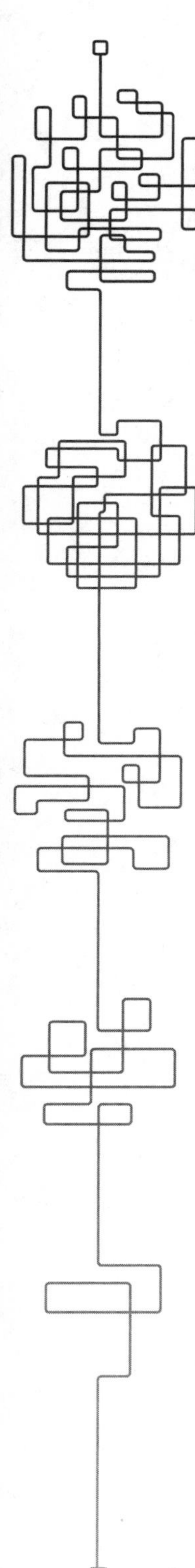

CHAPTER 2

ORGANIZATIONS & PROJECTS

A WORLD OF ORGANIZATIONS

Organizations are an inherent part of our contemporary lives. We are born in a hospital, attend schools, and become members, employees, or customers of all types of organizations, even nursing and funeral homes. Organizations are the bookends of our lives. We continuously interact with them to meet our needs for food, health, safety, education, finance, and spirituality. Public and private organizations have become unavoidable engines that shape our lives and transform society's very foundation.

Organizations change as they compete for space and influence. They are given legal status, with rights and obligations, so much so that we are inclined to perceive them as individuals. We ascribe them with traits of will and creativity, and they evoke strong feelings, like confidence or distrust. In the same vein, we view the projects they undertake with approval or suspicion.

What Is an "Organization"?

For Nancy Smart to acquire a more enlightened view of projects, organizations, and their management, she will need to understand organizations in fundamental ways. What is an organization? How does it come into existence? Why do we choose to be part of one?

A simple example is when two people, like Robinson Crusoe and Friday stranded on an island, form a partnership—a basic organization—and work together for years.[1] With its implicit contract, such long-term collaborative relationship is at the heart of the concept of what an organization is.

An organization is a place of internal and external exchanges and also of collaboration. Members exchange goods and services *internally* with one another, but they also trade with individuals and organizations beyond the *external* boundaries of their organization. Within their stable organizational framework, members can reliably collaborate, exchange economic resources, and also meet social, psychological, and security needs. In this context, the organizational setting provides a coherent collective solution to satisfy a wide variety of individual and common interests.

Let's consider the case of a farmer who has always worked alone and hires a farmhand. In this collaborative endeavor, with each person focusing on specific tasks, the division of labor is likely to pay off. If production and productivity increase, the farmer and helper will produce more food than they need for themselves. The money they receive from selling their surplus allows them to buy the things they need, and thus to maintain and expand the business. Cooks, hairdressers, and accountants can do the same.

Organizations enable their members to accomplish more when they join forces. Individuals can divide and share the workload, and do the tasks suited to their skills. Self-interest, increased productivity, and emotional and economic needs are the primary reasons individuals divide work and specialize in specific tasks (Smith, 1776).

As it endeavors to obtain needed goods and services with efficiency and effectiveness, each organization carries out certain activities internally through its employees and units, and some externally on the marketplace. For example, a restaurant owner could stop doing her own accounting or delivery and outsource these tasks.

BOX 2.1

Coffee Production from Ground to Grind

Consider the many activities needed to bring coffee from the ground to your cup: planting, processing, roasting, retailing, and brewing. There is also a host of less visible players like the transporters, insurers, financial agents, and government agencies. Your simple cup of coffee comes to you thanks to a complex web of business-to-business (B2B) suppliers and brokers performing specialized activities at every link of the coffee production chain.

That chain evolves over time. Responding to technological, economic, and social changes, individuals and organizations undertake novel ways of rewiring the production chain and consumption of coffee. Some of these individuals and organizations may insert themselves as intermediaries between two adjacent links; conversely, some will short-circuit existing parts of the chain and create new bridges, resulting in *disintermediation* between the links. In either case, their novel ways of participating give rise to new value chain configurations. This broader set of activities is what we call the *marketplace*.

As exchanges of goods and services become highly fluid and complex, it becomes difficult to assess the costs and benefits for the parties involved, since each exchange requires a payment or contract. Doing these transactions within the organizational framework may lower transaction costs, making them more efficient and effective than in the marketplace. The option of conducting these activities in-house, rather than on the open market, becomes even more advantageous when they involve people with common interests.

Carrying out these exchanges within an organizational framework overcomes the limitations of the *bounded rationality* of the individuals involved. Alone, each individual would have to find—in an open marketplace—the right supplier for what they need or the right buyer for what they can offer. Instead, the organizational framework allows each employee to concentrate on their tasks, further pushing task specialization and productivity. The organization finds the right balance of doing things internally versus externally. In a successful setting, the interests of the people involved are then better served.

Membership or employment in an organization is in part motivated by the benefits that stem from the division of labor and facilitation of exchanges. Thus, cooks, cashiers, soldiers, nurses, students, and teachers can satisfy their needs and focus on their areas of expertise. As they interact with fellow employees or members, they will be more influenced by one another in their organizational settings than by people in the external marketplace. The organizational framework also makes the coordination of individual efforts easier and more productive (Williamson 1975, 1985).

By coordinating their specialized tasks and organizing themselves, Robinson and Friday make deliberate and unconscious actions that will continually redefine their respective fields of influence and responsibilities within their two-person organization. In so doing, they draw an organizational space for their bilateral internal exchanges while trading jointly with external suppliers and customers (occasional visitors from neighboring islands). Over time, their activities clarify *where, how,* and *why* they will work together and *who* will do *what* in their organization. In this context, the organization is never static—it is a reality in the making.

Each organization is a link in one of the many production chains that make up modern societies. Indeed, the customers of most organizations are usually other organizations rather than ultimate consumers. For example, think of the many intermediary organizations that contributed to the book, tablet, or product you are currently using, from raw materials to finished products. Making the modest lead pencil involves coal mining, silviculture, paint manufacturing, and a host of other industries.

The division of labor operates simultaneously at two levels. First, it is *intra-organizational* because every individual performs distinct tasks. Second, it is *inter-organizational* since each organization provides different products and services than other organizations or serves distinct clienteles and regions. The two types of division of labor coexist in a complementary and conflicting manner.

The organizational setting provides a coherent collective solution to satisfy a wide variety of individual and common interests. Moreover, since organizations significantly impact society, human beings associate with them in different ways—as employees, members, customers, or beneficiaries. Finding these enclaves to make beneficial exchanges makes them feel more comfortable and secure.

As noted earlier, Robinson and Friday could have engaged in hunting, fishing, art, or agriculture individually and bartered their respective products and services. Instead, the small organization they formed allowed them to trade with each other in a closed environment and on a continuous and predictable basis. When we try either to buy or sell a used car or a house, we quickly find out it costs time and money to get the information we need. To make matters worse, whatever information we get can be elusive and is likely to change. Within the boundaries of an organization, employees and departments are constantly making ad hoc buying and selling transactions, evaluating the options and risks of these exchanges and contracts with the external environment. Members do not have to worry about the negotiation costs related to these market transactions. Therefore, the organization can provide a better environment to optimize the benefits of the division of labor and to contain the costs that result from it.

Self-interest → Collaboration → Division of labor → Specialization → Increased productivity

The Hidden Face of Organizations

An organization is not a peaceful oasis of collaboration within a hostile environment nor is it a panacea for the ills plaguing the marketplace. Working in a collective setting has many unexpected and challenging consequences that result from the steps taken to increase productivity and collaboration. First, resources are *allocated* to each individual or unit to help them accomplish their tasks. Second, activities are *coordinated* to achieve a coherent result. Finally, after selling the products or services, the benefits are *distributed* among the organization's members as compensation for their contribution; this is an essential condition to ensure their continued collaboration. However, profit sharing also has unintended and negative consequences.

The system used to *allocate* resources to different members inevitably leads to an unequal distribution of power. In our example, Robinson has the upper hand in their uneven partnership. But, like any organization, things are dynamic and the allocation of resources will change over time. Fluctuating resources (type and amount), and the power that accompanies their allocation, are constant sources of frustration and conflict.

The method used to *coordinate* the activities creates dependencies and hierarchies between the organization's members. Friday has a subordinate role, to begin with, as he is subject to Robinson's authority and power. For them, as is the case in a large organization, the stratification of their respective roles will fluctuate over time and will also be a source of conflict.

The formula used to *share* the benefits of their work can pit individuals and units within the organization against each other. For example, Robinson receives much higher rewards, which may frustrate his companion. Whether the sharing formula—salaries and other fringe benefits—is based on the effort, results, ownership, or risks attributable to the various members of the organization, many employees are likely to judge it to be inequitable or unfair.

When exchanges occur in the public arena, the many complex adjustments required for the allocation, coordination, and distribution of benefits are made by the *invisible* and implacable hand of the market (Smith, 1976). Theoretically, the freer the market, the more actors can choose what is right for them. Within an organization, these mechanisms operate through the managers' implacable but highly *visible* hand (Chandler, 1977). With less freedom of choice, participants can only accept the rules and practices, at least in the short and medium term.

Characteristics of an Organization

The first fundamental characteristic of an organization is that it is a collective (as opposed to individual) endeavor, with its inherent advantages and disadvantages. A second basic characteristic is that production activities occur within an *internal and hierarchical* framework, rather than in an open external market where each actor can act more freely.

The implicit and explicit contracts that bind the members of an organization include the products and services exchanged on the open market, along with other less tangible aspects. Forming an organization facilitates each member's contribution and pooling of economic, technological, and social resources much more than the market allows.

Before they met, Friday and Robinson had their own *economic resources* (their respective tools and materials) and *technological resources* (unique know-how and a set of skills). In addition, they each brought in *social resources* (personal contacts and affiliations outside the organizational framework) to their organization.

Obviously, *economic resources* are essential to the functioning of any organization. This is as true for a neighborhood soccer team or local grocery store as it is for a government service or global retail chain. These resources include the *organization's inputs* from the external environment, which they transform into *outputs* (its products and services). For a local soccer team, the inputs are a playground and a ball, and the outputs are the enjoyment of the players and spectators. The economic resources enable the organization to meet expectations of consumers and other organizations. In addition, what the organization receives from customers allows it to compensate the owners and employees for their contributions.

Every organization uses a combination of specific *technology* with unique means, processes, and sets of knowledge that define how that organization does things. This technology includes a combination of tools and machines (*hardware*), work methods and processes (*software*), and the particular characteristics and experience of its members (*liveware*). For the local soccer team, the technology is the players' skills, the software is the rules of the game, and the liveware is the players and spectators. Therefore, the technology can be more or less complex, depending on whether it is highly differentiated, concentrated in one unit, or widely disseminated across different parts of the organization.

Since an organization is made up of people, it is also a *social entity*. Indeed, the organization is an answer to the problem of collective action, which takes place when a group of people work together to achieve a common goal or some common good (Olson, 2009). As economic and technological resources are shared on a sustained basis, individuals will also use their social resources—values, networks, and affiliations—within the organizational environment they have created. Social interactions occurring within the walls of each organization are more frequent and intense than those that take place in market-type exchanges, where they are fewer and more limited. So the importance of the social dimension of an organization depends on the frequency, type, and intensity of the exchanges, and to what extent they are hierarchical.

Managers and organizational theorists often overlook the social character of organizations. This oversight is even more common in project management, where people are brought together on a temporary basis. But not in this book. We attach a great deal of importance to it in our three-dimensional perspective of project management.

Organizations Are Common but Unique

The size of an organization and the goods and services provided set them apart from one another in the general public's eyes. Less known, and albeit quite important, are also the facts that some are private or public, and regardless of their size they may employ a surprisingly limited number of people or, inversely, thousands.

As we explore them further, we can gain even deeper insight into any organization by assessing its social, technological, and economic dimensions. Keep in mind that the nature and relative importance of each of these three dimensions can vary greatly, as was the case for its visible characteristics, and give rise to diverse organizational configurations. We will explore these dimensions at length in the following sections and chapters.

Challenges Facing Organizations

Internal and External Pressures

Managers strive to ensure the viability of their organization in the face of internal and external pressures. As their organizations compete for favorable interactions with the external environment, they have to deal with changing power and threats within their specific industrial sector—customers, competitors, and suppliers. They must also consider the opportunities and threats that affect the larger environment—stemming from economic, social, technological, political, ecological, and legal factors. This macro-environment includes all relevant industrial sectors, including those of the organizations that supply them and to whom they sell. It is worth remembering that most organizations sell to other organizations as part of the long value chain of production of our modern world, as we saw earlier in the example on coffee production (see Box 2.1).

Efficiency vs. Effectiveness

As noted in Chapter 1, managers must ensure that the internal production of their organization is both *effective* (by "doing the right things") and *efficient* (by "doing things right"), to use the well-known definitions proffered by Peter Drucker (1966). However, since being efficient and effective do not always go hand in hand and may even run contrary to one another, managers have to contend with their organization being inefficient during certain periods. Strategically, being effective must take priority.

Efficiency requires stability, or at least predictability. Understandably, for production and marketing activities to be carried out efficiently, operational managers prefer to have consistency in the organization's volume and type of goods and services. However, as the marketplace changes, the organization must adjust or perish. As is always the case, such changes lead to periods of instability, decreased efficiency, and (at least temporarily) higher costs. Even thriving organizations will fail if they do not respond adequately to changes. In modern times, some may even resort to the process of *creative destruction*—when a new technology makes their existing products or systems obsolete. However, with adequate initiatives and learning, the effectiveness and efficiency can be restored and even increased.

The simultaneous management of efficiency and effectiveness and the resulting tensions are more pronounced in organizations that operate in highly competitive or fast-changing environments. In recent years, many companies have grown or shrunk rapidly through technological, economic, or social upheaval. Consider the burst of the dot-com bubble, the disintegration of companies in the game and movie rental industry, and the many companies that struggled to survive the COVID-19 pandemic by reinventing themselves.

As the organization strives to create an efficient internal environment and endeavors to outperform competitors, the organization's managers conduct activities that may seem contradictory in nature and purpose. This is a core characteristic of organizational change. The ExPlus Project is a good example. While the marketing and production departments are busy marketing and providing their current set of services, Nancy Smart and the research & development department are busy designing new ones to ultimately replace them.

THE WORLD OF PROJECT MANAGEMENT

What Is Management?

Looking at the many definitions of the term can guide our thinking and actions as managers. At its root, "manage" comes from the Latin word *manus*, meaning "hand." So in this sense, managing something originally meant to shape and control with your hands. This is likely the root of the older Italian word *maneggio*, which refers to the art of training horses.

Management is also likened to the idea of a *merry-go-round* or a *carousel*, because it is a process of carrying out routine activities over and over again. It takes control and skill to stay on course and to adjust to changes.

So, management also involves dealing with change, be it intentional or imposed by circumstances. Consider the analogy of household managers: they must use their family's assets fruitfully and keep things tidy. Periodically, however, managing a household requires some spring cleaning to *get rid* of stuff, reassign responsibilities, or *review* how things are done in the house. Such measures are much more disruptive than the day-to-day running of the house. The term "management" then takes on a more radical meaning when we undertake projects that effect real change.

This book subtly differentiates between "managing" and "management" (Mintzberg, 2009). We are more concerned with what managers *really* do than what they should do. While the functions of management are planning, organizing, directing, controlling, and coordinating, we take the essence of managing to be engaging with context, including stakeholders. In this instance, we do not separate between managing and leading as they go hand in hand. Notably, while the purpose of project management is getting things done, we consider that managing is all about making the best of the evolving context surrounding projects (Ika & Bredillet, 2016). We do not seek to tame the complexity, uncertainty, or wickedness inherent with fuzzy projects (Rittel & Webber, 1973), but instead we endeavor to embrace it. If the plan is not good enough to guide us toward project success, we change the plan or adjust the goals.

Managing the Future Through Projects

As discussed in the previous chapter, organizations are akin to living organisms striving to survive by design, or other means. They acquire inputs from their environment and process them to satisfy their needs and those of their clients. In the best circumstances, organizations perform timely adaptations to their products, services, operations, and processes as they assess internal strengths or weaknesses and external opportunities and threats. Again, in particular areas, some organizations practice the art of creative destruction by anticipating the future and continually revising their product lines or production systems.

From its earliest years, Apple offered striking illustrations of an ability to change and even challenge its own product line. When they launched the first iPhone, they ostensibly trounced BlackBerry, the flagship of Research in Motion (RIM). However, the new iPhone also cut into the market share of one of Apple's other products, the iPod. Both the iPod and now the iPhone allowed people to listen to music, but the iPhone offered even more: it let people communicate by phone, messages, and then email. Even with this success, Apple did not rest and has continued to launch newer lines of iPhones with more sophisticated features (photos, videos, etc.).

For an organization to make a positive difference in its sector, it must design and implement these types of strategies. In the next chapter, we will examine the role that projects play in dealing with these changes and implementing organizational strategy on a large scale. But first, why do we need projects?

Why Do Organizations Start Projects?

Projects are *coordinated activities* that organizations or other individuals put into place for a limited period to achieve a set goal outside the scope of their usual tasks or operations. They are undertaken for a variety of reasons: to comply with legal requirements; to optimize operational processes; to test an idea; to gain a competitive advantage; or to acquire the ability needed to produce a new good or service.

As with any organized activity, the project can be carried out internally by a special task force or externally by hiring services in the marketplace. Typically, the sponsor(s) will entrust an agent with a mandate to achieve what is required. In turn, the agent will set up a project team. In this way, sponsors and agent team members operate at arm's length, linked by interests that are partly common but also distinct, and delineated.

Key Project Challenges: Collaboration and Coordination

Like all organizations, projects face the double-edged challenge of ensuring *collaboration and coordination among team members internally and externally with their sponsors.* Moreover, like any new or large task, projects must deal with two opposing requirements: dividing the tasks into subtasks to gain the benefits of specialization and coordinating these subtasks to ensure they accomplish their larger purpose.

Coordination and collaboration among multiple stakeholders, over many years, with different businesses and institutional contexts, are more sociopolitically complex and have increased transaction costs (Manning, 2017). Many major or large-scale public and private sector projects are inter-organizational and even international, so they have significant economic, social, political, and environmental implications.

Collaboration requires that the parties work together to achieve common goals. The challenge in securing collaboration stems from the fact that team members have distinct roles, objectives, and interests. To deal with this challenge, the organization must take these kinds of actions at various levels:

- Use formal and informal contracts wisely.
- Understand and take into account the interests and motivations of all parties.
- Define the authority of the project members and partners.
- Share risks and benefits.
- Form alliances.

To illustrate this, let us turn again to Friday and Robinson. Though informal, the contractual relationship between them was hierarchical at the outset. However, their relationship evolved as they cooperated and took on challenges that made the most of their distinctive skills dealing with survival, enemies, and natural disasters.

The iPhone 1 project was a collaboration between Apple and a partner in China, Foxconn, which became the largest assembler of the subsequent versions of the smartphone over the years. At some point in their business partnership, Foxconn was in the spotlight because of low wages, employee suicides, explosions on its production sites, and serious safety negligence related to a highly flammable dust that accumulated from inadequate ventilation. Apple could not remain indifferent to these economic and sociopolitical considerations because they affected the delivery of their iPhones and created serious collaboration challenges for the company, in addition to the social responsibility issues.

Coordination challenges stem from the division of labor, since what is divided, at any level, must be reassembled at some point. Hence the need to synchronize various project activities. To this end, project managers use plans and schedules to optimize task completion and team management to communicate and take corrective measures. Depending on the circumstances and the existing organizational structure, the coordination mechanisms at the planning stage will include the standardization of skills and processes, based on the project's broad goals and specific objectives. Later on, managers will use direct supervision, and the team members will make some adjustments among themselves.

At an individual level, the participants' personal and professional affiliations with other organizations—religious, political, social, and so on—will affect their cohesiveness at work (Mintzberg, 1989).

The C Series project of the Canadian aircraft maker Bombardier, which sought to manufacture and market a 100-passenger jetliner is instructive (see Box 2.2). Collaboration challenges reached a peak when Montreal-based Bombardier received US$1 billion in subsidies from the Quebec and Canadian governments and entered into a partnership with European aerospace corporation Airbus. Coordination challenges were also unprecedented. As a result of the aircraft subsidy wars between Boeing and Bombardier, and the punitive tariffs imposed by the US Department of Commerce, Bombardier was forced to assemble the jets intended for the US market in the Airbus plant in

Alabama. In addition, the project experienced substantial delays and considerable quality issues, attributed mainly to engine supplier Pratt & Whitney and French interiors and seat maker Zodiac Aerospace.

BOX 2.2

The Complicated Life of Bombardier's C Series / A220 Project

In July 2004, Bombardier announced its US$2 billion project to manufacture and market a 100–150-seat aircraft with low operating costs and low environmental impact in six years. When they did not get enough orders for the so-called whisper jet, Bombardier had to adjust the plan. They entrusted the engine manufacturing to Pratt & Whitney, lightened the aircraft with more composite materials, and revised the budget and time-to-market. The C Series came to market years behind schedule and a couple billion dollars over budget. It regained its commercial credibility when Air Canada and Delta requested more than 100 aircraft, but delivery was put on hold awaiting certification in Canada, the United States, and Europe. The horizon darkened again when Boeing issued a formal complaint in the United States alleging that Bombardier was "dumping" and had gotten "illegal" subsidies from the Quebec and Canadian governments to help them stay afloat. After Boeing's lawsuit was dismissed in 2018, Bombardier closed its deal with Airbus, who rebranded the aircraft the A220 and won dozens of orders from JetBlue and a new carrier, Moxy. The A220 then performed well at the Paris Air Show and sufficiently increased its orders. In February 2020, Airbus was handed full control. In total, the C-Series gamble contributed to increasing Bombardier's debt to over US$9 billion.

Sources: Financial Post (December 14, 2015);[2] Montreal Gazette (February 8, 2020);[3] Reuters (April 11, 2018).[4]

Projects Are Everywhere

Although they are temporary by definition, projects big and small have profoundly shaped organizations and societies throughout the world. Not only do they seek to transform the natural environment, they also attempt to create a new human-built world (Davies, 2017). Over the years, projects have varied in scope and nature, with some being particularly ambitious and futuristic. The Biden administration's Build Back Better plan, "a-once-in-a-generation" investment in infrastructure in the United States, includes a number of major projects.[5] The Belt and Road Initiative, formerly known as the One Belt One Road or OBOR for short, is an ongoing Chinese infrastructure project that will physically link Asia, Europe, and Africa.[6] The Indian government plans to spend up to US$530 billion on public infrastructure[7] (see Box 2.3). These megaprojects drive the economy and undoubtedly have a significant sociopolitical impact.

BOX 2.3

Examples of Futuristic Projects from Around the World

- **The Biden administration's Build Back Better:** A plan to invest trillions of dollars in both economic and social infrastructure projects to fix no less than 20,000 miles of roads and 10,000 bridges, while also providing more access to childcare and home- or community-based care for seniors and people with disabilities, making education and housing affordable, and fighting climate change.
- **The Belt and Road Initiative:** Described as a twenty-first-century Silk Road, this trillion-dollar Chinese government project seeks to create a transportation route through land and sea that will link over 70 countries—from Southeast Asia through Eastern Europe to Africa. These countries include more than half of the world's population and half of global GDP.

- **The Great Wall of Lagos:** This wall is an 8.5-kilometer-long dike made of 100,000 concrete blocks being built to counter coastal erosion and protect the posh district and financial heart of Nigeria—Victoria Island in Lagos. In addition, this wall will enable another pharaonic project, the Eko Atlantic, to house the highest skyscrapers on the continent in the "Afrofuturist" district located between the wall and the coast. This district has already benefited from the re-silting of the ocean on more than 2.5 square miles, with more than 100 million tons of sand dredged from the bottom of the sea.
- **The Grand Paris Express:** The largest transport project in Europe is scheduled for completion in 2030. It consists of a 200-kilometer metro network loop serviced by automatic trains and flanked by 68 new stations, moving two million passengers daily and giving rise to whole new neighborhoods.
- **The Big Move:** This 25-year, US$50 billion regional transit plan seeks to improve the quality of life, environment, and prosperity in the Greater Toronto and Hamilton area (GTHA).
- **Sydney Metro:** Australia's largest transit project, a US$12 billion-plus project, will deliver 31 subway stations and 66 kilometers of rail.
- **Nigerian billionaire Dangote's oil refinery:** This US$20 billion-plus project with a capacity of 650,000 barrels per day could become the world's largest refinery.

Over the past half century, we have witnessed a proliferation of complex and large-scale projects driven by three factors: *globalization, accelerating technological progress, and the shortening of product life cycles*. As a result, today's organizations face a context of uncertainty and complexity to which they in turn contribute. They must do things faster, better, cheaper, and compete, alone or through alliances, by launching new products and services and delivering value to a widening variety of stakeholders.

One such case is Apple's decision to buy the Canadian startup Mobeewave, known for its expertise in mobile payment terminals. By offering Apple Pay, the smartphone manufacturer gained a share in a market dominated by large banks and payment service providers and increased the practice of cashless virtual transactions.

Apple has undertaken two other projects that will be transformational on a global scale. One aims to make Apple totally carbon neutral by 2030—their offices are already carbon neutral, and their operations and production will follow. The other multimillion-dollar project—the Racial Equity and Justice Initiative (REJI)—addresses systemic racism and expanding opportunities for communities of color. To these ends, Apple will focus on minority-owned businesses that positively impact Apple's supply chain and communities that are severely affected by environmental degradation.

Projects have become a popular way for organizations to achieve their objectives, giving rise to "projectification," which means the tendency to use projects as a way to organize work and deliver change in every sector of the world economy (Midler, 1995). We live in a "project society," where projects help coordinate human activities and thus shape personal, organizational, and societal lives (Lundin et al., 2015). As the project economy booms, projects (that which makes organizations change and prepare their future) seemingly trump operations (that which makes organizations run on a daily basis) as the leading economic engine (Asquin, Falcoz, & Picq, 2005; Nieto-Rodriguez, 2021). Notably, projects worth more than US$1 billion are multiplying worldwide at an accelerated pace in both traditional and modern sectors such as oil, gas, mining, aerospace, information and communication technologies (ICT), supply chains, and defense.

According to Bent Flyvbjerg (2014), the drivers behind such megaprojects may be:

- **Technological:** to increase speed and size, for example
- **Political:** to build infrastructure that supports causes and improves the lives of people

- **Economic:** to fulfill promises of substantial financial gains by organizations and businesspeople
- **Aesthetic:** to appeal to architects, engineers, and designers inspired by a desire to create remarkable or iconic works
- **Community pride** is a fifth driver, as it provides a sense of accomplishment to a given community about the great things it has been able to achieve (Frey, 2016).

In addition to these five factors, we suggest the impetus can also be:

- **Altrusim** on the part of the West (e.g., the United States, Europe), to help others help themselves, especially in the rest of the world (e.g., Africa, Latin America); this is a factor that has driven the proliferation of donor-funded international development assistance projects, which sought to combat extreme poverty over the last decades.
- A desire to **rescue**, to save the world from the damaging threats posed by grand challenges such as pandemics, climate change, and unsustainable development.

Unfortunately, the drivers behind the megaproject economy are so powerful that they lead decision makers to take greater risks. Indeed, though they are seen as shortcuts to success, megaprojects tend to create their own set of challenges not only in terms of their implementation setbacks but also their social, economic, and environmental impacts. As a result, these projects reportedly succumb to what Bent Flyvbjerg terms the "iron law of megaprojects": overrunning budgets and deadlines again and again.

Project Management: Two "Bane-and-Boon" Paradoxes

The idea that some companies are "too big to fail" gained popularity during the 2008 recession, and continues to be applied to major projects. When confronted with significant setbacks, stakeholders argue that it is too late to give up, given the large sums of money already invested and the alluring benefits for the economy and society. This escalation of commitment frequently results in substantial cost blowouts. Half of major transport projects exceed their planned budgets (Love, Sing, Ika, & Newton, 2019). In information technology (IT), major projects have virtually no chance of staying within their assigned budgets (The Standish Group, 2013), and, relative to their approved business case figures, average cost overruns are about 27 percent, according to some estimates (Flyvbjerg & Budzier, 2011). Two bane-and-boon paradoxes stand out in project management:

Paradox 1: Project management as a field of knowledge enjoys success, yet projects tend to fail. Consider these astonishing figures and trends. Some 95 percent of public policies are currently implemented through major projects. According to the World Bank, about US$20 trillion, or one-fourth of the world's GDP, is spent every year through projects. Projects are undertaken in both periods of economic growth and in downturns. During the COVID-19 pandemic, many countries were also facing economic hardship. So, they invested in the health care system by building hospitals, COVID-testing centers, and major infrastructure projects that ultimately boosted their economies..

Yet, almost three decades after *Fortune* magazine heralded project management as the number one career choice of the twenty-first century, the failure rate of projects, large or small, remains high, and the frustrations of practitioners are matched only by the disappointments of stakeholders.

No project is too big or too small to fail, and no industry is immune. Whether in IT, new product development, international development, or organizational change, it seems that roughly one in two major projects *fail* and do not produce the expected economic or social impacts (Ika, 2012; Eckerd & Snider, 2017). The Project Management Institute (PMI) estimates that more than 10 percent of the investment made in projects is wasted every year. Thus, major projects continue to proliferate and grow, despite substantial cost overruns and benefit shortfalls.

Paradox 2: While executives of public and private organizations excel in strategy formulation, they struggle with strategy implementation. Examples include new product development projects like Samsung Galaxy Note 7 and Amazon's Fire Phone. Conversely, project managers excel at implementing projects, but they often lose sight of the strategy they must implement, as noted by the CEOs of JP Morgan Chase and AlliedSignal: "Execution is not just tactics—it is a discipline and a system. It has to be built into a company's strategy, its goals, and its culture. And the leader of the organization must be deeply engaged in it. He cannot delegate its substance" (Bossidy & Charan, 2002). As a result, projects may be completed on time and on budget, yet fail to meet their strategic objectives or business case expectations. Google Glass and Microsoft Zune are key illustrations of this.

These apparent failures often conceal unacknowledged economic and political successes for some individuals or groups, within the respective organizations, as strategists, sponsors, or agents are motivated by personal, technological, economic, political, or personal interests and preferences. For instance, for every person fired, another was promoted.

The next chapter provides an overview of the challenge of strategy implementation and the role that project management can play in it. Why projects fail, succeed, or succeed in unexpected ways—the good, the bad, the ugly, including their hidden sides—must be brought to light, assessed, and reexamined from many angles by a manager.

DIVERSE PROJECT ORGANIZATIONS AND STRUCTURES

Organizations initiate all kinds of projects for all sorts of reasons, using various project organizations and diverse project structures. Here, we describe a few commonly used project organizations and structures.

Project Organizations

The Project Management Institute defines a project as "a temporary endeavor undertaken to create a unique product, service or result" (PMI, 2013). While projects are often considered as temporary organizations, most of them are undertaken by permanent (Winch, 2014) or process-oriented organizations which are often dominated by operations and functional lines (Müller, Drouin, & Sankaran, 2019). There are six main types of project organizations, based on how the project relates either to a single organization or multiple organizations (see Figures 2.1 and 2.2).

Type 1—Lonely Project Organization: This is a project with its own organizational and legal identity and where the structure set up for the project is dissolved at its end, as is the case for the ExPlus project. It is the model for major infrastructure projects, such as the construction of the world's tallest tower in Dubai, the Burj Khalifa (a project that cost more than a billion US dollars), or event projects, such as the World Cup or the Olympic Games.

Type 2—Project-Oriented Organization: Here, mass production is continuous and recurring, and activity tends to be standardized (e.g., automotive, pharmaceuticals, and electronics). The challenge is to launch new products or services, make the same products or services better and cheaper, or make organizational changes. While these endeavors may be run as business as usual, top management may devise

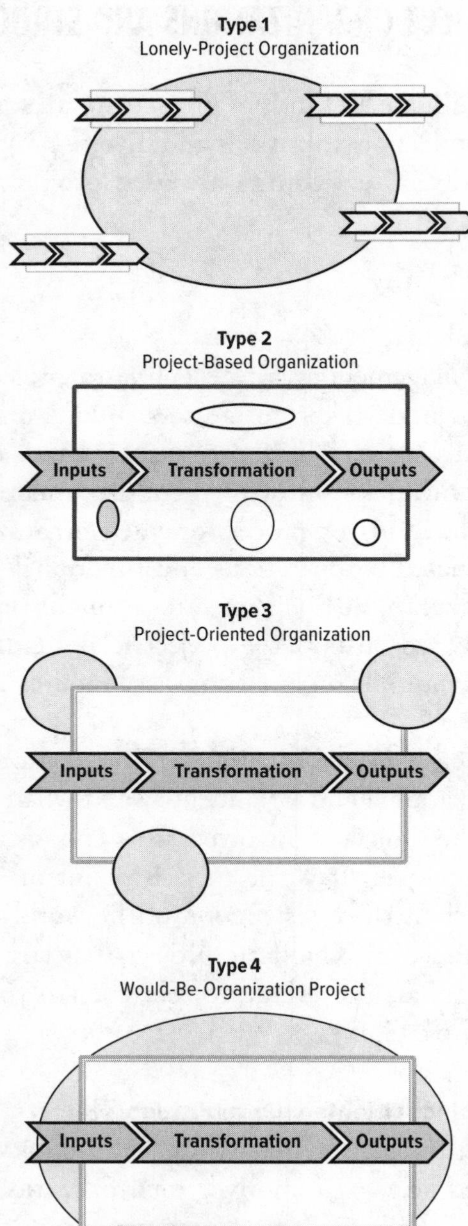

FIGURE 2.1 Four types of project organizations based on project-organization configuration

"a management by projects" strategy and make a deliberate choice to run them as projects (Turner, 2018).

Type 3—Project-Based Organization: This configuration is found in a sector such as construction, engineering, or consulting that gathers temporary or ad hoc resources to carry out regular assignments or one-off contracts. Projects are the essence of what these organizations do, making the former the unit of production of the latter (Müller et al., 2019). The challenge is to optimize the *portfolio* of ongoing projects and to ensure, in a process that is sometimes referred to as "stop or go" (i.e., to stop or continue the project), that resources are allocated to the most profitable projects, even if it means abandoning less attractive projects.

Type 4—Project as a Would-Be Organization: This is the case of *startup* projects, especially in the new economy, where the entrepreneurship project is the would-be organization, and the latter only survives when the former succeeds. The challenge is for the organization to survive the project and become permanent. A good example is a would-be-organization-project like Twitter at the time of its conception (Asquin et al., 2005).

The last two types account for the multiorganizational nature of projects:

Type 5—Inter-Organizational Project: In this scenario, a single inter-organizational project, namely a lonely project, involves multiple organizations. This project organization is sometimes called a "project network" and it may include dozens of contractors and thousands of subcontractors (Davies, 2017). For example, the US$70 billion Beijing Daxing Airport project in China, the largest transportation hub to date, includes 45 subprojects and involves 12 government departments,

24 investment agencies, and hundreds of contractors and subcontractors.

Type 6—Project Ecologies: This configuration refers to a dense constellation of organizations involved in multiple projects, using their individual and collective capabilities as well as their collaborative relationships. Some of these interconnected organizations may be involved in the delivery of a megaproject today as tier-one contractors and the others as subcontractors, and vice versa tomorrow. A case in point is the vast mobilization of people, organizations, and government agencies that typically takes part in the planning and delivery of the Olympic Games (Davies, 2017).

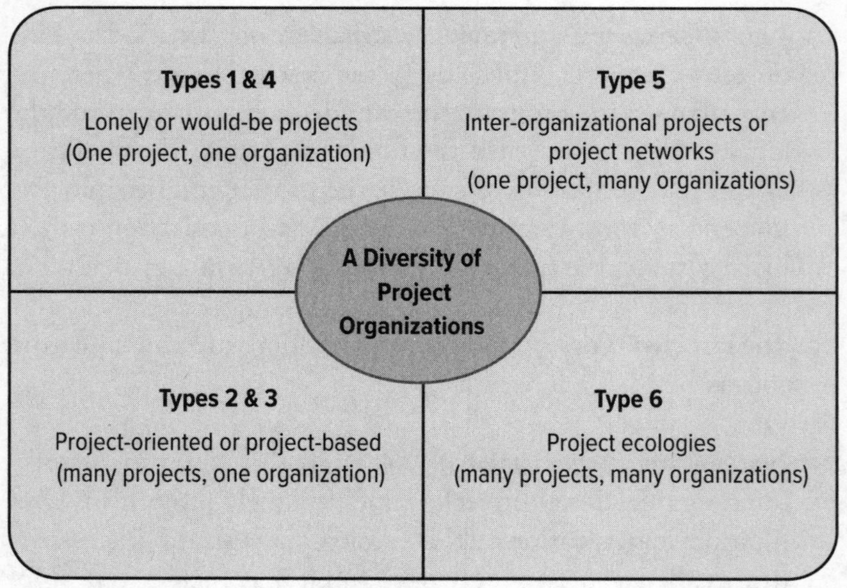

FIGURE 2.2 A two-by-two matrix of project organizations

Sources: Adapted from Söderlund (2004); Davies (2017).

Project Structures

In addition to the diversity of project organizations, there are many ways of structuring projects in organizations where they coexist with operations, which epitomize the functional logic of the organization. From the moment an organization adopts a strategy (what it wants to become) and designs its projects or the products or services it will produce (what it will do), it needs to think about the project structure, how it will affect the redistribution of scarce resources, and what authority and latitude project managers will have in relation to the functional managers. The choice of a good project structure is dictated in part by the organizational structure in place, the unique characteristics of the projects, and their anticipated contribution to the strategic objectives. Setting up a good project structure can be a challenge as businesses often operate in "organizational silos" (divisions that operate independently), whereas projects cut across all divisions, getting resources and specialists from different parts.

Different structures are inserted into the organization to meet these challenges and facilitate project deployment. For example, *functional structures* and *matrix structures* are differentiated by how the people in charge of the functional units and projects share the authority. A *projectized structure* gives the project manager the most autonomy. Next we provide an overview of the main types of project structures (for more information, see Larson & Gray, 2014; PMI, 2013).

The Functional Structure

The project is carried out in a specific department or *functional unit* (such as marketing, R&D, production) that will make the most important technical contribution to it or has a great interest in seeing it succeed. The project manager (rarely called the project leader) is under the hierarchical authority of the department manager, who is responsible for coordinating and allocating resources. The roles of the project manager tend to be limited to that of an instigator and facilitator (see Figure 2.3). Sometimes, several departments manage the project, and each one is in charge of a specific module assigned to them by senior management. In this case, the project is coordinated through the usual channels.

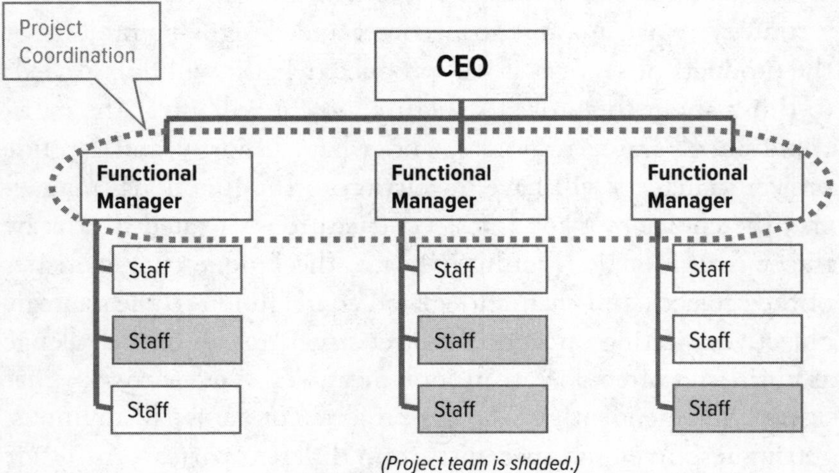

FIGURE 2.3 The functional structure
Source: PMI (2013).

The functional structure works well for small, low-budget, relatively simple projects of short duration. Its advantages:

- Clear structure thanks to well-defined departmental objectives and priorities
- Proven technical expertise
- Synergy within each department (or functional unit)
- Relatively easy transition for the employees after the project ends

On the other hand, the functional structure has notable disadvantages, especially when the project is multifunctional and no single department (or functional unit) plays a leading role in its delivery:

- Subordination of management to technical considerations
- Project delays when operations are given higher priority
- Gaps in project integration because each department is limited to its own module
- Administrative slowness

The Projectized Structure

The opposite of the functional structure is the *projectized structure.* In this case, the project is said to be taken "out," meaning that it is institutionally outside or physically separated from the organization. Major projects—such as the Saint-Gothard tunnel in Switzerland, the world's longest buried tunnel—tend to rely on this structure. These projects are often run by dedicated, self-managed, or "commando" teams. They are typically found in project-based organizations such as construction and consulting companies that make the project their production unit and get their functional departments to support it.

In all cases, senior management sets up a temporary organization with the necessary resources needed to complete the project. A project manager is given a "road map" and is in charge for the duration (see Figure 2.4). The project manager may recruit the personnel required for the project from inside and outside the organization. This structure tends to give the project manager greater freedom or authority.

The projectized structure avoids the pitfalls of the functional structure, and it has these additional strengths:

- Stronger accountability for results
- Greater flexibility
- Faster results
- Better team dynamic due to the guidance of an actual project manager
- Greater project integration

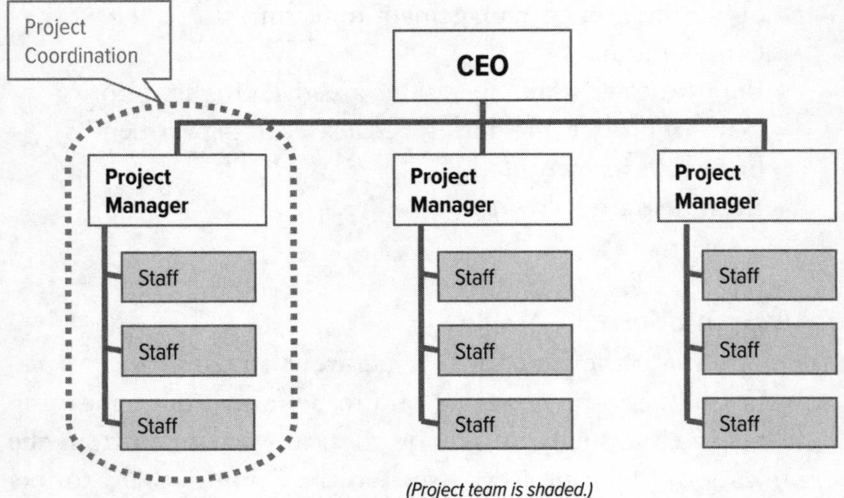

FIGURE 2.4 The projectized structure
Source: PMI (2013).

However, it also has challenges:

- Job instability for full-time seconded members, or a difficult transition after project completion.
- Loss of institutional memory.
- Underutilization of resources at given times, which increases the opportunity cost of the project for the organization.
- Abuse of project-based operations (sometimes called "projectitis")—a project pathology in which work is termed a project but requires little actual project management; in such a case, project team members may exhibit deep but inappropriate attachment to the project. This can lead to conflicts between project teams and the rest of the organization and even depression from individuals when the project is dismantled.

The Matrix Structure

Finally, hybrid organizational forms take advantage of the benefits of both functional and projectized structures while avoiding their drawbacks. The matrix structure crosses the responsibilities of project managers with those of functional managers and thus makes it possible to carry out many projects simultaneously with a limited number of resources mobilized, as needed, on a part-time basis as the project progresses. In other words, two chains of authority are set up, one for the functional hierarchy and the other for the project. Rather than entrusting project modules to several functional units as in the functional structure, resources are placed concurrently under the dual authority of functional managers and project managers. There are two basic scenarios: (1) the project manager is only a coordinator and does not have dominant control over project activities, and (2) the project manager plays a decisive role in driving the project. The former is referred to as a weak matrix structure (see Figure 2.5) and the latter as a strong matrix structure (see Figure 2.6).

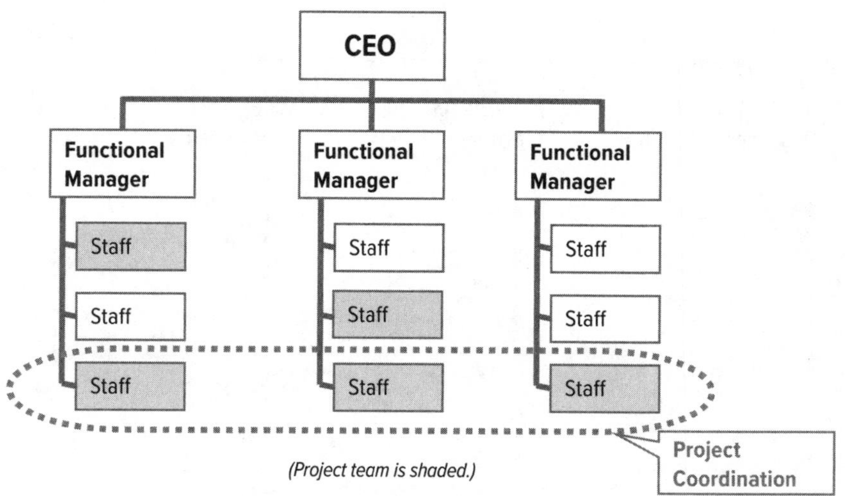

FIGURE 2.5 The weak matrix structure

Source: PMI (2013).

In the first case, the *project manager* has no real hierarchical authority over the project team members. Instead, the project manager's role is to establish schedules, facilitate the project's execution, and monitor its progress. The *functional manager* manages a project module, makes most of the decisions, and determines who does what and when.

In the second case, the project manager steers the project, assigns tasks to specialists, and determines who does what and when. While the functional managers are consulted as needed, the project manager has the final say on project decisions. In this configuration, the project manager has more influence and can therefore assess the performance of project team members.

In all cases, the matrix structure has the advantage of offering an efficient use of resources and a better compromise between time, cost, and quality. On the other hand, it has the disadvantages of administrative complexity and dual command, and as a result is often a source of conflict and stress.

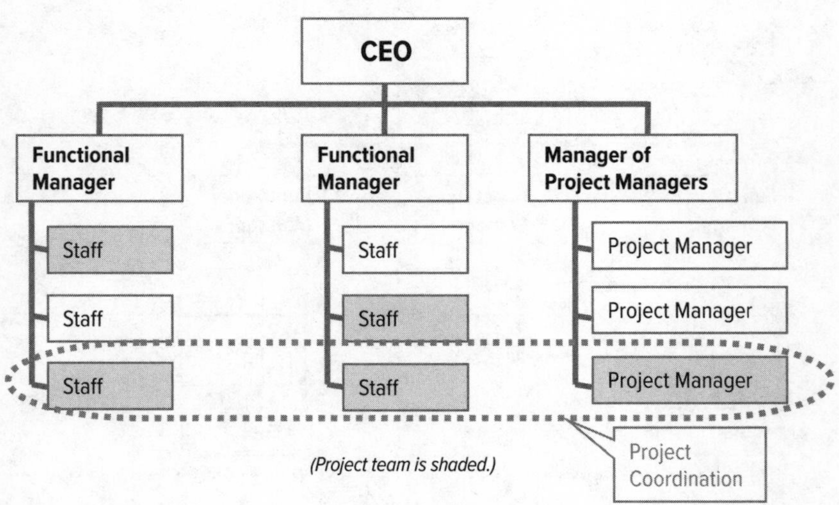

FIGURE 2.6 The strong matrix structure
Source: PMI (2013).

Figure 2.7 matches the different project structures with different project characteristics.

Organization Structure / Project Characteristics	Functional	Matrix			Projectized
		Weak	*Balanced*	*Strong*	
PM's Authority and Resource Availability					
Budget Control	Functional manager		Mixed	Project manager	
PM's Role	Part time		Full time		
PM Administrative Staff	Part time			Full time	

FIGURE 2.7 Matching project structures with project characteristics

Source: PMI (2013).

CONCLUSION

In the marketplace, individuals and organizations routinely exchange goods on a transactional basis. This process is flexible but time-consuming, as parties must find one another, negotiate, and secure payments and guarantees. When exchanges between some parties become standardized, a new organization is born. This new organization offers an alternative to the market by carving out a place where its members share resources and interact with the external environment on a sustained basis. As it evolves and redefines its relationship with the environment, the organization will launch projects to alter its internal operations, outsourcing some activities or, conversely, deciding to carry them out in-house instead of the marketplace. Since such changes entail reallocating resources and privileges among members and restricting their freedom in many ways, they inevitably create internal tensions and conflicts.

Consequently, organizations also impact society, playing a key role in creating and redistributing wealth and power among individuals and groups. This hidden side of organizations becomes evident in projects, where successes and failures shift the balance of power inside and outside the organization, with major rewards for some and negative effects for others.

While projects are temporary organizations with flexible structures, they are typically undertaken by permanent organizations with structures that are set to run operations along functional lines. Those differences make for awkward and tense relationships, depending on the rigidity of the organization and the fuzziness of the project. Organizations and projects can be an odd couple.

Four takeaways are suggested for project managers and sponsors:

1. The organization is a substitute for the market. Within its internal setting, collaborative activities take place on a longer-term, contractual basis. In that way, the organization is a nexus of contracts. Along with its primary purposes, the organization also impacts the interests of many individuals and groups at large.
2. Every organization is faced with a dual quest for internal efficiency and external effectiveness. To these ends, the organization allocates different resources to its members and distributes wealth and other benefits unevenly to them and to its external environment. As a result, the organization is a potential source of tension and conflict.
3. Given the projectification of the organization and of society, we are witnessing a project economy. Projects are proliferating all over the world under the impetus of globalization, the acceleration of technological progress, and the shortening of the product life cycle. In particular, there are seven "sublimes" that drive the business of megaprojects: technology, politics, economics, aesthetics,

community pride, altruism, and rescuing the world. Projects are enabling organizations to transform themselves and shape their future and the whole world.

4. Project management as a discipline is experiencing a boom and the use of projects is growing. Paradoxically, their failure rate is high and cost overruns are all too common.

Project organizations and project structures come in many forms, as they reflect the diverse organizational contexts in which projects are carried out. A particular project may answer to one or many organizations, just as a single organization may undertake a single project or multiple projects at a time. More variety in project organizations and in project structures stems from the strategy, the nature of the projects in question, how the organization allocates resources, and what authority is given to the project managers and functional managers. Project managers and sponsors who understand the contingent nature of these forms of structuring and organizing can navigate organizational complexity more effectively and deliver their projects successfully.

REFERENCES

Asquin, A., Falcoz, C., & Picq, T. (2005). *Ce que manager par projet veut dire.* Éditions d'Organisation.

Bossidy, L., & Charan, R. (2002). *Execution: The discipline of getting things done.* Crown Publishing Group.

Chandler, A. (1977). *The visible hand: The managerial revolution in American business.* Harvard Business Press.

Davies, A. (2017). *Projects: A very short introduction.* Oxford University Press.

Drucker, P. (1966). *The effective executive.* Harper.

Eckerd, A., & Snider, K. (2017). Does the program manager matter? New public management and defense acquisition. *American Review of Public Administration, 47*(1), 36–57.

Flyvbjerg, B. (2014). What you should know about megaprojects and why: An overview. *Project Management Journal, 45*(2), 6–19.

Flyvjberg, B., & Budzier, A. (2011). Why your IT project may be riskier than you think. *Harvard Business Review,* 89(9), 23–25.

Frey, T. (2016). Megaprojects set to explode to 24% of global GDP within a decade. https://futuristspeaker.com/business-trends/megaprojects-set-to-explode-to-24-of-global-gdp-within-a-decade/ (accessed 13 February 2022).

Ika, L. A. (2012). Project management for development in Africa: Why projects are failing and what can be done about it. *Project Management Journal, 43*(4), 27–41.

Ika, L. A., & Bredillet, C. N. (2016). The metaphysical questions every project practitioner should ask. *Project Management Journal, 47*(3), 86–100.

Jensen, M. C., & Meckling, W. H. (1976). Theory of the firm: Managerial behavior, agency costs and ownership structure. *Journal of Financial Economics,* 3(4), 305–360.

Larson, E. W., & Gray, C. F. (2018). *Project management: The managerial process.* Seventh edition. McGraw-Hill.

Love, P. E., Sing, M. C., Ika, L. A., & Newton, S. (2019). The cost performance of transportation projects: The fallacy of the Planning Fallacy account. *Transportation Research Part A: Policy and Practice, 122,* 1–20.

Lundin, R., Arvidsson, N., Brady, T., Eksted, E., Midler, C., & Sydow, J. (2015). *Managing and working in project society: Institutional challenges of temporary organizations.* Cambridge University Press.

Manning, S. (2017). The rise of project network organizations: building core teams and flexible partner pools for interorganizational projects. *Research Policy, 46*(8), 1399–1415.

Midler, C. (1995). "Projectification" of the firm: the Renault case. *Scandinavian Journal of Management, 11*(4), 363–375.

Mintzberg, H. (1989). *Mintzberg on management: Inside our strange world of organizatio*ns. Simon and Schuster.

Mintzberg, H. (2009). *Managing.* Berrett-Koehler.

Müller, R., Drouin, N., & Sankaran, S. (2019). *Organizational project management: Theory and implementation.* Edward Elgar Publishing.

Nieto-Rodriguez, A. (2021). *Project management handbook. How to launch, lead, and sponsor successful projects.* Harvard Business School Press.

Olson, M. (2009). *The logic of collective action.* Harvard University Press.

PMI (2013). *A guide to the project management body of knowledge (PMBOK® guide)*. Project Management Institute.

Rittel, H. W. J., & Webber, M. M. (1973). Dilemmas in a general theory of planning. *Policy Sciences, 4*(2),155–169.

Smith, A. (1976). *An inquiry into the nature and causes of the wealth of nations.*

Söderlund, J. (2004). On the broadening scope of the research on projects: A review and a model for analysis. *International Journal of Project Management, 22*(8), 655–667.

The Standish Group (2013). The Standish Group CHAOS Report. *CHAOS Manifesto 2013.* The Standish Group International.

Turner, J. R. (2018). The management of the project-based organization: A personal reflection. *International Journal of Project Management, 36*(1), 231–240.

Williamson, O. E. (1975). *Markets and hierarchies, analysis and antitrust implications: A study in the economics of internal organization.* Free Press.

Williamson, O. E. (1985). *The economic institutions of capitalism.* Free Press.

Winch, G. M. (2014). Three domains of project organising. *International Journal of Project Management, 32*(5), 721–731.

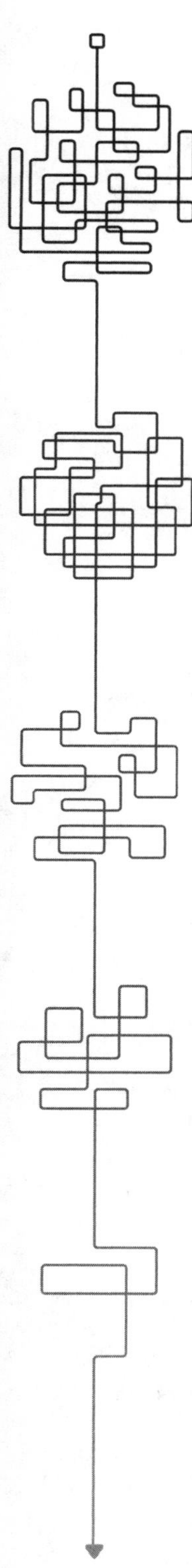

CHAPTER 3

STRATEGY AND THE ROLE OF PROJECT MANAGEMENT

Vision without execution is hallucination.

—attributed to Thomas Edison

Projects are key instruments to make and reorient an organization's strategy. However, the executives who set the strategy, the business managers who provide inputs, and the project managers who endeavor to reconcile these different interpretations of the strategy will face obstacles, at every stage of its conception, implementation, and assessment.

Having a good strategy is undoubtedly key to the survival and success of any organization and is a responsibility that is expected to fall on its senior managers. Indeed, surveys of thousands of executives in a variety of sectors have confirmed that strategic thinking is the skill they consider most important. Undoubtedly, strategy implementation is a complex task. Yet, in all contexts, including project management, several myths, half-truths, or hazardous assumptions can prevent organizations from achieving strategic success (Bungay, 2019).

MYTHS & REALITIES

Let us examine three common myths regarding strategy (see Table 3.1). Since they are widely held at many levels within organizations and even outside, these myths hinder strategy implementation in many ways.

TABLE 3.1 Three Myths and Facts About Strategy

MYTH (Reflecting a purely rational perspective)	REALITY (Reflecting political and social factors)
There is a one best way to formulate a strategy: Strategy is conceived through a rational process, by one individual (or a cohesive team) who sets the overarching goal and the appropriate course of action for the organization.	**There are many ways and means to arrive at a strategy:** Strategy is conceived by several individuals and groups (stakeholders) with distinct visions, interests, and power. Thus, it can be formulated in many ways, and can even "emerge" independently of what is intended.
Implementation follows formulation: With a clear mandate, the team tasked with implementing it will execute the strategy as planned or the project as planned (within reasonable variations), using proven tools and appropriate forecasting methods.	**Formulation and implementation are intertwined:** Implementers form a heterogeneous team that will evolve; the team is comprised of individuals with distinct interests and perceptions of the strategy (or the project); implementation will face unforeseen changes.
Success can be measured against one overarching goal: Success criteria are reliable measures that reflect the interests of the organization. They can be set to guide implementation as a linear, time-limited process.	**Success is measured progressively by various stakeholders:** Success (or failure) is the net sum of hits and misses in the implementation process, as it unfolds. The results can be assessed against the rank-ordered interests of various stakeholders.

THE CHALLENGES OF STRATEGY IMPLEMENTATION

When managers embark on the uncharted path of strategy implementation, they face three important challenges:

1. **How do we develop a good strategy?** Researchers have found as many as 10 distinct ways in which strategy is conceived and formulated (Mintzberg, Alstrand, & Lampel, 1998). Given that upper management and various team members will use the term "strategy" to mean different things, it can be challenging for them to agree on what they want to achieve and the best way to get there. A good manager needs to know how to build a strong strategy backed up by an action plan.
2. **How do we successfully integrate strategy formulation with implementation?** Implementing a strategy is about achieving an advantageous fit between the organization and its environment. However, few strategies are implemented as they were originally formulated. Moreover, studies have shown that most strategies fail to deliver the desired results and do not satisfy stakeholder expectations. Why?

   There is a tendency to separate thought from action, so strategy formulation gets separated from implementation in a unidirectional flow. The end goals of the strategy and how to achieve these goals are unclear and are understood differently by different parties. The people and units involved will change, further confounding the problems of communication and of execution. The implementation may stay on course but fail to meet the needs of shifting circumstances. Even after successfully slashing production costs and prices, Ford's Model T simply would not sell. Conversely, the implementation may exceed expectations and yet be deemed a failure because the original project strayed off course, as was Columbus's first voyage. Often, implementers lack direction on how to implement the strategy.

It is of dubious help that in theory and practice, project managers are encouraged to meet their objectives using either a *prescriptive and deliberate* process ("stick to the script, using proven techniques") or a *descriptive and emergent* one ("no handbook, do the best you can, incrementally"). Given this situation, it seems crucial to integrate strategy formulation and implementation more effectively—they should not be separated in time and scope.

3. **How do we measure success?** As a project unfolds, should success be measured against the initial implementation plan or the concrete results for the stakeholders? Unsurprisingly, managers find it hard to successfully implement the strategy, given the fuzziness of its end goal and the inevitable deviations from its original formulation. Delivering products and services, fulfilling promises made to stakeholders, and achieving strategic objectives is a challenge. Managers of all stripes and ranks should understand what drives strategic successes and failures.

Projects are used to implement organizational strategies (Cleland, 2007). They enable strategists to move from concept to specific actions by breaking down the overall strategy into concrete deliverables that can be managed separately and methodically. In an unpredictable world, a successful implementation requires that the strategy be designed at the outset with implementation contingencies in mind. The conceived strategy can then serve as a frame of reference, a beacon, at every subsequent stage of its deployment. Integrating project management within strategy formulation and implementation is the best approach to effectively make, break, alter, or reorient the organization's strategy (Miller & Lessard, 2000; Shenhar & Dvir, 2007).

Before we explore the specific role of project management in strategy implementation, we delve more deeply into strategy, lay out implementation challenges, and present potential solutions.

First Challenge: Developing a Good Strategy

Strategy is clear in a military context, as war historians and experts have noted for hundreds of years. As far back as 400 BC, Sun Tzu described strategy as the "art of management." Renowned military theorist Carl von Clausewitz (1832) also saw strategy as an art, constrained by political benefits rather than military costs and losses. Yet strategy remains a difficult concept to define for an organization (see Box 3.1). In the business world, a "battle" is a project and "war" is a set of projects, and in this context, "strategy" takes on many meanings.

BOX 3.1

Strategy: Definitions Used in the Business World

Strategy defines the organization and integrates its parts. The fundamental questions are: What will we do? What will we become? (Selznick, 1957).

Strategy is about matching the firm to its environment; it is primarily concerned with the firm's external problems (Ansoff, 1965).

Developing a competitive strategy is about creating a unique and valuable position involving a set of activities. It is not about operational efficiency, that is doing the same things better than competitors, but rather about doing things *differently* from them (Porter, 1996).

Strategy is a coherent set of policies and actions designed to address a challenge, often an overarching issue (Rumelt, 2011).

Mintztberg et al. (1998) studied the distinct views of strategy held by researchers and practitioners and grouped them into five *P*s:

- A **plan**—formulated through a formal process to determine where the organization should be and how to get there
- A **pattern**—a trail that results from past decisions and behaviors that have shaped its present
- A **position**—the niche for its products and services carved out in the marketplace
- A **perspective**—that aligns the organization's culture, values, and goals
- A **ploy**—or clever scheme to outwit its competitors

Depending on the researcher's or the practitioner's perspective, the organization is primarily constrained by its *environment*, propelled by the *aspirations and interests* of its members, pulled into different directions by *various stakeholders*, and framed by reason, future goals, and previous decisions.

As with all complex notions, the concept of "strategy" has many definitions. Mintzberg et al. (1998) identified *10 schools of thought,* each with a distinct perspective on anticipating the organization's future and its relationship with the internal and external environments. Three schools of thought are *prescriptive* and conceive of strategy as it *should be*: the design, planning, and positioning schools. Six schools are *descriptive* as they present strategy as it *is* in practice: the entrepreneurial, cognitive, learning, political, cultural, and environmental schools. Finally, the configuration school involves a *combination* of the other schools (see Box 3.2).

BOX 3.2

Schools of Thought on Strategy

Depending on the organization's particular circumstances and resources, it may have little or a lot of latitude in the formulation and implementation of strategy. So, it is not surprising that authors adhere to different schools of thought. The type of strategy used will directly impact the dominant or ancillary role of the project during strategy implementation.

Design School: Strategy *conception* is a deliberate *process* driven by strategists.

Planning School: Strategy is a *rational, formal,* and systematic step-by-step *process.*

Positioning School: Strategy is an *analytical selection process* undertaken to carve out a niche in the competitive landscape.

Environment School: Strategy is a *reactive process*, driven by external forces.

Cognitive School: Strategy is a *mental process* undertaken by leaders, and it reflects their way of seeing reality.

Learning School: Strategy is a *collective process* that produces many options. These "lessons learned" are integrated into their overall action plan.

Cultural School: Strategy is a *collective process* that reflects the *values shared* by the members of the organization.

Entrepreneurial School: Strategy is a *visionary process* that reflects the perspective of an individual.

Political School: Strategy is a *process of negotiation* among actors inside and outside the organization, taking into account their specific requirements.

Configuration School: Strategy is a *process of transformation* that results in periods of stability and instability within the organization.

Source: Mintzberg et al. (1998).

Collectively, these distinctions among the different meanings of strategy are very instructive. In short, they teach us that strategy is not just the organization's mission or a simple intention. Moreover, it includes the fit of the organization within its external environment and the internal choices and means used to achieve it. Consequently, strategies may be formal or informal, prescriptive or descriptive, deliberate or emergent.

Strategy formulation can be a process of creative design or systematic planning, and an individual or collective process. It can be *intended* (the result of thought-out deliberations) but also *emergent* (the result of unexpected adjustments or reorientations, opportunistic or not, as we witnessed on a large scale in the COVID-19 pandemic). An emergent strategy typically takes shape "along the way," with its share of hazards, pivots, and experimentation.

Strategy formulation is a *dynamic process*: a deliberate strategy may be formulated well or poorly at the outset; it may not be realized at all in the end; it may be poorly implemented; depending on the circumstances, the deliberate strategy may be overcome by emergent strategy; and in practice, what is realized may lie anywhere between these two extremes of the strategy spectrum (see Figure 3.1). Table 3.2 contrasts deliberate and emergent strategies.

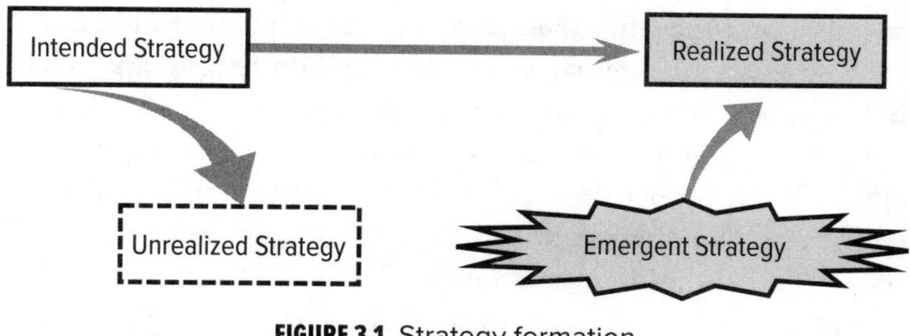

FIGURE 3.1 Strategy formation

Source: Mintzberg et al. (1998).

TABLE 3.2 Deliberate and Emergent Strategies: Two Contrasting Views

DELIBERATE STRATEGY	EMERGENT STRATEGY
Analyzed	Action-oriented
Planned	Opportunistic
Controlled	Spontaneous
Reflective	Intuitive
Focused on the future	Formed in the present
Top-down	Bottom-up
Episodic	Ongoing

Source: Adapted from Crossan, Rouse, Rowe, & Maurer (2015).

Most studies reach an alarming conclusion: there are very few successful strategies in organizations.[1] A major longitudinal study by PricewaterhouseCoopers (PwC) confirmed this. They surveyed 4,400 executives from 2010 to 2015, and more than half admitted to not having a winning strategy.

As mentioned, strategy is concerned with an organization's relationship with its environment, and this concept has many facets. Since our main interest is in the projects that contribute to that relationship, we use Rumelt's (2011) practical definition of *strategy as a set of policies and actions designed to address a challenge*. Strategy is about solving important problems and overarching issues, whether in the private or public sector. Some of these issues are internal and pertain to the strengths and weaknesses of the organization, while others reflect the threats and opportunities in its external environment. The latter may be specific to its sector, but they also include macroeconomic and social conditions. Notably, multicountry, multiorganizational, multi-program, and multiproject strategies are needed across the globe to address world scale and global challenges such as pandemics, climate change, and sustainable development (Ferraro, Etzion, & Gehman, 2015; Ika & Munro, 2022).

In this approach, any strategy that does not address the organization's current challenges or that is merely a sum of overly ambitious or vague objectives is considered "bad." A "good" strategy can be built using this three-step process (Rumelt, 2011):

- A **diagnosis** of the current situation—an assessment of the organizational issue to reduce the complexity of the reality and focus on the critical aspects of the current situation
- A **guiding policy**—a general approach to overcoming the challenge identified in the diagnosis
- A set of **coherent** actions—concrete and coordinated steps to support policy implementation

Rumelt's definition of strategy is of interest to fuzzy projects for three reasons: Strategy is a way for the organization to deal with its most complex, ill-defined challenges; it sets up an action plan for the project—this is critical for successful implementation; and it defines a "good" strategy as one that is designed to solve the problem at hand (see Box 3.4).

BOX 3.4

Good or Bad Strategy?

A good strategy:

1. Proposes how to deal with an issue of primary importance to the organization; it offers a response to a clearly identified and analyzed challenge
2. Focuses effort, resources, and skills on a few critical but achievable goals
3. Makes a clear link between the strategy and the actions to achieve it
4. Proposes a diagnosis of the current situation, a policy to guide action, and an execution plan

A bad strategy:

1. Sets one or many unclear goals, naively trying to achieve the impossible
2. Proposes a long list of activities or things to do.
3. Merely states the desired situation or the issue facing the organization
4. Focuses on superficial abstractions such as "maximizing customer satisfaction"
5. Proffers a vision or mission—but nothing more

See Rumelt, 2011

But having a good strategy is only the starting point—it must be well implemented.

Second Challenge: Integrating Strategy Formulation with Implementation

Too often, practitioners succumb to the lure of banalities such as "becoming the world's number one company in our field" or "maximizing customer satisfaction." Such vague so-called strategies are all too common in organizations, and, as a result, they fail to be implemented. This poses a considerable challenge to organizations.

Strategy formation and implementation are often separated in organizations. Moreover, strategists often excel at strategy formation but struggle with implementation. According to the PwC survey cited earlier, nearly half of executives believe there is a gap between strategy formation and implementation. Indeed, it is foolish to think that if an organization has a clear mission statement and a winning strategy, it will magically deliver quality products and services, meet the promises made to stakeholders, and achieve its strategic objectives. Unfortunately, reality is not that simple, and the challenge of implementation is critical.

A pivotal moment in the adventures of Robinson Crusoe illustrates the folly of segregating strategic concept from implementation. A century after the original version published by Defoe, Michel Tournier (1984) retold Robinson's adventures, recounting his daring attempt to leave the island of "Speranza" (the island of hope).

With great difficulty, Robinson built a boat that would be strong enough to withstand the high seas and allow him to reach the coast of Chile. Unfortunately, his ambitious project failed miserably as he could not get the 500-kilogram boat to the sea (see Box 3.3).

BOX 3.3

The Escape Project and the Failure of a Strategy

Shipwrecked on an island, Robinson built a boat called the *Escape*. He decided to do a test run to see how the boat would perform. Would the *Escape* hold up well in the water? Would it be watertight?

He built the boat up near the trees. To get it to the water, he decided to slide logs under the keel so he could roll it. After a few days of excruciating work, he realized that he could not drag the boat, which must have weighed half a ton, over the grass and sand to the sea. He then thought of digging a trench to slide the *Escape* to the shore, but he knew it would take years to finish this project. He gave up.

Robinson had utterly neglected the problem of getting the boat to the shore. Perhaps he had relied too much on the story of Noah's ark. Built far from the sea, the ark had only to wait for the water to come to it in the form of rain and runoff from the mountains.

Source: Inspired by Michel Tournier (1984).

While we know a lot about what strategy is, many organizations still know very little about translating strategy into concrete results. Indeed, the scorecard on strategic implementations seems at times bimodal. Some organizations have had outstanding achievements and great successes that last for decades. Other organizations (even experienced ones) have had resounding failures. A survey conducted in 2004 by Marakon & Associates (in collaboration with *The Economist Intelligence Unit*) among executives of nearly 200 companies with revenues exceeding US$500 million reveals that more than 60 percent of corporate strategies fail to deliver the expected financial performance. As we will see in the examples presented (see Table 3.3), both deliberate or emergent strategies can fail or succeed.

TABLE 3.3 Strategy Implementation: Successes and Failures

STRATEGIC SUCCESSES	STRATEGIC FAILURES
Examples: Apple's iPhone; Zara; Starbucks; Lego	**Examples**: NBA basketball changeover; Target Canada; Lehman Brothers; Galaxy Note 7; Walmart Seiyu

What can we learn about strategy implementation from companies using *winning strategies*?

Strategic Successes

Let us start with Apple and the emergence of the iPhone. By the mid-2000s, people were getting used to using smartphones—namely, the BlackBerry—to access emails and the internet. Steve Jobs and many others understood that people would want one device rather than two or three to read and send emails, make and receive phone calls, and listen to music. In short, they would need "a device that could be used to email while on the toilet," and that would allow Apple to enter and dominate the new smartphone market. The iPhone's launch in 2007 was a runaway commercial success! Apple had realized that people do not need any particular product. Rather they seek to satisfy a basic human need—in this case, their need for communication, be it via email, phone calls, or even music. The implementation of that strategy involved intense negotiations and involvement of service providers, such as AT&T.

Zara is a Spanish store specializing in ready-to-wear clothing for women and men. With more than 36,000 offerings per year and more than 1,900 stores worldwide, Zara has revolutionized the fashion industry. Gone are the days of once-a-season or twice-a-year collection renewals for ready-to-wear companies! Instead, with what is known as "fast fashion," Zara is setting the pace for all brands, including luxury clothing companies like Prada and Louis Vuitton. Zara emphasizes limited inventory and maximum collection updates, avoiding the risk that traditional retailers like Gap, Abercrombie & Fitch, Ann Taylor, and American Eagle face, of not being able to predict next year's fashion trends. For example, Zara stores receive new styles twice a week, encouraging customers to return to the store often or risk not finding the garment they want to buy later, creating a mini marketplace with constant updates. Its customers have access to dozens of merchants in one store, saving on the cost of acquiring, evaluating, and negotiating. The implementation of that strategy is supported by radio frequency identification (RFID) technology. With real-time tracking of garments, each store can offer the items that are most in demand and be informed of orders that could not be fulfilled.

The case of Starbucks is also instructive. While customers may have seemed "just to want coffee," CEO Howard Schultz realized that giving them "a third place to live or gather" in addition to their homes and offices would appeal to some segments. Of course, coffeehouses had existed for centuries in the Arab world (think Arabica) and had become common in Europe. Starbucks brought that idea to America, addressing two basic human needs, casual socialization and eating. The implementation of their strategy rested heavily on the delegation of responsibilities at various levels, down to the local store.

The Danish company Lego was losing about a million dollars a day in 2004. It cut costs, particularly in clothing and theme parks, to refocus on what it does best: providing fun for children and adults. So, they kept the traditional Lego toys and added some digital games. Thus Lego effectively made the transition from "bricks *to* clicks" to become one of the 10 best brands in the world! Adapting to social and technological changes, Lego continued to provide children with educational toys, a basic human need, likely to appeal to the users (children) as well as the payers (parents). The project was helped by the fact that Lego is a trusted name for the target segment.

In summary, in successfully delivering these winning strategies, these organizations were able to carve out or transition to a comfortable position in the competitive market by meeting customers' needs in a timely manner. But these success stories are not the norm.

Strategic Failures

Let us consider and learn from *failures.* Few organizations succeed in implementing their strategy effectively—while some fail to have any clear strategy at all.[2] The PwC survey reports that two-thirds of these leaders believe their organization does not have the resources or skills to implement the strategy well, even if it is well formulated. As a result, only 8 percent of them excel at both strategy formulation and implementation. *Implementation challenges are major obstacles to success.*

In the case of the National Basketball Association (NBA), why change a ball that works? Yet, that is precisely what the NBA did—without a clear strategy, goal, or need. Indeed, it was the first time in 35 years that the NBA changed its ball.

What was the idea behind this change? While NBA Commissioner David Stern said that it was time for the best basketball players to play with the best basketball in the world, the real motivation was unclear. Clearly, the new synthetic ball should provide a new design and a better grip, feel, and consistency than the old leather ball. Some, however, speculated that it was a way for the commissioner to assert control over the players during salary negotiations, or an attempt to project a more polished image for the league.

The implementation was disastrous for this key reason: the NBA did not consult with the players. After many complaints from influential players, the NBA had to withdraw the new synthetic ball and return to the leather one used for decades.

Other examples abound. Minnesota-based Target—the fifth-largest retailer in the United States by volume behind Walmart, Home Depot, Kroger, and Costco—was receiving more than two million Canadian customers a year in its US stores. Considering the strong attraction for Canadians, Target CEO Gregg Steinhafel, who had had a stellar career up to then—having increased sales by 8.3 percent during the 2008 recession—decided on a strategy to conquer the Canadian market.

After a pretty good start, the strategy ran into implementation difficulties. Canadian consumer expectations for local Target stores were high, based on the extraordinary experience they had shopping at Target across the border. They were quickly disappointed due to supply problems and the lack of competitively priced products. The organization had also neglected to factor in the existing competition Target would face in Canada. With operating losses of more than US$2 billion in 2013, Target was forced to close 133 stores in Canada in 2015 and put 17,600 employees out of work.

Another telling case is that of the Lehman Brothers investment bank. Until 2005, Lehman Brothers was a successful pioneer in mortgage securities in the United States. But things began to change; by mid-2005, home sales were peaking, home prices were starting to stagnate, and a slight increase in interest rates had led to foreclosures. Against this backdrop, CEO Richard Fuld devised a strategy to outgrow the rest of the industry and augment Lehman Brothers' market share: the plan was to increase their risk appetite by taking on mortgages that competitors would reject. In short, it was an ambitious, risky, and, as it turned out, an ill-conceived strategy that was not accompanied by adequate risk mitigation.

Like Robinson Crusoe, who could not drag the boat to sea, these organizations and others (e.g., Samsung for the Galaxy 7 Note and Walmart for the Seiyu expansion) tried hard but failed badly. Their strategies fell short, because they failed either to assess adequately in advance, or to adapt to the changing environment. This is a clear warning for C-suite executives (the top level management positions in the company) like Facebook's Mark Zuckerberg, who changed the name of his trillion-dollar company to "Meta" in 2021, betting that the multibillion dollar "Metaverse" strategy of "a virtual world where people can socialize, work, and play" is the future of the internet. Time will tell if this bold move is a case of "damned if you do or damned if you don't" for Meta's CEO. By understanding strategic successes and failures, organizations can improve their chances of success or limit the negative impact poor strategy implementation has on the organization.

Third Challenge: Understanding Poor Strategy Implementation

Since there can be no adequate cure without proper diagnosis, we need to look upstream at the common reasons for implementation failure:

- **Strategic planning, at the initial stages:** Poorly conceived plans; inadequate, unavailable, or misused resources
- **Project management, in the implementation team:** Unclear actions and responsibilities; communication problems; lack of leadership; organizational silos and an unsupportive organizational culture; poor consequences or rewards for failure or success; inadequate accountability; and people's resistance to change
- **Strategy implementation, as the project progresses:** Changing strategy or objectives, causing confusion; inadequate project performance monitoring (fewer than 15 percent of companies track their performance; performance bottlenecks are invisible to senior management; a culture of poor performance prevails); failures to synchronize strategy; and inability to deliver the right product, to the right customer, at the right time
- **Bad timing, poor cultural adaptation, and whirlwind problems throughout the implementation cycle**

Strategy or *objectives that change too often* create confusion. Hewlett-Packard's (HP) competitive strategy to outmaneuver Dell in the personal computer (PC) market offers a good illustration. After acquiring Compaq, HP focused on price one week and service the next while trying to sell through high-cost and often conflicting channels. As a result, CEO Carly Fiorina lost her job (Knowledge@Wharton, 2005).

Timing mishaps also contribute to implementation problems. When United Airlines decided to set up a low-cost subsidiary called TED to compete with "upstarts" like Southwest, it kept its old cost structure, which was the fundamental reason United was losing market share to low-cost carriers. Timing was also an issue, as the launch coincided with unexpected rising fuel costs. The steep cost of jet fuel jeopardized the profitability of TED and put United Airlines in a difficult financial situation. In the end, TED was successfully absorbed by United.[3]

Target also suffered from problems linked to *cultural adaptation*. In its strategy to conquer the Canadian market, Target used the same recipes that had succeeded in the United States, only to learn the hard way that Canada is not the United States. Cultural factors also played a role in Walmart's failure in Germany and Japan (Knowledge@Wharton, 2005).

For these reasons, some authors add the *"whirlwind" problem* to the list: the enormous amount of energy needed to deal with the company's day-to-day operations, which year in and year out leaves little time for strategy execution (McChesney, Covey, & Huling, 2012). To paraphrase a colloquial saying: When you are up to your neck in alligators, it is hard to concentrate on draining the swamp. Now that we understand why strategy implementation fails, how can better project management help us meet these challenges?

INSIGHTS FOR GETTING STRATEGY IMPLEMENTATION RIGHT

While the strategy implementation literature has provided many prescriptions, two schools of thought stand out, one focusing on the *people involved* in the implementation, the other on the *processes they use* (Knowledge@Wharton, 2015). In the first school, successful implementation requires the right people. Here, the perspective of former 3M CEO James McNerney is instructive. If you can increase the average performance of each individual (regardless of their role) by 15 percent, you will surely and sustainably improve your company's performance. In the second school of thought, to be successful you need to invest in the *implementation process*. This was the view promoted by Larry Bossidy (2012), former CEO of Honeywell.

Some of the best companies—Cisco, 3M, and GE—focus on the implementation process as well as the training of people, including executives, project team members, and stakeholders. The advice that follows is in line with this two-pronged approach.

Building and delivering successful strategies should be based on *six pillars*, according to Lepsinger (2010)—namely, (1) translate strategy into action, and align projects and programs with strategy; (2) establish high and clear expectations for performance, and expect people to deliver by tapping into the power of the Pygmalion effect[4] of self-fulfilling prophecies; (3) hold people accountable for their actions and results; (4) ensure that the right people can make the right decisions at the right time; (5) prepare for change and ensure that actions follow words; and, finally, (6) improve coordination and cooperation through clear communications, shared goals, and well-defined roles.

Other strategy experts (Knowledge@Wharton, 2005) suggest *five keys for more effective implementation by framing the process*: (1) develop an implementation model with guidelines including change management and not just a mandate to execute; (2) choose performance measures that reflect changing market conditions; (3) do not forget the plan and organize meetings to discuss the strategy in depth; (4) monitor performance and get real-time feedback on the effectiveness of the execution; and (5) communicate regularly with executives and everyone involved in implementing the strategy.

Strategists can also rely on precise "recipes" (Mankins & Steele, 2005): (1) make things simple and concrete; clarify what a strategy is and what it is not; (2) discuss the assumptions underlying the business case and ensure that they reflect market conditions; (3) use a rigorous performance measurement framework, agree on financial projections, and discuss resource allocation early on; (4) identify the right priorities at the right time, and communicate them; (5) monitor real-time performance continually, review assumptions, adjust, and reallocate resources as necessary; and (6) develop and reward excellence in implementation.

Still others take a very broad approach and urge companies to rely on *four disciplines to implement their strategic priorities* (McChesney et al., 2012): (1) focus on the critical objectives that will make a difference and have the most significant organizational impact; (2) act on predictive performance measures to know whether you are on track to meeting the goal; (3) maintain a credible scoreboard; and (4) create an accountability pace: a regular, recurring cycle of accountability that allows you to measure past performance and anticipate future performance.

Other authors (Leinward & Mainardi, 2016) have noted that companies that excel in strategy implementation set aside such conventional measures. Instead, they use the global concepts of *identity, culture, and fundamental capabilities*. Accordingly, they (1) develop an identity that allows them to focus on delivering value to their customers, developing distinctive and sustainable capabilities, while responding quickly to new opportunities; (2) translate their strategy into concrete actions that give substance to their identity; (3) put their culture to work, making good use of their ways of thinking and behaving to implement the strategy and promote performance; (4) do not reduce costs across the board, but rather focus on the few capabilities that matter most to their long-term success; and (5) refrain from responding too quickly to certain changes in the external environment—instead, they focus on shaping their future, leveraging their privileged access to customers, or making mergers and acquisitions to make the environment more favorable.

Undoubtedly, these ideas for successful strategy implementation are appealing. However, their reductionist approaches underestimate the complexity and importance of strategy implementation. In so doing, they restrain the contribution that project management can make. This should be cause for concern. Rigorous strategy implementation is not our purpose in this book. We can aim higher by managing projects in a manner that delivers benefits and value to organizations and stakeholders. To these ends, the next section examines how project management can help managers deal with the challenges of strategy implementation.

ROLE OF PROJECT MANAGEMENT IN STRATEGY IMPLEMENTATION

Approaches to Strategy Implementation

The challenges faced in implementing strategies successfully have been chronicled for centuries. In the past few decades alone, a host of prescriptions have been proposed in the organizational literature: management by objectives, results-based management (RBM), benefits realization management (BRM), total quality management (TQM), and the balanced scorecard. All of these approaches have been helpful in selected areas. They inform the ideas we put forth in this book, as we look at the organization fully, in three dimensions. Table 3.4 provides a brief overview of these initiatives and their relation to strategy implementation.

Of all these approaches to strategy implementation, two stand out for managing projects: results-based management and benefits realization management. Both approaches share a common focus on results, benefits, or value delivery, not traditional output-driven metrics such as time, cost, and quality. Put differently, they look beyond mere project inputs (what is spent), activities (what is done), and outputs (what is produced) and focus on actual results (what is the contribution of the project to the organization).

TABLE 3.4 Managerial Initiatives to Address Implementation

MANAGERIAL INITIATIVE	KEY ELEMENTS AND MAJOR AUTHORS (Adapted from Serra, 2016)
Management by Objectives	Achieve a set of key organizational objectives (e.g., Drucker, 1954).
Results-Based Management (RBM)	Align the conduct of projects and programs with short-, medium-, and long-term results (e.g., Binnendijk, 2000).
Benefits Realization Management	Align the projects, programs, and portfolios with the potential that each one has to contribute to the organization's strategy and to create value (e.g., Zwikael & Zmyrk, 2019).
Total Quality Management (TQM)	Involve the organization's members as much as possible in improving processes, products, and services; develop a culture that focuses on customer satisfaction and the organization's long-term success (e.g., Ishikawa, 1984).
Balanced Scorecard	Move from a measurement system to a management system that articulates the links between performance measurement, indicators, and the management process and thus strategically aligns the behaviors of the management units (e.g., Kaplan & Norton, 1996).

Results-Based Management

Results-based management has a two-pronged approach: *managing for results* and *tracking results*. In the context of international development projects where results-based management has been extensively used, keeping track of results entails gathering the performance information and reporting it to external stakeholders such as funders, parliaments, and oversight agencies in order to show "value for money"; managing for results means using such performance information to improve internal management decision-making processes and achieving better results (Binnendijk, 2000).

However, in practice, results-based management has focused too much on keeping track of results and too little on managing for results, leading to the *accountability-for-results* trap (Ika, 2012): lack of a long-term results orientation, reporting for the sake of reporting, lack of a strong results culture, and so on. While results-based management has held sway in the public sector for decades, benefits realization management has been gaining ground in the private sector for years (Zwikael & Smyrk, 2019). As results-based management is akin to benefits realization management applied to the public sector, we will gain more insight in terms of how benefits realization can help project management improve strategy implementation.

Benefits Realization Management

In a real sense, the organization itself is a project, since its past, present, and future are based on projects. To succeed in strategy is to carry out projects and deliver the value expected by the project stakeholders or the competitive advantage anticipated by organizations. Projects are privileged instruments to make or alter the organization's strategy and deliver value or gain a competitive advantage (Miller & Lessard, 2000; Shenhar & Dvir, 2007). They are used to develop new products or services such as Fairphone (the eco-friendly and fair-trade smartphone; see Box 3.5); to generate disruptive innovations such as Twitter, Nespresso, or Crocs; to improve operational processes by adopting ISO standards; or to make organizational changes such as restructuring the firm. A benefits realization approach to project management can help align these projects to the organization's strategy.

BOX 3.5

The Fairphone Project

Fairphone, a Dutch startup founded in 2010, launched the world's first "green" or "fair-trade" smartphone in 2013. In 2022, this eco-smartphone is now on its fourth version (currently selling for US$650) using Fairphone Open OS, an open operating system based on Android. It looks like a classic smartphone, but it is simply designed to avoid premature obsolescence. Like the iPhone, it is assembled in China, where most of the components come from.

Even if the fourth version is not yet 100 percent fair trade, Fairphone can count on healthy and long-term relationships with its suppliers and subcontractors (Chinese, Taiwanese, Japanese, German, American, and Czech) and a supply chain that puts human and social values first. Fairphone is careful to avoid minerals (such as tin or tantalum) that would finance local conflicts in countries like the Democratic Republic of Congo.

It includes 40 percent recycled products; it is modular, allowing you to simply change the screen, the battery, or the camera and is thus an antidote to programmed obsolescence; and it is ethical, in that it ensures the traceability of all components and promotes fair trade.

Sources: The Guardian (18 September 2019);[5]
Irish Times (16 December 2021).[6]

In essence, benefits realization management is the process of linking the organizational strategy with a project's intended benefits (e.g., cost savings, productivity gains, process improvements, increased returns on investment, increased market share, poverty reduction, lowered carbon emissions). It emphasizes the creation and delivery of benefits, which are the flows of value that emerge from a project and value, which is the sum of economic and wider social benefits to be accrued minus the costs incurred. Thus, in order to manage a project to yield benefits, the organization must identify:

- The target benefits assigned to the project at its initiation that would meet its strategic objectives

- The desired benefits that key stakeholders expect any time during the project life
- The likely benefits that an incomplete project will yield during execution, considering its resources and capabilities
- The actual benefits delivered by the project at completion, based on how it had evolved and where it ended up (Browning, 2019)

In so doing, benefits realization management helps ensure that benefits and value are achieved and sustained in a way that is consistent with the organization's strategy. A PMI survey reveals that while 9 out of 10 organizations implement benefits realization management practices, less than 1 out of 5 do so consistently. Another study by Boston Consulting Group reports that those organizations where benefits realization management is fully in place are about 1.5 times more likely to reach their benefits targets and 3 times more likely to meet their "goal value" targets, including return on investment (ROI) for their projects (The Boston Consulting Group, 2016).

Learning from these benefits-focused contributions, we suggest the organizations that excel in benefits realization rely on the following 10 successful practices:

- Engage C-suite executives who set and approve strategy, project sponsors who translate the strategy into projects with targeted "goal value" and benefits for their unit, and project managers, like Nancy Smart, who are tasked with the implementation of the projects to realize these benefits.
- Select the right projects.
- Define target benefits and anticipate the stakeholders' desired benefits.
- Ensure that the right conditions for success are in place by setting up clear expectations in terms of behavior, project managers' skills, and project sponsors' level of engagement.

- Keep project sponsors and managers engaged and encourage and reward the right behaviors throughout the project and make them accountable to benefits creation and delivery.
- Keep track of benefits by measuring likely benefits during project execution compared to target benefits identified in the approved business case, and apply corrective measures during project execution.
- Link project success systematically with project benefits and value.
- Measure actual benefits at project completion, compared with target benefits at project completion; learn lessons; and ensure benefits are sustained after project completion.
- Put in place early-warning systems to detect problems proactively and course-correct.
- Invest in long-term benefits realization management training for project sponsors, managers, and teams.

Given the many potential benefits of projects, it is easy to see why a benefits realization approach to project management is important. What are the risks if such a strategy-implementation-oriented project management approach is ignored or not given enough attention?

THE NBA DROPPED THE BALL: HOW PROJECT MANAGEMENT FAILS STRATEGY

It is easy to find projects that miss their target benefits or fail to contribute to organizational strategy (Shenhar & Dvir, 2007; Zwikael & Smyrk, 2019). Let us consider again the case of the NBA basketball changeover project. Its failures illustrate how project management can thwart strategy implementation. Unfortunately, this project lacked a focus on benefits realization and on what Rumelt (2011) would call a proper diagnosis of the situation: (1) the purpose, need, and target benefits for the project were unclear; (2) the key project stakeholders were not consulted; and (3) stakeholder benefits were not anticipated.

In 2004, Stu Jackson, the NBA's vice president of operations, pointed out that the NBA's official leather ball could be improved. In 2006, the NBA decided to switch to a synthetic ball.

In hindsight, what reasons did they give for the change? The leather ball lacked consistency, had an irregular color and shape, slipped too much in the players' hands, and took teams six to seven months to break in before being used in official games. In addition, the leather ball could not be used for outdoor basketball. Changing it would improve the game, reduce ball break-in time, and boost sales of the new ball.

The NBA and Spalding worked together to develop the new synthetic ball. They put it through a rigorous evaluation process that included laboratory and court testing, and also got feedback from *retired* players Steve Kerr and Mark Jackson.

Things did not go well for the NBA. They excluded the players from the ball's development process and did not explore these key stakeholders' desired benefits. They did not consider the comments that players had made during training camps before the official season began (perhaps because of the poor relationship between the league and the National Basketball Players Association, the NBPA). Shortly after introducing the new ball, stars like LeBron James and Shaquille O'Neal were complaining publicly. For example, LeBron opined: "The only thing that we love the most is the basketball . . . That's your comfort. I mean, without your basketball, it does not work. That was my biggest problem. Why would you change something that means so much to us?" O'Neal added: "It feels like one of those cheap balls you buy at the toy store. . . . I look for shooting percentages to be way down and turnovers to be way up, because when the ball gets wet you can't really control it. Whoever did that needs to be fired. It was terrible, a terrible decision. Awful."

Many players found the basketball hard to handle—too slick when dry, too sticky when wet, and it bounced awkwardly—and worse, it caused a rash of minor hand injuries. Another influential player, Steve Nash, also expressed disappointment that the NBA did not consult with them before changing the ball.

Despite player pushback, the new ball exceeded Spalding's sales expectations, and it became one of the bestselling products on Amazon. It was so popular that it was hard to find in sports stores. However, the players would not relent. In December 2006, the NBPA filed a grievance against the NBA for not involving the players in developing the new ball. The NBA withdrew the ball on January 1, 2007—they had to revert to the old ball mid-season. The NBA commissioner eventually admitted that the NBA and Spalding should have consulted the players, as is typically done in the soccer (FIFA) and field hockey (NHL) leagues.[7]

How Can Good Project Management Help Save Some Initiatives?

If the NBA had taken the time to do one or more of these steps at the start of the project, it could have made a significant difference:

- Create a project charter: a document that formally approves the project and highlights the business need or rationale for the project (see Appendix 3.1)
- Develop a business case that states the business need and justifies the investment in the project (see Appendix 3.2)
- Complete a project frame that includes the needs, options, and stakeholders (see Appendix 3.3)

For the NBA, a good stakeholder analysis would have taken into account the players in a changeover process. It would have highlighted the importance of including the star players in the change process, and of securing their buy-in from the start.

Most successful major projects start off with preliminary thoughts and conversations during their front end or initiation, which may last several years, if not decades. This covers the period between when the project idea is conceptualized to when the final decision to fund the project is made. A business case—which tends to be solution-free—states a timeline and provides measures of the target "goal value" of the project; it is developed and approved during the front end. For formal authorization purposes, a project charter or frame may then follow. Executives and senior managers are the target audience for the business case, the project charter, and the project frame. Project sponsors, who oversee the initiation (and later the execution of the project) or the "management of project management," might lead the call. In some instances, project managers may be involved in the elaboration of the project charter or frame. During the initiation phase, project sponsors assess the needs (what are the objectives?), analyze the feasibility (can we do it?), weigh the options (is there more than one way of doing it?), and examine the risks (what can go wrong?) of the proposed project.

CONCLUSION

In implementing strategies, managers face obstacles in three main areas: First, at the stage of strategy formulation, there is no broad consensus on what "strategy" means, so it is challenging to develop a clear one. Second, strategy formulation is not integrated with the implementation process. The people who develop the initial strategy expect the team to implement it "as is" but do not adjust it as the project evolves. Many believe that the strategy cannot subsequently be altered due to the amounts of time and money that have been invested. A mission statement or vision has proven to be insufficient for a strategy to succeed. Third, at the final stages of implementation, it is hard to measure the strategy's success given that the project's circumstances usually change, and implementation faces so many challenges.

Better approaches to project management focused on benefits realization can help fuzzy projects deal with these strategy implementation challenges and improve the chances of success. To this end, six takeaways are proffered for project managers and sponsors:

1. Projects are privileged instruments that organizations use to make/break or alter/reorient their core strategy. While there are many successes, strategies (deliberate or emergent) fail more often than they succeed.
2. There is no consensus on what strategy is, but it could be defined as a coherent set of policies and actions designed to address an overarching challenge or issue. Strategy has different meanings and different schools of thought.
3. The kernel of a good strategy is a diagnosis of the current situation, a policy to guide action, and a coherent plan of action.
4. It is a mistake to separate strategy formulation from strategy implementation because strategy is a dynamic process.
5. The reasons for strategy implementation failure are many and varied: failures in formulation and implementation, poor organizational culture, and lack of capacity.
6. Managers need to invest in the implementation process and in training people. Project management can best contribute to strategy implementation by focusing on benefits realization and value delivery. In doing so, managers can make better use of the tools of the trade, such as the project charter, the project frame, and the business case.

REFERENCES

Ansoff, I. H. (1965). *Corporate strategy: An analytic approach to business policy for growth and expansion*. McGraw-Hill.

Bhide, A. (2000). *The origin and the evolution of new businesses*. Oxford University Press.

Bossidy, L., & Charan, R. (2002). *Execution: The discipline of getting things done*. Crown Publishing Group.

Browning, T. R. (2019). Planning, tracking, and reducing a complex project's value at risk. *Project Management Journal, 50*(1), 71–85.

Bungay, S. (2019). Myths about strategy. *Harvard Business Review*. https://hbr.org/2019/04/5-myths-about-strategy. Zugegriffen, 18.

Cleland, D. I. (2007). *Project management: Strategic design and implementation*. McGraw-Hill Education.

Crossan, M. M., Rouse, M. J., Rowe, W. G., & Maurer, C. (2015). *Strategic analysis and action*. Ninth edition. Pearson.

Ferraro, F., Etzion, D., & Gehman, J. (2015). Tackling grand challenges pragmatically: Robust action revisited. *Organization Studies, 36*, 363–390.

Ika, L. A. (2012). Project management for development in Africa: Why projects are failing and what can be done about it. *Project Management Journal, 43(*4), 27–41.

Ika, L. A., & Munro, L. T. (2022). Tackling grand challenges with projects: Five insights and a research agenda for project management theory and practice. *International Journal of Project Management, 40*(6), 601–607.

Knowledge@Wharton (2005). Three reasons why good strategies fail: Execution, execution . . . https://knowledge.wharton.upenn.edu/article/three-reasons-why-good-strategies-fail-execution-execution/ (accessed 15 February, 2022).

Leinward, P., & Mainardi, C. R. (2016). *Strategy that works*. How winning companies close the strategy-to-execution gap. Harvard Business Press.

Lepsinger, R. (2010). *Closing the execution gap: How great leaders and their companies get results*. John Wiley & Sons.

Mankins, M. C., & Steele, R. (2005). Turning great strategy into great performance. *Harvard Business Review, 83*, 7(8), 64–72.

McChesney, C., Covey, S., & Huling, J. (2012). *The 4 disciplines of execution: Achieving your wildly important goals*. Free Press, Simon & Schuster.

Miller, R., & Lessard, D. R. (2000). *The strategic management of large engineering projects. Shaping institutions, risks, and governance.* MIT Press.

Mintzberg, H., Alstrand, B., & Lampel, J. (1998). *Strategy safari: a guided tour through the wilds of strategic management.* Simon & Shuster.

Peters, T. (2004). Nix the spreadsheet. *PM Network, 18*(1)19, Jan.

Porter, M. (1996). What is strategy? *Harvard Business Review, 74*(6), 61–79.

Rivkin, J. W. (2006). Why do strategies fail? Advanced Competitive Strategy, Module note 9-706-433 for students. Harvard Business School. February 27.

Rosenthal, R., & Jacobson, L. (1968). *Pygmalion in the classroom: Teacher expectations and pupils' intellectual development.* Holt, Rinehart, & Winston.

Roth, D. (2017, 23 February). The NBA ball that everyone hated: Throwback Thursday. Vice.Com. The NBA Ball That Everyone Hated: Throwback Thursday (vice.com) (accessed 2 September, 2022).

Rumelt, R. P. (2011). *Good strategy. Bad strategy. The difference and why it matters.* Crown Business.

Selznick, P. (1957). *Leadership in administration.* Harper & Row.

Serra, C. E. M. (2016). *Benefits realization management.* Taylor & Francis, CRC Press.

The Boston Consulting Group (2016). *Connecting business strategy and project management.*

Tournier, M. (1984). *Friday, or the other island* (D. Norman, Trans.). Penguin.

Sun Tzu (1984). *The art of war* (R. D. Sawyer, Trans.). Westview Press.

Von Clausewitz, C. (1989). *Carl von Clausewitz on war* (M. Howard & P. Paret, Trans.) Princeton University Press.

Zwikael, O., & Smyrk, J. R. (2019). *Project management: A benefit realisation approach.* Springer-Verlag.

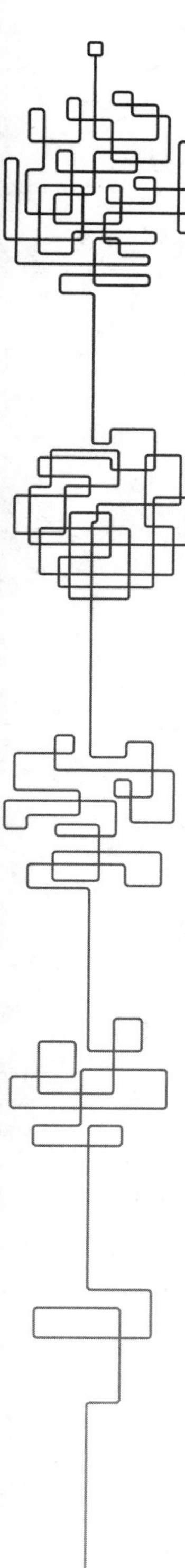

CHAPTER 4

PROJECTS AND MANAGEMENT

If you are planning for a year, plant rice; for 20, plant a tree; for 100, develop people.

—Guan Zhong (720–645 BCE)

This chapter focuses on the strategy-project-operations triad. First, we examine the nature of projects and how they relate to strategic and operational management. Next, we highlight the key characteristics of projects and project management. Then, we examine the roots of project management to gain insight into how it informs but also impairs how it is practiced today.

SIMILARITIES AND DIFFERENCES BETWEEN PROJECT AND STRATEGY

Project and strategy have striking similarities and marked differences, which are sources of synergy and of tension. As with strategy, a "good project" requires a comprehensive diagnosis of the situation, a clear policy to guide action, and a coherent action plan (Rumelt,

2011). In practical terms, a good project has a clearly identified problem/opportunity or business need, a clear scope of what must be accomplished, and clear direction and objectives embedded in a thorough implementation plan (see Figure 4.1).

In the case of the original iPhone, given that it was not the first smartphone, the *business need* (or opportunity in this case) could have been expressed as follows: "There is no device on the market that can make phone calls, browse the web, write emails, *and* listen to music. Such a smartphone would have a high-growth market potential."

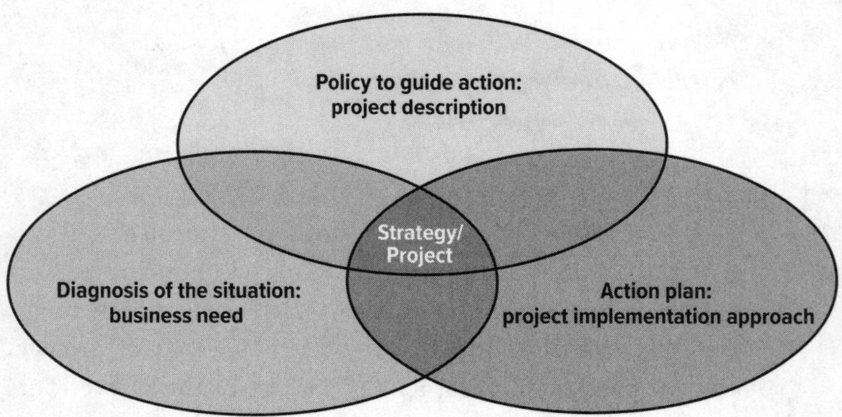

FIGURE 4.1 The project overlaid on the core strategy

This business need led the company to initiate a major project in 2007, which was very successful. Over the next two decades, Apple undertook other projects to enhance the original iPhone. Newer versions included photos and movies, and addressed personal health, lifestyles, and security concerns. They also offered safe access to apps, information storage, and seamless integration with other Apple devices.

As previously mentioned, the business need may be included in the *project charter,* a document that formally authorizes the project and gives its manager the authority to use the organization's resources for the project. The *project description* section of the project charter provides information about the project and gives it concrete direction to guide implementation. For the series of iPhone projects, we would have described the project as a smartphone that is easy to navigate, stores a large amount of data, and has user-friendly software. Though most consumers might not have given it any thought, Apple thought consumers would prefer having many functions in one device. This description stems from an assessment of the project environment and the assumptions underlying the project idea (see "Project Charter" in Appendix 3.1).

Finally, as is the case for strategy, a project cannot succeed without good execution. A project needs a methodical implementation approach—concrete, feasible steps that are likely to succeed. Undoubtedly, Apple's implementation approach included a trial-and-error process where you experiment, innovate, and learn as you go. It also included making prototypes to reduce the project's complexity.

As noted in the previous chapter, Mintzberg, Alstrand, and Lampel (1998) identified five ways in which strategy is conceived (five Ps): Plan, Pattern, Ploy, Perspective, and Position. Nearly the same characterization holds for projects. Both strategy and project are driven by deliberate thinking, past decisions, and vision, as well as contexts. A project could be viewed as an action that is (Joffre, Aurégan, Chodétel, & Tellier, 2006):

1. Deliberately wanted **(plan)**
2. Formalized and structured **(pattern)**
3. Designed to achieve, by certain means and tricks, a specific objective **(ploy)**
4. Deemed favorable for the future of the organization **(perspective)**
5. Potentially able to strengthen the position of the organization within its environment **(position)**

As these authors argue, a project should help execute the strategy; but it can also make or break the organization's strategy. That is, a project is not just a variation of the strategy. Quite the contrary: a dual relationship exists between the project and the strategy. Sometimes they are in sync, sometimes they are not; the project may submit to the strategy, shape it, or even strongly influence or alter it.

Like strategy, a project can be a *deliberate* and intentionally part of the organization's strategy, or it can *emerge* gradually without being expressly desired by senior management. The Frappuccino is an iced coffee drink that has become an important Starbucks trademark. However, when an employee first submitted the idea, the Starbucks bosses rejected it: "We do not do that at Starbucks. . . . We are in the coffee business!" However, a few people who believed in the project did not relent, and the Frappuccino significantly contributed to the company's strategic growth and direction (see Box 4.1).

Even the initial strategy that gave some well-known companies their fundamental orientation could have also emerged in ways that were quite low-key, with limited deliberation and intent. After being dumped by his girlfriend, Mark Zuckerberg created a website called FaceMash, where viewers could vote on the attractiveness of women. The site evolved into "The Facebook," an online social network exclusively for Harvard students. It gained popularity, and Facebook became the social media site we know today, accessible to everyone (except in China, Iran, North Korea, and Russia).

BOX 4.1

The Starbucks Frappuccino Project: The Art of Perseverance

In 1992, looking for a way to increase sales, Boston coffee shop owner George Howell caught wind of a trend on the West Coast to blend iced drinks with an Italian espresso-based cappuccino. Andrew Frank, his young marketing manager, came up with a recipe for the Frappuccino, which was inspired and named after the New England milkshake called "frappe." It was a unique blend of coffee, sugar, milk, and ice with a smooth, creamy consistency. With this recipe, coffee consumption in Boston increased, and Howell doubled the number of coffee shops he owned to 23. In 1994, Starbucks bought Howell's coffee shop chain and the Frappuccino brand's rights for US$23 million.

Later, Dina Campion (one of Starbucks' first district managers in Southern California) and Howard Behar (the former president of Starbucks International) figured if they made their own version, they could sell about 30 a day for a 5 percent bump in average store volume. However, despite Behar's belief in the project, senior executives Howard Schultz and Orin Smith outright rejected it.

Despite this resounding "no," Behar quietly commissioned Campion to test the new drink in his stores. It was a huge success! So, once again, Behar presented the new drink to the management team, and this time Schultz agreed to a 90-day test. Starbucks then modified the old Frappuccino recipe, prepared the drink in a blender instead of a frozen yogurt machine, and struck a deal with Pepsi to manufacture the small, ready-to-drink milk bottles. By 1996, annual sales of Frappuccino were more than US$52 million. Starting in 2002, Starbucks began releasing a new Frappuccino each spring, coordinating the flavor to match trendy colors. Since 2012, Frappuccino has accounted for up to 20 percent of Starbuck's sales.

Sources: Boston Magazine.com (7 December 2012); Fields (2011).

So, it is clear that specific projects can alter the overall strategy of an organization. However, a *project* differs from a strategy in many ways (see Table 4.1):

- A project has a preset timeline, while strategy is never-ending.
- It focuses on the implementation of a specific objective.
- It has tangible, specific, and relatively easy-to-measure deliverables.
- It is subject to relatively strict time, cost, quality, and scope constraints.
- It involves clearer and more circumscribed accountability for results than the strategy.

Although a project is a temporary endeavor, its implementation can take years. *Time constraints* are usually assumed to be the project deadline (a given date), but they can refer to a project's duration (such as a marketing campaign linked to the launch of a product), or its sequence (like the long-planned state funeral of Queen Elizabeth II).

TABLE 4.1 Contrasting Project and Strategy

PROJECT	STRATEGY
Temporary	Continuous
Targeted business problems or needs	Complex business problems or needs
Relatively stable environment	Dynamic environment
Relatively low complexity and uncertainty	Relatively high complexity and uncertainty
Focused on implementation	Focused on problem formulation
Specific objective	Several goals
Limited scope	Wide scope
Limited options for action	Many options for action
Specific deliverables	Broad deliverables
Often strict constraints on scope, time, budget, and quality	Few constraints on scope, time, budget, and quality
Clear and focused accountability for results	Broadly shared accountability for results
Responsibility of project managers	Responsibility of upper managers

KEY DIFFERENCES BETWEEN PROJECTS AND OPERATIONS

Aside from project and strategic activities, the management of an organization also includes operations that are characteristically recurrent, predictable, and relatively stable. Together, these activities form a *strategy-project-operations triad.* Specifically, the *project* differs from operations in that it is generally time-bound, temporary, innovative, multidisciplinary, and dependent on exogenous constraints and negative cash flows. Conversely, *operations* are characterized by routine and continuous work that consists of the repetitive execution of identical or similar tasks. Table 4.2 contrasts projects and operations.

TABLE 4.2 Contrasting Projects and Operations

PROJECTS	OPERATIONS
Singular	Repetitive
Temporary, limited in time	Continuous, routinized
Irreversible decisions	Reversible decisions
High uncertainty	Low uncertainty
Multidisciplinary, more heterogeneous	Standardized tasks, more homogeneous
New systems	Existing systems
Outside the organization's hierarchy	Within the organization's hierarchy
Externally constrained	Internally constrained
Negative cash flows	Positive cash flows
Disrupts the status quo	Preserves the status quo
Challenges well-established practices	Relies on well-established practices

Sources: Adapted from Declerck, Debourse, & Navarre (1983); Pinto (2013).

Contrary to operations and strategies, all projects come to an end that has been envisioned from the start. As Christophe Midler notes, "The project has no future, it has an end." The project results get embedded in operations and strategy, one way or another. When a project fails, operations and strategy can be adversely affected by the fallout. Conversely, when a project succeeds, the organization reaps the benefits, such as higher revenues or a brighter future. For example, the success of the first iPhone went beyond the excellent implementation of one project. Within a year of launching the iPhone, Apple's share price increased dramatically, providing the company with excellent liquidity that it used to finance its strategic and operational endeavors. Although operational efficiency is not a competitive advantage in itself, successful projects can create resources and assets to achieve the organization's strategies.

Considering the many benefits of project management, it should be everyone's priority. In the implementation stage, where strategy often falters, project management's disciplined approach can help it succeed. Implementation or getting things done is the alpha and omega of project management. Action-oriented project management embodies the Nike slogan: *Just do it!* Moreover, as we have seen, important managerial trends—like management by objectives, results-based management, total quality, or the balanced scorecard—rely on project management to complete their projects.

Yet many business and management authors still ignore projects and project management when discussing the challenge of strategy implementation. In his bestselling book *Managing,* Mintzberg (2009) devotes only 5 pages out of 306 to project management. Crossan, Rouse, Rowe, and Maurer (2015) devote two chapters to strategy implementation in their book, but they do not mention project management. It is time to make use of the potential of project management in implementation, especially in the field of strategy—this is one of the fundamental premises of this book. So, what do we mean by a project and project management?

WHAT IS PROJECT MANAGEMENT?

A project is neither strategy nor operation. What is it then? Like strategy, a "project" is a catchall concept with a highly contextual definition that garners little consensus. Indeed, a project can be a blueprint, a foresight, a problem-solving approach, a practice, a set of tasks, or a deliverable. Like inkblots in a Rorschach test projects are perceived differently by different observers, and may reveal more about the perspectives and experience of the observers than about what they are describing.

It is tempting to think that almost everything in the organizational universe is a project. Some authors point out that the word "project" has many meanings and is elusive. So, it is more constructive to define a project by its characteristics. For example, Midler (1996) sees the *project* as a set of activities that are:

- Aimed at achieving a global goal that responds to a need.
- Specific, singular, or nonrepetitive with regard to its goals.
- Combinatorial and multidisciplinary in its deployment, since achieving the goal depends on several parameters determined by a preset beginning and end.
- Subject to exogenous variables. As an open system, the project is sensitive to the influences of events and actors and prone to risk and/or uncertainty.

Project management is often defined as the application of knowledge, skills, tools, and techniques necessary for the delivery of a temporary, singular, nonrepetitive effort carried out under constraints of time, cost, quality, scope, resources, and satisfaction of stakeholders' expectations. In recent years, two useful views of project management have emerged (see Table 4.3).

First, an analytical, structured, and professional view of project management sees it as the initiation, planning, implementation, monitoring, and control of the project—*the management of the project life cycle*. So, planning is the essence of project management, and the project plan is its cornerstone. Here, the dominant project management approach, which is essentially execution focused, is deliberate or planned. Tools and techniques are used to manage the project's scope, time, cost, resources, and specifications. In this context, the project succeeds when delivered within those time, cost, and specification constraints. It fails when there is weak planning, inadequate resources, or poor implementation. The focus of this project management approach is *efficiency.*

An alternative view of project management is more eclectic, political, and even ecological. The objective is not to simply do things but to make the most of the project's *evolving context and deliver value* for the different stakeholders. Here, project management tries to understand the context from the viewpoints of the project team and stakeholders. The project succeeds when it meets stakeholders' expectations and also aligns with their rhetorical and symbolic evaluations (Ika and Bredillet, 2016).

TABLE 4.3 Two Contrasting Project Management Perspectives

FEATURES OF PROJECT MANAGEMENT	TOOL-BASED AND EXECUTION-FOCUSED PROJECT MANAGEMENT	CONTEXT-BASED AND VALUE-BASED PROJECT MANAGEMENT
Central Role	Getting things done (efficiency)	Make the best of the evolving context (effectiveness or value delivery)
Purpose	Seamless execution	Adaptive execution
Criteria	Time, cost, specifications	Benefits; symbolic and rhetorical evaluations of stakeholders
Roadblocks	"Weak links," poor planning, inadequate resources	"Missed opportunities," bad luck, unexpected events
Project Management Approach	Planned	Emerging
Paradigm	Efficiency, rationality, objectivity, stability, reductionism, and planning	Effectiveness, change, value, uncertainty, complexity, politics, improvisation, creativity, managing and organizing
Thinking Style	Analytical	Holistic

Source: Adapted from Ika & Bredillet (2016).

Managing is about dealing with a plurality of objectives, expectations, needs, complexities, and uncertainties. Altogether, it means making the best of the various contexts that will emerge during the implementation of the project, without a set handbook. Thus, an emergent management approach prevails, as luck and unexpected events (or "externalities" as economists would have it) may affect the project's success or failure. The focus of this alternative project management approach is *effectiveness or even value creation and delivery*. This book is in keeping with this current approach.

The academic literature has produced multiple definitions of a project and project management (see Box 4.2 for a summary of the main definitions). However, given our interest in *fuzzy projects* and the confusion that often surrounds the use of the words in practice, we use the following definitions for the concepts of project and project management:

- A **project** is a temporary and singular effort to deliver value to stakeholders or give a specific competitive advantage or relevance to the organization that is driving it.
- **Project management** is the set of initiation, planning, implementation, evaluation, and meaning-making activities used to structure a future reality or perform a temporary and singular effort to deliver value to stakeholders or provide a specific competitive advantage or relevance to a given organization.

These definitions suggest that the project may not be "lonely" or single within an organization. It can be part of a portfolio, a program, or even a business strategy. Moreover, not all projects are pioneering ventures like the first iPhone, which steered the company away from its focus on computers. Sometimes, projects are multiple and repetitive. The iPhone series is an example, with the regular update of its models. It has relied on principals and agents who know what to do and how to do it. It has also benefitted from best practices in terms of bidding, cost control, and risk management, which have been streamlined over the years. These managers are learning from the past and preparing for the future. Though repetitive, the iPhone series consists of projects with unique strategic positioning within the environment as technology and the competitive landscape have, for example, shifted over the time. In this sense, these projects, which include some unique but incremental elements, still represent something that has never been done before (Davies, 2017).

BOX 4.2

Definitions of Project and Project Management

Five useful definitions of a "project":

1. An organizational unit dedicated to achieving an objective, or the delivery of a product on time, on budget, and according to predetermined performance specifications (Gaddis, 1959)
2. A specific, new action that methodically and progressively structures a future reality for which we do not yet have an exact equivalent (Le Bissonnais, 2000)
3. A temporary organization and process set up to achieve a specific goal within constraints of time, budget, and other resources (Shenhar & Dvir, 2007)
4. A temporary effort undertaken to create a product, service, or outcome (PMI, 2013)
5. Any action subject to prior review by a validating or funding authority (Graber & Giraudeau, 2018)

Five useful definitions of "project management":

1. A long journey of discovery in various fields, from technology to politics (Hirschman, 1967)

2. The art and science of turning a vision into reality (Turner, 1996)
3. The discipline of managing projects for success (APM, 2000)
4. A set of managerial activities needed to make a project successful (Shenhar and Dvir, 2007)
5. The application of knowledge, skills, tools, and techniques to project activities to meet project requirements (PMI, 2013)

THE EVOLUTION OF PROJECT MANAGEMENT

The history of project management has yet to be written (Garel, 2013; Morris, 2013). However, we can sketch out a brief history of project management to help us understand the major stages and critical moments of its evolution.

Period 1: The Early Days—Fifteenth Century to the 1940s

Projects date back to earliest human civilizations; the ancient cities of Mesopotamia, the pyramid of Giza in Egypt, the Great Wall of China, the English monument Stonehenge, and the Roman war fleet used to destroy Carthage are remarkable examples. But project management as a distinct profession is only a few decades old.

Projects existed long before they were labeled as such. Indeed, the term was not part of Greek or Latin vocabulary. It became part of the common language in the fifteenth century, meaning "that which is thrown forward," since it mainly referred to architectural elements placed in the front of a building, like balconies on a façade. While the French later saw a project as something being built (the content), Anglo-Saxons singled out the processes and means utilized (the way to get there).

Architectural projects proliferated in the Middle Ages. In these projects, execution was separated from conception, moving from an initial design to an anticipated outcome. The practice of project management was based on the division of labor among the various trades: the architects acted as designers and project managers, the masons and other skilled workers as project professionals, and the clients and bankers as project sponsors. Essentially, this view has come to characterize how project management was viewed up until the early 1950s (post-WWII).

Some other project characteristics gained importance during the last decades of that first period:

- The idea of a **matrix organization**—a project structure where team members report to two bosses: the project manager, for the duration of the project, and the head of the department in which they normally work.
- The prevalence of **engineering projects**, which included major state projects, colonial projects, and later on international development projects. These included military projects, shipyards, dams, oil rigs, highways, universities, and industrial sites.

During this period, project management prioritized achieving socioeconomic objectives over project efficiency. The mastery of project management methods, tools, and techniques was left to engineers and the know-how to a few companies whose processes and tools were neither standardized nor disseminated. These companies carried out *projects* but did not see themselves doing *project management*; that is, there was no specific project management model.

These projects were essentially carried out almost like any other operation. "Everyone lives in splendid isolation, convinced of the extreme singularity of their expertise" (Navarre, 1993, our translation). In these earlier times, projects were being carried out, but *not* project management per se.

Period 2: The Emergence of a Pioneering, Traditional, and Instrumental Approach (1950s–1980s)

Project management as we know it today emerged in this second period, with the realization of major North American military, aeronautical, and space programs such as the Polaris and Atlas rockets and later the Apollo program. The notion of project management "officially" entered the organizational world around 1953 with the Atlas rocket development program. It became formalized with the introduction of project management tools and techniques.

The essential tools include PERT (*Program Evaluation and Review Technique*) in 1957, CPM (*Critical Path Method*) in 1957–1959, *earned value* in 1967, and the WBS (*Work Breakdown Structure*) in 1968. The project management "toolbox" was completed with feasibility studies and economic evaluation tools such as *cost-benefit analysis* and the *internal rate of return*. These tools were added to the Gantt chart, which has been used by production management since the 1920s to improve efficiency and control deadlines and costs. Along with the use of these tools, we also witnessed the extension of *scientific management,* heavily inspired by the works of Frederick Taylor.

These founding ideas of project management circulated in academic circles in the 1960s and early 1970s and contributed to what is known as the "systems approach" to project management (Cleland & King, 1968). First, each project has a life cycle and it should be managed. The project's activities should be well integrated throughout that life cycle. Second, the project manager and team are key. In 1959, the *Harvard Business Review* published a seminal article that highlighted the role of the project manager as the chief integrator. It also recognized the importance of the team's contribution to the project's success (Gaddis, 1959).

With the advent of large professional associations such as the Project Management Institute (PMI) in 1969 and the International Project Management Association (IPMA) in 1972, the *PMI Instrumental and Standard Model* emerged. It focuses on (1) what projects have in common, rather than what makes them different and (2) the execution of a single project. This model took on a life of its own thanks to an analysis of exemplary projects by NASA, the Department of Defense (DOD), and later, the Department of Energy (DOE).

During this pioneering period, key success factors, methods, and now-famous "best practices" emerged and an *instrumental approach* garnered a lot of interest. It focused on successful project *execution* (as opposed to a successful project): delivering the project as planned, within the constraints of scope, time, cost, and specifications. This approach made central the project management tools and techniques in use, and highlighted that a good project manager should prioritize planning, much like any good architect.

Projects often performed poorly during this period. It was common to have substantial time and cost overruns and poor-quality deliverables. An analysis of 34 studies covering 1,536 projects and programs completed in the 1960s and 1970s, and 8 other projects (including the Concorde, Thames Barrier, and Fulmar North Sea Oil) shows an average cost overrun of between 40 and 200 percent for one out of two construction projects (Morris & Hough, 1987). In addition, one out of two international agricultural and rural development projects in the 1970s failed (Ika & Hodgson, 2014).

Surveys conducted 50 years later confirmed these findings, illustrating that the need for greater project efficiency had not diminished. For example, it has been shown that about half of major transport infrastructure projects are not delivered within their assigned budget (Love, Sing, Ika, & Newton, 2019).

Period 3: Contingent Approaches (1980s–1990s)

While project management successfully delivered many major projects in the relatively stable economic, political, and technological environment that characterized the 1970s (Levitt, 2011), it really gained prominence in the 1980s (Garel, 2013). The 1980s marked the appearance of a project management control system specific to the engineering field and project management software such as MS Project and Primavera. Project management was then institutionalized with these developments: the establishment of knowledge repositories such as PMI's *Project Management Body of Knowledge* (PMBoK), first published in 1996; professional certifications such as PMI's *Project Management Professional* (PMP); and the push to make project management a profession, which gained ground.

However, a slew of disappointing project outcomes between the 1950s and the 1980s left many disillusioned with the traditional project management approach. In response, organizations wanted project management to refocus on how the project team functions and the crucial role of the manager in the project's success. Indeed, with the advent of what some authors call the "speed economy"—which refers to innovation as a source of competitive advantage for the organization—organizations needed to do a better job designing projects and launching products or services more quickly to take market share from their competitors.

Organizations began seeing projects and project management differently. Delivering new products within the constraints of time, cost, and specifications was no longer enough. The quality of products and services, and the satisfaction of customers and end users, needed to be emphasized. Some suggested adding to the triangle of time, cost, and specifications the perceived quality of the project and client satisfaction as key measures of success (Pinto & Slevin, 1987). To do this, organizations had to think more about the clients' true expectations. Furthermore, this would allow the project team and its manager to learn from their successes and failures.

Other projects, however, failed during implementation. This was the case with the Franco-British Concorde, a supersonic airliner with cutting-edge technological advances that later failed commercially. Many projects failed because they continued to rely on the traditional instrumental approach to project management. Indeed, some say this is why the Western world had trouble keeping pace with the Japanese in terms of speed and variety. In the 1980s, the Taylorian model of *sequential project management* was still being used by many Western organizations. Like a relay race, the project moved from one business line to another, or from one function in the company to another, resulting in significant delays.

Concurrent engineering gained popularity and proved its worth in new product development projects, especially in the automotive, chemical, and pharmaceutical sectors. Since the idea was to go fast, projects started as soon as possible. To that end, tasks that required heavy and strategic resources were delayed in favor of other priorities, thus taking advantage of the degrees of freedom open in the early stages of the project. The project manager had a stronger mandate, unquestionable legitimacy, and a leading role that included reading market trends and consumer needs. Some called it being a *heavyweight project manager* (Clark & Wheelwright, 1992).

The idea that a project is a *temporary* organization emerged during this period—it was a core view of the Scandinavian school of project management (Packendorff, 1995). A project's link with the environment became very important as well. "Soft" factors such as communications, customer satisfaction, team satisfaction, and project actors took precedence over "hard" factors like planning—organizations tried to "plan less and communicate more."

Another shift was the increased focus on the *project context*. This change explains why the *Project Management Body of Knowledge* (PMBoK) was expanded to include the government, construction, and military sectors. While the PMBoK emphasized project management processes (such as defining project scope and estimating time and cost), other project management standards emphasized the skills of project team members. The latter is the case with the IPMA's *Individual Competence Baseline (ICB)* standard.

Despite placing greater importance on a project's hard and soft aspects, organizations continued to overrun deadlines and costs, and disappoint stakeholders. For example, the Standish Group routinely reported that 7 out of 10 IT projects over the years were either canceled or failed to meet time, cost, and specifications. Three out of four new product development projects that entered the development phase were found to end as commercial failures (Cooper, 1993). Engineering projects performed better in terms of efficiency (time, budget, scope) than effectiveness (achieving the client's objectives) (Miller & Lessard, 2000). The World Bank reported that one out of two investment projects it had funded over the years in Africa failed (Ika & Hodgson, 2014). As a result, problems relating to a project's organizational and strategic effectiveness became increasingly acute. These realities fueled the shift from single to multiprojects and reinforced the need to consider the project's impact on both the organization and its environment.

Period 4: More Strategic and Ecological Approaches—from the 1990s Onward

This period was marked by an unstable environment; a highly competitive economic context; stricter standards in terms of health, safety at work, environment, and ethics; and stronger requirements in terms of social responsibility for organizations. In short, project management from the 1990s onward evolved in a context of great complexity and uncertainty that required flexibility, agility, and adaptability in implementing projects.

Today, organizations need to do things better, faster, and cheaper in order to:

- Beat the competition and remain relevant.

- Develop the individual and collective skills of the project actors.
- Modify organizational structures or redesign business processes.
- Meet the expectations of the project team.
- Satisfy the clients and customers (since there may be several).
- Deliver value to stakeholders (there is often more than one).

Within the organization, project sponsors and managers must be aware of rivalries between projects, make the necessary trade-offs in terms of resources, and manage (upstream and downstream) the impacts of projects on other projects, programs, or initiatives; the entire organization; and society in general. This is quite a challenge!

In these turbulent times, and in what is commonly referred to as a "project economy" (Joffre et al., 2006; Nieto-Rodriguez, 2021), project management has infiltrated banking, insurance, tourism, and municipal governments. In addition to the traditional construction, engineering, and entertainment sectors, new project-oriented or project-based organizations are emerging. Project management is no longer just about execution. The front-end phase is paramount to ensuring that the "right" projects are well initiated and planned. Unfortunately, the artificial separation between design and execution that characterized the emergence of project management and established the project manager as an architect has led to projects that consume scarce resources but create little or no value for stakeholders.

The project manager no longer operates from an ivory tower, determining and negotiating the "big stuff," while others faithfully execute "on the ground." Instead, depending on the context, the project manager is more like a jazz conductor, facilitator, or entrepreneur who knows how to find and mobilize resources to create value. The new rules of thumb include "no project is an island" (Engwall, 2003); internal and external environments are equally important; and efficiency, effectiveness, and "doing the right things well" are priorities for today's project managers.

These changes have led to *organizational project management* or *management by projects*. Some good news: this approach has improved project performance. By managing programs and portfolios, managers have ample opportunity to learn from past and present endeavors. To this end, organizations set up project management offices—that is, bodies or entities responsible for the centralized and coordinated management of their projects. For the HP-Compaq merger, they set up a joint project office with more than 40 dedicated people responsible for no fewer than 3,000 active projects among the 10,000 employees of the IT department.

To stimulate organizational learning, communities of practice are emerging, project management training and certifications are multiplying, and more project evaluations are being conducted to learn from them. Maturity models such as PMI's OPM3 appeared in the early 2000s. New project management methodologies are becoming popular such as PRINCE 2 for public sector project management, agile approaches in IT, and PM4DEV and PMD PRO in international development. The International Standard ISO 21 500 was published in 2012. In the United Kingdom, APM recently became a Chartered Association, thus putting the profession alongside other long-established managerial professions. However, like Mintzberg (2003), author of the book *Managers Not MBAs,* many voices question professional certifications like the PMP and PRINCE 2 because they provide knowledge but do not really make project managers (Morris, 2013).

Project management approaches that focus on benefits realization management through the whole investment life cycle of the project have gained momentum with their inclusion in the *Managing Successful Projects* standard. It is no longer enough to deliver the project within the constraints of time, cost, and quality or to satisfy the client. The project must meet the organization's strategic objectives for sales, market share, return on investment, and long-term benefits (Shenhar & Dvir, 2007).

This approach is sometimes referred to as *strategic project management,* in that the project must be deployed with a good deal of flexibility while taking into account its internal and external environments. If a project seems to be going poorly, for example, it can be set aside without being scrapped for good. Later, it can be revisited and adapted to the emerging circumstances, when it may succeed.

In the late 1990s, concerns about project governance emerged, particularly after the Enron and WorldCom scandals. In 2002, these types of situations led to the Sarbanes-Oxley Act, designed to protect shareholders, employees, and the public from accounting errors and fraudulent financial practices. To deal successfully with issues surrounding their strategic alignment and transparency in monitoring their progress and risks, the responsibilities and roles of senior executives, managers, members of project steering committees, and the team delivering the projects become crucial (Morris, 2013).

Many observers have recognized the role that politics plays within the project team and the organization, and how it affects stakeholder engagement and the tensions that emerge among them. This prompted the PMBoK to add "stakeholder management" as a new knowledge area in 2013. This recognition has contributed to the "projectification" of organizations and of society as a whole.

Increasingly, projects are viewed in their broader political and sociological context. Consequently, the impact of project management on the organization, its members, and society is taken into account. These related issues have gained salience: power, domination, ethics, and moral responsibility; the tensions between standardization and creativity in project-oriented or project-based organizations; and the dysfunctions of the hyper-rationalization of projects, overridden by timetables and charts.

Finally, the complexity and uncertainty of projects are being given greater consideration. In this context, more complex models are being used in project management. The PMBOK has added “agile” approaches in its recent versions. The seventh edition of the PMBOK, published in 2021, emphasizes tailoring project management to context. It proffers not a mechanistic but a principles-based approach, and focuses on the effective delivery of value. Managers are asked to pay attention to the project’s organizational management approach, sustainability, and impact on the project team, the organization, and society. The central idea of this new approach is that project management should be about ensuring the organizational and social relevance of the project. This view is related to the so-called project studies movement (Geraldi & Söderlund, 2018).

Box 4.3 provides an overview of the three generic approaches that have characterized project management from its emergence to the present. Then, Table 4.4 summarizes the characteristics of these approaches.

BOX 4.3

Overview of the Evolution of Project Management

Chronologically, three generic approaches to project management stand out:

1. **A pioneering, traditional, scientific, instrumental, and standardized approach** (from the 1950s), inspired by Taylorism of earlier years, with a paradigm rooted in architecture, engineering, and construction. The widespread belief that inspired this dominant approach is that project management is limited to project execution. In this context, it is a set of tools and techniques used to achieve specific organizational objectives under time, cost, and specifications constraints.

   This approach influenced the activities of professional associations like the Project Management Institute (PMI), the identification and codification of best practices and key success factors for projects. In addition, it prioritizes the project plan, which must first be developed and then followed methodically during the project's implementation.

2. **Contingent approaches** (the 1980s onward) exposed the limits of the traditional approach. They emphasized the importance of the project team, and thus sought to give fuller context to the project-as-organization, albeit temporary. Inspired by the social sciences, and not solely by the "hard" factors of engineering and construction, these contingent approaches emphasize "soft" factors such as communication, customer satisfaction, leadership, and politics within the project team.

   The Scandinavian school of project management embraced this approach. The general idea is to *adapt* project management approaches to the project's context and the types of projects being conducted. This perspective led to multiple schools of thought in project management. It also justified expanding the PMBoK to include the government, the military, and so on. The same is true of the proliferation of project management standards from other professional associations such as the *Individual Competence Baseline* of the European *International Project Management Association* (IPMA), which, rather than emphasizing processes as does the PMI, focuses on the skills of the project manager.

3. **More strategic, ecological, and eclectic approaches** (the 1990s onward) consider the project in a broader organizational, sectoral, and societal context. They take into account the impact of projects and their management approaches on ongoing or future projects of the organization, the project teams and their members, the organization itself, the sector of activity, and on society in general. They incorporate "project studies" and include contributions from multiple disciplines: strategy, organizational theory, psychology, sociology, politics, economics, geography, and ecology. They pay particular attention to strategic project alignment;

project, program, and portfolio management; project management offices; maturity models such as PMI's OPM3; and organizational project management, or what is also known as project-oriented or project-based management.

As a result, new approaches are emerging: PRINCE 2 in the public sector, agile approaches in IT, approaches focused on delivering project benefits such as *Managing Successful Projects*, and PM4DEV and PMD PRO for international development projects. Other critical issues include organizational learning; project politics; governance, ethics, and moral responsibility; social relevance of projects and their societal impact; and project complexity and uncertainty.

TABLE 4.4 Characteristics of Generic Project Management Approaches

	PIONEER, TRADITIONAL, AND INSTRUMENTAL APPROACH: ONLY THE TOOLS COUNT!	CONTINGENT APPROACHES: PEOPLE MATTER MOST!	STRATEGIC, ECLECTIC OR EVEN ECOLOGICAL APPROACHES: THE EFFECTS OF THE PROJECTS MATTER MOST!
Periods	1950s–1980s	1980s–1990s	1990s–present
Project Types	Infrastructure projects	New product development projects	Organizational change projects
Project Metaphor	The project is the best way to achieve a specific product or service.	The project is the best way to launch useful products or services for a specific client.	The project is a way to create and share value between the organization and the involved stakeholders, with both expected and unexpected consequences on society.

(*continued*)

TABLE 4.4 *(continued)*

	PIONEER, TRADITIONAL, AND INSTRUMENTAL APPROACH: ONLY THE TOOLS COUNT!	CONTINGENT APPROACHES: PEOPLE MATTER MOST!	STRATEGIC, ECLECTIC OR EVEN ECOLOGICAL APPROACHES: THE EFFECTS OF THE PROJECTS MATTER MOST!
Key Questions	What is the best way to achieve the product or service?	What is the best way to achieve the product or service given the context?	How to create and share benefits between the organization and the project stakeholders?
Basic Philosophical Concepts	Rationality, objectivity, efficiency, planning, and reductionism	Experience, involvement, communication, satisfaction, negotiation	Effectiveness, change, value, strategic and societal impact, adaptation, uncertainty, complexity, power
Project Manager Archetypes	Architect, homo economicus, planner	Negotiator, communicator	Animator, jazz conductor, entrepreneur, political, ethical, and moral, homo heuristicus
Key Tools	CPM, PERT, WBS, CBA (cost-benefit analysis), earned value, project plan	Organizational structures, monitoring and evaluation reports, communication and leadership tools	Benefit Realization, complexity models, governance models, communities of practice, institutional analysis, societal and ecological impact analysis

(continued)

TABLE 4.4 *(continued)*

	PIONEER, TRADITIONAL, AND INSTRUMENTAL APPROACH: ONLY THE TOOLS COUNT!	CONTINGENT APPROACHES: PEOPLE MATTER MOST!	STRATEGIC, ECLECTIC OR EVEN ECOLOGICAL APPROACHES: THE EFFECTS OF THE PROJECTS MATTER MOST!
Criteria for Success	Time, cost, specifications, internal rate of return	Satisfaction of the staff, the project team, and the client	Stakeholder satisfaction, achievement of strategic objectives, minimization of societal and ecological impacts, symbolic and rhetorical stakeholder evaluations
Motto	Think product and plan accordingly	Think client, plan less, communicate more	Think systems, act, and adapt to the environment

Source: Adapted from Ika & Hodgson (2014).

CONCLUSION

Operations, strategy, and projects are the sets of activities that characterize the lives of organizations. Operations cover the routine activities meant to produce the organization's goods and services efficiently. Strategy aims to align the organization with the environment and focuses on its global and long-term effectiveness. Projects are typically temporary activities, focused on implementing and achieving specific objectives related to strategy and operations. Thus, project management helps reconcile the pursuit of two basically contradictory goals: efficiency and effectiveness. It can help the organization implement change or do things better. Its practice has undergone significant changes over time. We reviewed the four key stages of project management evolution in this chapter and drew significant lessons for our young century.

Although major projects were realized in ancient civilizations and in all continents, structured and formalized project management with standardized techniques represents a more recent development in many parts of the world where major public sector projects were undertaken from the fifteenth century onward. The context changed radically during and after WWII. Project management experienced rapid growth from the 1950s to the 1980s, relying on a mix of pioneering, traditional, and instrumental approaches, with the advent and use of computers. A third period (1980s–1990s) emerged, characterized by project management approaches that recognized the importance of the actors involved. The fourth period, from the 1990s onward, has been dominated by more strategic and ecological approaches that consider the project's beneficial and harmful effects. The chapter provides project sponsors and managers with six takeaways:

1. Like strategy, a project relies on a comprehensive diagnosis of the situation, a clear policy to guide action, and a coherent action plan. It can be deliberate or emergent; it can make or break, submit to, or alter the strategy.
2. Unlike strategy, a project is typically temporary and focused on implementing a specific objective; it has tangible, specific, and easy-to-measure deliverables; it is subject to tighter time, cost, quality, and scope constraints; and it involves clearer and more circumscribed accountability for results than the strategy.
3. Projects differ from operations in that each project is typically singular and challenges well-established practices within the organizations where they are carried out.
4. Since operational efficiency alone is not a competitive advantage, project management can help ensure strategic effectiveness.
5. A *project* is a temporary and singular endeavor to deliver value to stakeholders or give a specific competitive advantage or relevance to the organization.

Project management is the set of initiation, planning, implementation, evaluation, and meaning-making activities used to structure a future reality or perform a temporary and singular effort to deliver value to stakeholders or provide a specific competitive advantage or relevance to a given organization.

6. There are two contrasting views of project management: one is tool based and efficiency focused with a planned delivery approach, and the other context based and value focused with an emerging delivery approach.

Project management has evolved through four major periods: the early days when projects were carried out but implementers did not see themselves as doing project management; the emergence of a pioneering approach dominated by tools; the advent of contingent approaches where actors matter the most; and more recently, the occurrence of more strategic, eclectic and even ecological approaches where the effects of projects become the most important.

REFERENCES

Association for Project Management, APM (2000). *Body of knowledge.* Fourth edition. APM, UK.

Cleland, D. I., & King, W. R. (1968). *Systems analysis and project management.* McGraw-Hill.

Cooper, R. G. (1993). *Winning at new products.* Addison-Wesley Publishing.

Crossan, M. M., Rouse, M. J., Rowe, W. G., & Maurer, C. C. (2015) *Strategic analysis and action.* Ninth edition. Pearson.

Davies, A. (2017). *Projects: A very short introduction.* Oxford University Press.

Declerck, R., Debourse, J-P., & Navarre, C. (1983). *Méthode de direction générale: Le management stratégique.* Hommes et Techniques.

Engwall, M. (2003). No project is an island: Linking projects to history and context. *Research Policy, 32*(5), 789–808.

Fields, J. (2011). *Uncertainty: Turning fear and doubt into fuel for brilliance.* Penguin.

Gaddis, P. O. (1959). The project manager. *Harvard Business Review,* May–June, 89–97.

Garel, G. (2013). A history of project management models: From pre-models to the standard models. *International Journal of Project Management, 31*(5), 663–669.

Geraldi, J., & Söderlund, J. (2018). Project studies: What it is, where it is going. *International Journal of Project Management, 36*(1), 55–70.

Graber, F., & Giraudeau, M. (2018). *Les projets: Une histoire politique* (XVIe–XXIe siècles). Presses des Mines.

Hisrchman, A. O. (1967). *Development projects observed.* Brookings Institution.

Ika, L. A., & Bredillet, C. N. (2016). The metaphysical questions every project practitioner should ask. *Project Management Journal, 47*(3), 86–100.

Ika, L. A., & Hodgson, D. (2014). Learning from international development projects: Blending critical project studies and critical development studies. *International Journal of Project Management, 32,* 1182–1196.

Joffre, P., Aurégan, P., Chodétel, F., & Tellier, A. (2006). *La gestion stratégique par le projet.* Édition Economica.

Le Bissonnais, J. (2000). *Le management de projets—Principes et pratique,* 2ème édition. Éditions Afnor Gestion.

Levitt, R. E. (2011). Towards project management 2.0. *Engineering Project Organization Journal, 1*(3), 197–210.

Love, P. E. D., Sing, M. C. P., Ika, L. A., & Newton, S. (2019). The cost performance of transportation projects: The fallacy of the planning fallacy account. *Transportation Research Part A: Policy and Practice, 122,* 1–20.

Midler, C. (1996). Modèles gestionnaires et régulation économique de la conception. In G. Terssac & E. Friedberg (Eds). *Coopération et conception.* Éditions Octares, Toulouse, pp. 63–85.

Miller, R., & Lessard, D. R. (2000). *The Strategic management of large engineering projects.* MIT Press.

Mintzberg, H., Alstrand, B., & Lampel, J. (1998). *Strategy safari: A guided tour through the wilds of strategic management.* Simon & Shuster.

Mintzberg, H. (2003). *Managers not MBAs. A hard look at the soft practice of managing and management development.* Berrett-Koehler Publishers, Inc.

Mintzberg, H. (2009). *Managing.* Berrett-Koehler Publishers, Inc.

Morris, P. W. G., & Hough, G. H. (1987). *The anatomy of major projects. A study of the reality of project management.* John Wiley & Sons.

Morris, P. W. G. (2013). *Reconstructing project management.* John Wiley & Sons.

Navarre, C. (1993). Pilotage stratégique de la firme et gestion de projet: de Ford et Taylor à agile et IMS. In C. Midler and V. Giard (Eds). *Pilotages de projet et entreprise: Diversités et convergences.* Economica, pp. 181–215.

Nieto-Rodriguez, A. (2021). *Project management handbook. How to launch, lead, and sponsor successful projects.* Harvard Business Review Press.

Packendorff, J. (1995). Inquiring into the temporary organization: new directions for project management research. *Scandinavian Journal of Management, 11*(4), 319–333.

Pinto, J. K., & Slevin, D. P. (1987). Critical factors in successful project implementation. *IEEE Transactions of Engineering Management, 34* (1), 22–27.

Pinto, J. K. (2013). Lies, damned lies, and project plans: Recurring human errors that can ruin the project planning process. *Business Horizons, 56,* 643–653.

Project Management Institute, PMI (2013). *A Guide to the Project Management Body of Knowledge.* Fifth edition. PMI Inc.

Rumelt, R. P. (2011). *Good strategy. Bad strategy. The difference and why it matters.* Crown Business.

Shenhar, A., & Dvir, D. (2007). *Reinventing project management.* Harvard Business School Press.

Turner, J. R. (1996). Editorial. International Project Management Association global qualification, certification and accreditation. *International Journal of Project Management, 14,* 1–6.

Wheelwright, S. C., & Clark, K. B. (1992). *Revolutionizing product development.* Harvard Business School Press.

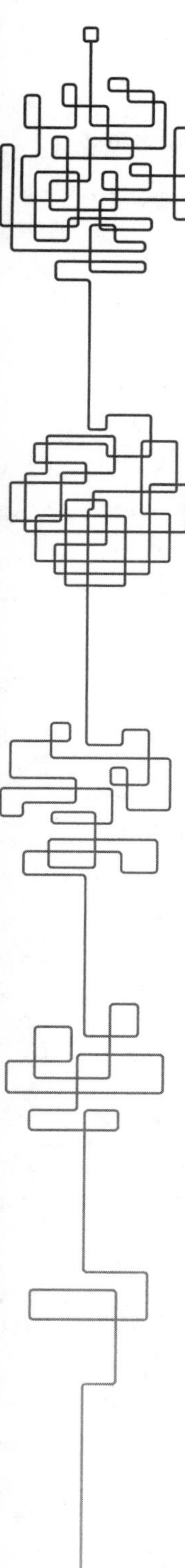

CHAPTER 5

PROJECT SUCCESS AND FAILURE

I have not failed. I've just found 10,000 ways that won't work.

—attributed to Thomas Edison

SUCCESS OR FAILURE?

In recent decades we have witnessed an unprecedented boom of projects in organizations, as project managers and their professional associations promise to deliver efficiency and effectiveness. *Fortune* magazine's 1995 prediction that project management would become the profession of the twenty-first century is coming true. According to some estimates, upper managers and their staff may soon spend more than 60 percent of their time working actively on the initiation, planning, and execution of projects (Nieto-Rodriguez, 2021).

Nancy Smart is passionate about her profession and follows its evolution closely. In project debriefings, she often wonders whether sponsors get value for their effort and money, and whether beneficiaries are ultimately satisfied with the results. She also thinks about the major successes and the resounding failures reported in the press, wondering whether their fates are inevitable.

Regardless of its size or sector, no project is immune to failure. This holds true for projects led by people known for their successes. Although Woody Allen is a renowned filmmaker, three-quarters of his films have gone unnoticed in the United States. James Dyson made more than 5,000 different prototypes of his high-end vacuum in 15 years before having one that was good enough to pitch. Even then, British retailers rejected it, so he sold it by catalog in Japan, which was very successful. Only then was he able to conquer other markets worldwide. Always thriving on innovation, Dyson designed a ventilator to fight COVID-19 in early 2020 in only 10 days.

Oprah was fired from her first job as a TV news anchor for being too "emotionally invested" in her reporting. She eventually became one of the world's most influential businesswomen and TV personalities. Harry Potter creator J.K. Rowling was rejected by 12 major publishing firms who deemed that the public "had no interest in wizards and witches." Arianna Huffington was turned down by 36 publishers before she created the Huffington Post empire. Soichiro Honda, Elon Musk, Steve Jobs, and Mark Cuban have all had their share of failures, successes, and failures again.

As we have seen in the first chapters, whether in construction, information technology (IT), new product development, organizational change, international development, or the arts, half of projects fail to deliver the expected impact[1] (Ika, 2012; Matta & Ashkenas, 2003). This assessment of project success considers the long-term nature of the project, its rationale, or the underlying strategic intent (Shenhar & Dvir, 2007). We come back to this broader perspective later in this chapter.

The notions of project success and performance are often conflated. In this book, we take project success to be the end point or the achievement of a goal the organization and relevant stakeholders seek to reach. In contrast, project performance, strictly speaking, concerns the extent to which, during execution or completion, the project's target goal and objectives and stakeholder expectations are being met (Ika & Pinto, 2022). For convenience, we speak of both project performance in the short term and long term. Hence, from a strategic point of view, stakeholders may assess project success in the long term with the benefits realized, but in the short term time and cost underperformance often make the news; this is even more likely when the general public is affected or foots the bill. So, what does research tell us about project cost overruns?

Cost Performance of Projects

Albert Hirschman, an international development economist and a well-known pioneer in project management, was one of the first authors to study major projects. After analyzing 11 World Bank projects in Europe, Latin America, Asia, and Africa, he noted significant cost overruns (Hirschman, 1967). These international development projects went over budget or performed poorly because their objectives were broad and intangible (e.g., poverty reduction, capacity building, improved governance), and they had to deal with the sociopolitical context of the countries in which the projects were implemented. The following data shows that cost overruns are significant, recurrent, and widespread in *almost* all types of projects (see Table 5.1).

Twenty years later, Morris and Hough (1987) found that the average cost overrun was 40 to 200 percent for one out of two construction projects. In contrast, military acquisition projects had a much lower average cost overrun of only 15 percent (Meier, 2008). Research on transportation projects confirms this general cost overrun trend even though about half are delivered within budget (Love, Ika, Matthews, & Fang, 2019). While the numbers vary widely across the research and types of transportation projects, according to some estimates,[2] the average cost overrun is around 40 percent (Flyvbjerg, 2016). Transportation project cost overruns have occurred in 20 countries, on five continents, and covered periods of up to 70 years (Flyvbjerg, Holm, & Buhl, 2002). In addition, an analysis of the costs of 30 major transportation projects, including the Boston Central Artery/Tunnel Project (also known as the "Big Dig"), the Athens subway, and the Valencia-Marseille high-speed train, found an average cost overrun of 22 percent (OMEGA, 2012). These examples of cost overruns in the transportation sector, where there has been more comprehensive research, underscore the magnitude of the phenomenon and thus the immense challenge it represents for researchers and practitioners.

TABLE 5.1 Project Cost Overruns

AUTHORS	TYPE OF PROJECT	SCOPE OF THE STUDY	PROPORTION OF PROJECTS WITH COST OVERRUN
Morris & Hough (1987)	Construction, aeronautics, and miscellaneous	34 studies covering 1,536 projects, including 8 major projects. Examples: the Concorde and Fulmar	40% to 200%
Miller & Lessard (2000)	Engineering	60 projects	1 project out of 5
Meier (2008)	Military acquisition	26 projects in the United States	15%
Flyvbjerg, Holm, & Buhl (2002)	Transportation: Roads, tunnels, bridges, railroads	258 projects totaling US$90 billion; mainly in Germany, Denmark, France, Sweden, and the United Kingdom	9 out of 10 projects; 20% for railways; 34% for bridges and tunnels; 20% for roads
Hertogh, Baker, Staal-Ong, & Westerveld (2008)	Infrastructure	15 European Commission projects	All 15 projects

(continued)

TABLE 5.1 *(continued)*

AUTHORS	TYPE OF PROJECT	SCOPE OF THE STUDY	PROPORTION OF PROJECTS WITH COST OVERRUN
Omega (2012)	Transportation	30 major projects including Boston's Artery/ Tunnel aka Big Dig, Valencia-Marseille TGV	22%
Flyvbjerg & Budzier (2011)	Information Technology (IT)	1,471 projects; average cost US$167 million; most expensive US$32 billion	27%
Jergeas & Ruwanpura (2010)	Oil and gas projects	Alberta Oil sands	50% to 100%
Terrill & Danks (2016)	Transportation: Roads and railways	836 projects from Australia	24%
Love, Ahiaga-Dagbui, Welde, & Odeck (2017)	Transportation: Railways	16 projects	23%
Odeck (2004)	Transportation: Roads	620 projects	8%
Flyvbjerg (2016)	Infrastructure: Dams, urban transport, railroads, tunnels, power plants, buildings, bridges, and roads	2,062 projects in 104 countries on six continents, from 1927 to 2013	40%
Love, Ika, Matthews, & Fang (2019)	Transportation: Roads, tunnels, bridges, universal accessibility such as crossings, expressways, escalators, elevators, subways, and ancillary road facilities	85 projects in Hong Kong for a total cost of approximately US$14 billion	13% of which 40 exceeded their budget by 33% and 27 were under budget by 19%; 3 delivered at cost

The cost overrun phenomenon extends to IT projects. The Standish Group (2013) analyzed a database of more than 50,000 IT projects and found that overruns hovered around 50 percent from 2004 to 2012. More importantly, the Standish Group concluded that major projects had virtually no chance of coming in under budget. Oil and gas projects in the oil sands in Alberta (Canada) had cost overruns of 50 to 100 percent (Jergeas & Ruwanpura, 2010). But how accurate are these cost-overrun figures? (See Eveleens & Verhoef, 2010, who question the statistics reported by the Standish Group for IT projects.)

Timing matters. The magnitude of cost overruns varies depending on whether the approved project budget was set *before* or *after* the feasibility studies, project planning, or contract signing. The cost overrun is less likely to be significant if a project's budget is estimated after the planning, then updated and finalized just before the project implementation starts. On the other hand, it is normal for a project to experience cost overruns proportional to changes made to its scope and sanctioned by sponsors during implementation (Love et al., 2019). In Chapter 6 we will examine the relationship between the baseline forecast and its accuracy.

Cost overruns are neither new nor limited to certain sectors, but are rather pervasive and widespread. Indeed, beyond these statistics, there are countless examples of projects that experienced cost overruns throughout the world.

A well-known case is the Boston Big Dig, one of the largest and most expensive infrastructure projects in US history. Initially pegged at US$2.35 billion in 1983, the megaproject was delivered at the end of 2007 at a reported cost (including interest) of more than US$24.3 billion. The VA Aurora Hospital (in Colorado), one of the most expensive hospitals in the world, is another illustration. Originally budgeted at US$328 million in 2004, and reestimated at US$678 million in 2011, the costs of the state-of-the-art medical facility to treat veterans suffering from a variety of disabilities grew to about US$2 billion at its completion in 2018 (Ika, Pinto, Love, & Paché, 2022).

What Explains Cost Overruns and Benefit Shortfalls?

Nancy Smart wants to understand the causes of project drift or cost overruns and/or benefit shortfalls, and what can be done about it.

Researchers and practitioners have generally taken two approaches to explain the cost overrun and benefit shortfall phenomenon. The first is a *rational approach* that focuses on factors that can be predicted or corrected: design or planning errors, changes in project scope, variations in inflation rates, political bargaining, problems stemming from organizational structures, project environment or context, and complexity and uncertainty. This rational, traditional project management perspective applies "best practices" for cost forecasting, project monitoring and evaluation, and risk management to reduce the chances of cost overruns (Love et al., 2019). When confronted with the ballooning of the costs of the VA Aurora Hospital megaproject, Congress took its oversight role seriously and insisted on after-the-fact cost cutting, leading to the abandonment of the initially planned US$20 million PTSD building from the project and thus the reduction of its initial scope (Ika et al., 2022).

In the last two decades, a *behavioral approach* has emerged, with the work of former Oxford professor Bent Flyvbjerg, inspired by the psychologist Daniel Kahneman, winner of the Nobel Prize in Economic Sciences. This recent approach purports that psychological and political factors, not technical and rational factors, can explain project drift. For example, these thinkers argue that cost overruns are in great part due to the *planning fallacy* phenomenon (excessive discounting of the future; Kahneman, 2011) or the tendency to promise too much, even if it means delivering little (Flyvbjerg, 2016). Notably, they both point out the tendency to make plans using the most optimistic or even manipulated forecasts, rather than using past data from similar projects to yield more accurate results.

As authors of this book, we saw firsthand what Kahneman experienced early in his career with his own book. As we embarked on our journey and projected ourselves into the future, it seemed reasonable to think that we could write this book in two years while attending to our work at the university. Prudently, we had already decided to cut back on other research work and keep our consulting activities to a minimum. To be safe, we added 50 percent to our two-year forecast to account for uncertainties and contingencies, giving ourselves three years to finish the project.

As was the case for Kahneman, we were wrong. It took much longer than three years. The lesson learned by Kahneman, us, and so many others is that in estimating how long a project will take, one should refrain from using forecasts based solely on one's own judgment. These forecasts are inevitably biased. Rather than looking forward, as is done in forecasting, we should turn to the past and rely on the actual experiences of those who have carried out similar projects (Kahneman, 2011).

A key component of the planning fallacy is *optimism bias*. For example, decision makers unintentionally underestimate project costs and believe that they are less likely than anyone else to be wrong in their forecasts. Optimism bias is akin to "delusion" on the part of decision makers. NASA's Space Shuttle project is an excellent example of optimism bias as it experienced substantial cost overruns.

At times, however, the planning fallacy can also be intentional. It involves deliberate ignorance or *strategic misrepresentation,* a ploy that underestimates the project's costs and overestimates its benefits to gain acceptance and obtain the necessary funding to carry it out. Strategic misrepresentation is thus akin to "deception" on the part of the promoters of the project. A good example is the CLEM-7 tunnel project in Brisbane, Australia. A class-action lawsuit proved to the Australian Federal Court that traffic forecasts the project had presented were falsified. Within 18 months, the actual daily ridership volume was about 22,780, rather than the 100,285 formally forecasted (Love, Ika, Matthews, & Fang, 2021).

When the planning fallacy is at play, projects that "look good" on paper are chosen over those that are "actually good," a kind of reverse natural selection (Flyvbjerg, 2016). Consider the case of the Sochi Winter Olympics. Its budget was pegged at US$10 billion, knowing that the London Olympics officially cost more than US$18 billion (six times more than budgeted), yet it ended up costing more than US$50 billion. This estimate was probably due to optimism bias and strategic misrepresentation.

Like Occam's razor, the behavioral approach has become popular with many governments, including the United Kingdom. Accordingly, the solution to the cost overrun problem is to "de-bias" the cost estimates of projects under consideration with statistics drawn from the results of past—and similar—projects, using reference class forecasting (RCF). Put simply, RCF is a method developed by Flyvbjerg (2008) and based on the work of Kahneman and Tversky (1979) that consists of adding an "uplift" to project cost estimates and contingencies.

In sum, two schools of thought prevail when it comes to explaining project drift. The *error school* connects cost overruns and benefit shortfalls to the use of deficient management techniques, making honest mistakes during the forecasting and execution process (e.g., judgment and decision making), inexperience, lack of knowledge, and having access to incomplete data (e.g., knowledge and rule-based errors when confronted with complex and uncertain problems). Key errors include scope changes, complexity, and uncertainty. In contrast, the dominant *bias school* associates cost overruns and benefit shortfalls with a systematic distortion of logical thinking, or a deviation between the (average) judgment of a person or a group and a true value or norm (e.g., a statistical principle), whether intentional or not, leading to misjudgments and inappropriate decision-making. Key behavioral factors include delusion and deception, which form the core of the planning fallacy (Ika, Love, and Pinto, 2022).

Proponents of the bias school argue that biases trump rational explanations or errors (Flyvbjerg et al., 2018). Given this duality of errors and biases, a more effective approach for reducing cost overruns and benefit shortfalls is to address both rational and behavioral causes (Ika et al., 2022). Both errors and biases were at play in the case of the Aurora VA Hospital project. When charges emerged of a willingness to obscure the facts from the Congressional Budget Office, the responsibility to complete the project was handed over to the Army Corps of Engineers. Other observers suggested instead that the overarching reasons behind the significant overruns were the snowballing of errors, misjudgments, and poor communication and collaboration among key stakeholders. A media and legal battle between the Aurora VA and its primary contractors arose as a result of the project's cost overruns setting off a long legal battle. In any case, solely addressing biases or errors may not be sufficient to avoid cost overruns and benefit shortfalls.

The US$600 million Edinburgh Trams project, a 14-kilometer light rail between Newhaven and Edinburgh Airport in Scotland, also had cost overruns, despite the "de-biasing" of its cost estimates using RCF. In this instance, actual data from the London Docklands Light Rail project was used, thereby increasing the projected budget from £300 million to £400 million. Still, the costs of the project grew to over £1 billion at the time of its completion (three years late) due to unforeseen risks including the location of underground utilities, contract errors and omissions, and contractual disputes.

These examples show that a more effective approach is to combine both schools and their respective solutions: best practices *and* de-biaising (Ika et al., 2022). Still, important as they are, cost overruns are not the only problems that plague project delivery.

DIAGNOSIS AND REMEDIES FOR PROJECT FAILURE AND UNDERPERFORMANCE

Project Planning and Implementation Failures

In addition to the cost, the criteria of time and quality should also be of concern to stakeholders and clients. The VA Aurora

Hospital project illustrates the importance of "the iron triangle" of time, cost, and quality in assessing the performance of a project. Box 5.1 illustrates the setbacks of the VA Aurora Hospital.

BOX 5.1

The VA Aurora Hospital Setbacks

Scope: A massive US$2 billion, 11-building, 1.2-million-square-foot, 31-acre, state-of-the-art medical center to treat veterans suffering from a variety of disabilities.

Long ideation period: Seven years. Year 1 was 1995, when the Department of Veterans Affairs decided to take over the closing Fitzsimons Army Medical Center. The idea of a shared hospital between the VA and the University of Colorado came up in Year 4 and was recommended in a VA consultant report in Year 7.

Long initiation and planning time: Nine more years were added when the project concept shifted from a shared hospital to a stand-alone hospital campus in Year 14 (2009). The project cost was pegged at US$328 million in Year 9 (2004) and US$604 in Year 16 (2011).

Execution: Year 16 (2011) to Year 23 (2018).

Changes to the scope of the project: From an initial 13-building project to 11 because a post-traumatic stress disorder treatment (PTSD) center and a nursing home were cut from the plan due to the rising project costs.

Time performance: A decade behind schedule.

Cost performance: The final cost at completion (US$1.7 billion) was about three times the budget at the start of construction

(US$604 million); equipment costs to fill the hospital after completion are not included.

Quality performance: A series of malfunctioning, poorly installed, or missing elements. Examples include deficiency problems with sewers, elevators, and fire doors; the sidewalks were inaccessible to the disabled.

Management problems: Scope changes, mismanagement of construction, charges of deliberate deception from the Congressional Budget Office, poor communication and collaboration with stakeholders.

Contextual problems: The project spanned four presidencies and more than six VA secretaries.

Institutional problems: A culture of incompetence in VA construction management; congressional hearings and corruption investigations were held, which let to the project being handed over to the Army Corps of Engineers in Year 21 in an attempt to keep the rising costs under control.

Unexpected consequences: As a result of the above institutional problems, the US House of Representatives passed bill H.R. 3996 in Year 24 to change the way construction megaprojects are managed. The bill was then sent to the US Senate.

Sources: Migoya (2021); Ika et al. (2022).

Major projects, whether they are large or complex, often pose significant management challenges and recurrent difficulties, and can turn into horror stories. And for good reason. They are shrouded by uncertainty and have long planning and execution times, as well as complex interfaces with a number of internal and external stakeholders who have conflicting and changing interests. The VA Aurora Hospital project took 23 years to complete, including 7 years of ideation, 9 years of planning and 7 years of execution.

While there are many problems in managing major projects, the causes of failure are revealing: unclear success criteria; changes in strategy or scope by the project *sponsors*; shortcomings in the design, planning, or implementation; technical and design uncertainties; and unfavorable conditions in the physical environment. On top of a poor time and cost estimation, we can add weak quality assurance; haphazard contract and procurement management; inexperienced or overly rotated staff; poor risk and change management during implementation (Morris & Hough, 1987). There are many factors that cause project failure. To gain clarity, we can look at failures that occur during certain stages of the project life cycle, or stem from the nature of the problems themselves.

Let's begin with the project life cycle. It is possible to distinguish planning factors (including design) from factors related to implementation and the project environment (including stakeholders). While there are many examples to illustrate the effect of changes in the environment on projects, the case of Bombardier stands out. In 2015, Bombardier—a leading manufacturer of business jets—abandoned the Learjet 85 project due to prolonged market weakness and laid off more than 1,000 workers in parts manufacturing in Mexico and assembly in the United States. A mere six years later, during the COVID-19 pandemic, the demand for private and business jets increased exponentially as the wealthy flocked to private jets to avoid airport line-ups and crowded commercial flights. The demand was so high that there were not enough planes and pilots to serve them (Sullivan, 2021).

The life cycle often offers practitioners the opportunity to blame one another. Some may claim that a project was well planned but poorly executed (e.g., project sponsors); others may say it was well executed, but the environment made it ineffective or inefficient (e.g., project managers). Either way, while there are escape hatches for planners and managers, the beneficiaries tend to lose out.

Managerial, Contextual, and Institutional Problems

Grouping project challenges according to the nature of the problems they face—*managerial, contextual, and institutional*—as is done in international development, gives us further insights (Ika, 2012). First, let's look at some examples of *managerial problems.* Software and integration issues plagued the Airbus A380 project, causing time and cost overruns, including penalties of over US$6 billion. Poor management eventually led to the restructuring of the Airbus company and the departure of two CEOs. Project management shortcomings also plagued the Concorde as it was delivered late and over budget. Underestimating its complexity and mismanaging the automated baggage handling system derailed the Denver International Airport construction project. In addition to mismanagement and poor communication and collaboration with critical stakeholders, the VA Aurora Hospital project reportedly suffered from both optimism bias and strategic misrepresentation.

Now let us look at examples of *contextual and institutional problems.* The Tata Nano project aimed to build the world's cheapest car (US$2,200). However, the decision to locate the factories in Singur (the West Bengal region of eastern India) resulted in violent protests by farmers in the region. This project also faced institutional problems due to allegations of corruption of some civil servants. All of this resulted in delays of more than a year and a half and additional costs of US$350 million. Faced with contextual problems in a context of tight public finances, Governor Chris Christie of New Jersey terminated a US$9 billion-plus transit project—the *Commuter Rail Tunnel*—in 2010 because the anticipated cost overrun was already US$5 billion.

On the *institutional side*, as the costs of the Aurora VA Hospital project continued to rise, the FBI was asked to investigate allegations of corruption. It was found that VA construction management was plagued by enduring incompetence. The project was handed over to the Army Corps of Engineers in 2016, which removed the US$20 million PTSD center from the project scope in an effort to curb rising costs.

Solutions to Reduce Project Failures

There are many well-documented efforts to better understand the issues facing projects. For example, specialized methods for estimating project schedules and costs have been developed and have proven useful in projects such as the NASA Polaris Missile. Today, PERT (*Program Evaluation and Review Technique*), CPM (*Critical Path Method*), and *earned value* calculations are used to some extent to measure a project's time and cost performance. In addition, project management software, such as MS Project and Primavera, and artificial intelligence–backed tools have become popular. Beyond this toolbox, project managers can rely on best practices in project management, "de-biasing" tools such as RCF, the growing contribution of international professional associations such as the Project Management Institute (PMI), and the development of project research.

Navigating project complexity and uncertainty can increase the chances of success. Broadly speaking, this entails being more flexible in our project management approach. Specifically, it means using the tools and techniques less rigidly. For example, IT project practitioners have moved away from using the "waterfall" approach that follows steps, from features development to system introduction. They reckoned that efficiency usually trumps user satisfaction, leading to dismal project performance, including project underutilization or outright cancellation. More and more, IT projects now opt for agile approaches. In so doing, they shorten planning cycles, emphasize system acceptance and use over development efficiency, and improve delivery success (Serrador & Pinto, 2015). Unfortunately, agile approaches alone may not help turn things around when it comes to project underperformance and failure. For instance, practitioners have been calling for more flexibility in managing major projects for over 30 years in the field of international development (Rondinelli, 1983), but either these calls have not been answered or the answers have been insufficient. In any case, many major international development projects still fail to deliver intended impacts (Ika, 2012).

Considering project management tools, and all we now know about success or failure factors, why do many projects still fail? Two important reasons stand out. First, as we search for the root causes, the list of contributing factors only gets longer, and the mystery surrounding success or failure becomes foggier. Increased knowledge has not improved things, and this is why we say (tongue in cheek) that researchers should eliminate two old factors for every new one!

A second reason for project failure relates to not placing enough importance on the human factor and underestimating a project's sociopolitical complexity. Major projects often exceed time and cost targets (the "hard" aspects of their performance) because we manage the "soft" aspects poorly, such as (external) stakeholder engagement, beneficiary participation, communications, motivation, and social acceptability. In addition, much depends on how success is defined and measured, and when the evaluation is done.

WHAT MAKES A PROJECT SUCCESSFUL?

Project success is an important topic for project management researchers and practitioners, as well as the general public. It is also a topic of worldwide interest in many sectors, as a Google search will confirm. *So, Nancy Smart wonders, what is project success?*

The Concept of Project Success

Although it is a common word, "success" is difficult to define. Merriam-Webster dictionary says that success is "the *correct* or *desired* result of an attempt." So, what does success mean when it comes to a full-fledged project? First, it is important to note that the "desired" result (what is wanted, preferred) may be different from the "correct" result (what is appropriate, suitable).

Furthermore, there is no consensus on what constitutes "project success" or "project failure" in practice and theory (Jugdev & Müller, 2005). After decades of research, project success still remains an ambiguous and elusive concept. The words written by Pinto and Slevin (1988) still ring true today: "There are few topics in the field of project management that are so frequently discussed and yet so rarely agreed upon as the notion of project success."

As a result, we have a conundrum. Without a standard or a definition, any project may be deemed a success or a failure. On the other hand, it is unreasonable to claim that we can objectively measure the success or failure of projects. Notably, the concepts of success and failure are multidimensional, with several measures, and we must contextualize their use.

In project management, our assessment of success is mainly based on criteria set in the beginning (ex ante) to measure results at the end (ex post). This approach is a slippery slope since it can result in what psychosocial theorists call a *fundamental attribution error*. It leads us to assess success using subjective assessments of what we observe while ignoring external and contextual factors that occur or fall outside our purview.

For example, in an invitation for tender, the proposals reflect the results each firm vows to achieve. However, these proposals cannot be used at face value to determine the winners of the competition. Similarly, the project plan can hardly be used to evaluate the success of a project. Actual projects encompass the contrasts between expectations and plans, decisions and actions, outputs and deliverables, performance targets and actual performance, and internal and external measures of performance, all of which can change between the short term and the long term. These contrasts cannot be ignored, and they explain why fuzzy projects fail so often. As we have learned from social psychology, we tend to underestimate the complexity of both the project and its context (Kreiner, 2014).

Since context (including stakeholders) plays a major role in the project's performance, it should be considered when evaluating the project. Project success is, in great part, a matter of perception and perspectives among project actors or stakeholder groups (Davis, 2014).

As far back as 1974, Baker, Murphy, and Fisher warned that there is no such thing as "absolute success," only "perceived success," and there is little consistency in assessing success over time. Furthermore, stakeholders have dissimilar viewpoints that cannot always be reconciled. A particular client may not care as much about the project's success or failure as the community does about its economic, social, and environmental impacts. Success and failure of projects are not necessarily two opposite or binary, "black and white" notions. Success is not the absence of failure, and there is more than one way for a project to be deemed successful.

Philosophers make a helpful distinction between the notion of a *successful life,* which focuses on efficient causes and emphasizes performance, from a *good life,* which considers final causes and emphasizes transcendence (Ferry, 2002). Similarly, we need to distinguish between the notions of efficiency and effectiveness of the project (see Chapter 1). Again, efficiency means "doing things with a minimum of resources," or maximizing outputs for a given level of inputs or resources. Effectiveness is about "doing the right things"—that is, achieving the objectives or goals of the project. Peter Drucker made these distinctions, and he thought effectiveness was more important than efficiency. While we could assume that a successful project is both efficient and effective (Ika, 2009), we will see in the following chapters that being both efficient and effective is not enough in some cases, especially now that the sustainability imperative is winning ground.

Project Management Success or Business Case Success?

Given the distinction between project efficiency and effectiveness, there is a dichotomy between the concepts of *project management success* and *business case success,* as the project management targets are not the same as those associated with the business case (Ika & Pinto, 2022). Business case success may include the delivery of target benefits at some point after completion (Zwikael & Meredith, 2021). Indeed, business case success is much broader than project management success, and the two dimensions of success do not have the same time scale either. The first is short term, the second long term.

The evaluator's task is essentially internal and retrospective when assessing *project management success,* as it involves comparing actual performance with the project plan. Conversely, external and prospective considerations are inherent in measuring *business case success,* which entails assessing the project's future impact on the client, for example. Therefore, this measure is not objective nor definitive—at best, it is descriptive. So there is a difference between project management success and business case success (Kreiner, 2014). Though they represent two sides of the same coin and have been shown to be positively and moderately correlated (Serrador & Pinto, 2015), project management success may not lead to business case success (Ika & Pinto, 2022; Shenhar & Dvir, 2007). While a project may succeed despite poor project management, it may fail notwithstanding outstanding project management.

It has been a long-standing practice to measure project success considering time, cost, and quality targets. The time-cost-quality triangle—dubbed the "iron triangle" by Martins Barnes back in 1969, or the "golden triangle," the "holy trinity," or the "virtuous triangle" by others—has long been the go-to formula used to define and measure project success. However, this triangle is no longer enough, as many projects that deliver on time, on budget, and with the required specifications are still considered failures. Conversely, other projects that exceeded time and cost projections are seen as successes.

A percussion effect can be observed: projects perceived as successes at first are seen as disasters later on, and vice versa. As a result, the project team may be wrongly praised or blamed, depending on when the evaluation is conducted. This observation led de Wit (1988) to advocate for a distinction between *project success* (i.e., meeting the target benefits that flow from the product or service delivered by the project) and *project management success* (i.e., getting the process right). Our distinction between business case success and project management success is in line with such reasoning.

However, prioritizing project management success over business case success means sacrificing effectiveness for the benefit of efficiency. In so doing, we fall into the trap of the "anomia of success" (Cohen, 1972), a societal disease where using the stick of rules without the carrot of common sense undermines good project management practices. We then lose sight of the project's purpose, its shared ethos and true meaning, and, of course, the expectations of its stakeholders (Kreiner, 2014). We will explore this further in Chapters 7 to 9, focusing on the interests of stakeholders. Having gained insights on measuring success, we need to shed light on how to achieve it, using the distinction between criteria and factors of project success.

Criteria and Factors for Project Success

Practitioners also blur these two concepts: success *criteria* and success *factors*. Merriam-Webster dictionary defines a *criterion* as "a standard on which a judgment or decision may be based," whereas a *factor* is "something that helps produce or influence a result." Similarly, project success criteria refer to standards or principles for assessing project deliverables and benefits. In contrast, the critical success factors refer to conditions, facts, and circumstances contributing to the delivery of project deliverables and benefits (Ika, 2009). Let us look further at project success criteria.

The traditional solution to the challenge of measuring project success has been to use a formula that is simple and unequivocal and likely to garner a broad consensus among professionals, namely, the time-cost-quality triangle, with the first two criteria being described as "best guesses" and the latter akin to a "phenomenon" (Atkinson, 1999). Note that some authors argue that "quality" means conforming to the functional and technical specifications of the project.

Criticisms of the narrowness of this trilogy led Baker et al. (1974) and Pinto and Slevin (1988) to add *client satisfaction* to the list. Thus the "triangle" of criteria became, for some at least, a "square": time, cost, quality, and client satisfaction. It then evolved into a "hexagon" as more criteria were added to the initial triangle: achievement of the strategic objectives of the client organization, satisfaction of the end users, and satisfaction of other stakeholders (Ika, 2009).

For example, over time the evaluator may assess the performance of the project manager, the funder, and the owner (the senior manager accountable to the funder for the business case realization). So, project success can be judged in at least three different ways, depending on the main focus of the evaluator (Zwikael & Meredith, 2021):

- The project owner measures project management success against the plan (the delivery of the plan by the project manager).
- The project funder measures project ownership success against the business case (the achievement of the business case by the project owner).
- The project funder measures project investment success or the actual value generated by the project (the return on investment for the funder).

These last two judgments together measure what we previously called *business case success* (Zwikael & Meredith, 2021). To these relatively objective criteria, we must add the subjective, symbolic, and rhetorical judgments of project stakeholders, the kinds of narratives or generic recurring themes across the diverse stories they tell themselves about the project's progress and outcomes (Ika, 2009; Davis, 2014).

Table 5.2 presents these criteria and groups them into the two main dimensions of project success: project management success and business case success.

TABLE 5.2 Two Main Dimensions of Project Success

PROJECT MANAGEMENT SUCCESS (Short Term, or at the End of Project Execution)	BUSINESS CASE SUCCESS (Long Term, or at the End of Benefits Realization)
Time Cost Quality	Achieving client's strategic objectives (e.g., business case and return on investment) Satisfaction of end users Satisfaction of other stakeholders Subjective, symbolic, and rhetorical evaluations of project stakeholders

Source: Adapted from Ika (2009); Zwikael & Meredith (2021).

While the above criteria and dimensions apply to all types of projects, some are specific to particular types of projects. For example, Shenhar and Dvir (2007) propose five dimensions of success for new product development projects but with different time frames over the course of the project and product life cycles: efficiency (during execution or at completion); impact on end users (months after completion); team impact (months after completion); business and direct success (often one or two years after completion); and preparation for the future (likely three or five years after completion). Table 5.3 details these dimensions and the underlying success criteria. It highlights the importance of the more strategic criteria for project success, such as the return on the investment, market share, development of new organizational capabilities or product lines, etc.

TABLE 5.3 Measures of Success in New Product Development Projects

Efficiency	Schedule; budget; yield and other relevant efficiency measures
Impact of the Deliverables on End Users	Requirements/specifications; benefits; degree of use; satisfaction and loyalty; brand name recognition
Impact on the Project Team	Team satisfaction, morale, and skill development; team member retention
Business and Direct Success	Sales; profits; market share; return on investment; return on equity; cash flow; quality of service; cycle time; organizational measures; regulatory approvals
Preparation for the Future	New technologies; new markets; new product lines; new skill sets; new organizational capabilities

Source: Adapted from Shenhar & Dvir (2007).

Critical success factors are the elements project sponsors and managers use to increase the chances of success. Much of what has been written about success factors cannot be covered here (Jugdev & Müller, 2005). Of particular interest is the work of Pinto and Slevin (1988), who scientifically developed and validated an empirical list of 14 key success factors (Table 5.4). For decades, these factors have been a good guide for the project manager and are sufficient for this discussion. The first 10 factors are more or less under the control of the project team. But the other four factors are external to the project implementation process, so they are out of their hands.

Different key success factors may be relevant at different phases of the project's life cycle. In the *design phase*, project mission and client consultation appear to be the most important factors. In the *planning phase*, the key success factors are project mission, top management support, client acceptance, and urgency. In the *execution phase*, project mission, characteristics of the project team leader, troubleshooting, project schedule/plan, technical tasks, and client consultation matter the most. Finally, in the *closing phase,* the key success factors are technical tasks, project mission, and client consultation.

TABLE 5.4 Critical Success Factors for Projects

A LIST OF 14 PROJECT CRITICAL SUCCESS FACTORS	
Factors that are more or less under the control of the project team:	**Factors that are rather outside the control of the project team**:
1. Project mission	**1.** Characteristics of the project team leader
2. Top management support	**2.** Power and politics
3. Schedule/Plan	**3.** Environmental events
4. Client consultation	**4.** Urgency
5. Personnel	
6. Technical tasks	
7. Client acceptance	
8. Monitoring and feedback	
9. Communication	
10. Troubleshooting	

Source: Pinto & Slevin (1988).

Research has shown that stakeholders have different views on project success. Indeed, there is no consensus on success criteria and success factors among the various groups of upper managers, the core team, or even project beneficiaries (Davis, 2014). Table 5.5 traces the evolution of the criteria and critical success factors of projects from the 1960s onward. We illustrate the rise of strategic concerns and the emphasis placed on business case success and even green success.

TABLE 5.5 Project Success Over the Decades

	PERIOD 1 1960s–1980s	PERIOD 2 1980s–1990s	PERIOD 3 21st century
Success Criteria	Iron Triangle of time, cost, quality	Triangle + Client satisfaction Business case benefits End-user satisfaction Benefits to key internal stakeholders (e.g., project staff)	Triangle + Business case benefits and return on investment Benefits to internal stakeholders (project staff and other organizational employees) Benefits to external stakeholders Symbolic and rhetorical success/failure assessments Economic, environmental, and societal impacts or sustainability considerations
Critical Success Factors	Anecdotal lists	Empirical lists (e.g., the 14 factors of Pinto and Slevin, 1988)	More comprehensive empirical lists
Emphasis	Project *management* success	*Business case* success	*Green* success

Source: Adapted from Ika (2009); Ika & Pinto (2022).

THE FOUR QUADRANTS OF PROJECT PERFORMANCE

In *The Iliad,* Achilles failed the initiation rite that would move him from adolescence to adulthood; he failed to kill either a dangerous wild animal in the middle of the forest or an enemy in hostile territory. However, this failure was offset by passing another kind of test that gave him superhero status: he won a fight with the Trojan Scamander. So, Achilles achieved immortal glory after his double initiation (see Wathelet, 1992, 2000).

A similar double jeopardy also applies to projects and their performance. As we have seen, experts agree on two dimensions of project success: *management success* and *business case success.* They also agree that timing matters in the evaluation of success. Finally, experts proffer that typically, project management success provides a short-term assessment and business case success a long-term assessment. The first test of success is management success, which is usually assessed after project completion looking at time and costs. The second test is business case success, which relates to the usefulness, value, and contribution of the project deliverables and benefits; it is usually assessed at the end of the benefits realization phase of the project (Zwikael & Meredith, 2021).

Using this dual measure of success that occurs over time, projects offer (like Achilles and his double initiation in *The Iliad*) a mix of success and failure. Table 5.6 combines the two dimensions of success and proposes four quadrants for measuring project performance. It also gives relevant examples for each (Ika, 2018).

First, some projects are outright failures (Quadrant 4). These are resounding failures in terms of both project management and business case, or the management process failed in the short term, and the project failed to meet the expected business case benefits in the long term. The Ciudad Real International Airport, 200 kilometers from Madrid, illustrates this. Although it boasted the longest runway in Europe (4,200 meters long), this "ghost airport"—airport without passengers—did not host a single commercial flight between 2008 and 2012! Nicknamed Don Quixote's airport, this US$1.5 billion infrastructure was put up for auction, but failed to receive any offer above US$15,000. The same is true of the infamous multibillion-dollar Canadian Federal Government Phoenix Pay System, which was delivered late, over budget, and under quality. Tens of thousands of civil servants were overpaid, underpaid, or not paid at all, leading to costly and desperate attempts to fix the system, only to eventually abandon it altogether.

TABLE 5.6 The Four Quadrants of Project Performance

Business Case \ Project Management	FAILURE (–)	SUCCESS (+)
SUCCESS (+)	**Quadrant 1** *Key examples:* Hoosac Tunnel; the first-generation Taurus (Ford Taurus 1) *Other examples:* Rideau Canal; Sydney Opera House	**Quadrant 2** *Key examples:* The Golden Gate Bridge; NASA Apollo project *Other examples*: The Empire State Building; the Guggenheim Museum in Bilbao
FAILURE (–)	**Quadrant 4** *Key examples:* Ciudad Real Airport; Airbus A380 *Other examples*: United Kingdom's FiReControl project; Canadian Federal Government's Phoenix Pay System	**Quadrant 3** *Key Examples:* The second-generation Taurus (Ford Taurus 2); Los Angeles Red Line Metro *Other examples*: Iridium from Motorola; Chad-Cameroon pipeline

Source: Adapted from Ika (2018).

There are also examples of project management failures but great business case successes (Quadrant 1). Although the Hoosac Tunnel project sponsors estimated that it would cost about US$2 million in 1851, it was delivered after 24 years at a final cost of more than 10 times the initial budget, with unprecedented set-backs including the loss of more than 100 men. Yet it turned out to be one of the greatest engineering feats of the nineteenth century and was instrumental for trade growth between the state of Massachusetts and the West. The first-generation Ford Taurus (1986) had major project delays, leading Ford to fire the project manager. However, a few years later, the car was a huge commercial success, with over two million cars sold!

Some major projects are successfully managed but do not deliver target business case benefits (Quadrant 3). It reminds us of the well-known medical irony: "The operation was successful, but the patient died." The project manager of the second-generation Ford Taurus (1995), perhaps learning from the setbacks of his predecessor, delivered the project on time. Although more than one million units were sold, the car did not live up to expectations, and it was seen as a commercial flop. The ExxonMobil-led Chad-Cameroon pipeline project (1993–2003; US$3.7 billion) was delivered ahead of schedule, and the World Bank saw it as a model for managing infrastructure projects in Africa. Unfortunately, it did not have the expected developmental impact in terms of poverty reduction. Instead of helping the poor, the Chadian government used the oil revenues to rearm and get rid of the rebels threatening to overthrow it.

Finally, some projects are all-around successes, in terms of both their management process and business case target benefits (Quadrant 2)—this is the "Holy Grail" to which every project manager aspires! NASA's Apollo project (1966–1972) was delivered on time—before "the end of the decade" and, more importantly, before the Soviets—and it was a great strategic success for the United States. The San Francisco Golden Gate Bridge, a US$35 million project, was the longest suspension bridge in the world at the time. This bridge was delivered on time (1933–1937) and US$1.3 million under budget. It is now one of the most picturesque bridges in the world and an iconic symbol for San Francisco and the United States.

PROJECTS REQUIRE PATIENCE AND TRIAL AND ERROR

Successful projects sometimes require patience, tinkering, and an iterative process of trial and error. Take the case of the famous

Windows operating system project. In the opinion of Steve Ballmer, cofounder of Microsoft, Windows 1.0 was not a success, Windows 2.0 was not a success, but Windows 3.0 was a home run! Bill Gates, the other cofounder, points out that Microsoft's successful software products such as Excel and Access derive their successes from the dismal performance of a spreadsheet program that could not stand up to the competition of Lotus 1-2-3 and a database called OMEGA that cost millions of dollars in vain.

The (apparent) failure of some projects can lead to the success of others. Christopher Columbus's plan to reach the Indian Ocean failed as he missed his geographical target, timeline, and budget. However, the rather fortuitous discovery of the New World was a colossal success, at least for the project sponsors! The first *Harry Potter* novel had many rejections before finally succeeding. Multiple studios turned down Mark Millar's *Kick Ass* movie, but it eventually grossed at least three times its budget.

CONCLUSION

Despite their widespread usage, projects often experience delays, cost overruns, and benefit shortfalls. Underperformance can be a serious problem even in projects that are successful in some respects. As a result, many projects do not meet the expectations of sponsors, beneficiaries, or other stakeholders.

Project outcomes are difficult to assess. Often, the results observed are a mix of successes and failures. Projects face contextual, institutional, and managerial problems that lead to disappointing results. Planning and implementation factors can also hinder optimal project success: forecasting errors; complexity, uncertainty, or changes in the environment or project scope; and biases.

There are two main dimensions of project success. One assesses project management success in the short term, measured by time, cost, and quality. The other judges business case success; here, the results can only be seen and evaluated in the long term. Since these two assessments are at different points in time, project performance can fall into one of four quadrants: (1) management failure, but business case success; (2) all-around success; (3) management success, but business case failure; and (4) outright failure. To increase the likelihood of success in both the short and long term, project sponsors and managers need to use "best practices," a good dose of patience, a little tinkering, and an iterative process of trial and error.

The chapter offers six takeaways for project sponsors and managers:

1. Project performance often leaves much to be desired with delays, cost overruns, benefit shortfalls, and even business case or strategic failures. This underperformance also occurs in projects that are successful in some ways.
2. Cost overruns and benefit shortfalls are notable, recurrent, and generalized to almost all sectors of activity, even if researchers do not agree on the degree of precision.
3. There are two competing explanations for cost overruns and benefit shortfalls. Rational explanations mainly focus on changes in scope, complexity, and uncertainty. In this case, the recipe for limiting cost overruns is to apply "best practices" in project management. On the other hand, behavioral explanations focus on biases, notably the planning fallacy which is the tendency to overpromise and underdeliver. Consequently, we select "bad" projects from the start—that is, those most likely to underperform. The solution is to de-bias project forecasts with tools such as the reference class forecasting (RCF).
4. A project's underperformance is mainly due to planning, implementation, and environmental failure factors, or management, contextual, and institutional issues.

5. Success is difficult to define, and there is no consensus on its meaning or measurement. However, we can distinguish between criteria and factors. The former refers to objective or subjective measures of success and the latter to circumstances that contribute to the realization of the project's deliverables and benefits.
6. Two dimensions of project performance are commonly recognized: project management performance and business case performance, yielding to four possible combinations.

Achieving project success is a major challenge. Prioritizing management success over business case success often means sacrificing effectiveness for the sake of efficiency and shortchanging stakeholders, the community, and society at large. Moreover, explaining project underperformance by deviations from the agreed-upon ex ante plan and targets leads to what psychosocial theorists call an attribution error: blaming project team members while underestimating the complexity of both the project and its context.

REFERENCES

Atkinson, R. (1999). Project management: cost, time and quality, two best guesses and a phenomenon, it's time to accept other success criteria. *International Journal of Project Management, 17*(6), 337–342.

Baker, BN., Murphy, D. C., & Fisher, D. (1974). Factors affecting project success. In Cleland, D. I., King, W. R. (1988) (Eds.). *Project management handbook*. Van Nostrand Reinhold, 902–919.

Barnes, M. (1969). Email dated 14/12/2005 and interview on January 2006. Quoted in Weaver, P. (2006). A brief history of project management. *APM Project, 19*(11), June 2007.

Cohen, H. (1972). The anomia of success and the anomia of failure: A study of similarities in opposites. *The British Journal of Sociology, 23*, 329–343.

Davis, K. (2014). Different stakeholder groups and their perceptions of project success *International Journal of Project Management, 32*(2), 189–201.

de Wit, A. (1988). Measurement of project success. *Project Management Journal, 6*(3), 164–170.

Eveleens, J. L., & Verhoef, C. (2010). The rise and fall of the Chaos report figures. *IEEE Software*, January/February, 30–36.

Ferry, L. (2002). Qu'est-ce qu'une vie réussie? Éditions Bernard Grasset.

Flyvbjerg, B. (2016). The fallacy of beneficial ignorance: A test of Hirschman's hiding hand. *World Development, 84,* 176–189.

Flyvbjerg, B. (2008). Curbing optimism bias and strategic misrepresentation in planning: Reference class forecasting in practice. *European Planning Studies, 16*(1), 3–21.

Flyvjberg, B., & Budzier, A. (2011). Why your IT project may be riskier than you think. *Harvard Business Review* (September), 23–25.

Flyvbjerg, B., Holm, M. K.S., & Buhl, S. L. (2002). Underestimating costs in public works projects: Error or lie. *Journal of the American Planning Association, 68*(3), 279–295.

Flyvbjerg, B., Ansar, A., Budzier, A., Buhl, S., Cantarelli, C., Garbuio, M., Lavallo, D., Lunn, D., Molin, E., Ronnest, A., Stewart, A., & van Wee, B. (2018). Five things you should know about cost overruns. *Transportation Research A: Policy and Practice, 118*, 174–190.

Hertogh, M., Baker, S., Staal-Ong, P.L., & Westerveld, E. (2008). *Managing large infrastructure projects—Research on best practices and lessons learnt in large infrastructure projects in Europe*. Netlipse.

Hirschman, A. O. (1967). *Development projects observed.* Brookings Institution.

Ika, L. A. (2009). Project success as a topic of project management journals. *Project Management Journal, 40*(4), 6–19.

Ika, L. A. (2012). Project management for development in Africa: Why projects are failing and what can be done about it. *Project Management Journal, 43*(4), 27–41.

Ika, L. A. (2018). Beneficial or detrimental ignorance: The straw man Fallacy of Flyvbjerg's test of Hirschman's Hiding Hand. *World Development, 103,* 369–382.

Ika, L. A., & Pinto, J. K. (2022). The "re-meaning" of project success: Updating and recalibrating for a modern project management. *International Journal of Project Management,* 40(7), 835–848.

Ika, L. A., Love, P. E. D., & Pinto, J. K. (2022). Moving beyond the Planning Fallacy: The emergence of a new principle of project behavior. *IEEE Transactions on Engineering Management,* 69(6), 3310–3325.

Ika, L. A., Pinto, J. K., Love, P. E. D., & Paché, G. (2022). Bias versus error. Why projects fall short. *Journal of Business Strategy*. https://doi.org/10.1108/JBS-11-2021-0190.

Jergeas, G. F., & Ruwanpura J. (2010). Why cost and schedule overruns on mega oil sands projects? *ASCE Practice Periodical on Structural Design and Construction, 15*(1), 40–43.

Jugdev, K., & Muller, R. (2005). A retrospective look at our evolving understanding of project success. *Project Management Journal, 36*(4), 19–31.

Kahneman, D., & Tversky, A. (1979). Intuitive prediction: Biases and corrective procedures. In Makridakis, S., Wheelwright, S. C. (Eds.). Studies in the management sciences: Forecasting, Vol. 12, pp. 313–327. Amsterdam: North Holland.

Kahneman, D. (2011). *Thinking Fast and Slow.* DoubleDay.

Kreiner, K. (2014). Restoring project success as phenomenon. In Lundin, R. A., Hällgreen, M. (Eds.). *Advancing Research on Projects and Temporary Organizations.* Copenhagen Business School Press & Liber, pp. 21–40.

Love, P. E. D., Ahiaga-Dagbui, D., Welde, M., & Odeck, J. (2017). Cost performance light transit rail: Enablers of future-proofing. *Transportation Research A: Policy and Practice, 100,* 27–39.

Love, P. E. D., Sing, M. C. P., Ika, L. A., & Newton, S. (2019). The cost performance of transportation infrastructure projects: The fallacy of the Planning Fallacy account. *Transportation Research A: Policy and Practice, 122,* 1–20.

Love, P. E. D., Ika, L. A., Matthews, J., & Fang, W. (2021). Shared leadership, value and risks in large scale transportation projects: Re-calibrating procurement policy for post COVID-19. *Research Transportation Economics, 90,* 100999.

Matta, N. F., & Ashkenas, R. N. (2003). Why good projects fail anyway. *Harvard Business Review* (September), 109–114.

Meier, S. R. (2008). Best project management and systems engineering practices in pre-acquisition practices in the federal intelligence and defense agencies. *Project Management Journ*al, *39*(1), 59–71.

Migoya, D. (2021). Cost of Aurora VA hospital complex tops $2 billion; becomes one of world's most expensive health facilities. *The Denver Post,* 27 August. Available at www.denverpost.com/2021/08/27/va-hospital-aurora-building-budget-expenses/ (accessed 3 February 2022).

Miller, R., & Lessard, D. R. (2000). *The strategic management of large engineering projects*. MIT Press.

Morris, P. W. G. (2013). *Reconstructing project management*. John Wiley & Sons.

Morris, P. W. G., & Hough, G. H. (1987). *The anatomy of major projects*. John Wiley and Sons.

Odeck, J. (2004). Cost overruns in road construction—what are their size and determinants. *Transport Policy, 24,* 43–53.

OMEGA (2012). *Mega projects executive summary. Lessons for decision makers: An analysis of selected large-scale transport infrastructure projects*. Omega Centre, December.

Pinto, J. K., & Slevin D. P. (1988). Project success: definitions and measurement techniques. *Project Management Journal, 19*(1), 67–72.

Rondinelli, D. A. (1983). *Development projects as policy experiments. An adaptive approach to development administration*. Methuen.

Serrador, P., & Pinto, J. K. (2015). Does agile work? A quantitative analysis of agile project success. *International Journal of Project Management, 33*(5), 1040–1051.

Shenhar, A., & Dvir, D. (2007). *Reinventing project management. The diamond approach to successful growth and innovation*. Harvard Business School Press.

Sullivan, P. (2021, 1 October). *Private jet market grapples with surge in get-me-away Demand. New York Times*. https://www.nytimes.com/2021/10/01/your-money/private-jets-demand.html (accessed 27 April 2022).

Terrill, M., & Danks, L. (2016). *Cost overruns in transportation infrastructure Projects*. A Grattan Institute, Melbourne, Victoria, Australia. Available at https://grattan.edu.au/report/cost-overruns-in-transport-infrastructure/ (accessed 2 July 2019).

The Standish Group (2013). *CHAOS Manifesto 2013. Think big, Act small*. The Standish Group.

Wathelet, P. (1992). Rites de passage dans l'Iliade : Échecs et réussites. In A. Moreau (Ed.). *L'initiation*, Montpellier, Université Paul Valéry, I, 61–72.

Wathelet, P. (1999). La double initiation d'Achille dans l'Iliade. In *Héros et Héroïnes dans les Mythes et les Cultes Grecs*. Actes du colloque organisé à l'Université de Valladolid, du 26 mai au 29 Mai 1999.

Zwikael, O., & Meredith, J. (2021). Evaluating the success of a project and the performance of its leaders. *IEEE Transactions on Engineering Management, 68*(6), 1745–1757.

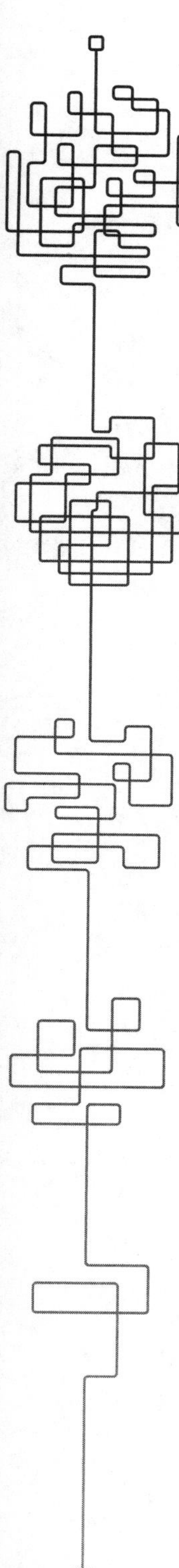

CHAPTER 6

THE RATIONAL PERSPECTIVE (IN VITRO)

BACK TO THE ROOTS

Project management is old, but its study is young. It emerged as a distinct discipline over the last few decades, even though great projects have been carried out throughout history. Some of these historic projects still stand: pyramids in Africa and the Americas, the Great Wall of China, the palaces and places of worship throughout Asia and Europe, and the lesser-known Ngunnhu dry-stone fish traps in Australia (over 3,000 years old and still in use). These projects are called "hard" projects because they are tangible. But there are also records of remarkable "soft" projects. Historians tell us of organizational projects carried out on a grand scale in the management of cities, and also for wars and conquests like the great fleet the Romans assembled to destroy the city of Carthage. Today, we use "soft" and "hard" projects to shape our world. They are conducted in every sector of our physical and social environment—in business, arts, and entertainment—to explore outer space or to fight microscopic viruses.

Historically, project management has been the preferred method of organizing construction work because each building, road, and bridge addresses specific needs in unique geophysical circumstances. Unsurprisingly, the construction industry has one of the world's oldest companies. Kongō Gumi Co, Ltd. was founded in Japan in 578 and operated for 14 centuries. The fortified walls built under the dynasties and kingdoms of China over a period of 22 centuries exceeded 12,000 miles (20,000 km) in length. Construction also has one of the longest-running projects in modern history: the Sagrada Familia Cathedral in Barcelona, Spain. Its construction began in 1882, stopped during the Spanish Civil War, and resumed in 1952. The long-unfinished "masterpiece" is slated for completion in 2026, while its total construction cost remains unknown (Abend, 2019).

Construction traditionally calls for customized solutions that cannot be found in the *standardized management methods* used in operations management to manufacture goods and deliver services on a continuous basis. In construction, the human, material, and financial resources required to undertake purposeful activities must be configured and mobilized to meet unique requirements. Once the goal is achieved, these resources are dismantled and reassigned to other projects with new configurations.

TACKLING CHANGE

Offering a better way to implement change through "best practices," the standardized approach has been adapted to many industrial sectors and, over the past 80 years, has extended to new fields like international development. It has also taken root in the emerging fields of R&D and IT, in which changes are the norm, not the exception. Incursions into these new areas faced new challenges because, unlike construction, these sectors do not aim for material strength or durability but rather for intangible objectives, innovation, and change.

Later, project management was used in industrial sectors (where continuous production had been the norm) that needed to adjust to constant and increasingly constraining technological, economic, and social changes. Driven by the need to innovate, the insertion of project management in these new sectors occurred at first tentatively, through the back door, and today with fanfare and visibility.

In these new environments, project managers no longer wear construction hard hats, computer scientist's sneakers and jeans, or researcher's lab coats. Instead, they are more likely to wear ties or high heels! Even if these project managers, like Nancy Smart, try to blend in within these new environments, they operate differently and, consequently, often come into conflict with managers working in traditional sectors. The new relationships that arise are far from symbiotic, and for good reason: project managers inevitably upset the established order.

Before the intrusion of project management, strategic management and operations management had coexisted in relative harmony with a clear hierarchy. Strategists set the overall, long-term direction of the organization, while operations managers of the various units ensured its smooth operation. In short, there were executives and implementers. There was a clear differentiation of roles, and everyone knew their place.

The arrival of project management in this environment introduced a flatter hierarchical structure in which managers "coordinate" much more than "command"—this is a new way of managing. Indeed, a project may involve many organizational units and spread out spatially, within the organization, and over time. As a result, its effects are often felt far beyond its initial scope and temporary presence. The organization's reporting relationships are altered for the project's duration and often for a longer period than expected.

Using project management to deal with change in new sectors means taking on a unique role in environments where stability and reliability were core principles. However, since project management is not well known in these new settings, its practical application and unusual methods are often misunderstood. Indeed, their insertion has been a double-edged sword. At the heart of the problem is the *temporary* and *cross-functional* nature of the project manager's field of action and its implications for the relationships that ensue. The *strategy-operations* dyad that traditionally oversees the management of organizations has evolved into the threesome we know today: *strategy-projects-operations* (presented in Chapter 1, Table 1.1).

NEW MANAGERS, NEW PERSPECTIVES

Unlike strategy and operations, project management is used at many levels of the organization due to its promise of solving problems and effecting change. The changes project managers deal with—large or small—may be driven by strategic and operational needs. What distinguishes project management from the other two types of management is its *temporary* nature and *transversality*.

Project managers face major challenges and have limited room to maneuver because they must accomplish a novel task with a predetermined objective, specific resources, and often tight constraints. They have neither the luxury of the long-term horizon enjoyed by strategic managers nor the ability to draw on the industry-specific experience of production managers. Instead, their goal is to get the project "up and running" as fast as possible.

They must rely on their own tools to carry out projects in low-tech sectors and relatively stable markets, as is the case for quality circles and product changes. However, the same tools and practices may be inadequate for radical innovation projects with high complexity and uncertainty. The latter require a more flexible and adaptive management approach, possibly involving trial and error (Loch, 2017). Put simply, the iPhone project manager could have relied on best practices when dealing with the technological improvements needed for the *n*th version of the iPhone, but not for the first iPhone, which was an unprecedented technological breakthrough for Apple.

To overcome the constraints inherent to their ill-defined role and their temporary status within the organization, project managers use a specific arsenal of tools to define and circumscribe all the phases of the project. They begin with the traditional methods of planning, organizing, directing, and controlling, adapting them as best they can to the specific reality of the project. Modern tools are then added to this classical approach to help mitigate uncertainty and structure the work more efficiently (see Chapter 4).

This newer form of management was applied to projects to compensate for the structural shortcomings of traditional *strategic or operational management*. These latter types of management were too slow, too costly, and unreliable when dealing with innovation/change or operating in a climate of high uncertainty. As a result, this new project management approach pays particular attention to time, cost, and quality management to counter the slow processes, resources consuming, and unpredictable results typically found in traditional general management. The time-cost-quality (TCQ) triangle thus supplants concerns about stability and reliability as cardinal virtues in management.

Project management endeavors to fulfill the mandate efficiently by adopting a focused and time-bound approach rather than a circular and continuous operations management approach. In essence, this new approach manages organizational change without shortchanging the organization. Moreover, it offers an orderly vision of the environment whose parameters are relatively circumscribed and controlled. Strategic management executives do not see this project-based environment as fuzzy and limitless.

They structure the work according to the task at hand and nothing more. Human and material resources are mobilized and demobilized for this sole purpose. In short, it is a focused and rigorous approach.

A RIGOROUS APPROACH

How does a field of human activity get overtaken by rules? An antecedent in classical literature, in another century and in the field of literature and art, illustrates how the practice of a well-established profession came to be circumscribed by imposing operational rules.

In the traditional Baroque theater, a plot could unfold over many years, take place in different countries, have many subplots, and move from humorous to tragic. To contain this unbridled format, the classical theorists of seventeenth-century Italy, France, and England promoted a steadier set of rules, grounded in Aristotle's *Poetics*: a unit of time, a unit of place, and a unit of action. As Boileau wrote in his *Art poétique*: "Let in one place, and in one day, a single deed be done, to keep the theater full to the end." The new rules of classical drama reduced a play to one day, limited the location to a single place, and included one central plot with no subsidiary events to divert the audience's attention. The driving force behind the rule of three—a unit of time, place, and action—was to establish order and reason.

We can draw a parallel between this evolution and what we witnessed in project management. The manager's room to maneuver (the equivalent of the playwright) is restricted by constraints known in advance, in order to better meet the expectations of clients and owners (the audience and the theater owners). Project management thus aims to constrain managerial action to the strict parameters of time, cost, and quality that guarantee success.

The expected advantages are that it will save money and increase efficiency.

Table 6.1 shows the parallels between the rule of three units in the theater and the time-cost-quality triangle in project management.

TABLE 6.1 The Triangulation of Plays and Projects

IN THE THEATER, THE THREE-UNIT RULE:		IN PROJECT MANAGEMENT, THE TIME-COST-QUALITY TRIANGLE:	
That in one place . . .	(Location)	That within budget . . .	(Costs)
In one day . . .	(Time)	And on time . . .	(Time)
One plot . . .	(Action)	Within scope . . .	(Quality)
The theater is filled until the end.		The project is delivered as promised.	

The project management profession has evolved to the point where it no longer has free rein and is subject to constraints. These safeguards, which strictly delimit the field of action, aim to make project management more effective and efficient. As a result, this field now has a more functionalist, task-oriented vision.

AN EMERGING DISCIPLINE

Project management has experienced remarkable growth over the past 80 years. One of the first projects to use modern management principles was the Hoover Dam, built in the 1930s in the United States. It delivered expected benefits within time, cost, and quality, using practices that are now called critical success factors, such as top management and stakeholder engagement (Kwak, Walewski, Sleeper, & Sadatsafavi, 2014).

Over the years, the TCQ triangle has been studied and promoted in-depth in the project management literature. These constraints are central to the body of knowledge taught in textbooks and required in certification exams. With this specialized knowledge, project management has been able to counterbalance a more generalist managerial approach.

The modernization and standardization of project management practices have led to the formation of professional associations in the field, such as the European-based International Project Management Association (IPMA) in 1965 and the US-based Project Management Institute (PMI) in 1969. Their goal has been to raise the profile of the discipline, standardize it, promote a formal certification process, and even make it a profession on par with medicine, law, accounting, or engineering. Nothing similar has occurred in operations or strategic management, although formal training was first given at business schools and later at colleges/universities. Throughout, the formal training provided by these institutions was independent of the practice of the profession. In this context, the process of certifying project managers is relatively new and growing in importance.

Project management is emerging as an actual scientific field, with its own research topics and conferences. It is also gaining recognition and credibility in the academic world of business and management. For several years, PMI has invited and sponsored the active participation of project management researchers in the annual meetings of the US Academy of Management (AOM). The same is happening with the European Academy of Management (EURAM), the European Group for Organizational Studies (EGOS), and the British Academy of Management (BAM), which now offer a Project Management section in their annual conference.

Project management researchers are publishing in leading business and management journals such as the top 50 *Financial Times* journals, giving the discipline the credibility that it lacked in the eyes of some informed observers and its staunch detractors. In the view of Thomas Kuhn (1996), we are witnessing the emergence of a paradigm (with its own language, societies of specialists, and periodicals), a special scientific status, and an important field of knowledge in the area of business and management. Appendix 6.1 identifies some of the key professional associations and the standards and certifications they offer, and Appendix 6.2 lists a few leading project management journals and magazines.

AN IN VITRO APPROACH

To achieve efficiency and effectiveness simultaneously, project management researchers and practitioners strive to clearly define the scope of their discipline and reduce gray areas as much as possible. For example, expected results are defined explicitly and well in advance, so that project managers can measure the activity's effectiveness. Similarly, the resources needed must be approved early to make it easier to measure their efficiency.

Once the TCQ targets are known, the project managers can work—*in vitro,* as in the isolation of a laboratory—on project initiation, the deployment of material and human resources, and then project execution. By focusing on these constraints, managers can effectively organize the project so that it represents a well-oiled process designed to deliver a product or service that meets a specific need.

In the *rational approach,* the project has one client, one mandate, and one dominant goal, and the organization is a stable and closed system. Thus, initiation and execution of the project is carried out methodically, in vitro. As the main challenge is meeting TCQ targets, the managerial process adheres strictly to these constraints, as stated in the mandate. Just like the organization where it is implemented, the project is reified—that is, perceived and treated as if it were an objective, unified "thing"—a concrete entity with its own functions, structure, and relations with the environment. In that perspective, a project can be launched with a specific and predetermined objective, which is called a *mandate*. The latter is formally described in the terms of reference, the project management plan, or the project charter, which outlines the business need or rationale for the project. The project sponsors and managers must officially endorse the plan. In so doing, the project acquires an independent existence that transcends that of its individual members. Even though the project team's composition and dynamics (with their different views and expertise) are likely to fluctuate as the project progresses, they are seen as "the team."

THE PROJECT AS A WELL-DEFINED AND MANDATED ACTIVITY

The mandate allows the project manager to establish a quasi-equality among the project objectives (po), its management (pm), and stakeholders (sh):

$$0_{po} \rightarrow 0_{pm} \rightarrow 0_{sh}$$

We presume that there is equifinality in this system because the desired results can be achieved regardless of the circumstances. First, it assumes that the mandate documented in the terms of reference, project charter, or project management plan reflects all that is required and nothing superfluous. So the mandate represents a brief but complete statement of what is *to be achieved in the project* (the specific objective).

From there, the project manager's training determines the path and every step taken. The objectives of project management are limited to applying knowledge, skills, tools, and techniques to project activities in order to meet the requirements of time, cost, and quality (PMI, 2017). Furthermore, since the objectives of the project are stable, the project can be managed methodically: $0_{po} \rightarrow 0_{pm}$. Project management indicates, without ambiguity, *how to manage the project*.

Finally, the various stakeholders are treated as a relatively homogeneous group with compatible and stable interests, who hold similar views that will not change over time. The stakeholder expectations are explicitly expressed in the mandate given to the project manager. To satisfy them, the project manager need only apply the proven tools and methods: $0_{po} \rightarrow 0_{pm} \rightarrow 0_{sh}$. Since there is no ambiguity about *for whom* and *why* the project is carried out, the project manager can see the stakeholders as "things" or "objects" that they can manipulate in the best interest of the project, according to their help or harm potential. Therefore, they can "manage" stakeholders like they do time and cost constraints, to optimize their net impact on the project to ensure its success. Their attitude: keep stakeholders up to date on the project's progress, and all will be fine.

A project mandate clearly identifies what must be delivered and typically remains stable over time. The project's mandate binds the different stakeholders into a stable and closed system. This system can be managed in isolation, with few unexpected interactions with the rest of the organization and the outside world. The efficiency criterion requires that project management be free from the fragmentation that characterizes organizations and their different subunits, such as production, sales, and accounting (Ika & Saint-Macary, 2011).

From this perspective, the project is only confronted with managerial and technical challenges. The manager can rationally and objectively plan the project and ensure its success, free from political or social disruptions, whether internal or external. Therefore, project managers can be chosen based on the technical and managerial skills needed to meet the requirements of the project. Similarly, they can expect their team members and external stakeholders to behave the same way and view the project from a purely rational point of view, free of subjective considerations.

The project manager relies on proven tools to ensure that the result obtained is the one that was desired at the outset. But the theory of bounded rationality shows that the decision-making process is doubly impaired: (1) by people's inability to collect and process all the information they require, and (2) by the fact that they often change their minds about the assessment of the information gathered. The *principals* (the sponsors, clients, suppliers, and external contributors) and *agents* (the project team members) are likely to change their preferences as the project progresses. These shifting preferences can affect the achievement of objectives (as they may change) and the efficient use of resources (as they may have to be modified). Safeguards are needed to compensate for these cognitive deficiencies and limit potential irrational impulses.

A clear and fixed mandate makes it possible to avoid deviations from the work to be done, as well as complications that may ensue. The project is thus shielded from the unstable preferences of the parties involved. Consequently, the only shortcomings of bounded rationality result from the inability of the parties to collect, process, and store a large amount of information, such as the project scope and the numerous tasks to be distributed. Fortunately, project management techniques such as scheduling can help in this regard. In the mandate, the project is treated like an activity intended to produce predetermined deliverables or achieve a specific organizational objective. Project management is simply the means to ensure that this happens. In short, the project defines the mandate, and the mandate defines the project. To succeed in one is to succeed in the other.

ALIGNMENT FOR EFFICIENCY AND EFFECTIVENESS

In the rational perspective, the project focuses on the mandate or specific objective of the project. To illustrate this approach, consider a bill advocated by a newly elected governor that aims to stimulate the state economy during a pandemic and boost health by improving access to outdoor activities. The overall, strategic goal of such a bill might be to accelerate the execution of some key projects using a sizable budget. Once the governor sponsors the bill, legislative aides will oversee its passage by the state legislature, working with the budget and policy directors. Later, the State Office of Recreation and Parks will oversee the project implementation. From a rational perspective, that is the project in a nutshell.

The rational perspective would lead one to believe that the project's objective is well defined in the mandate entrusted to the project manager—that is, to get the bill passed by the state legislature. Therefore, it may be argued that there is no need to redefine the rationale for the project or specify the needs to be met (i.e., the problem to solve or the opportunity to seize). One might assume that if the bill is passed, the project's overall goal (to accelerate construction and stimulate the economy) will de facto be achieved and the needs met.

Unfortunately, without a clear and precise understanding of the mandate, the project manager cannot adequately answer these kinds of questions: What is the project meant to do? How can it be effective and efficient? What will the project look like once the deliverable is complete (in this case, the bill)? In other words, how will the project transform its inputs (e.g., the proposed bill) into outputs (e.g., the passed bill) and measure its efficiency (e.g., debate time in the legislature)? In such a case, the degree of accountability for project outcomes (efficiency and effectiveness) is hard to decipher. While the "goal" of the governor's chief of staff is to get the bill passed, the governor's "goal" is to stimulate the economy. So, success for the chief of staff is getting the bill passed, and success for the governor is meeting the overall goal and then achieving other projects to keep his or her election promises.

The alignment between the inputs, outputs, and mandate should reflect the rationality or logic of the project. This logic is based on an assumption of certainty. It assumes that if one can gather the inputs, one can certainly deliver the outputs, achieve the specific objective, and contribute to the overall goal of the project.

To better understand the desired level of efficiency of the project, it is common to consider the *descriptive aspects* (inputs, outputs, specific objective) and *performance indicators* (e.g., time taken to debate it, the number of votes in favor, if the law passed or not). These indicators can measure and translate the constraints of the project in concrete terms (whether they relate to efficiency or effectiveness).

The governor's office may underestimate the risks posed by some contentious sections of the bill regarding, for example, the environment and public procurement, two subjects that may be considered sensitive by the other political parties. Another mitigating factor could be the project manager's (governor's chief of staff) lack of political experience. Since nothing is certain in projects, the goal of the rational approach is to identify, in a risk context, what could go wrong with the project before execution.

While the rational approach recognizes the importance of identifying the invisible part of the iceberg (project needs), it is only interested in its visible part (the mandate or specific objective). Why? Knowledge of the mandate is considered sufficient for the project manager to execute the project well and duly contribute to the achievement of the overall goal in the long term. Project initiation and planning tools such as the project charter, the logical framework, and the project management plan, which are often used by practitioners, help probe and confirm the project's logic before execution. Table 6.2 lays out how project alignment, through the use of a logical framework, can help improve project efficiency and effectiveness (the first column of the logical framework is appropriately nicknamed "project logic").

TABLE 6.2 Logical Framework and Project Alignment for Efficiency and Effectiveness

Project Start: ____________________

Project End: ____________________

Date of the Log Frame: ____________________

Project Name: ____________________

DESCRIPTIVE LEVELS OF THE PROJECT	KEY PERFORMANCE INDICATORS	SOURCES OF EVIDENCE	CRITICAL CONDITIONS
Overall goal			Specific Objective → Overall goal
Specific objective			Outputs → Objective
Outputs			Inputs → Outputs
Inputs			Prerequisite conditions

THE AUTHORITY OF THE PROJECT MANAGER

Nancy Smart does not have the authority of a hierarchical position at ExPlus. Her management role is temporary, and at the end of the project, her team members will return to their previous jobs unless they are working on another project. As a project manager, she does not have the authority that generally comes from having superior technical skills than her collaborators: her role is not *to lead, but rather to coordinate the work of the specialists on her team. Thus, the project manager's authority is continually at risk of being challenged. Experience shows that this is often the case, especially if the team members have not been introduced to project management or informed of their new duties and responsibilities.*

At first glance, the project manager can only count on *legitimacy* based on personal qualities and distinctive skills. Therefore, the mandate received from the principals—for example, the project's clients—helps establish *rational and legal authority* within the project team and the other organizational units involved in implementing it. In the next chapter, we take a deeper look at the project manager's authority when examining a project's political dimensions.

THINK FIRST, THEN ACT?

One of the basic principles of the rational project management approach is to plan the work carefully and then execute it as planned—*Plan your work and work your plan*. The necessary steps are well known to project management professionals: define the problem, diagnose its causes, design feasible solutions, choose the "best" solution to address the identified needs, and implement it.

Define → Diagnose → Design → Decide → Do

Many critics point out that this approach does not work when needs are complex or unclear. In these cases, solutions cannot be formulated, designed, and structured in advance of their execution (Mintzberg, Ahlstrand, & Lampel, 2013). Mintzberg and his collaborators, well-known authors in strategy, argue that there are sound alternatives to this universal "thinking first" rational approach. Notably, "seeing first" by observing what has been done in a similar way, or "acting first" by managing incrementally.

These practices can be advantageously combined since they are not mutually exclusive. In fact, they are found in both our personal and organizational lives. Mintzberg illustrates this point by identifying the different ways we find a spouse. The *think first* approach fits "marriages of reason" or arranged marriages. Here, the decision to marry is rational and based on criteria used by the two parties, their friends, or their respective families. The *see first* approach includes couples that come together as a result of chance or social encounters. A third type is cohabitation (*act first*) before marriage.

Similar practices are found in organizations and, increasingly, in projects. Managers plan first (*think first*), of course. But they also observe what is going on in their organizations, MBWA-style (management by walking around), or observe what other organizations are doing (*see first*). As well, managers also launch pilot projects (*act first*). In real life, managers think in order to act; however, they also see and act in order to think. This ties in with Henri Bergson's maxim (1937): "One must act as a man of thought and think as a man of action" (our translation).

Astute project managers, like Nancy, will correctly suggest that the starting point of relationships or of projects can be a combination of thinking, seeing, and doing first. Our main point is that, contrary to orthodox views, projects originate in a variety of ways, and how they start off will cast long shadows on how they will evolve, as it is the case with marriages. Evidently, couples who are formed based on objective criteria (*think first*), chance encounters (*see first*), or after living together (*act first*), start off not only with different advantages and knowledge bases, but with handicaps as well. The same holds for projects.

The TCQ constraints impose limitations on projects. Because they are interdependent, as noted earlier, a change in one affects the others, leading to trade-offs among time, cost, and quality. Another problem stems from the fact that projects are usually presented as if they originated from a rational (*think first*) approach. In reality, the decision to initiate the project and establish any of the TCQ constraints may result from a combination of the three approaches discussed in the previous paragraphs, not solely of "think first." When this occurs, the reliability of the TCQ's "solid and stable" foundation should be questioned. It is therefore important to examine these constraints carefully, each in turn.

The iterative or even adaptive *see first* process makes it easier to assess the impacts of different options. While this process lets managers choose the solution that will best meet the perceived needs, it can also redefine the nature of the needs. As a result, it influences the choice of the options to be considered and the perception of the needs to be met. By embracing seeing or doing first, choices can be modified through observation and experience. The iterative process enriches the decision-making process and allows one to choose the most appropriate option given the context.

In project management practice, we cannot rule out the possibility that deliverables will be organized and phased in unpredictably because of what we see and do. Therefore, quality cannot be fixed in a closed contract, as in a mandate-based approach. Changes in one constraint will affect the others. This is why iterative and adaptive options (such as agile approaches) have emerged with different life cycles and planning styles. These newer methods challenge the dominant rational, mandate-based approach as they strive to consider the complexity and uncertainty surrounding projects.

THE IMMUTABLE NATURE OF THE PROJECT LIFE CYCLE

The project goes through different phases from initiation to closure. This development process is commonly referred to as the *project life cycle,* which is central to the rational approach based on the mandate. It structures the project management process which makes it predictable, and assigns roles and responsibilities to team members. In short, it uses a proven recipe for delivering projects, regardless of their nature, based on the broad assumption that most projects are similar. The project life cycle provides this standard frame of reference for all projects, regardless of their specificity or complexity. These phases are sets of related activities that lead to the completion of project deliverables. The life cycle varies depending on the industry, the organizational context, the technology used, the type of project, and the specific life cycle of the deliverable to be achieved. However, a generic life cycle generally consists of four phases that expand in length and intensity depending on the project's scope and complexity:

- The **initiation phase** examines the needs, identifies the specific and strategic objectives, outlines the options for responding to the project needs, and summarizes the project's feasibility and expected results in a document like a *project charter.*
- The **planning phase** determines the project's scope and estimates the times, costs, and resources. It ends with a project management *plan.*
- The **execution phase** is where the plan is implemented, the project is monitored and controlled, and the deliverables are produced.
- The **closing phase** is when the work is completed and delivered to the client. Then, the project may be evaluated, lessons learned compiled, and findings summarized in an evaluation report.

The rational, mandate-based approach favors a life cycle that could be described as predictive (see Figure 6.1). This life cycle is rather rigid and essentially sequential, although phases may overlap. Approval of the project charter marks the end of the initiation phase, approval of the plan marks the end of the planning phase, and acceptance of the deliverables by the client marks the end of the execution phase.

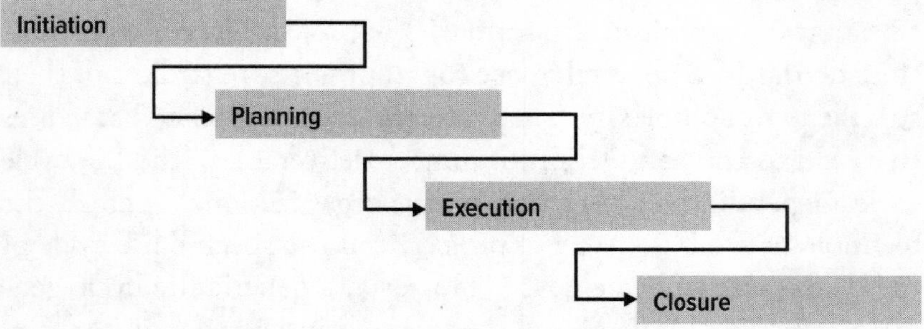

FIGURE 6.1 The waterfall project life cycle

The *predictive life cycle* is effective in a reasonably stable or predictable environment where the project's needs and scope can be identified in advance. While the predictive life cycle is commonly used in the construction sector, it is less common in software engineering, for example, where *iterative life cycles* are preferred.

Agile approaches are proving to be good alternative approaches because they embrace complexity and uncertainty in a dynamic environment and integrate feedback from stakeholders from one iteration to the next for efficiency purposes. In contrast, the predictive life cycle operates in a stable environment, and it aims to reduce complexity and uncertainty, and to increase efficiency; this is why the project plan must be methodically followed and project phases deployed in cascades.

In the *predictive approach,* the project's scope, times, and costs should be determined as early as possible. Any changes to the project's scope should then be carefully managed and communicated through a project change request form that documents the proposed changes and the levels of authority to approve them (PMI, 2017). Thus, this approach leads to a paradox: the risks, times, resources, and costs of the project must be estimated when this knowledge is most lacking. This weakness explains why the rational approach has developed planning tools that purport to reduce complexity and uncertainty, and help managers quickly process a large amount of information about the project.

IS PROJECT PLANNING THE BEST PRACTICE?

The words "If you fail to plan, you are planning to fail," attributed to Benjamin Franklin, could be a good motto for project management. The rational perspective considers the project as a reasoned and purposive human action. It is not a quest, an experiment, or a discovery (Hirschman, 1967), but rather a deliberate leap into a planned future (Kreiner, 2020). This explains why planning plays a central role in any project (see Appendix 6.3 for a project management plan template). Although planning is not insurance against project failure—and too much planning can kill creativity—it can reduce complexity and uncertainty and increase the chances of success.

In this context, planning is used in the term's broadest sense, which includes the activities in the initiation and planning phases. Planning is generally seen as a major success factor, and is therefore *the* project management practice *par excellence.*

While it is customary to separate the initiation phase from the planning phase, initiating the project means anticipating the future and as such requires planning. To this end, project initiation includes a clear, precise, and rational definition of the project's scope, objectives, starting and end dates, along with the proposed resources and budget to deliver the product or service.

It considers TCQ constraints, with the paramount goal of meeting the expectations of project stakeholders.

Of course, no project flows like a smooth river, since numerous obstacles, difficulties, and setbacks can alter its course. In the *rational approach,* however, these uncertainties are assumed to be anticipated in the project plan, keeping the successful completion of the project mandate as a constant objective. In theory, nothing relevant to the project's overall objective should happen between the initiation stage and the start of operations. Through planning, the project's success criteria, duration, costs, and risks can be established at the outset. Should any of these deviate from the plan, corrective measures can redress the project's course. This is no easy task; in Box 6.1, we discuss the limitations of detailed planning using the example of the US company Biogen[1].

BOX 6.1

Biogen's rBeta Project and the Limitations of Detailed Planning

The Recombinant Beta Interferon (rBeta) project undertaken between 1991 and 1996 by the US biotechnology company Biogen offers a good example of the limitations of detailed planning. The rBeta project aimed to produce interferons: proteins with mammalian cells to fight cancer or treat hepatitis B and C. At the end of the summer of 1992, the company prepared a detailed project plan using Microsoft Project software. However, this 30+-page plan only included the project tasks scheduled to be completed by mid-1993.

The company then identified 1,500+ specific project tasks, their sequence, resources, and timelines for completion. In this way, they wanted to highlight the interdependent relationships between the tasks assigned to each of the small work teams involved in the project. Finally, the company planned to monitor progress monthly, by function, by the person in charge, and other variables. It would then take corrective measures if necessary.

The company quickly realized that some teams embraced detailed planning, but others did not because it added to their everyday responsibilities. They settled on an eight-page rough project plan that focused on the critical tasks of process development, facilities, and production, rather than documentation, quality assurance, and quality control.

Work teams whose tasks were not on the critical path began to experience difficulties and faced bottlenecks early on. For example, documentation took too much time, even though it was important to meet Food and Drug Administration (FDA) time requirements. Due to a poor project management culture and weak planning skills, this project was delayed and it was only launched commercially in June 1996.

Source: Wheelwright (1996).

These words used by President Eisenhower (1957) speak volumes: "Plans are worthless, but planning is everything." When changes (e.g., in scope) are made or occur along the way, the plan remains an important project management tool to ensure that best practices are used to carry out the mandate. "Plans are nothing, changes in plans are everything" (Dvir & Lechler, 2004) sums up what keeps the project mandate and objectives on course.

More specifically, the *project mandate* serves as a compass for the project team. It sets the course for reasoned human action, while the *project plan* serves as a road map. In theory, there is a presumption of a causal relationship between project efficiency and effectiveness, where one implies the other. But in practice, since the project is not carried out in a "bubble of certainty," efficiency and effectiveness are in essence decoupled, since the former does not necessarily lead to the latter. For example, as we saw in Chapter 5 it is not uncommon to have *management* successes that are *strategic* failures, or efficient but ineffective projects. Two examples will illustrate this project performance paradox between efficiency and effectiveness.

Iridium was a limited liability company that Motorola established to develop an ambitious US$5 billion project for a wireless handheld satellite telephone system to make and receive calls from anywhere on earth, including polar and ocean regions. The project required 77 low-orbiting satellites—science nerds will have noted that 77 is the atomic number for the element iridium! Over 11 years, the project sponsors consulted over 200,000 people, interviewed 23,000 individuals in 42 countries, and surveyed more than 3,000 companies. This planning effort paid off handsomely in terms of efficiency, because the project was delivered on time and within budget (Shenhar & Dvir, 2007).

During that same decade, the competitive landscape had evolved with the advent of the cellular market, 2G (second-generation cellular) and GSM (Global System for Mobile Communications) standards, and smaller phones. Unfortunately for Motorola, effectiveness did not follow efficiency: Iridium's technology could not be used in cars, buildings, and many urban areas because it required a direct line of sight between the phone's antenna and the satellite. Ten years into the project, people saw the Iridium satellite phone as bulky and expensive by new phone standards. With 10,000 subscribers instead of the projected 500,000, Iridium was forced into bankruptcy within a year of launch (Finkelstein & Sanford, 2000). The US government bailed out Iridium and it was bought by private investors who adopted a different business model.

As discussed in Chapter 5, the Chad-Cameroon pipeline, a US$4 billion pipeline construction project stretching over 650 miles, took six years to design and plan. The World Bank championed this project as a model for managing infrastructure projects in Africa, using strict and responsible scrutiny. For example, the environmental plan prepared by ExxonMobil, the leader of the oil consortium that built the pipeline, comprised 19 volumes of documentation, was debated for 18 months, and responded to World Bank project supervisors' 66 separate requests for clarification. ExxonMobil and the other consortium members successfully managed the structural complexity of the project, which stemmed from the number and diversity of the different components of the project deliverables and their interconnections.

However, the sociopolitical complexity in Chad got the better of the project. Although the pipeline was delivered months ahead of schedule, it was an international development fiasco. The plan was to use the money to deliver education and health services to Chad's poorest people, but the Chadian government used the oil revenues to rearm and win the battle against the rebels that threatened the government (Ika & Saint-Macary, 2012).

In the public and private sectors, good planning does not guarantee that the project's strategic objectives will be met. Project management success does not necessarily lead to strategic success. Yet the tenets of rational project management are unambiguous. There are proven tools, methods, and standards available. The project team is expected to use these tools and knowledge to carry out the project successfully. They need to use them wisely, prepare the project plan accordingly, and implement it methodically. In short, the project team has everything it needs to complete a project successfully; ignorance is no excuse.

Unfortunately, many projects are "over budget, over time, again and again" (Flyvbjerg, 2014). When this occurs (and especially in cases of perceived inefficiency), the rationale offered by the proponents of the rational approach is that the project team misused the tools, or did not use them at all. But either way, poor project performance is not a reason to give up on the ideal. Instead, the solution is to bring practice as close as possible to the ideal (Kreiner, 2020).

The project team must explain the project to the stakeholders, giving them the opportunity to modify the project plan before or during implementation. To that end, the project team has a complete toolbox with proven ways and means, rules, principles, and skills to get any job done. Of the more than 70 project management tools used by practitioners (Besner & Hobbs, 2004), the vast majority are initiation or planning tools.

In the strict sense of the word, planning tools include the work breakdown structure (WBS), the responsibility matrix, coding of activities and work packages, budgeting of the packages, the Gantt chart, the critical path method (CPM), and the PERT (Program Evaluation and Review Technique). In addition, companies regularly use tools such as whiteboards, 3M Post-it Notes, milestone planning tools, and project management software like Microsoft Project (Dvir & Lechler, 2004).

Monitoring tools such as earned value analysis (EVA), balanced scorecard, and performance indicators can help align the project with the plan or keep it on track. For their part, *evaluation tools* such as stakeholder satisfaction surveys help managers learn from the experience, which benefits future project planning.

Almost everything revolves around planning, the cornerstone of project management. The central idea is to go from the most complicated to the simplest by fragmenting the overall project into smaller chunks. Then, the project can be structured based on the rational preferences of project sponsors and managers. Consequently, while there are many robust and valuable project management tools to deal with the technical aspects of projects, there are few tools to address the "soft" concerns such as quality, risk, communication, and stakeholder management. Yet these aspects are proving to be more critical in managing large-scale or complex projects (Ika, Diallo, & Thuillier, 2010).

We touched on project initiation in our discussion of the logical framework and project alignment with project efficiency and effectiveness. Now, we will examine project planning and its tools (see Table 6.3). Figure 6.2 provides an overview of the *project planning cycle.* Planning in the strict sense can be broken down into four aspects:

- **Structural planning** (*What?*) involves establishing an exhaustive list of activities or tasks, describing them, and organizing them into work packages to achieve the project deliverables; it leads to a work breakdown structure.
- **Organizational planning** (*Who?*) defines the roles and responsibilities for the tasks to be performed; it leads to a responsibility matrix.
- **Operational planning** (*When?*) is used to schedule tasks and determine the estimated project duration; it leads to a project schedule.
- **Budget planning** (*How much?*) consists of estimating the total realization cost; it ends with an estimate of the budget necessary to deliver the project.

TABLE 6.3 Structural, Organizational, Operational, and Budgetary Planning

MANDATE	DIMENSION	DETAILS	KEY TOOLS
What is it?	Structural planning	Make an exhaustive list of tasks Describe the tasks Specify the work packages	Work breakdown structure (WBS)
Who is it?	Organizational planning	Identify resources Assign resources to tasks Prepare the charter of responsibilities	Responsibility matrix
When will it happen?	Operational planning	Estimate the duration of tasks Estimate start and end dates of tasks	Critical path method (CPM)
How much is it?	Budget planning	Estimate the budget for each task Estimate the budget for each resource Estimate the total cost of the project	Budgeting the work packages

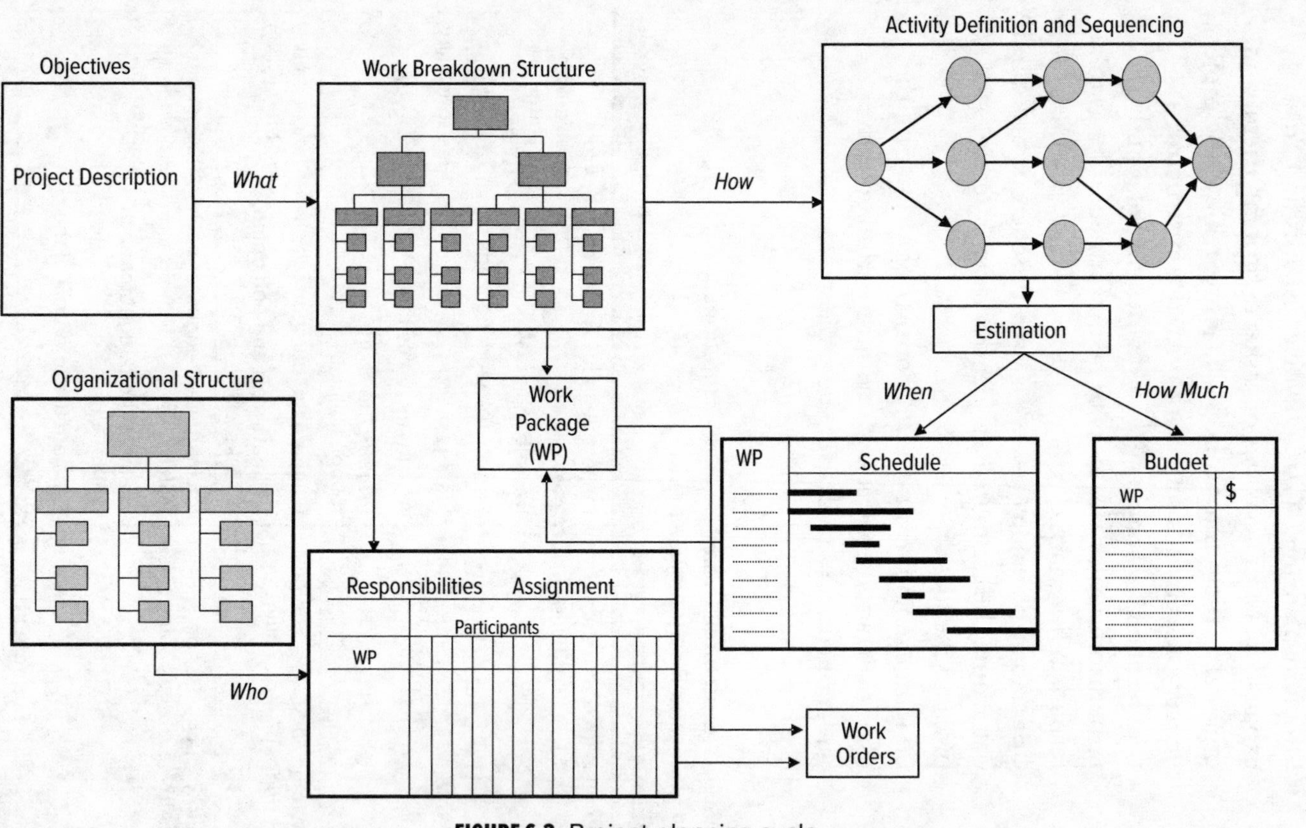

FIGURE 6.2 Project planning cycle

PROJECT CONSTRAINTS UNDER THE MICROSCOPE

A Precarious Balance

Ideally, the TCQ constraints provide a clear picture of what the project must achieve, why, how, for whom, and at what cost. They also delineate the importance of each of these key project management issues. The objective is to avoid excesses and minimize ambiguities. That way, the project's scope can be determined at the outset, once and for all.

However, it is important to remember that TCQ constraints and the project scope are all interrelated, and any change in one affects the others. An increase in costs, for example, must be compensated by adjustments in time, quality, or project scope. Yet the overriding precept of classical project management—based on a rational, mandate-based approach—is to achieve all three aspects simultaneously: quickly, cheaply, *and* done well.

Consider the relationship between these three constraints using the famous moon landing project. This excerpt from President Kennedy's speech to a joint session of the US Congress in 1961 sums up a project mission: "This nation should commit itself to achieving the goal, before this decade is out, of landing a man on the Moon and returning him safely to the Earth."

The challenge was great. Kennedy's time constraint was clear and explicit (*December 31, 1969*), as was the quality constraint (*a safe return trip*). Fortunately for NASA, created three years earlier, the president did not mention the project cost, acknowledging that "none will be so difficult or expensive to accomplish." So, NASA had financial leeway to carry out this large-scale project, and they could focus on meeting the very demanding time and quality constraints.

The president was careful to repeatedly emphasize the importance of this space journey. He said the United States should assume a "leading role in space achievement . . . which in many ways may hold the key to our future on Earth." Yet a safe return trip to the moon by December 31, 1969—an extraordinary feat in itself—would not be enough for NASA or the United States to claim strategic success. What remained vague, yet crucial, was that this project had to be done *before the Soviets*!

When seen in that light, the moon landing project was not a classic mandate-based project, with an iron triangle of time, cost, and quality. Instead, it had a hidden agenda, no cost constraints, and an ambiguous deadline—was it 1969, or before the Soviets? Such projects, with unclear or unstable goals and constraints, are common in the world of organizations. We refer to them as *fuzzy projects* in this book. Often, important expectations are unstated or not fully agreed upon, or the project's goal goes far beyond a specific, execution-focused objective. Elected for a first four-year term in 1960, Kennedy would no longer be president by 1969. However, it can be reasonably argued that the Kennedy administration, as a stakeholder, reaped immediate benefits from the project by simply announcing it, as is often the case in politics (and discussed further in Chapter 7).

The rational, mandate-based approach fails to recognize these fuzzy features in projects, or endeavors to straighten them out by squaring the circle, as it were. These flaws in the mandate-based approach are not trivial since many projects cannot be fully understood or properly managed from the perspective of the mandate.

Contrary to what is postulated in the mandate-based approach, it can be perilous to treat the three basic constraints—time, cost, and quality—in the same way by blindly adhering to the stipulations of the "contract." The "plan your work and work your plan" attitude may prove to be unwise along the way. We will come back to this idea in the next chapters.

Equivocal Concepts

A Question of Time

The time constraint is usually understood as a *date* or a *deadline* (e.g., employee training or the launch of a new service must be completed by December 31, 2025). But a time constraint can also be expressed in terms of *duration* (e.g., complete the training or launch within 90 days). Furthermore, time constraints can also be linked to an *event in a given sequence* (e.g., finish the employee training or new product launch before opening our offices in Mexico).

These different forms of time are not mutually exclusive. In the most restrictive case, one could have a project with a customary deadline in the form of a target date. This project could also have a maximum (or minimum) duration (i.e., a period of time that must be respected). Furthermore, this same project could be subject to an event or a sequence of events (i.e., before or after another critical event).

These different types of time are common when several projects are conducted concurrently, share similar resources, or have interdependent goals. Other situations may impede compliance with more important constraints, but which cannot be made public for strategic reasons.

Let us go back to the moon landing project. Completing it before the end of the decade—the official deadline—would have been a success by the criteria of the mandate. Yet if the Soviets had managed to beat the Americans, this so-called (managerial) "success" would have been a humiliating (strategic) failure in the eyes of the principals. The unofficial watchword was thinly veiled: roll up your sleeves and shorten the timeframe. To say so officially would have been at best childish, at worst belligerent. So, the Kennedy administration's strategists decided to phrase the deadline in veiled terms.

As shown earlier, the three basic TCQ constraints may need to be scheduled in a way that allows managers to make tradeoffs between them after the contract is signed. Moreover, it is equally imperative to determine what kind of time constraints should be prioritized as the project moves through its various stages. For example, should the *deadline for one event* be pushed back or brought forward? Should the *duration* of another feature be extended or shortened? Or, should a *sequence of events* be modified?

What are the challenges with quality and cost constraints that are incompatible with a strict mandate-based approach? In practical terms, to what extent can the quality and costs of a project be fixed ahead of time, once and for all? If that is not feasible, to what extent can we really anticipate variations since projects are by definition novel undertakings that often involve new products and services?

From Costs to Costs?

As we have seen in the previous chapter, cost overruns for projects, large and small, are common in almost all public and private sectors and on all continents (Flyvbjerg, Holm, & Buhl, 2002). Cost overruns are usually attributed to the misuse of traditional project management tools for cost and schedule forecasting and monitoring. However, the accuracy of the overrun figures depends on the baseline forecast, and it varies depending on whether the approved budget was set before or after the feasibility studies, or once the project planning was done. As we mentioned in the previous chapter, we can reasonably expect a small overrun when a budget is estimated after planning, then judiciously updated, and finally set just before project implementation. It is also normal for a project to experience a cost overrun if there are scope changes during execution.

The Canadian federal government's Department of Defence *Capital Project Cost Estimation* framework has a nine-year life cycle (see Figure 6.3). It includes a two-year options analysis phase where an indicative project value forecast is established; a two-year definition phase when a forecast of procurement costs is approved; and finally, a five-year implementation phase when approval is required to validate any cost increase of 10 percent or CA$10 million (National Defence Canada, 2013).

In addition, although there exist different guidelines for estimating projects (e.g., American Association of Cost Engineers), there are generally four classes of project estimates used at different times in the project life cycle:

- **Class D—Rough Estimate:** This rather rough estimate is made before the feasibility studies and is based on cost statistics of similar past projects; its accuracy is therefore generally low at approximately ± 30 percent.
- **Class C—Preliminary Estimate:** More elaborate, it is based on feasibility studies, and its accuracy is ±15 to 20 percent.
- **Class B—Control Estimate:** It is based on the preliminary project plans and allows the team to set the preliminary project budget; its accuracy is ±10 percent.
- **Class A—Detailed Estimate:** It is based on detailed plans and is used to determine the final project budget once the bids in response to calls for tenders are analyzed; its accuracy is ±5 percent.

The aforementioned cost overrun figures show that, in practice, cost estimates tend to be inaccurate, raising questions about the suitability of the estimation approaches (Love, Ika, & Sing, 2022).

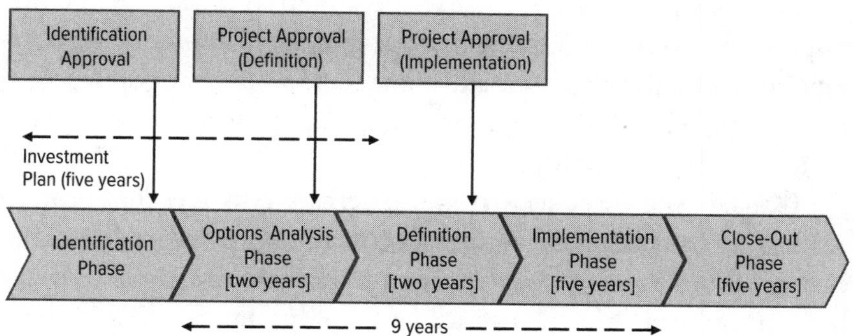

FIGURE 6.3 Canadian Department of National Defence project cost estimation process

Source: National Defence Canada (2013).

PLANNING SETBACKS

Project planning failures abound. Many bona fide errors plague project forecasting and execution, including misused tools and techniques, lack of experience, and inappropriate data. Cost forecasting for the preliminary design, for example, can vary due to price escalation or inflation (e.g., increases in labor, material, plant, and equipment costs), interest rates on loans, availability of labor, and other market conditions. Another factor to consider is the geotechnical conditions for some infrastructure projects (Love, Sing, Ika, & Newton, 2019).

Cost overruns can result from *premature announcements* made by politicians or businesspeople who do not wait for feasibility studies. The most critical factors (especially for large-scale projects) are changes in scope—which can account for approximately 10 to 90 percent of the budget overrun—complexity, and uncertainty.

Consider the case of Perth in Western Australia. An audit of 20 large-scale projects (over A$6 billion in total) revealed that government announcements of public projects were premature—that is, based on incomplete business cases or feasibility studies. As a result, about 90 percent (A$2.95 billion) of the budget variance occurred during the ex ante appraisal phase (i.e., before implementation) due to project scope or design changes that were sanctioned by the client. In addition, there were changes in scope during implementation, quality issues, and delays due to bad weather (Love et al., 2021).

Considering these recurring problems, many feel that project management should do better, specifically with regards to forecasting. Fortunately, new findings by behavioral psychologists have brought to light the pervasiveness of human biases and their consequences on our ability to make reliable forecasts.

SHORTCUTS TO NOWHERE

Cognitive scientists have studied how we estimate and process quantitative data. Extensive research has shown that we routinely use mental shortcuts. These unconscious processes are quick and save time, but they may also have perverse effects that lead to erroneous conclusions.

Cognitive biases are misleading and distort time and cost estimates at all project stages: initiation, planning, implementation, and monitoring. As a result, the way the tool is used, and the users themselves, must be questioned. Indeed, the governance of the project is as much part of the problem as it is the solution, at least according to some authors (Flyvbjerg, 2014; Flyvbjerg et al., 2002). This represents a real paradigm shift from the "error school" to the "bias school."

Since costs are related to future actions, they cannot be known in advance and must be estimated based on scenarios that assume future risks. Fortunately, project management offers a toolbox for forecasting future revenues and expenses, discounting their value, anticipating and mitigating risks, and so on. With these forecasting and discounting tools, a project manager can bring future and hypothetical events into the realm of the present and the certain; the virtual becomes real. This toolbox is an embodiment of the rational, mandate-based approach. But is it reliable?

It turns out that cost forecasting is rife with cognitive biases. In a *Financial Times* article (March, 2008), former chairman of the Federal Reserve, Alan Greenspan, made a public mea culpa at the height of the financial crisis, admitting that he and his team had erred because of *overconfidence* (a common cognitive bias). The man who had held this prestigious position for almost 20 years also warned that human factors explain why risk management and econometric forecasting models failed to detect the global mortgage crisis in time.

Three years later, Daniel Kahneman—psychologist and winner of the Nobel Prize in Economic Sciences—pointed out that we tend to over-estimate our ability to predict the future and thus err on the side of overconfidence. Indeed, he noted that overconfidence is common among financial forecasters, doctors, and other specialists. Given its consequences on decisions, optimism bias is one of the most important cognitive biases that need to be addressed (Kahneman, 2011).

As we saw in Chapter 5, behavioral pitfalls are omnipresent in projects, and they include the *planning fallacy* and its psychological determinants like *optimism bias,* and political determinants like *strategic misrepresentation*. Flyvbjerg (2014) is a strong supporter of this view, and he is the researcher who popularized Kahneman's work in project management. These biases manifest themselves in global and local events, and the small and large projects that individuals and organizations undertake.

Although project managers are accountable, it is easy to see how projects fail strategically or miss deadlines and budgets because of poor planning and weak governance. Clearly, with these biases and consequently naively optimistic or fraudulently manipulated cost estimates, projects move ahead in a kind of "death march," as project managers have the virtually impossible task of delivering projects within budget (Kreiner, 2020). While these two biases are the most discussed in project management theory and practice (Flyvbjerg, 2014; Flyvbjerg et al., 2002), an academic debate rages over their prevalence.

Although many projects go over budget, many are also delivered within budget—that is, actual total costs are below planned costs. Based on this observation, Love et al. (2021) studied transport projects and concluded that the planning fallacy (to the extent that it can be detected empirically in project management) affects at most 57 percent of projects, not 90 percent as Flyvbjerg et al. (2002) suggest.

While the planning fallacy is critical, it is not the only bias that comes into play. Indeed, many others haunt the daily lives of practitioners! To get a clearer picture of the cognitive pitfalls, let us take a quick look at the typical process of developing a mandate for a given project using the ExPlus project as an example (see Box 6.2).

BOX 6.2

A Road Paved with Biases

As the ExPlus project manager, Nancy Smart must assess the work to be done, the anticipated costs, the required deliverables, and the time required. Her core estimates will include the project duration, the number of person-hours needed for the team, the material and informational resources required, and the risks to consider.

The right information is needed to evaluate the time and cost estimates in advance. To that end, project managers like Nancy must consult various sources and experts to validate the information they accumulate. When the data is uncertain, they should assess the probability and impact on the project. In this preliminary process, it is dangerous to jump to conclusions. They need to tread carefully!

During their first meetings, Nancy noticed that many participants kept referring to a "similar" recent project that only took 18 months to complete (though it had a different organizational context). So, their first cognitive bias relates to *easier recall of recent memories*. People tend to favor information that comes easily to mind because it is more striking or more recent, though it may not be relevant.

Given this bias, Nancy runs the risks of locking in the 18-month timeframe as an anchor for the new project. This type of *first impression bias* has a pernicious but lasting influence on timing predictions. Subsequently, she and her colleagues will be subject to confirmation biases, as they will tend to seek and accept data that reinforces what they have come to believe. Based on research, we can hypothesize that if the completion period for the "recent" project had been twice as long, the timeframe for the ExPlus project charter and the mandate would have been longer too.

Nancy Smart also needs to gauge the level of interest in the new service. To this end, she will consult with the underwriters and, more importantly, account managers, since this group has more regular interactions with potential service customers. However, these employees—as would be the case for any team—are susceptible to a *group compliance bias,* making them more likely to proffer options that keep the organization together.

As a professional, Nancy cross-checks this information with the banks that deal with the potential project end users. In doing so, she reasons that they will be in a better position to make an objective judgment about the end users. Unfortunately, *confirmation bias* leads everyone—Nancy, the underwriters, account managers, banks, and those involved in the forecasting process—to retain information confirming opinions they had already formed.

She also needs to know more about the risks facing ExPlus's customers regarding the fluctuating peso exchange rate. Out of caution and professionalism, she decides to consult ExPlus's treasury department, and her boss approves. This department had accurately forecasted the value of treasury bills five years in a row. It was an exceptional performance, and ExPlus was very proud of this division. Unfortunately, by the *extrapolation and halo effect,* Nancy and her boss assume that the treasury department will give an accurate assessment of the exchange rate risk, thereby giving undue weight to the opinion of "experts."

Biases as Far as We Can See

Nancy also consults with several departments on various aspects of the project. Unfortunately, many managers, employees, and stakeholders offer biased opinions about the project in good faith, regardless of their expertise. Some have a *status quo bias,* preferring to leave things as they are, making the assumption that change will bring more risks and disadvantages than potential benefits. Others exhibit a *risk-averse bias.* Still others are prone to *overconfidence, optimism,* or *shortsightedness bias,* showing an exaggerated preference for present rather than future gains and costs.

The scientific evidence is quite strong on the subject notably at the individual decision maker level, and Nancy Smart's estimates run a high risk of being tainted from the outset. She should have made similar predictions at each project stage to avoid this. While her steps are paved with good intentions, her planning process is littered with conflicting cognitive biases.

If the project faces setbacks (a real possibility, given the many pitfalls), ExPlus managers will try to recover the costs of a disappointing project. However, they might not be able to "cut their losses" in time (escalation of commitment bias), and thus they will incur even more significant losses.

If senior management changes during the project, things could get even more complicated. Why? New leaders often do not hesitate to terminate a project prematurely, even if such a decision is not objectively justified. Projects are always associated with the people who work on them. Projects are subjective constructs to a large extent—their planners' and managers' decisions are not always based on facts.

Whatever the outcome, many people will feel that the result was obvious in hindsight. Again, once an event has occurred, *hindsight bias* leads them to overestimate how predictable or highly likely it was.

Source: Inspired by Kahneman (2011).

Are Biases Unavoidable?

Even if Nancy and her colleagues know about these biases, they will still be subjected to them (Kahneman, 2011). Psychologists consider that cognitive biases, for example, may be as pervasive as optical illusions. For instance, in Figure 6.4, which of the two straight lines is longer, A or B? Which of the two center circles is bigger, the one in group C or in group D?

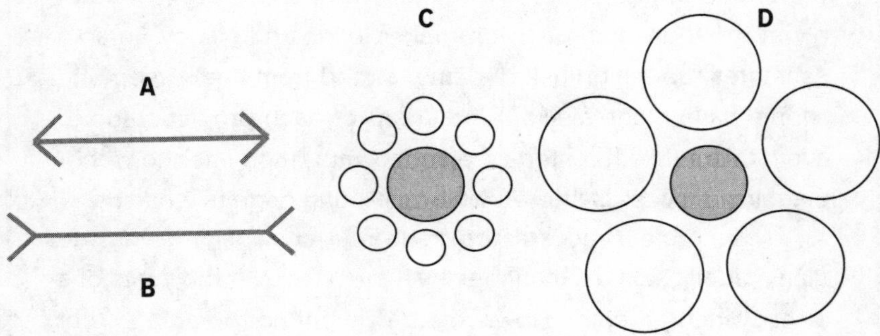

FIGURE 6.4 Illusions due to context

Most of us get it wrong, most of the time. We "see" that line B is longer than line A, and that the gray circle in group C is larger than the gray circle in group D. Why? Line B and the gray C circle make a stronger impression on us because of their respective contexts. Even if we measure and realize that the two lines are the same length and that the two gray circles are the same size, we cannot escape the optical illusion. We continue to "see" that line B is longer and that the central gray circle in set C is larger.

Kahneman (2011) cites a problem of a different order. It goes like this: *A bat and a ball cost $1.10 in total. The bat costs $1.00 more than the ball. How much does the ball cost?* Take a few seconds to work out this simple problem in your mind, and write down how much the ball costs. Your answer is likely to be a nice round number. If your answer is 10 cents, you are wrong. But, don't feel bad! Most people make the same mistake.[2]

At best, we can learn not to rely blindly on these snappy but faulty "judgments" we make most of the time. Once we understand this, organizational mechanisms can be put in place to curb the effect of such biases. We can then improve our collective ability to assess situations, forecast and predict, and ultimately make decisions. Improving governance can improve decision-making, and managers may be more likely to abandon "bad" projects and select "good" ones. It can also enhance implementation strategies and their chances of success.

Projects may be construed as a deliberate leap into a planned future. Good project management practices or guidelines exist, particularly in terms of governance. For projects to succeed, these guidelines simply need to be applied. When it comes to project costs, the forecasts must be "de-biased" (Flyvbjerg, 2014). As we saw in Chapter 5, a forecasting and risk management method called *reference class forecasting* could be very helpful (Flyvbjerg, 2008). But is it a panacea?

A Small Critique of the Bias Thesis

As interesting as they may be, de-biasing methods such as RCF quickly find their limits in complex and uncertain project contexts. The Edinburgh Trams project in Scotland is a particularly instructive example (see Chapter 5).

On the other hand, one must also avoid "bias of bias" and guard against seeing biases everywhere, like the proponents of the planning fallacy theory in project management (Ika, Love, & Pinto, 2022). Psychologist Gerd Gigerenzer (2014) of the Max Planck Institute in Germany is a longtime critic of the bias thesis. He shows that the probability theory that Kahneman (2011) advocates, and on which de-biasing methods are based, only works well when the manager is in a risk context—that is, when faced with "known unknowns." Unfortunately, this is rarely the case for major or large-scale projects, which are new and innovative and uncertain by nature. When dealing with high uncertainty or "unknown unknowns" in large-scale projects, probability theory responds poorly and managers may fall into a kind of "illusion of certainty" (Gigerenzer, 2014).

When facing complexity and uncertainty, avoiding the bias pitfalls is not a panacea for avoiding cost overruns. We proffer instead that heuristics, those smart rules of thumb, could help managers make better decisions, especially if they can trust their hunches and intuition.

If, however, projects fail strategically or go over time and budget, as the Edinburgh Trams project did, then we can still assume that these practices of de-biasing cost estimates have not been well applied or applied at all. Again, poor project performance is not a reason to give up on the ideal. The solution is to bring practice as close as possible to the ideal (Kreiner, 2020). Year in and year out, the rational, mandate-based approach remains in place, despite its recurring setbacks.

LIMITATIONS OF THE MANDATE-BASED APPROACH

The mandate-based approach is based on precepts of formal rationality. Its practitioners advocate a process of decision-making and execution based on known parameters. Complexity and uncertainty must be reduced at all costs. The project is essentially seen as a technical challenge entrusted to experts. The way the project is structured, as well as all decisions and actions, must be based on reason and logic, and not on personal experience or emotion. Managerial actions must focus on efficiency, which should result in effectiveness. The best performance criteria are clear, actionable, and easily measurable—notably time and cost.

People and interests outside the mandate are obscured within the framework of substantive rationality, which is supported by supposedly perfect[3] information (Weber, 1921). The project manager and their team are thus inclined to focus on *what should be* rather than on *what is being done.*

The same precepts of formal rationality also guide specialized project management journals. Little is described, but much is prescribed. They argue that attention and energy *must* focus on the concrete and measurable aspects of scope, time, and cost as stipulated in the mandate. This implies that we should focus on project management's scientific objective (Irwin, 2008) to the detriment of the subjective, political, and social aspects that exist both within the project and in the external environment.

It is tempting to use the rational, mandate-based approach in all circumstances and the predictive life cycle that embodies it because it is essentially a solution in search of a problem to solve. However, it quickly finds its limits with large-scale or complex programs and projects. Complexity is much more than a sum of complications. One can seek to further optimize project management within the framework of the rational, mandate-based approach. But this will not be enough. As Ronald Reagan (1964) cautioned, "The more plans fail, the more planners plan." It is doubtful that the problem can be solved by doing more of the same. A way out of this conundrum is to challenge the framework itself, without "throwing the baby out with the bathwater."

To sum up, focusing primarily on the mandate (excluding all other considerations) means sacrificing organizational effectiveness for efficiency, thus risking strategic or political failure. This is particularly unfortunate when one considers that project drift is often predictable in the early stages of the project. It is in part attributable to the project manager's refusal to recognize the nonrational dimensions of the project and failure to cultivate political links with clients, both internal and external (Pinto, 2000). For more information about project management periodicals and associations, and a useful template for project management see Appendices 6.1, 6.2, and 6.3.

CONCLUSION

Project management is widely used in the industrial and social sectors because its rigorous methods help organizations deliver the changes required to address new needs. These needs are fully spelled out in the mandate given to the project manager and are presumed to be clear, precise, and stable. In theory, the project can be carried out effectively by meeting the time, cost, and quality targets set out in the project plan. Implementation is thus fine-tuned into a sequential, organized, and controlled process to create a predetermined deliverable that meets a specific need. The project is seen as a reasoned and purposive human action designed to make a deliberate leap into a planned future. In this paradigm, *thinking* precedes and controls *doing*. If the project deviates from the expected trajectory, it must be realigned with the plan.

However, this reductionist approach falters in the face of complexity and uncertainty. When best practices face political and psychological hurdles, significant setbacks are bound to occur. Against all expectations and by an adverse effect, project managers can *successfully manage* a project but *fail to deliver a successful project*. When the project's plan becomes an end in itself, it will likely fail the stakeholders who are overlooked in the process.

To this end, this chapter proffers seven takeaways for project managers and sponsors:

1. Project management is gaining momentum in the industrial and social sectors, which thrive on innovation, change, and intangible objectives. These objectives differ from its traditional base in construction, where solidity and durability are paramount. Notwithstanding the promises of project management, its "flat" structures present coordination and cooperation challenges due to their focused, functionalist, and efficiency-oriented methods.

2. Standard project management practices have proved successful for projects with small innovations or continuous improvements, as well as in low-tech sectors and relatively stable markets. But they have proved inadequate in more complex and uncertain projects that require a more flexible, adaptive, trial-and-error management approach.
3. The rational approach is the traditional way of managing projects. The project is seen as an activity clearly defined in the mandate—the project's specific, and predetermined, objective. The project manager focuses on time, cost, and quality constraints and implements the project in vitro, as in the closed environment of a laboratory, reducing it to a well-oiled, organized, and controlled process. With a unique deliverable conceived to meet a specific and stable need, the mandate becomes the project's focal point. Its manager oversees its efficient and effective implementation with proven tools such as the project charter, the logical framework, and the project management plan.
4. Under the rational approach, everything must be thought out beforehand, as the project is seen as a purposive and reasoned human action and a deliberate leap into a planned future. Planning becomes the best practice *par excellence* in such cases. The predictive, rigorous, and sequential life cycle renders the management approach predictable in a stable environment. The idea is to determine the project's scope, times, and costs as early as possible. Planning and its battery of tools allow the project team to reduce complexity and uncertainty and process the maximum amount of information possible.
5. The rational approach, despite project setbacks, assumes that the team knows how to run a project, has the knowledge to prepare a plan, and just needs to implement it methodically. In case of underperformance, they will assume that the best practices were not used properly. However, underperformance should not lead us to

question the ideal, as the goal is to get as close as possible to it, despite the incidence of bias and error. If you miss the bull's-eye, don't move the target—aim better.

6. The mandate, a kind of compass, sets the course for reasoned human action and the project plan serves as a road map. The plan contains contingencies to anticipate any circumstances that may affect the project's execution. The planning process systematically establishes the criteria for success, forecasting, times, costs, and risks. If the project deviates from the plan, corrective measures must be applied to bring it back on course (i.e., "as planned").
7. While the project planning and management process can be successful, the project itself may be a failure if it disappoints the stakeholders.

As we saw, the rational approach to project management has many advantages, but many disadvantages as well. It may fall short in complex projects that require careful attention to stakeholders. There, it needs to be complemented by approaches that address the psychosocial and political aspects of projects.

REFERENCES

Abend, L. (2019). Inside Barcelona's unfinished masterpiece. *Time.* June 27. https://time.com/magazine/south-pacific/5615705/july-8th-2019-vol-194-no-2-international/ (accessed 22 August 2022).

Bergson, H. (1937). *Message au Congrès Descartes*. Paris.

Besner, C., & Hobbs, B. (2004). An empirical investigation of project management practice: In reality what tools do practitioners use? In Slevin, D. P., Cleland, D. I., & Pinto, J. K. (Eds). *Innovations: Project management research.* Project Management Institute, 337–351.

Dvir, D., & Lechler, T. (2004). Plans are nothing, changing plans is everything: the impact of changes on project success. *Research Policy, 33,* 1–15.

Eisenhower, D. D. (1957). Remarks at the National Defense Executive Reserve Conference. 14 November. https://www.presidency.ucsb.edu/documents/remarks-the-national-defense-executive-reserve-conference

Finkelstein, S., & Sanford, S. H. (2000). Learning from corporate mistakes: the rise and fall of Iridium. *Organizational Dynamics, 29*(2), 138–148.

Flyvbjerg, B. (2008). Curbing optimism bias and strategic misrepresentation in planning: Reference class forecasting in practice. *European Planning Studies, 16*(1), 3–21.

Flyvbjerg, B. (2014). What you should know about megaprojects and why: An overview. *Project Management Journal, 45*(2), 6–19.

Flyvbjerg, B., Holm, M. K. S., & Buhl, S. L. (2002). Underestimating costs in public works projects: Error or lie. *Journal of the American Planning Association, 68*(3), 279–295.

Gigerenzer, G. (2014). *Risk savvy: How to make good decisions.* Penguin Books.

Hirschman, A. O. (1967). *Development projects observed.* Brookings Institution.

Ika, L. A., & Saint-Macary, J. (June 1–4, 2011). *Paradigm lost: The concept of strategy in project organizing.* Proceedings of the 11th European Academy of management Conference, Tallinn, Estonia.

Ika, L. A., & Saint-Macary, J. (2012). The project planning myth in international development. *International Journal of Managing Projects in Business, 5*(3), 420–439.

Ika, L. A., Diallo, A., & Thuillier, D. (2010). Project management in the international industry: The project coordinator's perspective. *International Journal of Managing Projects in Business, 3*(1), 61–93.

Ika, L. A., Love, P. E. D., & Pinto, J. K. (2022). Moving beyond the Planning Fallacy: The emergence of a new principle of project behavior. *IEEE Transactions on Engineering Management*, 69(6), 3310–3325.

Irwin, B. (2008). *Managing politics and conflicts in projects.* Management Concepts.

Kahneman, D. (2011). *Thinking fast and slow.* DoubleDay.

Kreiner, K. (2020). Conflicting notions of a project: The battle between Albert O. Hirschman and Bent Flyvbjerg. *Project Management Journal, 51*(4), 400–410.

Kuhn, T. S. (1996). *The structure of scientific revolution.* Third edition. University of Chicago Press.

Kwak, Y. H., Walewski, J., Sleeper, D., & Sadatsafavi, H. (2014). What can we learn from the Hoover Dam project that influenced modern project management? *International Journal of Project Management, 32*(2), 256–264.

Loch, C.H. (2017). Creativity and risk taking aren't rational: Behavioral operations in M.O.T. *Production and Operations Management, 26*(4), 591–604.

Love, P. E. D., Sing, M. C. P., Ika, L. A., & Newton, S. (2019). The cost performance of transportation infrastructure projects: The fallacy of the Planning Fallacy account. *Transportation Research A: Policy and Practice, 122*, 1–20.

Love, P. E. D., Ika, L. A., & Sing, M. C. P. (2022). Does the planning fallacy prevail in social infrastructure projects? Empirical evidence and competing explanations. *IEEE Transactions on Engineering Management*, 69(6), 2588–2602.

Mintzberg, H., & Westley, F. (2001). Decision-making: It's not what you think. *MIT Sloan Management Review, 42*(3), Spring.

Mintzberg, H., Ahlstrand, B., & Lampel, J. B. (2013). *Management? It is not what you think!* Pearson.

National Defence, Government of Canada (2013). Internal Audit of Capital Project Cost Estimating. https://www.canada.ca/en/department-national-defence/corporate/reports-publications/audit-evaluation/internal-audit-capital-project-cost-estimation.html (accessed 21 October 2020).

Pinto, J. K. (2000). Understanding the role of politics in successful project management. *International Journal of Project Management, 18*, 55–91.

Project Management Institute, PMI (2017). *A guide to the project management body of knowledge.* Sixth edition.

Reagan, R. (1964). A time for choosing. In A. A. Bolitzer et al. (Eds), *A time for choosing: The speeches of Ronald Reagan,* 1961–1982, pp. 41–57. Chicago: Regnery. 1983.

Shenhar, A., & Dvir, D. (2007). Project management research—the challenge and opportunity. *Project Management Journal, 38*(2), 93–99.

Weber, M. (1921). *Economy and society.* (G. Roth, & C. Wittich, Trans.) Bedminster Press.

Wheelwright, S. C. (1996). Biogen, Inc: rBeta Interferon manufacturing process development. Harvard Business School Case 696-083, January.

Zwikael, O., & Smyrk, J.R. (2019). *Project management: A benefit realisation approach.* Springer-Verlag.

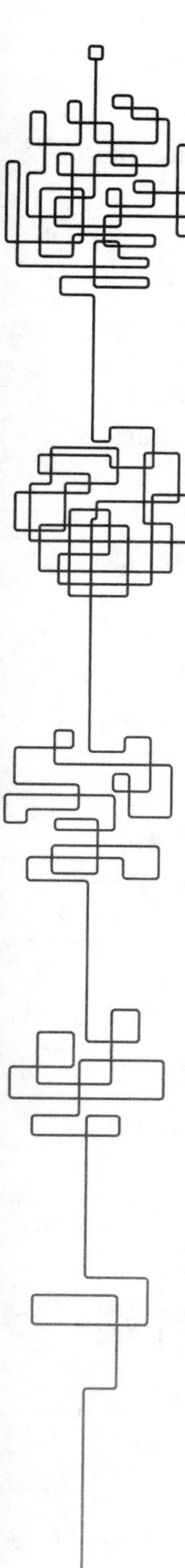

CHAPTER 7

THE POLITICAL PERSPECTIVE (IN SITU)

POLITICS MAKES OR BREAKS PROJECTS

"In the main, project management subscribes to an objective view of the organization, relatively free of political and psychosocial tensions. But, this may be misleading in the context of projects where the stakes are numerous and complex . . . the rational perspective may be sufficient to assess and manage a project when efficiency prevails in both the parent and the client organizations. However, the project manager would be better served to use an integrative approach that also includes the political perspective when the organizations involved have differing expectations regarding the project" (Saint-Macary & Ika, 2015).

From a political perspective, the organization and the project become instruments used by various groups of stakeholders. We use the term "stakeholders" in its broadest sense—those who are affected by the project, positively or negatively, even if they are not directly involved in its execution (Freeman, 1984).

Let's delve into the political dimension of projects from the point of view of the CEO of a very large engineering firm seeking to win a contract.

"[W]hile the competing firms were focused on solving the engineering problems involved in the most efficient and cost-effective way, SNC-LAVALIN's managers first looked at the project as a whole, including its political dimension. Since the first pillars of the bridge were located on Amerindian territory, prior to any technical feasibility study, our negotiators began discussions with the First Nations leaders [. . .] When the time came to submit bids, SNC-LAVALIN had a major political advantage over rival firms" (Saint-Pierre, 1995).

The surprising thing about this example is that a key group of stakeholders was consulted right from the start. Remarkably, this is not the norm in project management, where scant attention is usually paid to stakeholders, especially when these individuals and groups are *external to* the organization (Lehtinen & Aaltonen, 2020). Concrete examples include the NBA basketball changeover where the players were not consulted, and India's Tata Nano low-cost car project that did not consider the farmers' expectations in the region where the factory was located (see Chapters 3 and 5). These are not isolated cases; politics is often present in projects, whether they are small or large, public or private.

Politics can make or break projects in surprising ways. An example is President Barack Obama's proposed presidential library on Chicago's South Side, which riled up the residents in the targeted neighborhood (see Box 7.1).

BOX 7.1

Obama, "No, You Can't!"[1]

"Barack Obama is no longer a prophet in Chicago."[2] This newspaper headline describes the unexpected resistance faced by

Obama's Presidential Library project in Chicago. Residents, including supporters of the former president, took to the streets to express their concern about the gentrification of their neighborhood.

At first sight, the project seemed quite ordinary and should have gone smoothly. It is traditional for outgoing presidents to build a library to house their archives, so Obama's project was not unexpected. Though he was born in Honolulu, Obama partnered with the University of Chicago and decided to build his library on the city's South Side. That location probably seemed ideal to his team: the neighborhood was 93 percent African American, and it was where Obama had worked for years as a community organizer, made his debut in politics, and received overwhelming support in the 2008 and 2012 elections. On the face of it, the library was in the perfect place and should have been seen as a boon to the community.

Despite broad support for Obama in this neighborhood, the African American community strongly opposed this project. "Stakeholders," in Freeman's (1984) broad definition, mobilized against it, including neighborhood and tenant associations. In addition, professors and staff at the University of Chicago described the project as socially regressive. Other opponents argued that the presidential complex would only accelerate the gentrification of the area, and they denounced the support it received from the mayor's office and the university. Worse, some even spoke of "ethnic cleansing." In addition, there were complaints about the exorbitant cost and the large parcel of land needed to build it, offered to Obama by Chicago City Hall and Mayor Rahm Emanuel, Obama's former chief of staff.

Considering the support given to Obama when he was a presidential candidate, the project designers wrongly assumed they knew the stakeholders well and took their support for granted. They erred in assuming that the Chicago community would support anything Obama did. Clearly, their support was not unconditional. "(While) we trusted him enough to elect him to the White House, not once but twice, we would not trust him or Michelle to do good in their community," said one local citizen. For the South Side community, this project presented different stakes than the election and reelection of Obama: "Yes, you can," at the national level, was "No, you can't!" at the municipal level. The well-respected Reverend Finley Campbell opined that Barack Obama's presidency brought positive change for the black elites and bourgeoisie, but his presidency had failed the working class.

Source: Ika, Saint-Macary, & Bandé (2020).

In politics, where "politicians campaign in poetry, but . . . govern in prose," as New York Governor Mario Cuomo famously said, many projects do not survive the aftermath of elections due to the reorientation of public policy and rivalries within and among political parties and regions. Indeed, regime changes are often followed by a flurry of projects being shelved as new ones are put forth.

Consider the common example of building a road. For many politicians, it is about meeting the travel needs of the people and serving their political ambitions. In some contexts, populism infects the political debate especially with large-scale projects: they become overblown and take on underhanded objectives.

Some of Hungarian Prime Minister Victor Orbán's big projects seemed to be politically motivated in the eyes of some observers. Hundreds of millions of euros were spent to build soccer stadiums for the enjoyment of soccer fans in one of the poorest countries in Europe (Lawrence, 2018). The political saga of the US$8 billion-plus Keystone XL pipeline project is also instructive. The project was delayed in 2011 due to opposition from environmentalists and indigenous groups. It was then denied by President Obama in 2015, endorsed by President

Trump in 2017, and rejected by President Biden in 2021. The Canadian province of Alberta supports this project, but it does not have unanimous support in Canada, causing Canadian Prime Minister Justin Trudeau to walk on eggshells when discussing it (Thomson, 2017).

Political interference means that many large projects are announced publicly with an anticipated budget and completion date *before* their appraisal is completed, needs are validated, and local populations are consulted. As the chairman of the Public Administration Committee in the United Kingdom lamented about the need for input from local communities in big projects, "Developing large infrastructure projects must not become an end in itself" (BBC, 2020).

Pork barrel politics plagues major projects to such an extent that even if the general public funds them, these projects benefit only a small group of people due to crony capitalism between politicians and business people. This phenomenon is so damaging that the US Congress imposed a moratorium on the common practice of *earmarking funds* for initiatives in a congressman's home state.

Let's revisit the SNC-Lavalin project that we introduced earlier in this chapter. It triggered polarized reactions among our class of Masters of Project Management students (all with practical experience). Some felt that the engineering firm had "cheated" by deviating from standard bidding practices, while others thought that the engineering firm had "thought outside the box."

The students' opinions converged, however, with regard to external stakeholders. A strong majority felt that the federal government had been shortsighted in failing to anticipate "political" obstacles, as SNC-Lavalin had done. Some students went further, saying the political aspects are the responsibility of the government, not the project managers.

Though some lamented the harm done to the competing firms, others argued that what SNC-Lavalin did was fair game.

However, they all agreed that the unusual approach taken by SNC-Lavalin's managers benefited their firm, the federal government, the Amerindian community, and society in general. Regardless of whether they supported or criticized SNC-Lavalin's approach, the students concluded that SNC-Lavalin had spared these groups from thorny and costly problems in the future.

Was this a case of managers overstepping their role in project management? Or was it a case of poor strategic oversight by the government, which failed to anticipate the potential concerns of the Amerindians and their implications for the project? In the words of the former SNC-Lavalin CEO, "The manager of a consulting engineering firm that did not have this sensitivity to political and cultural dimensions would not have been as effective from a purely professional standpoint" (Saint-Pierre, 1995).

In her professional career, Nancy Smart has faced these thorny political questions and struggled with how they should be handled. She doesn't think it is wise to ignore the political aspects of organizations and projects. In this context, shouldn't the "exceptional" approach taken by SNC-Lavalin be the norm in project management?[3] Let's explore this further in the next section.

MANDATES, AGENTS, AND PURPOSES

As noted in the previous chapters, the dominant viewpoint in project management is that the organization is a *rational entity* in all respects and should act accordingly. Moreover, it assumes that organizational action is motivated by *a common goal* because the organization is immune to political or psychosocial tensions that might divert it from that goal. Thus, the organization's alignment with the environment—its strategic management—is essentially guided by reason and analysis. The same is true of the management of the operations and projects that the organization undertakes. Adhering to this notion of the organization as a *homogeneous* entity allows it to orient and focus its efforts harmoniously, but it also circumscribes the role that managers can and must play.

This view of the *unified* organization with a *single agent* and a *single goal* has dominated project management since it emerged as a distinct professional field in the 1950s. This perspective stems directly from classical economic theory that purports that a business organization's ultimate and only legitimate goal is profit maximization. This generic goal is clear, and the success measurement is unambiguous: *profit.*

Classical strategic and operations management strongly contested the idea that the organization only pursues a single goal. As early as 1938, Barnard introduced the *theory of equilibrium,* which considers the trade-offs that must be made due to the presence of several actors within the firm (not just one). For example, this theory singles out the preferences of employees and suggests the owners of the firm should offer incentives in return for their contributions. With this in mind, we discuss the importance of treating project team members as *internal stakeholders* in the next chapter. In addition to employees, there are owners, suppliers, and customers with whom the "Peak Coordinator" (as economist Papandréou called it in 1952) must negotiate on behalf of the company. The organization is a market where all these groups interact and exchange.

Twenty-five years after Barnard, March and Cyert (1963) concluded that the single organizational goal is an illusion. Instead, the organization does and must pursue *many goals,* since it strives to satisfy a collective of individuals and groups. More precisely, these individuals and groups may have clear goals, whereas the organization itself might not. At best, the organization sets in motion collective action that enables individuals and groups to achieve their particular goals through value creation and distribution (McGahan, 2021). At the same time, it influences each of them to support the achievement of the others. In effect, they trade off between goals.

In this context, the objective of maximizing a single goal is unattainable. At best, organizational "goals" become "constraints" that administrators must satisfy. They cannot simply focus on achieving the single goal of profit maximization of a "unified" organization as understood by classical economists. Sociologists such as Crozier and Friedberg (1977) reinforced this perspective that the organization should be seen as an *instrument* serving distinct groups.

DIVISION OF LABOR MEANS DIVISION OF POWER

As discussed in Chapter 2, building an organization involves dividing labor and allocating the resources needed to accomplish the related tasks and functions. This allocation is necessarily differentiated. To perform their work, each employee, department, and subunit receives distinct resources. The division of labor, characteristic of any organization, thus leads to diverse sources of power. In this instance, an organization is inevitably a breeding ground for tensions and even power struggles.

Depending on their sector and particular circumstances, organizations have critical dependencies that create uncertainty, like access to some raw materials and access to markets or political connections. Those who have a say or control over those dependencies have power. Sociologists Crozier and Friedberg (1977) underline three prime sources of power: control over an essential resource, technical know-how, or a general body of knowledge.

These power sources vary with the type of work done and its context. They confer *direct* power to some members by virtue of their legal standing in the organization (e.g., a shareholder or an executive). Other members get *indirect* power if they have privileged access to those who hold direct power. Each source—production factors, know-how, and legal prerogatives—creates different configurations of influence and power within each organization.

Employee compensation is a good indicator of the relative power of certain units of the organization, in both the public and private sectors. We expect salaries to be higher in units and levels of the hierarchy that are highly technical or possess knowledge critical to the organization. On the other hand, we expect a more even wage distribution when there are coalitions, such as unions, that can exercise countervailing power. This latter situation is typically found in capital-intensive industries where large amounts are allocated to employee productivity and income generation.

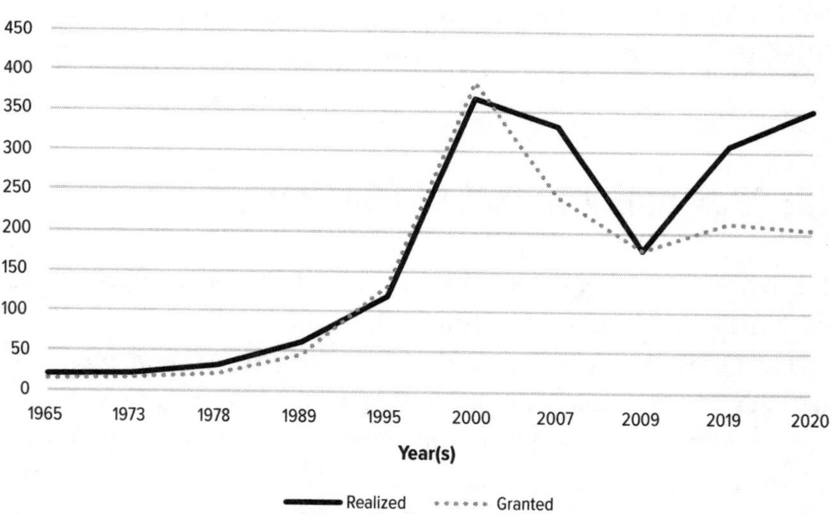

FIGURE 7.1 CEO-to-worker compensation ratio (1965–2020)

According to the Economic Policy Institute (Figure 7.1), the compensation gap between CEOs and the typical worker widened dramatically between 1978 and 2020. The 18.0 percent growth in the typical worker's compensation pales in comparison to the 1,322.2 percent increase in their CEO's "realized" compensation, which includes the salary, bonus, and value of stock-related components. Other studies reveal marked differences in salary distributions between organizations in different sectors. Researchers found "that relative pay is higher in firms belonging to homogeneous industries, where employees are likely to be more interchangeable and thus less powerful relative to managers. In contrast, it declines with employee unionization and capital intensity" (Faleye, Reis, & Venkateswaran, 2013).

World-renowned economist Thomas Piketty (2018) found that the gap between the rich and poor has widened beyond income since the middle of the twentieth century. A massive amount of data confirms that the rate of capital return is consistently greater than the rate of economic growth, which causes wealth inequality to increase over time. This development establishes the clear benefit of simply owning shares in a company.

THE PROJECT IS A SOURCE OF POWER

For better or worse, power affects projects, including their initial or emerging strategy, funding, approval, implementation, and termination. As we saw in Chapter 6, the direct use of power by decision makers may lead to strategic misrepresentation, where figures of planned budgets and/or benefits are deliberately manipulated to approve (e.g., CLEM-7 tunnel project in Brisbane), fast track (e.g., Sydney Opera House), keep running (e.g., Motorola's Iridium), or even alter projects and their strategy (e.g., Chad-Cameroon pipeline), leading to poor project outcomes. To avoid project failure and ensure smooth project delivery, upper management may use power to alter the behavior of the project team through surveillance, discipline, and punishment when new standards and procedures are not being practiced, in true Foucauldian tradition (Wynn, Smith, & Killen, 2021).

Since a project is about effecting change, it affects the interests of different individuals and groups and hence alters the balance of power in the organization. The project is usually associated with an official sponsor, a champion, and a client. These individuals and groups have vested interests in the project's benefits and value. They may assert power over other stakeholders including the project team and they may have power asserted over them, as we have seen with external stakeholders in the case of the Tata Nano (Chapter 5) and the NBA basketball changeover (Chapter 3) (Clegg & Kreiner, 2013). They will have different gains or losses, during implementation and depending on the value of the project. The project's completion will lead to a long-lasting reallocation of financial, material, and human resources. Power will shift in some form or degree.

Often, a project marks the end of one way of doing things and the beginning of another. As a result, some individuals and groups benefit from these reallocations and changes, while others feel hurt, rightly or wrongly. For these reasons, one cannot expect a project to be unanimously supported throughout the organization or even within groups where (formally at least) there seems to be a consensus.

The design and production of the Ford Mustang in the early 1960s illustrates the struggles between individuals and administrative units that can arise from a major project within the same organization. It was a true saga of *organizational politics* (Ika et al., 2020).

Launched in 1964, the Ford Mustang was a commercial success from the start. So much so, that today the words "Ford" or "Mustang" no longer appear on the car: its iconic logo is enough. Unfortunately, the project faced formidable opponents, including Henry Ford II, company CEO and grandson of its famous founder.

Managing Director Lee Iacocca led this ambitious project to offer "an affordable sports car." He cajoled, neutralized, bypassed stakeholders, and built coalitions to bring his project to fruition. He even succeeded in finding entirely new stakeholders, within and outside the organization. Why was the CEO initially opposed to the project? In the early 1960s, Ford was finally recovering from the Edsel disaster of a decade earlier. To put this into perspective, Henry Ford II's "Edsel" was later defined by Webster's Dictionary as "a product, project, etc., that is not accepted by the public despite high expectations and costly promotional efforts" (Carlson, 2007). This setback cost the company half of the US$650 million it had raised when it went public in 1956.

At this time, two visions prevailed at the Ford Motor Company: a production vision deeply rooted in the company's history, and a marketing vision to come up with a home run after the Edsel fiasco. The production vision was to offer new models that Ford could produce with limited modifications to its assembly line. Financial specialists fiercely shared this vision. However, it favored models more adapted to production demands than the customer. A bolder marketing vision focused on innovative products that would meet the needs and wishes of customers, increase market share, and conquer new market segments. These competing visions had their supporters and triggered clashes within the company. The infighting over the new Mustang's production illustrates the strong differences of opinion within the organization.

The Mustang was conceived as an affordable alternative to GM's Corvette, targeting the expanding youth market of the 1960s. Developed by two of Ford's top designers, the Mustang had the unconditional support of Don Frey, the company's chief engineer and project manager. Passionate about cars and technical performance, he was brilliant but unconcerned with conventions and administrative procedures. So Lee Iacocca, his immediate boss, oversaw the more mundane aspects of the project—"How do I get the finance guys to support it?" and "Is there a customer for this product?"

Ford analysts initially estimated potential annual sales at 50,000 units, just below the threshold that their financial experts thought would guarantee good profit margins at low risk. As a general rule, unless a new product exceeded that threshold, it was deemed risky and problematic. Fortunately, Iacocca knew how to use power and influence to advance his agenda. To counter their resistance, Iacocca decided to add bucket seats and convinced the marketing department to raise their estimates to 100,000 units. This new sales projection helped get the finance experts on board.

Iacocca believed that "all business operations can be reduced to three words: people, product, and profit." Early on, he felt that product and profit were a given for the Mustang, so he decided to tackle the other more challenging "p"—people (and their politics). His first strategy was to interest Henry Ford II in the project, and in informal meetings he tried to get Ford to see the Mustang as his idea. Unfortunately, Henry Ford II was exasperated by Iacocca's insistence and made it clear he did not want to hear any more about the project.

So, Iacocca took the major risk of talking about the Mustang to people at Ford's head office and members of the board of directors. He also leaked information about the Mustang to the specialized automotive press. Journalists, major car dealers, and potential buyers began asking Ford executives about the car and the release date. New stakeholders gradually emerged and made themselves heard: the general public, Ford dealers, the production department, the union, board members, and shareholders. This widespread buzz eventually forced the hand of Henry Ford II, who confronted Iacocca directly: "I am tired of hearing about this damn car. Is it salable?" Iacocca said, "Yes!" To which Ford retorted, "Then make sure you sell a lot of them" (Mowen, 1994).

The results were astounding. More than 400,000 units were sold in the first year, catapulting the company's net profits to US$1.1 billion the following year. With this success, Iacocca made the cover of *Newsweek* and *Time* in the same week. He had become a public figure, something that Henry Ford II had failed to achieve. On the strength of his success, Iacocca became president of the Ford Motor Company in 1970. Bad feelings lingered and Iacocca was fired in 1978, even though the company posted record profits of US$2 billion. Iacocca later gained even more notoriety as CEO of Chrysler, which he saved from bankruptcy (Carlson, 2007; Ika et al., 2020).

This Mustang project was a clear success in terms of the mandate. However, it did not go smoothly, nor was it a success in the eyes of all stakeholders. Indeed, it poisoned relationships between individuals, and there is a lingering perception that the Mustang was both a (mandate) success and a failure (for some stakeholders).

POWER AND POLITICS: TABOO WORDS IN PROJECT MANAGEMENT?

The Mustang and the SNC-Lavalin bridge construction projects seemed to have occurred in a different universe than the hyperrational framework of the mandate described in Chapter 5. While the reality of politics in projects is generally accepted, it is rarely discussed in the project management literature, except perhaps with public sector projects where political decision-making is part and parcel of the project's process to ensure legitimacy in the eyes of local communities, groups of citizens, or potential electors (di Maddaloni & Davis, 2018; Matinheikki, Aaltonen, & Walker, 2019). Even when the subject is broached, the discussion is so superficial or theoretical that it is of little use to project managers (Pinto, 2000; Sense, 2003).

The word "politics" has such negative connotations that it has become highly pejorative to talk about the political dimension of the project (Irwin, 2008). "I am not a politician, I am a project manager" is a commonly heard refrain among practitioners. Therefore, the project manager prefers to avoid discussing or openly considering the effects of politics on their project

(Clayton, 2007; Irwin, 2008; Pinto, 2000). But what does politics really mean in project management?

Politics is the art of achieving project goals through compromise[4] or influence[5] (see Sense, 2003; Sense & Antoni, 2003; Irwin, 2008). We use this definition because project managers often have limited formal power to impose their will.[6] They lack the hierarchical authority associated with the manager's position since they are not in the traditional hierarchy of the organization. Furthermore, their projects are often of limited scope. Only big projects give them visibility and, by the same token, confer a certain amount of power and control (Pinto, 2000).

For example, managers of international development projects, especially those with more experience, understand the inherent role of politics in their work. They know that politics is the *art of the possible,* as Bismarck and Napoleon are often quoted as saying. Therefore, as a practical matter (RealPolitik), they see project management as the art of dealing with the project's political situation (Ika & Saint-Macary, 2012). "A project, considered under a political angle, is as valuable a tool for governmental action as it is for the professional career of the project manager. Projects that run effectively are often publicised by the government for political purposes. This is beneficial for the project manager as well as for the government" (Diallo & Thuillier, 2004).

With his political savvy, Iacocca had only a few arrows in his quiver but used them well. Project management is also the *art of politics*. The project manager's ability to learn, understand, and influence the political dimension of the project and the organization is a significant asset. Too often, however, the political awareness and competence of the project manager are mistakenly taken for granted (Buchanan & Badham, 1999; Pinto, 2000; Sense 2003; Irwin, 2008).

"As a compromise between what is possible and what is doable according to the situation, the project requires mediation of its operating objectives, and of the motives, drives, and desires, often implicit, of many stakeholders" (Boutinet, 2005, our translation).

These many extraneous pressures pull the project apart and the multiple, even contradictory, objectives must be reconciled and negotiated.

Can we take the project out of the politics (of the organization) or the politics out of the project? Most likely, no. Like the organization, the project is a political arena where questions of power, influence, authority, and resources constantly collide with the interests of the various stakeholders.

When is a project likely to face major political issues? How can they be taken into account? What do we gain if we do? In addressing these questions, we examine project management through two lenses, one focused on the *mandate* and the other on the *principals*. In the next chapter, we explore the agents' perspective or the team members who are internal stakeholders, as opposed to principals who may be external stakeholders (Lehtinen & Aaltonen, 2020). Table 7.1 provides more examples of internal and external stakeholders. Table 7.2 shows the general parameters of the political perspective, focused on the principals.

TABLE 7.1 Internal and External Stakeholders

INTERNAL	EXTERNAL
■ Senior management, functional directors ■ Project team members ■ Employees, departments, unions ■ Sponsors	■ Customers, distributors, end users ■ Suppliers, sources of funds or information ■ Competitors ■ Political, governmental, social groups ■ Sponsors

Source: Adapted from Ika et al. (2020).

TABLE 7.2 The Political Perspective, Focused on Principals' Expectations

The Organization	An open system, with formal and informal mandates, balkanized by its many clients
The Process	Optimizing trade-offs among external forces
The Challenges	Reconciling divergent and variable objectives
The Approach	Managing the project contextually, in situ

PROJECT POLITICS AND PERFORMANCE: A MATTER OF PERSPECTIVE

The Vancouver 2010 Olympic Winter Games is a telling example of how politics can influence our perspective on the performance of a project. We also chose the Olympics because this type of project has a large and complex scope, with public records that are accessible and verifiable.[7]

Though the International Olympic Committee (IOC) guidelines say the games are all about sport, not politics, politics has featured prominently in the international competition since the first modern-day Olympics in 1896. The Olympic Games are not short of boycotts, protests, and political disputes. They have had their fair share of controversies about whether or not (or the extent to which) they suffer a triple whammy of cost overruns, benefit shortfalls, and stakeholder dismay (Flyvbjerg, Budzier, & Lunn, 2020; Preuss, 2022). As with other major projects, two key characters in the world of the Olympic Games projects, the Cassandras (the overpessimists) and the Pollyannas (the overoptimists) clash about the benefits and costs of hosting them (Ika, Pinto, Love, & Paché, 2022). When Virginia Raggi, mayor of Rome, withdrew her city's bid to host the 2024 Olympics citing past evidence of substantial cost overruns, Giovanni Malago, president of Italy's Olympic Committee (CONI) vehemently disagreed.

Here, our purpose is not to undertake an exhaustive review of the 2010 Winter Games and its controversies. Rather, we focus on a few salient aspects, such as the hot button French language issue in Canada and the lack of snow. The latter problem may seem nonpolitical and unpredictable. Yet the political lens provides useful "explanations"[8] for certain decisions made regarding risk and stakeholder management. However, before examining these phenomena through the lens of the mandate and then the principals, let us set up the context for these Olympic Games.

From February 12 to 28, 2010, fans around the world focused on Vancouver, the site of the XXI Olympic Winter Games.

Project management enthusiasts were paying particular attention because the Olympic Games are complex, large-scale projects whose success is never guaranteed. Nearly 3,000 athletes from 82 countries competed in 15 sports and 86 events. Canada, hosting the Olympic Games for the third time in its history, not only won its first gold medal as a host country, but also broke the record for the most gold medals won by a country in a single Winter Olympics (14 in total). Seen from the perspective of the mandate, this great Canadian project is therefore an undisputed success.

On the other hand, an athlete's[9] tragic and perhaps unavoidable death overshadowed the games from day one. Later, the games were criticized for not giving French enough prominence since it is one of Canada's two official languages. Finally, as with any large-scale project, this one had its share of unexpected events, such as the mildest winter ever officially recorded in Vancouver, which threatened certain events and raised the specter of the first cancellation of the Olympic Winter Games.

With a well-defined time, scope, and budget, the Vancouver Organizing Committee (VANOC) had a rather conventional mandate that involved "planning, organizing, financing, and staging the Olympics and Paralympics Winter Games 2010." But it was also expected to "foster and promote the development of sports in Canada," to "touch the soul of Canada," and to "inspire the world." For their part, committee members formulated their vision of "building a stronger Canada, driven by its passion for sport, culture and sustainable development."

While the Olympic spirit is universal and noble, the games inevitably face parochial issues on the national, provincial, and even local stages. Remember that although cities (not countries) are officially selected to host Olympic games, many levels of government are involved in the project. Thus, a 20-member board of directors governed VANOC: 7 appointed by the Canadian Olympic Committee, 3 by the Canadian government, 3 by the province of British Columbia, 2 by Vancouver, 2 by the Resort

Municipality of Whistler, 1 by the Canadian Paralympic Committee, 1 by local First Nations, with the twentieth member being appointed by the 19 other members. In sum, there were seven primary *agents* and 20 team members for the games.

Was the Vancouver 2010 Olympic Winter Games a successful project? The answer is clear if we are using standard *rational* criteria: the project was delivered on time and within the allocated budget, complying with International Olympic Committee standards.[10]

Let us broaden our assessment to consider the costs of building the site and the infrastructure. According to VANOC, the project was completed on budget, with no deficit or surplus. PricewaterhouseCoopers corroborated this evaluation, and demonstrated that the games had been successful in terms of tourism benefits and job creation.

But did the project live up to the federal government slogan of the games, "Own the podium/*À nous le podium*"? How did other stakeholders evaluate the games? Here, things get more complicated since there are at least seven formal stakeholders to consider, each potentially with different criteria. Much depends on whose perspective is taken to "explain" and evaluate such phenomena as the key decisions made by VANOC regarding the planning, organization, and financing of the sports venues, and the languages used during the Olympic Torch Relay and in the opening and closing ceremonies.

TAKE I: IN VITRO, THROUGH THE RATIONAL LENS

A conventional, *rational* evaluation of the organization of the games typically focuses on how well the project met the time, cost, and quality (and scope) constraints defined in VANOC's mandate. For both the project manager and any external observer wishing to assess the actions of the committee members, the frame of reference of choice is the *Terms of Reference,* the blueprint for the games planning.

Parlez-Vous Français?

The French language has a special status in the Olympic Games because France revived this event in 1896.[11] French is also one of Canada's two official languages—English being the other. In this context, VANOC was contractually required to use French and have both official language groups represented in major events, like the opening and closing ceremonies and the national anthem. However, after VANOC carried its first few public events, the Office of the Commissioner of Official Languages (OCOL) denounced the "lack of sensitivity on the part of VANOC with regard to linguistic duality at cultural events. The entire ceremony was conducted in English, with the exception of a song translated into French at the last minute."

VANOC used cost constraints to justify the limited use of French, relying on the rational project management perspective with regard to best practices. However, an internal evaluation made earlier in the summer of 2009 had made it clear that the resources set aside could not handle the significant volume of texts to be translated before and during the games. VANOC, which had six translators at the time, estimated that it would need approximately 40 additional translators. VANOC estimated the cost of the translation requirements at C$5.3 million. VANOC considered not translating the athletes' biographies and certain manuals, since they represented a significant volume of translation (Office of the Commissioner of Official Languages, 2010).

Consequently, the much-publicized opening ceremony was conducted entirely in English, except for one song. OCOL expressed its dissatisfaction, noting that "VANOC clearly gave less prominence to French during the cultural component of the ceremony [and, as a result] 38 admissible complaints regarding this issue were submitted . . . each deploring the glaring disparity between English and French" (OCOL, 2010).

Let There be Snow

An alarming situation occurred at Cypress Mountain in North Vancouver because there was not enough snow. It was even too warm to make artificial snow. At first glance, it may appear that such an unfortunate scenario and its impact on the games were entirely out of VANOC's control, since the vagaries of the weather are an external risk situation that project managers must accept and assume. True, the committee had no control over the weather, but it did have complete control over the choice of sites. So why were these key events held at Cypress and not at Whistler, further north, dependably colder and with plenty of snow?

Under the rational lens of the mandate, two explanations were proferred. First, "Whistler was already over capacity with five stadiums, an Athletes' Village, a Celebration Plaza and other facilities" (Furlong & Mason, 2011). Second, "[Cypress] was a lot closer to more people, for starters. That allowed us to get more Olympic tickets in the hands of more spectators" (OCOL, 2010). According to the people in charge, the mandate was faithfully executed: choosing Cypress was in line with the standard rules of project management: to level activities (avoiding peaks and valleys) and respect cost constraints.

Was the mandate faithfully executed? Again, we may gain more insight by using the political perspective.

TAKE II: IN SITU, THROUGH THE POLITICAL LENS

Taking a different perspective to explain the decisions made by VANOC may reveal aspects that were not previously understood. The political perspective assumes that the mandate is not as static, consensual, or explicit as the rational perspective claims. It acknowledges that the mandate evolves, is remotely negotiated, and is pulled in different directions by the principals. Inevitable ambiguities and contradictions also taint the mandate.

Since stakeholder expectations are expressed only *partially* and at the *outset,* the mandate—a signed document, drafted at the outset—cannot be used to "explain" or "understand" phenomena that are unexpected or overlooked, at least by the participants. Gaining a better understanding of the stakeholders (rather than the mandate itself) can help explain the phenomena mentioned—in the case of the 2010 Winter Olympics, this is the choice of languages used in the ceremonies, and the locations for the games.

Let us look at the French language issue through the *political lens of the principals*. The criticisms made by OCOL (2010) were based on the mandate and its formal contractual obligations: "There were also language clauses in the contribution agreements that accompanied the federal government's US$20 million contribution." For its part, VANOC argued that the use of French "was proportional to the size of the French-speaking community in these localities" (OCOL, 2010), in a country where French speakers are a minority at 23 percent, but less than 2 percent in the province of British Columbia. In contrast, the political perspective reveals that VANOC's decision was political, and their logic was based on local stakeholders' needs, which were over-represented in the committee.

Similarly, the political lens provides different answers to this question: Why choose Cypress over Whistler for the events? Based on weather statistics, Whistler gets more snow and has lower temperatures, so it was a much better site than Cypress, even in the view of committee members. So why did they opt for Cypress?

Here, a dose of *geopolitics* may prove helpful. Cypress is a "rather modest" mountain in Greater Vancouver. Politically, however, Greater Vancouver is a Canadian metropolis with a population of over two million—half of the entire province. Whistler, 75 miles away in the same province, is a municipality visited by over three million tourists annually, but it has only 9,000 voters. Vancouver's mayor repeatedly used this fact (2,000,000 vs. 9,000 voters) to influence the selection process (Furlong and Mason, 2011). As a result, it is no surprise that VANOC's federal and provincial members, pressured by Vancouver's municipal representatives, carried more political weight than Whistler in allocating events.

An organization has many individuals and coalitions with divergent and even conflicting expectations. Similarly, far from being consensual, a project is an instrument that these individuals and coalitions use for different ends. Multiple external pressures come from all sides, and thus the project has numerous contradictory objectives. Consequently, the project's objectives must be reconciled and negotiated.

The project is more than the mandate because the principals ultimately define it and give it meaning beyond the words written in the mandate. The participation of the principals in defining the mandate reflects their partial involvement. They may also have unstated goals, or ones that will evolve after the mandate is drafted.

The Mandate: An Open Contract

It is difficult to reduce the project to its mandate because it is filtered through each coalition's representation system. Each has "its own project within the project," "its own mandate within the mandate," and "its own agenda within the project's agenda." The project is best perceived as a political process that prioritizes one value system over another. The project's relationship with other projects, including counterprojects, also needs to be considered (Joffre, Aurégan, Chodétel, & Tellier, 2006). Major projects often operate in pluralistic institutional settings. The public sector and the private sector often hold differing, if not conflicting, views when it comes to the means and/or ends of organizing. While governments tend to focus on accountability, transparency, due process, and value for money, companies emphasize efficiency, innovation, effectiveness, and profits (Orr & Scott, 2011). Local communities, for their part, are generally concerned about the expected and unexpected impacts of the project including its sustainability (Di Maddaloni & Davis, 2018; Ika & Hodgson, 2014).

These perspectives are necessary because "no project is an island." A project is not isolated and self-sufficient: it is immersed in and takes place within a historical and political context (Engwall, 2003). Consequently, the ideal of a single, precise objective does not reflect the reality of projects, and is not unanimously accepted. Projects often have multiple, unclear, divergent, and even contradictory objectives.

Moreover, coalitions no longer agree on a common objective performance measurement (including cost and time). As a result, satisfying stakeholder expectations becomes the criterion par excellence for the project's success (rather than executing the contract well). For this reason, a dialectical method and debates between coalitions are often used to advance the project (Asquin, Falcoz, & Picq, 2005).

An analysis of the coalitions that evolve within and around organizations shows that organizations are far from rational entities and that power plays a fundamental role. In this perspective, projects are political arenas where the organization is a political instrument that fundamentally serves the needs and interests of coalitions (Di Maddaloni & Davis, 2018; Saint-Macary, 1989). What will determine the success of each coalition is its ability to manage the project agenda, block this or that potential item, and withhold information that does not serve its interests.

In these arenas, the objectives are usually imprecise and multiple. Some objectives are visible, and others are hidden—"what is must become what should be." Project stakeholders compete to set and manipulate the agenda for public discussion to benefit themselves. Informal trade-offs between different parties are common. Before any agenda receives serious consideration, stakeholders search for a consensus in the "chaos of purposes and accidents" (Hulme, 1995; Ika & Hodgson, 2014).

Bearing in mind their needs, expectations, objectives, and requirements, and their support or resistance to the project, the manager must deal with internal and external coalitions and stakeholders. According to experts, the ability to deal with stakeholders is a critical success factor (Lehtinen & Aaltonen, 2020). This view stems from *stakeholder theory* (Freeman, 1984) which claims that: "the organization has relationships with many principal groups and that it can engender and maintain the support of these groups by considering and balancing their relevant interests" (Aaltonen, 2011).

Like Freeman (1984), the Project Management Institute (PMI) defines stakeholders as "individuals, groups, or organizations that may affect or be affected by the project" (PMI, 2013). Each one has their own perspective on the ins and outs of the project and, of course, its performance. The same is true of the different perceptions between different stakeholder groups regarding the factors and criteria for project success (Davis, 2014).

Like a savvy politician, the project manager must address the interests of various coalitions in an arena of conflict, negotiation, and compromise. This work environment can be chaotic. Indeed, the *garbage can model* shows that an organization is much more like an organized anarchy than a rational agent. Solutions and decisions are not always well thought out. In the context of any organization, many problems linger on, unsolved, unattended, and eventually set aside, thrown in the garbage can, as it were. At the same time, there are many pet solutions proffered by individuals or groups, with no identifiable use. They too end up in the metaphorical garbage can. Periodically, some of these solutions and problems get fortuitously linked in this large organizational trash can (March & Olsen, 1976). This is especially true for large projects operating in pluralistic institutional settings, where the reasons for underperformance are different for the internal (e.g., project managers) and external (e.g., suppliers) project stakeholders (Steen, Ford, & Verreynne, 2017)—thus, between *agents* and *principals,* to use our preferred terms. As well, as newer scholarship on stakeholder theory suggests (McGahan, 2021), in the collective action context of major projects, scope change requests from external stakeholders such as local communities may significantly improve value distribution but increase costs (Gill and Fu, 2022).

Successful project delivery is not just about getting the mandate right. Instead, it is about making it work for the stakeholders—but for which stakeholders? "Such political perspectives on projects tend to suggest the need for a wider picture which considers what goes on in the social construction of projects and project management by focusing on who and which agendas are included or excluded from decision-making processes" (Cicmil, Hodgson, Lindgren, & Packendorff, 2009).

As we saw in Chapter 4, a faulty management of stakeholders can lead to unexpected consequences. For instance, when the sponsor is the sole beneficiary, the project may fail the community at large, lose its societal meaning and undermine the sociological balance (Kreiner, 2014). Furthermore, few stakeholders will have the attention of the project manager throughout the project. Internal stakeholders, with a formal, official, or contractual relationship with the project are naturally inclined to be advocates; but external stakeholders who are negatively impacted are freer to act against it unless they are part of some inter-organizational coalition (Lehtinen & Aaltonen, 2020).

CONCLUSION

In the rational approach, scant consideration is given to the role of politics in and around projects and organizations. Yet politics is often blamed for project failures. Can we take the project out of politics or the politics out of the project? No—nor should we. Politics in projects is inevitable and necessary.

Projects are fertile terrain for politics because they effect change. Thus, they alter the status quo, positively affecting the interests of some groups to the detriment of others. So, although politics is sometimes an impediment to change, it is also a critical agent of change, especially in democratic contexts.

To implement the project successfully, project sponsors and managers should pay attention to the political context and seek to achieve stakeholder buy-in by using some of the theoretical models presented in this chapter. The chapter provides project sponsors and managers with five takeaways:

1. Politics is omnipresent. Politics, the art of achieving project goals through compromise or influence, is a *constant in projects,* large or small, public or private. Politics can make or break a project—as supported by extensive evidence.
2. Politics means conflicts. The project, much like the organization, is a political arena where issues of power, influence, authority, and resources foster *continual conflict* among stakeholders. You cannot take the project out of the organization's politics, nor the politics out of the project.
3. Politics is paradoxical. Since it has negative connotations, many are uncomfortable discussing the political aspects of a project. The project is also subject to external pressures, and it is torn between contradictory objectives. Yet for a project to succeed, the implicit and explicit expectations of various stakeholders must be addressed.
4. There are more stakeholders than we generally think. They are inside and outside, formal or informal, and new ones will emerge. Key *external stakeholders* who are not members of the project coalition are often left out of projects. Every stakeholder has its own agenda and its own idea of the mandate.

5. Stakeholders often coalesce. Each coalition strives to impose its value system over those of others, to *influence the project agenda* to suit its interests. Along with the principals they strive to give the project a collective or even societal meaning. The project team should pay attention to context and stakeholder buy-in by using the dialectical methods and ideas discussed in this book.

The rational approach adopts a unified conception of the organization, with a single agent and a single goal defined in the mandate (i.e., the realization of the project within time, cost, and quality constraints). This idea of a single, clear, and stable objective is neither real nor ideal. Rather, the project has multiple, vague, divergent, and even contradictory objectives. The political perspective reveals the project as an instrument used by several groups and principals who pull it in different directions. Beware of stakeholders, but more importantly, be *aware* of stakeholders. This understanding is essential if we are to make satisfying stakeholder groups the overarching criterion for project success.

REFERENCES

Aaltonen, K. (2011). Project stakeholder analysis as an environmental interpretation process. *International Journal of Project Management, 29,* 165–183.

Asquin, A., Falcoz, C., & Picq, T. (2005). *Ce que manager par projet veut dire*. Éditions d'Organisation.

Barnard, C. I. (1938). *The functions of the executive*. Harvard University Press.

BBC (2020). Infrastructure: More local input needed in big projects, say MPs https://www.bbc.com/news/uk-politics-53554666 (accessed October 29, 2020).

Boutinet, J-P. (2005). *Anthropologie du projet*. Quadrige.

Buchanan, D. A., & Badham, R.J. (1999). *Power, politics, and organizational change: Winning the turf game.* Sage.

Carlson, P. (2007). The flop heard round the world. *Washington Post.*

Cicmil, S., Hodgson, D., Lindgren, M., & Packendorff, J. (2009). Project management behind the façade. *Ephemera, Theory & Politics in organization, 9*(2), 78–92.

Clayton, M. (2017). The game of projects. How to win at project politics. https://onlinepmcourses.com/project-politics/ (accessed 29 October 2020).

Clegg, S., & Kreiner, K. (2013). Power and politics in construction projects. In N. Drouin, R. Müller, & S. Sankaran (Eds.). *Novel approaches to organizational project management research: Translational and transformational* (pp. 268–293). Copenhagen Business School Press.

Crozier, M., & Friedberg, E. (1977). *L'acteur et le système.* Seuil.

Cyert, R., & March, G. (1963). *A behavioral theory of the firm.* Prentice-Hall.

Davis, K. (2014). Different stakeholder groups and their perceptions of project success *International Journal of Project Management, 32*(2), 189–201.

Diallo, A., & Thuillier, D. (2004). The success dimensions of international development projects: the perceptions of African project coordinators. *International journal of project management, 22*(1), 19–31.

Di Maddaloni, F., & Davis, K. (2018). Project manager's perception of the local communities' stakeholder in megaprojects. An empirical investigation in the UK. *International Journal of Project Management, 36*(3), 542–565.

Engwall, M. (2003). No project is an island: Linking projects to history and context. *Research Policy, 32*(5), 789–808.

Faleye, O., Reis, E., & Venkateswaran, A. (2013). The determinants and effects of CEO–employee pay ratios. *Journal of Banking & Finance, 37*(8), 3258–3272.

Flyvbjerg, B., Budzier, A., & Lunn, D. (2021). Regression to the tail: Why the Olympics blow up. *Environment and Planning A: Economy and Space, 53*(2), 233–260.

Freeman, J. (1984). *Strategic management: A stakeholder approach.* Pitman.

Furlong, J., & Mason, G. (2011). *Patriot hearts: Inside the olympics that changed a country.* Vancouver: Douglas & McIntyre.

Gil, N., & Fu, Y. (2022). Megaproject Performance, Value Creation, and Value Distribution: An Organizational Governance Perspective. *Academy of Management Discoveries*, *8*(2), 224–251.

Halberstam, D. (2012). *The reckoning.* Open Road Media.

Hulme, D. (1995). Projects, politics and professionals: Alternative approaches for project identification and project planning. *Agricultural Systems*, *47,* 211–233.

Ika, L. A., & Hodgson, D. (2014). Learning from international development projects: blending critical project studies and critical development studies. *International Journal of Project Management, 32*(7), 1182–1196.

Ika, L. A., & Saint-Macary, J. (June 1–4, 2011). Paradigm lost: The concept of strategy in project organizing. Proceedings of the 11th European Academy of management Conference, Tallinn, Estonia.

Ika, L. A., Saint-Macary, J., & Bandé, A. (2020). Mobilizing stakeholders for project success. *PM World Journal*, IX(VIII), August. Available online at https://pmworldlibrary.net/wp-content/uploads/2020/07/pmwj96-Aug2020-Ika-Saint-Macary-Bande-mobilizing-stakeholders-for-project-success.pdf.

Ika, L. A., Pinto, J. K., Love, P. E. D., & Paché, G. (2022). Bias versus error. Why projecst fall short. *Journal of Business Srategy.* https://doi.org/10.1108/JBS-11-2021-0190.

Irwing, B. (2008). *Managing politics and conflicts in projects.* Management Concepts.

Joffre, P., Aurégan, P., Chodétel, F., & Tellier, A. (2006). *La gestion stratégique par le projet.* Édition Economica.

Kreiner, K. (2014). Restoring project success as phenomenon. In Lundin, R. A., Hällgreen, M. (Eds.), *Advancing research on projects and temporary organizations.* Copenhagen & Stockholm: Copenhagen Business School Press & Liber (pp. 21–40).

Lawrence, C. (2018). Infrastructure populism: on the politics of building big, or failing to. https://citymonitor.ai/government/infrastructure-populism-politics-building-big-or-failing-4350 (accessed 29 October 29 2020).

Lehtinen, J., & Aaltonen, K. (2020). Organizing external stakeholder engagement in inter-organizational projects: Opening the black box. *International Journal of Project Management, 38*(2), 85–98.

March, J. G., & Olsen, J. P. (1976). *Ambiguity and choice in organizations.* Universitetsforlaget.

Matinheikki, J., Aaltonen, K., & Walker, D. (2019). Politics, public servants, and profits: Institutional complexity and temporary hybridization in a public infrastructure alliance project. *International Journal of Project Management, 37*(2), 298–317.

McGahan, A. M. (2021). Integrating insights from the resource-based view of the firm into the new stakeholder theory. *Journal of Management, 47*(7), 1734–1756.

Mowen, J. C. (1994). *Judgment calls. High-stakes decisions in a risky world.* Simon & Schuster.

Office of the Commissioner of Official Languages (2010). *A golden opportunity: Vancouver 2010. Final report on the olympic and paralympic games.* Cat. no.: SF31-106/201.

Orr, R., Scott, W., Levitt, R., Artto, K., & Kujala, J. (2011). Global projects: Distinguishing features, drivers, and challenges. In W. Scott, R. Levitt, & R. Orr (Eds.), *Global Projects: institutional and political challenges* (pp. 15–51). Cambridge University Press.

Papandreou, A. G. (1952). Some basic problems in the theory of the firm. In B. F. Haley, *A survey of contemporary economics*, II, Irwin.

Piketty, T. (2018). *Capital in the twenty-first century.* Harvard University Press.

Pinto, J. K. (2000). Understanding the role of politics in successful project management. *International Journal of Project Management, 18,* 55–91.

Preuss, H. (2022). Re-analysis, measurement and misperceptions of cost overruns at Olympic Games. *International Journal of Sport Policy and Politics, 14*(3), 381–400.

Project Management Institute, PMI (2013). *A guide to the project management body of knowledge.* Fifth edition. PMI.

Saint-Macary, J. (1989). What is the use? An appraisal of the functionalist approach in strategic management. Concordia University Working Paper Series, Faculty of Commerce and Administration, #89-08-18, Montreal, Quebec.

Saint-Pierre, G. (1995). *Le monde en mutation : implications pour les gestionnaires et les entreprises.* Gestion.

Sense, A. J. (2003). A model of the politics of project leader learning. *International Journal of Project Management, 21,* 107–114.

Sense, A. J., & Antoni, M. (2003). Exploring the politics of project learning. *International Journal of Project Management, 21,* 487–494.

Steen, J., Ford, J., & Verreynne, M. (2017). Symbols, sublimes, solutions and problems: A garbage can theory of megaprojects. *Project Management Journal, 48*(6), 117–131.

Thomson, S. (2017). The slippery politics of pipelines: Canada's biggest projects and the political lives that depend on them. *National Post.* https://nationalpost.com/news/politics/a-look-at-pipeline-projects-in-canada-and-the-political-livelihoods-that-depend-on-them (accessed 29 October 2020).

Wynn, C., Smith, L., & Killen, C. (2021). How power influences behavior in projects: A theory of planned behavior perspective. *Project Management Journal, 52*(6), 607–621.

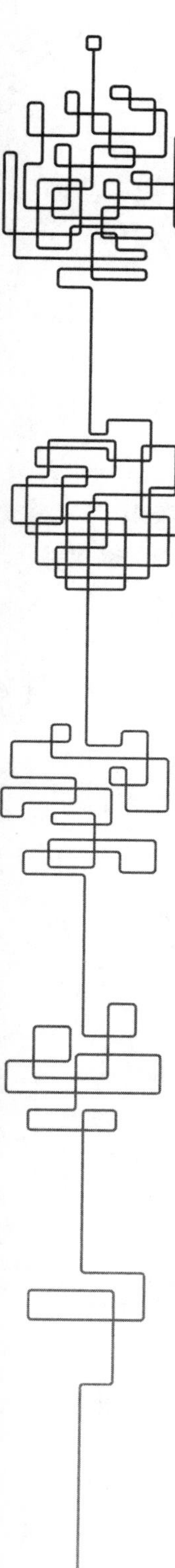

CHAPTER 8

THE PSYCHOSOCIAL PERSPECTIVE (IN VIVO)

Whether it stems from a business opportunity or out of necessity, a project is an emergent process. Its seed takes root *in vitro,* nurtured in the hearts and minds of a few people. It is subsequently "projected," *in situ,* by principals who will provide the necessary resources and formulate a mandate. The project then becomes visible to the outside world when it is implemented, *in vivo,* by agents. Some of the same people may be involved in its various phases such as design and implementation, or in mobilizing the necessary resources. This process is iterative, not linear.

In previous chapters, we looked at projects from a rational perspective, embodied in the mandate, and then from a political perspective, focused on the principals. In this chapter, we view projects from a psychosocial perspective—that is, the interrelation of social factors, individual thoughts, and behaviors. In that third dimension, we will see that the agents are not just well-disciplined implementers of projects. The ways in which they carry out their work are shaped by their expertise and experience, of course, but also by their personalities and own understanding of the mandate. While serving the interests of the principals, agents also seek to reconcile their own interests with the mandate.

A THIRD PERSPECTIVE ON PROJECTS

The *rational perspective* prevails in project management because of its success in some traditional areas, despite its shortcomings in others. Focusing on the objectives set out in the mandate helps managers design and implement a well-ordered workflow, even in an environment where there are risks.

With this approach, any project can be defined neatly, clearly, upfront, once and for all. The resulting mandate can fully consider the client's expectations, the available resources, and the constraints to be met. Resources earmarked for the project can then be deployed toward the orderly execution of the mandate, which is the sole overarching objective. With this process you can *plan your work, and work your plan.*

It is not an easy path, however, as it involves a lot of preparatory work. In theory, the rational perspective anticipates all relevant obstacles that could hinder the proper implementation of the project. Some obstacles may be *internal,* stemming from the characteristics of the project or from the organization's inherent shortcomings. There are also *external* threats that may seem to be beyond the manager's control. In either case, they can be detected and mitigated since their probable occurrence and impact can be measured and managed.

The main challenges are to assess the risks by estimating the probability of their occurrence and the possible impact on the project's time, cost, and quality targets. Managers can then design contingency plans with countermeasures and corrective solutions, like insurance and pilot projects. As a result, the project can be carried out in a relatively isolated organizational context, in vitro, protected from the consequences of unwanted changes. Moreover, the uncertainty is deemed manageable because, even if the implementation context changes, it is not chaotic: the agents are disciplined, the principals are circumspect, and everything has been covered in the mandate.

In a stable environment, with one goal, one principal, one mandate, reliable agents, the rational approach is ideal for executing projects. This economical, proven approach allows managers to focus on implementation since they have considered all reasonable risks. Managers can then confidently use the project management tools discussed in Chapter 6.

In Chapter 7, however, we questioned the premises and assumptions inherent to the rational perspective—the foundation for the classical project management approach—regarding the stability of the principals' preferences and predictability of the future. We then looked at situations where the *principals* (individuals and groups) do not form a homogeneous, stable block, as their interests may clash or change over time. Principals are human beings who are called upon to navigate a complex world and make decisions for the future, despite their limited cognitive abilities.

But the rational perspective does not allow us to anticipate ex ante, nor explain ex post, the evolution of a project carried out under complex circumstances. Except for projects with clear and precise objectives, the so-called rational perspective leads managers to take actions based on a "rationalized" view of the real world.

What should Nancy Smart do? First, she must evaluate the context of the project early on. Then, she must determine whether the conditions justify using the rational perspective as the main lens. Does she have a clear mandate with a clear outcome in mind? Has ExPlus done anything like that before?

To those ends, we assessed in the previous chapter how power and influence in and around organizations impact how projects are really implemented, in situ. Now, we will examine *who the project agents are,* and how their psychological and social characteristics influence how they view their role within the organization and the project.

AGENTS UNDER THE MICROSCOPE

To underscore the importance of personal psychology and social connections in organizational settings, we use the example of a courtroom, an arena supposedly shaped strictly by the rational-legal perspective (Weber, 1921). A judicial trial can be viewed as a project initiated by a *principal* (the "prosecutor" acting on behalf of the state or the plaintiff in a civil case) and implemented through *agents* (judges, lawyers, and jurors), whose *mandate* is to determine the guilt, innocence, or liability of the accused. Each party plays a distinct role, and each pursues its own objective within the broader mandate of the project. To that list of key stakeholders (to use the language of project management), one must add defendants, litigants, and the public.

In a process similar to a feasibility study, public prosecutors examine the circumstances of the case, ascertain whether they can prove guilt or liability with the evidence likely to be available at trial, and if so will lay formal charges, and move to the next phase. Specifically, they determine which charges would be appropriate (i.e., define the project's scope). If they go to trial, it will be subject to time, cost, and quality constraints (like any project).

It might seem that trials should be guided entirely by rational-legal procedures. After all, is Lady Justice not blindfolded as she weighs the facts fairly? Yet in trials, rational as they are purported to be, a lot of time and resources are devoted to selecting the agents: prosecutors, defense attorneys, and especially jurors.

In the complex jury selection process, the prosecutor and the defense attorney stand on opposite sides. As each party vies for a jury they can convince of their respective cases, they carefully examine the sociodemographic profiles and backgrounds of potential jurors (agents). Accordingly, they consider the presumed or expressed views of these individuals by analyzing their social network and by conducting social media background research, analyzing, for instance, their social media posts and responses regarding social and political questions.

The process is so important and complex that the parties involved may hire consultants who are experts in the field. This example highlights the importance of the actors (agents) in complex and fuzzy situations, and illustrates how psychosocial factors can generate and influence team dynamics in complex projects whose progress and outcomes are uncertain.

Human biases and group dynamics cannot be suppressed or ignored. In the following chapters, we will continue to explore how their detrimental effects can be kept in check and their contribution optimized, by structuring the decision-making process and defining the checks and balances and the roles of individuals and groups. In our courtroom example, the jury selection process should foster fairness and impartiality, for the greater good. In fuzzy projects, checks and balances may help keep the project aligned with its own higher purpose.

As we broaden our analysis, we will consider the agents and their influence on the project management process. This focus will enable managers, like Nancy Smart, to better understand the realities of fuzzy projects, which do not lend themselves to the strict application of the rational approach.

With these objectives in mind, we looked at the first two components of the mandate-principal-agent triad in Chapters 6 and 7. Now, in Chapter 8, we will see how agents behave under the banner of the mandate, in a politicized context inside the project. Are they simple executants who individually and collectively follow their marching orders? Like principals, can agents also be individualistic, undisciplined, or unpredictable?

By questioning the premises of the rational perspective, we move further away from the image of an orderly organization where all activities and projects converge toward a single, consensual organizational goal under the harmonious guidance of reason. Instead, what emerges is a divided organization torn by divergent and even conflicting interests.

The agents, whose official task is to serve the organization and its projects, may at times put their interests first. For example, they may adjust their contribution according to the task at hand, prioritizing certain issues over others. As individuals and team members, they can thus influence the use of resources and put their own stamp on the projects. So, we explore when and how agents can thus influence the project.[1]

Our analysis focuses on the project and on certain groups in the organization. Although organizations may have dozens or even thousands of employees, agents interact with a limited number of people in their daily work life. In other words, each agent's work environment is much smaller than the entire organization.

In this context, we focus on the *project team* from the perspective of its members (the agents) and their immediate working environment. In our foray into the heart of the project team, we are particularly interested in the *roles of the agents*. Furthermore, projects are fertile and revealing ground for analyzing the individual and social behaviors of project team members since interactions are intense, fueled by a very dynamic organizational framework (Chiocchio, Kelloway, & Hobbs, 2015). Let's consider an example to illustrate this point. Inadequate incentives may create a toxic environment in which managers and team members are pressured into violating safety procedures in order to speed up delivery. Such deviant behavior may become normalized (Pinto 2014). When even more pressure is exerted by upper management through new standards and procedures, individual agents will not react uniformly. Some team members may accept these new ways of doing things, but others may resist. Their differing behavior in this context depends on how they answer these two key questions: (1) "How will this action make me feel?" and (2) "What are the chances this course of action will be good for me?" (Wynn, Smith, & Killen, 2021).

To this end, we use a *psychosocial approach* that focuses on individual actions of a *psychological nature* and the *social interactions* between team members who have emotional connections to one another and toward the project. This approach complements the political perspective that focuses on the interests the principals have in the project. The defining parameters of a psychosocial perspective focused on agents' expectations, are:

- **The organization:** permeable to the environment, with fairly autonomous actors
- **The process:** reconciling the views of the principals regarding the mandate
- **The challenge:** justifying and channeling the actions of the agents within the mandate
- **The approach:** managing the project *and* the agents incrementally, in vivo

GIVE AND TAKE

An organization is a means by which its members and some people in society get things done. It is an instrument, not an end in itself. Its role is not neutral. It "cannot be equated with society in general, because it defends the particular interests" of some individuals and social groups (Séguin-Bernard & Chanlat, 1987, our translation). Organizations are *instrumentalized* by external forces and by their own members, who are motivated by personal needs and wants. Employees, employers and beneficiaries are engaged in a process of exchange. The same janitor, accountant, or HR manager could work for a factory, hospital, or the US Army with a low or high degree of commitment to the goals of these organizations. The interests of employees and employers do not need to be identical, they only need to be complementary.

In the marketplace, employees play a dual role when they interact with people outside the organization, selling, buying, or making exchanges of all kinds. In so doing, these individuals serve both their employers and themselves, and are paid accordingly. This duality may be less visible in the workplace where employees advocate for their organization *and* themselves, but it is just as true. While the exchanges between employees and employers—*agents and principals*—work out well most of the time, the risk of conflict is very real since these interests are not fully compatible. Indeed, when power is exercised, there is compliance but also resistance. Some project team members may be willing to adopt the new culture being fostered by upper management, while others may resist if they deem that benefits do not outweigh costs (Wynn et al., 2021). And since projects entail change, they necessarily involve the reallocation of resources that could benefit some people and groups but not others.

A*gents* are those who are formally tasked with carrying out the project. They have *extrinsic* motivations stemming from what they will gain by participating, such as salary, security, power, prestige, and promotion (rewards). Their motivations are also *intrinsic,* as they also derive satisfaction from the work they do (recognition) (Schmid & Adams, 2010). They may be motivated by the purpose of their work—be it in a factory, a hospital, or the army. In summary, each agent in the project team has a set of extrinsic and intrinsic motivations that serve their self-interests. Consequently, their motivations are different from those of other agents or principals.

Project managers may be motivated by as many as six key factors: (1) interpersonal interaction, (2) task, (3) general working conditions, (4) empowerment, (5) personal development, and (6) compensation. "A clearly defined, interesting task, working with a supportive and goal-oriented team, getting the necessary information and financial and personnel resources, and having the possibility to influence important decisions have been identified as the most important motivators for project managers working in Switzerland. Factors related to compensation were the least important motivators" (Seiler, Bogdan, Malgorzata, & Pinazza, 2012).

MANAGERIAL DISCRETION

How can an organization operate coherently if the opportunism of its members is pervasive? This issue is overlooked in the rational perspective that sees the organization as having overriding objectives such as maximizing profits, ensuring public safety, or providing exemplary customer service. In theory, to fulfill the overarching organizational goal, the various actors must put the organization's interests before their own.

It is possible that organizational and personal interests coexist, however, if the "organizational objectives" do not override all other concerns. While employees and team members are expected to contribute to organizational objectives, they do not always seek to maximize them. Rather, they may treat these objectives as constraints that must be met. Once these objectives are satisfied or on their way to being satisfied (even *before* optimal performance is achieved), the agents are free to pursue personal goals (Williamson, 1963). This pattern is observed in strategic, operations, and project management.

Research has consistently shown that, in practice, maximizing profits or any single organizational objective is not an all-consuming concern for managers on a sustained basis. Once managers reach a certain production level, they exercise more latitude in allocating budget surpluses and resources. They interpret rules and modify organizational actions to suit their personal values and interests. They also make trade-offs between their own interests and those of the organization. These various forms of managerial discretion are found in both the public and private sectors.

Managerial discretion refers to the latitude agents are given (or take) to pursue their own economic, power, status, or prestige objectives instead of those put forth by the principals (Williamson, 1963). A high level of discretion means that managers have a great deal of latitude to pursue personal goals. This latitude is facilitated or hindered by their work context. For example, assembly-line work or other rigid workflows allow for little freedom, whereas teleworking (which gained popularity during the pandemic) affords employees much more latitude.

Managerial discretion also depends on the separation of roles between managers and owners. Indeed, even though managers represent their departments or organizations, they are clearly not owners. Aside from smaller organizations, which may be managed by owner-operators, the separation of ownership and management is the norm in modern organizations, whether they are publicly traded, cooperatives, public, or not-for-profit.

The role of managers varies with the level at which they exercise their responsibilities. This may be at the level of the whole organization, when dealing with other organizations, within one of its units, or in the context of projects. Sometimes, a manager takes on the role of an agent; sometimes an owner takes on the role of a principal; it all depends on the context in which they perform their duties. *Discretionary latitude* varies greatly with organizational context and individual employees. It is proportional to certain external and exogenous factors—such as the political and financial autonomy of managers, or their hierarchical level (Gangloff, 1998). Managers who are in high-level positions or who are financially independent obviously have more discretion than others.

However, a manager's propensity to be independent at work is not entirely driven by exogenous and objective factors. It is also enhanced or inhibited by certain endogenous factors that stem from the individual's character and personality traits.

DISCRETIONARY LATITUDE OF AGENTS

With experience, Nancy Smart has become aware of the trade-off that individual employees must make between: what they bring to the job and what they get out of it. This was a major factor in her decision to take on the project at ExPlus. She can expect her teammates to do the same on their own terms.

Managerial discretion, like the trade-offs we discussed before, is part of organizational life. In a project, it means that agents first try to meet the contractual requirements of their positions vis-à-vis the organization or the project. These requirements will translate into profitability or performance objectives. Failure by managers to meet these obligations can threaten their standing. However, once they achieve the required level of profit or performance, managers are free to exercise some discretion and pursue more personal objectives (Migué & Bélanger, 1974).

When managing a project, the latitude of team members lets them shape the project, take it in a particular direction, independent of external constraints (Hirschman, 1967). However, Hirschman, one of the founders of project management, has also stressed that project team members are often caught between the propensity to take initiatives (latitude) and the limitations imposed by the project structure (pressures).

The implementation of a fuzzy project should rely on a dialectical approach that bridges the formalization imposed by the project structure (see Chapter 1) and the flexibility needed to respond to complexity and uncertainty (Sun, Zhu, Sun, Müller, & Yu, 2020). Some agents will be more willing to accept things in the organization and adapt the project to fit within its context. Others will take more risks, demonstrate autonomy and creativity, develop innovative solutions to the challenges posed by the project, and thus endeavor to change the organizational context. While the former exercise a narrow latitude, the latter take on more. Some will conform to a stricter discipline, the latter will be less inclined to do the same (Hirschman, 1967).

Limited managerial latitude is well suited to a rigid structure set up for efficiency. It has a high degree of formalization, close project supervision, tight control over task execution, and a directive project management style. That is how a construction company can build a series of row houses efficiently. However, wide latitude is useful in the face of complexity and uncertainty. Fuzzy projects require a more flexible structure, autonomous and flexible agents, and a participatory project management style to encourage cooperation and prompt initiative (Naveh, 2007; Sakka, Barki, & Côté, 2013); that's how unique projects come into being.

In practice, when given a great deal of latitude, the project manager can choose the most appropriate project management tools and techniques given the nature of the project and the sociopolitical context that surrounds it (Morris, Crawford, Hodgson, Shepherd, & Thomas, 2006). They tend to adapt more effectively to changing project circumstances and are better equipped to counter threats and seize opportunities as they emerge. They also tend to give the other team members more latitude and let them choose how to carry out their assigned tasks, including selecting the tools and techniques they will use. Agents working on fuzzy projects may need high discretionary latitude (see Table 8.1).

The examples shown earlier illustrate the various levels of discretionary latitude of project agents. Employees such as Dina Campion of Starbucks and Barry Bertiger of Motorola had a lot of latitude to carry out the Frappuccino and Iridium development projects, respectively, even when their supervisors or top management initially rejected their initiatives (see Chapter 3). Similarly, Arthur Fry (3M Post-it sticky notes) and Richard Drew (Scotch tape) both faced repeated setbacks while developing their products. At some point, each was ordered by senior management to cut their losses and move on. However, despite many roadblocks, they kept working on their pet project, which eventually became a great success for their respective companies (Govindarajan & Srinivas, 2013).

TABLE 8.1 Discretionary Latitude of Agents in Various Contexts

	NARROW LATITUDE	WIDE LATITUDE
Organizational Structure	Rigid	Flexible
Degree of Formalization	High	Low
Project Supervision or Managerial Control	Narrow	Ample
Project Management Style	Direct	Participatory
Autonomy of Agents	Low	High
Operating Word	Control	Managerial discretion
Flexibility of the Managerial Approach	Low	Strong
Discipline	Strong	Low
Appropriate Managerial Approach	Rational	Political or psychosocial

Source: Adapted from Ika & Söderlund (2016).

The wide latitude and persistence exercised by these four project actors led to "successful failures." They allowed their organizations to break free of a trap, which could be called "Catch-22 Success," in reference to Joseph Heller's classic 1955 American novel *Catch-22*.[2] "Wanting to be very successful can translate into a tendency to play it safe and not suffer any kind of failure" (Mans, 2002).

There is a downside to agents having too much discretionary latitude. Google had to halt its controversial search engine project in China, Dragonfly, because some project agents with a high degree of autonomy and latitude "leaked" information about it (Google was trying to keep it confidential). They mobilized Google employees and formed a coalition that fiercely opposed the project. It was the same for Google's Maven project. Also secretive and controversial, this US$9 million-plus project between the US Department of Defense and Google aimed to use artificial intelligence software to analyze video footage shot by US military drones. Though *Forbes* magazine reported that the Maven project might still live on with a group of startups associated with a Google sister venture capital company, Google was forced to back out publicly due to the opposition of rebellious agents with strong latitude (Brewster, 2021).[3]

LOCUS OF CONTROL

The degree of autonomy exercised by managers is also a function of their values and subjective assessment of their situation. Specifically, it depends on their *locus of control* (Paquet, 2006)—that is, the extent to which they individually feel they can control their careers and personal destinies. Since each individual's internal or external locus of control is a matter of degree, many combinations of exogenous and endogenous factors are possible for each manager (see Box 8.1).

BOX 8.1

Some Notes on Locus of Control

In personality psychology, the "locus of control" refers to an individual's perception about what drives the main events in their life (Rotter, 1971). One's locus is *internal* if they believe they have a great deal of control over their destiny (thanks to perseverance, for example), as opposed to *external,* if they believe that what happens to their life is essentially beyond their control (such as fate or luck).

A person's locus of control can be measured using psychological tests along a scale with two extremes, internal and external. This measure is predictive of individual performance in many spheres of activity, including work. Whether in organizations, academic settings, or sports, individuals with an internal locus of control are more likely to attribute their successes and failures to the effort they put in ("I worked really hard" or "I did not give 100 percent"). On the other hand, those with an external locus of control perceive themselves as rather powerless pawns on a chessboard. For them, the environment, luck, and "others" have a predominant influence on their lives.

The locus of control appears to be a stable psychological trait that is not significantly affected by life experiences, either positive or negative (Buddelmeyer & Powdthavee, 2016). Tests were given to individuals whose lives changed radically—following natural disasters, bankruptcies, or long illnesses, or conversely on those who had a peaceful life, won the lottery, or experienced professional success. Follow-up tests showed that these individuals did not significantly change their point of view on how and why their lives changed. Their locus of control was the same prior and after the life-changing events.

People with a high internal locus of control are more likely to attempt to influence organizational policies, their working conditions, and their relationships with supervisors and subordinates. As P. E. Spector refers to them in Levitin (2014), "Externals make more compliant followers or subordinates than do internals, who are likely to be independent and resist control by superiors and other individuals.[. . .] Externals, because of their greater compliance, would probably be easier to supervise as they would be more likely to follow directions." A combination of high autonomy and high internal control is associated with high productivity. *Internals* consider that "*they* get things done," while externals tend to think that "things are getting done." Internals perform better in a project that requires adaptability, more complex learning, initiative, and motivation.

Managers with a high internal locus of control are more likely to feel satisfied at work and believe that their quality of life depends more on their actions. Because they are less likely to think that success is mainly a matter of luck, they are more likely to feel that they have a high degree of discretionary latitude. Their personal perceptions influence how they act and make decisions in the workplace.

While it is not clear that locus of control determines the performance of team leaders (Keller, 2017), it does affect how teams execute projects. Projects may need managers with different loci of control. For example, those with a high external locus of control assess more realistically the skills needed to meet challenges. On the other hand, managers with a high internal locus of control can tap into their emotional and mental resources to complete projects successfully (Berg & Karlsen, 2016). Most projects need this duality or ambidexterity. This speaks volumes about the various psychosocial profiles needed in a project.

In strategic and operations management, employees with similar profiles are grouped together within specialized units, such as departments of information technology, human resources, marketing, production, or finance. This approach is quite different from what happens in project management. There, the multidisciplinary nature of projects requires the formation of heterogeneous teams. The project team members are chosen for their distinctive know-how, experience, and interpersonal skills. Far from being random, this variety is desired and sought after since projects are by nature multidisciplinary.

In Chapter 7, we saw how much the expectations of principals can vary. Expectations differ from one agent to another and also between the groups of principals and of agents. The potential for disagreement, discord, and the formation of coalitions is very real. At the beginning of the project, it is less likely that the agents share the same perspective since they do not have common skills, backgrounds, or history. Moreover, they are not likely to benefit from the project in the same way. These subjective and objective differences surface periodically as the project unfolds.

iPhone 1 is a good example of the *political tribulations* that can develop within a project team. The new phone was launched in 2007, after three years of effort and costing over US$150 million. It sold 270,000 units in its first two days and 3.4 million units in just six months. However, this technological and commercial success overshadows the trepidation and political scheming that occurred within its team and sometimes in full view of Steve Jobs, chairman and CEO of the Cupertino firm, Apple.

The primary battle was between two Apple executives whom Jobs let compete to see who would come up with the best product. The first was Tony Fadell, a brilliant man with little tolerance for poor quality work or ideas. Fadell was the head of the iPod division representing 40 percent of Apple's revenues. At the beginning of the project, he was responsible for the software engineering for the phone. His rival was the engaging and dramatic Scott Forstall, who had worked with Jobs longer than any other executive. At the time of the iPhone's development, he oversaw the development of Safari and Mail, and used his engineering expertise to help develop the phone's hardware.

Fadell and Forstall had two different visions for the iPhone. Fadell and his engineers wanted to develop the iPhone from the iPod. But Forstall's engineers secretly created an operating system based on the Mac OS X version. This is the unlikely option that Jobs finally chose, allowing Forstall to control the project and recruit some of Fadell's best engineers. As a result, the work climate became poisonous for the engineers working under the two men. Some described it as a "snake pit" (Vogelstein, 2013a, 2013b, 2017). Furthermore, the relentless pace for the several hundred engineers who worked 80 hours a week and sometimes seven days a week took its toll. Some project team members experienced burnout, and others left Apple shortly after the project was completed.

THE ORGANIZATION: A CONVERGENCE OF INTERESTS

As we underscored with the political perspective, project management cannot be reduced to simply executing the mandate or satisfying the principals. The project also serves the personal interests of the agents who implement it. A project is a place where individual motivations converge with organizational objectives:

> [W]e can only note that all collective projects are characterized by the central and determining role, but not the exclusive role, of an individual actor, or a small group of individual actors, playing the role of a catalyst. This individual actor, if necessary equipped with a charismatic authority, will exploit pre-existing social expectations within an organization. From this meeting, or rather from this conjunction, the collective action will be born. (Translated from Boutinet, 2005)

From a political perspective, the project is conducted in an influential *external environment* with which it has a dynamic relationship. However, when we focus on the agents, we can appreciate their importance as well. The project turns out to be also dependent on its *internal environment,* a psychosocial milieu in which individuals with distinct profiles and interests operate.

The team must come to agree somewhat on the meaning of the project and the mandate it receives since the latter cannot simply be imposed as in the rational perspective. For example, architects do not have the same conception of a project's success as do engineers, accountants, or market analysts. But as the work progresses, team members interpret and reevaluate the project's goals, individually and collectively. They constantly reinterpret what they are doing in the project and thus make sense of it. They clarify what they are learning and create the reality of the project through their individual and collective actions (Weick, 1969; Katz & Kahn, 1978). In so doing, they gradually redraw the shape and scope of the project (see the just described roles of Fadell and Forstall in shaping the iPhone 1 project).

A successful project must also satisfy the expectations of its agents. Since communication is a primary function of management, rhetoric and symbolism help stimulate the agents, channel their energies, and highlight their achievements. In turn, each person makes their own assessment of the project and uses personal communication tools to highlight their individual contribution and their contribution to the collective effort. This multifaceted assessment becomes the criterion of success par excellence because the project's "success" is a social construction, and the members' stories give meaning to the actions taken and to the results achieved (see Ika, 2009).

SENSEMAKING BY AGENTS

The organization is by essence a system of coordinated actions. It "is what is being constructed or deconstructed through interactions among people" (Vidaillet, 2009). In this social dynamic, employees, managers, and leaders do not just fit into organizational molds and play predetermined roles. Instead, they progressively "enact" their organizational environment according to their personal values and beliefs, the choices they favor, the decisions they make, and the sense they give to their work.

The manager's influence is often greater in major projects. This is because, unlike the organization's day-to-day activities, project-related activities are designed *de novo*, free from the burden of the actions and deeds of yesterday's actors. Given the risk of anomia posed by an often "unattainable success" (as measured by the time-cost-quality triangle) and its attendant loss of meaning (see Chapter 5), project team members (agents) cannot simply do their job and deliver the goods, without considering themselves. For a project to be successful, agents need to have the sense of having succeeded personally. Success is, therefore, much more than meeting the expectations imposed by others (such as principals or teammates) regarding efficiency (e.g., time, cost, quality triangle) or effectiveness (e.g., increasing market share) (Kreiner, 2014).

The perspective that we need to consider is that the role played by the organization's employees and leaders is not limited to *what they do,* as workers, managers, or salespeople within a particular project or organization. Their role also includes *who they are,* as individuals and as members of society. We should remember that many upper managers are hired because of their roles and connections in the external environment. They serve as a bridge between the internal and external environments of the organization, since it is their strategic role to anticipate, interpret, and mediate the respective requirements of these environments. Leaders also act on the entire organization to integrate its various parts (Hambrick, 1989; Keck & Tushman, 1993).

The ambiguity inherent in how work is performed and the uncertainty of their environment places "sensemaking" as the central organizational issue for managers (Weick, 2001). Therefore, team members interpret and, if necessary, "create the reality" of the project. Each member tries to carve out their place, and together they shape the project through their individual interpretation and actions.

But how do you know what matters to your teammates? Although she may not have access to the psychological profiles of her team members, Nancy Smart can get some insights about who they are and what matters to them from their résumés, career histories, and even social media platforms, where people express their views on different matters.

THE IMPACT OF STRUCTURES AND OTHER EXTRINSIC FACTORS

The *structure of an organization* refers to the various ways of *dividing* and *coordinating* collective work to create an enduring pattern of behavior. First, the division of labor allows for increased productivity through specialization and economies of scale, to be *efficient*. From this division stems the need to coordinate, which ensures that the different activities lead to coherent results, to be *effective*. The purpose of coordination is to try to put the various pieces back together again, just like the pieces of the legendary Humpty Dumpty after he fell off the wall.

The work carried out in the organization can be divided in a variety of ways, depending on the technology used and its corresponding body of knowledge and practices (e.g., farming by hand or with tractors). This technology varies with the organization's size, strategy, sector, environment, and so on. Mintzberg (1993) identified five types of structural configurations:[4]

1. The **simple structure** is typical of young or small organizations, with limited resources and a focused market that can adapt quickly to changes in their environment.
2. A **machine bureaucracy** is characterized by centralized control and regulated decision-making, to offer standardized goods and services on a very large scale, like electricity or mail services. It is the typical structure of government agencies, manufacturers, and banks.
3. A **professional bureaucracy** is also standardized, but by the rules of the profession. Vis-à-vis the organization, employees have more autonomy and decision-making is largely driven by the practices of their respective professions. Professional bureaucracies are common in health care, education, engineering, and law firms.
4. A **divisional structure** is common in large, diversified organizations, like GE and Walt Disney. That structure offers an umbrella of funds or brand name to its divisions, each with its distinct products, markets, organizational structure and coordinating mechanism.
5. An **adhocracy** is a structure that is temporary (i.e. ad hoc). It is commonly used in projects, high-tech industries, arts and

entertainment, for example. Innovation and decentralized decision-making are two of its distinguishing features.

These five basic structures (see Table 8.2) represent "pure" types of organizational structures. With these basic archetypes, we can describe the full range of organizational structures, just as we can produce almost any color with three primary colors. Although there are many variations and combinations, the number of viable structures is limited because only specific configurations are coherent and manageable in the long term. For instance, a simple structure could not be used for a large hospital or in a company the size of Walmart.

In the first two chapters, we saw that the *division of labor* is a fundamental characteristic of any organization, regardless of the strategic, operations, or project management methods used in its various parts. The structure of the sponsoring organization and of the project itself have a significant impact on the amount of discretion the agents will have.

TABLE 8.2 Organizational Structures and Their Coordination Mechanisms

STRUCTURAL CONFIGURATION	DOMINANT COORDINATION MECHANISMS (supported by the others)
Simple Structure	**Direct supervision of employees** through instructions and monitoring; common in entrepreneurial organizations
Machine Bureaucracy	**Standardization of processes** with precise job descriptions (e.g., the McDonald's "bible" of procedures, regulations in the civil service or in banking)
Professional Bureaucracy	**Standardization of skills** which relies primarily on professional training, or licensing by regulatory bodies (e.g., accountants, lawyers, nurses, engineers, pharmacists)
Divisional Structure	**Standardization of outputs** through coordination by objectives rather than processes; common in diversified organizations
Adhocracy	**Mutual adjustment** through coordination by informal communication among employees; common in innovative organizations and projects

Source: Based on Mintzberg (1993).

THE ROLE OF INTRINSIC FACTORS

While the organizational structure constrains the manager and other employees, it is not a straitjacket for them. Based on Mintzberg's (1973) on-site observations of top executives, and corroborated by other researchers in other contexts, it is more folklore than fact to view managerial work as a plan, organize, direct, coordinate, and control (PODCC) sequence. Similarly, the rational model outlined in Chapter 6 is more a prescription than a real description of what managers actually do. It is also a myth that the project manager primarily makes and executes plans methodically by applying a PODCC approach.

The modern manager wears different hats, as a leader, liaison, symbolic representative of the unit, and allocator of resources. Whether gathering or sharing information and interacting with people, the manager constantly makes and influences decisions. The fuzzier the project, the more salient the internal, external, and inter-organizational issues become. Indeed, the manager must lead and coordinate the project politically and socially, dealing with tensions between the different levels of objectives implied by their mandate and the divergences between internal and external stakeholders (Ika & Saint-Macary, 2012).

Most decisions made by managers have a psychosocial component because they affect people personally and in the workplace. It is particularly important to understand the coordination mechanisms in place in the organization and in the project. The manner in which supervision is exercised in the simple structure of a factory, for instance, will be quite different from how it happens in a hospital, which is a professional bureaucracy.

Some mechanisms are formal and put into place to guide the work done in different units and at different levels. Others are practiced informally by the employees. Whether formal or informal, these mechanisms are also distinguished by their scope: while some are organization-wide, others are used in interactions limited to two or three employees. Figures 8.1 and 8.2 highlight the coordination mechanisms, nature, and scope of the types of interactions used in organization. Figure 8.3 examines the latitude of agents in relation to the role of intrinsic and extrinsic factors.

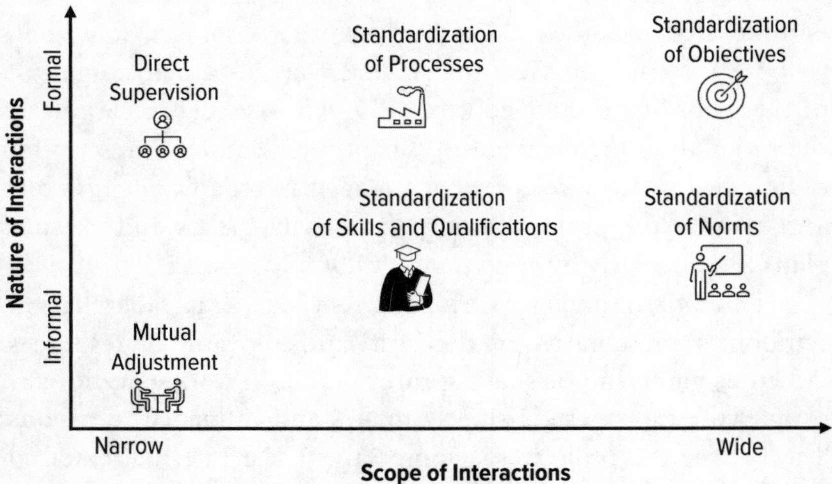

FIGURE 8.1 Coordination mechanisms and types of interaction between employees

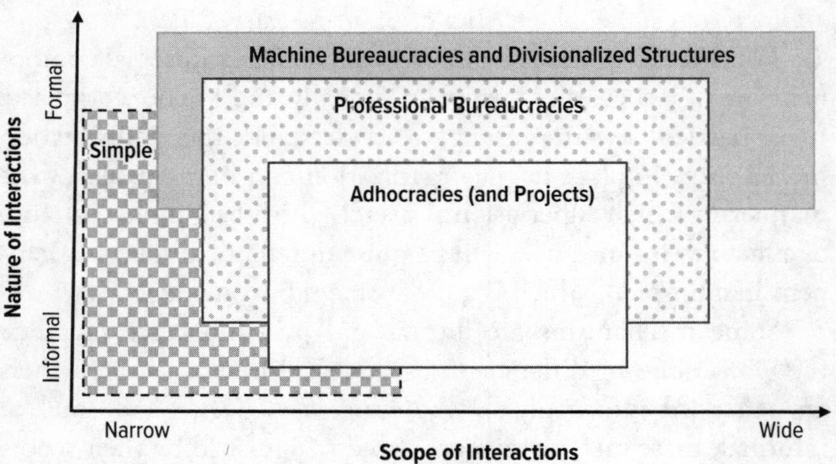

FIGURE 8.2 Employee interactions by type of organizational structure

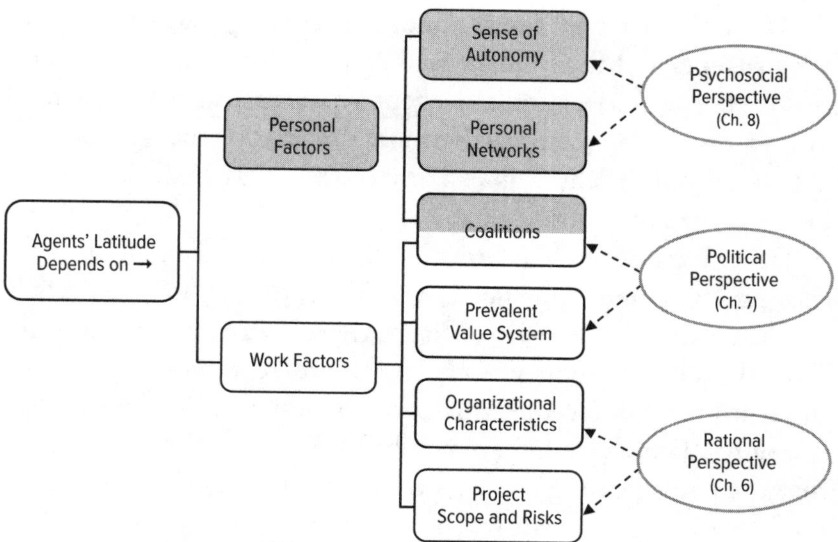

FIGURE 8.3 Determinants of agents' discretionary latitude

In Chapter 7, we saw that expectations vary a lot among principals. Now, we see that the same is true among agents in the project team. Hence, the potential for disagreements within each team, and between the two, is very real.

VANOC TAKE III: FOCUS ON THE AGENTS[5]

First, a brief recap. The *rational perspective* (Chapter 6) is based on the *mandate,* which is assumed to reflect the purpose of the project and the stable preferences of the *principals.* The *political perspective* (Chapter 7) focuses on the *principals,* taking into account their changing interests and roles. In turn, the *psychosocial perspective* (Chapter 8) puts the spotlight on the *agents* (i.e., the project team members). It asserts that who the agents *are*—not just what they *do* formally—impacts the project's evolution and performance.

By considering the influence of the *psychological characteristics* of the agents and the *social dimension* of their work environment, we can better understand the agents' actions and their potential impact on the project. Furthermore, analyzing the agents' profiles at the outset may help explain, or even anticipate, key events in the evolution of the project.

The psychosocial lens brings to light a number of factors concerning the language issues at the Vancouver Olympics. A key psychosocial characteristic of the VANOC team stands out right from the start: though French Canadians represent a quarter of the country's population, this pan-Canadian project committee had only 1 French Canadian member out of 20. It is not surprising that the committee ignored its contractual obligations regarding French-language content when implementing the games.

Here are some of the specific *language issues* that emerged during this project:

- The opening ceremonies were criticized concerning the lack of French. As the project evolved, Opening Ceremonies Producer-Director David Atkins became "increasingly annoyed with the French argument" (Furlong & Mason, 2011). Similarly, VANOC was criticized for minimal use of French during the Olympic Torch Relay across the country. (Their "rational" explanation: the low proportion of French-speaking residents in the cities.)
- Committee President John Furlong's inability to express himself in French was an issue even before he got elected to that position (which got delayed for that very reason).
- The committee failed to involve francophone organizations like Cirque du Soleil and iconic French Canadian celebrities like Céline Dion and Gilles Vigneault.

Criticized for insufficient use of French, VANOC members rectified the situation in time for the closing ceremonies. This illustrates how agents give meaning and direction to the mandate, though it remains formally unchanged.

The psychosocial lens also sheds light on why VANOC originally scheduled most competitions at Cypress, although Whistler was a better choice meteorologically. Cypress was close to Vancouver, but this meant the site was constantly overcrowded, and lines were ridiculously long even to buy hot drinks. It turned out to be a poor choice logistically, as well: buses had difficulty climbing the steep hills, and many broke down (Furlong & Masson, 2011). It can be inferred that the wrong choice was made because the committee was stacked against Whistler. The federal and provincial governments were each represented by three VANOC members, and an additional two more from the City of Vancouver, for a total of eight. In contrast, Whistler (the alternative site) only had two members on the committee.

Furthermore, the eight-member pro-Vancouver coalition was tightly knit. First, the three members appointed to VANOC by the provincial premier of British Columbia were closely connected. Many knew each other personally and had developed social, and sometimes nebulous, ties through a shared relationship with British Columbia's Liberal premier, Gordon Campbell. These prior relationships fostered an *esprit de corps* or coalition inside the pro-Vancouver group. In addition, they all had a high degree of personal autonomy, and many were financially self-sufficient—an important factor for asserting managerial discretion. More specifically:

- Ken Dobell, a former member of Parliament for the premier of British Columbia, was the city manager of Vancouver.
- Following the election of John Furlong as VANOC's chief executive officer,[6] the *Vancouver Sun* ran the headline "Premier 'rigged' 2010 games competition and endorsed inferior candidate."

- Jack Poole, who received only $1 per year for his role in VANOC, agreed to join only if John Furlong did the same (Furlong & Masson, 2011).
- Peter Brown was the cofounder of the country's largest securities firm.
- Rusty Goepel and Richard Turner were major donors and fundraisers for the B.C. Liberal Party.

EXECUTION SUCCESS, BUT NOT FOR ALL?

Projecting beyond their formal mandate, members of the committee formulated their own vision that reflected their own sensemaking of "building a stronger Canada, driven by its passion for sport, culture and sustainable development." Indeed, Canada broke the record for most gold medals won by a host nation in a Winter Games. The games were delivered on time and within budget, a major feat for sure. Yet to deem the project an overall success solely under a purely rational lens is to overlook that it underperformed in important areas for some key stakeholders.

From a rational perspective these failures, which cast doubt about the overall success of the project, might be dismissed as regrettable or outside the scope of managing the project. By taking into account the agents' personal views of the project, their discretionary latitude, and the composition of their team we can explain certain important issues that are overlooked or seem unavoidable.

First, the linguistic composition of the team made it less likely that it would be very concerned with meeting the contractual obligations regarding the use of French. Second, Cypress may have been chosen over Whistler because the latter carried little political weight.

There was another thorny issue that made the headlines worldwide and cast a dark cloud over the games: the tragic death of a Georgian luger at the start of the games. It raised questions about the speed of the track, its design, and its level of safety. The psychosocial perspective would bring us to consider that the committee was under pressure to set speed records and that it had been warned regarding that specific track. In the coroner's report, the president of the International Luge Federation indicated that "in his opinion, the track was not supplied as ordered. However, he also offered that there was no expectation on his part that VANOC would try to do anything to lower the track speed." For their part, the VANOC members saw the death of the athlete as a tragic but unavoidable "accident" (Furlong & Mason, 2011). The wall on the last curve of the Whistler Olympic track was promptly raised, preventing any further accidents.

CONCLUSION

The *psychosocial perspective* holds that how agents perform their work is in part guided by *who they are* as individuals, in interaction with others, and that objective and subjective factors guide their actions. Some agents believe that the forces shaping their personal and professional lives are *internal* and within their control (such as their actions and effort). Others believe that the course of their lives is determined primarily by *external* factors beyond their control (such as chance or "other people").

These psychosocial factors play out within the constraints and opportunities set by the structures of the project and of the parent organization. How work is divided and coordinated at these two levels will determine in part how freely the agents can act. The structures reflect the technology used, the leaders' preferences, the age of the parent organization, its size, and the importance of the project. The compatibility between the organizational and project structures and the psychological profiles of the agents are a source of both synergy and conflict. Managers should consider these factors in dealing with fuzzy projects. The chapter proffers five takeaways for project sponsors and project managers:

1. The psychosocial approach focuses on the agents in the project team and their perspectives and interests. It considers their profiles as individuals and their social interactions within the project and outside. Though they work to achieve the project's common goal, they are also motivated by individual, subjective, and even selfish considerations. These interests are distinct from but not entirely congruent with those of the project and its principals.
2. The agents contribute to the objective of the project while exercising some personal discretion, formally known as managerial discretion. Once they meet their contractual requirements and the project is on target, agents use their discretion to pursue their interests and personal objectives.
3. Managerial discretion is exercised more freely when the organization's structure is compatible with the project's structure. For instance, managers of innovative projects find it harder to exercise their discretion in a project carried out within a bureaucratic organization. The greater the discretionary latitude of the agents, the more they can shape the project to reflect their views and interests, within the constraints imposed by the project's structure and its degree of formalization. It is important to understand structures and, in particular, how work is divided and coordinated within the organization and the project.
4. Given the multidisciplinary and temporary nature of projects, they are staffed with individuals who have diverse psychosocial profiles. In addition, they have little time to adapt to one another. The degree of latitude of each agent varies according to their personal values and their subjective assessment of the situation. Much will depend on each person's *locus of control*. The more internal an

agent's locus of control, the more managerial discretion the agent is likely to exert.

5. Agents with a strong external locus of control assess more realistically the skills needed to meet challenges. But those with a strong internal locus of control draw on their emotional and mental resources to do their job. Should every agent be ambidextrous? No, for that is neither possible nor optimal. As in sports, teams with both left- and right-handed players have a big advantage.

A project is where individual and organization rationales and interests overlap in part. The project occurs in a social milieu in which individuals, with different interests and psychological profiles, interpret and evaluate the project through individual actions and perceptions. The project becomes a social construction borne out of their collective sensemaking. For a project to be a real success, each agent must also feel like the project has been a personal success.

REFERENCES

Berg, M. E., Karlsen, J. T., & Sarkis, J. (2016). A study of coaching leadership style practice in projects. *Management Research Review, 39*(9), 1122–1142.

Boutinet, J-P. (2005). *Anthropologie du projet*. Quadrige.

Brewster, T. (2021, 8 September). Eric Schmidt and James Murdoch are building AI and facial recognition surveillance tools for the pentagon. *Forbes*. https://www.forbes.com/sites/thomasbrewster/2021/09/08/project-maven-startups-backed-by-google-peter-thiel-eric-schmidt-and-james-murdoch-build-ai-and-facial-recognition-surveillance-for-the-defense-department/?sh=4ba460466ef2 (accessed 29 April 2022).

Buddelmeyer, H., & Powdthavee, N. (2016). Can having internal locus of control insure against negative shocks? Psychological evidence from panel data. *Journal of Economic Behavior & Organization, 122,* 88–109.

Chiocchio, F., Kelloway, E. K., & Hobbs, B. (Eds.). (2015). *The psychology and management of project teams.* Oxford University Press.

Furlong, J., & Mason, G. (2011). *Patriot hearts: Inside the Olympics that changed a country.* Douglas & McIntyre.

Gangloff, B. (1998). Niveau hiérarchique, style de management et infortunes de la norme d'internalité. *Revue québécoise de psychologie, 19*(2), 29–45.

Govindarajan, V., & Srinivas, S. (2013). The innovation mindset in action: 3M Corporation. *Harvard Business Review,* 6 August. https://hbr.org/2013/08/the-innovation-mindset-in-acti-3.

Hambrick, D. C. (1989). Putting top managers back in the strategy picture-introduction. *Strategic Management Journal, 10,* 5–15.

Hirschman, A. O. (1967). *Development projects observed.* Brookings Institution.

Jensen, M. C., & Meckling, W. H. (1976). Theory of the firm: Managerial behavior, agency costs and ownership structure. *Journal of Financial Economics, 3*(4), 305–360.

Katz, D., & Kahn, R.L. (1978). *The Social psychology of organization.* Wiley.

Keck, S. L., & Tushman, M. L. (1993). Environmental and organizational context and executive team structure. *Academy of Management Journal, 36*(6), 1314–1344.

Keller, R. T. (2017). A longitudinal study of the individual characteristics of effective R&D project team leaders. *R&D Management, 47*(5), 741–754.

Kreiner, K. (2014). Restoring project success as phenomenon. In R.A. Lundin, & M. Hällgreen (Eds.), *Advancing research on projects and temporary organizations*, Copenhagen Business School Press & Liber (pp. 21–40).

Ika, L.A. (2009). Project success as a topic in project management journals. *Project Management Journal, 40*(4), 6–19.

Ika, L. A., & Saint-Macary, J. (2012). The project planning myth in international development. *International Journal of Managing Projects in Business, 5*(3), 420–439.

Ika, L. A., & Söderlund, J. (2016). Rethinking revisited: insights from an early rethinker. *International Journal of Managing Projects in Business, 9*(4), 931–954.

Levitin, D. J. (2014). *The organized mind: Thinking straight in the age of information overload.* Penguin.

Manz, C. C. (2002). *The power of failure: 27 ways to turn life's setbacks into success*. BerrettKoehler.

Maurel, D. (2010). Sense-making: un modèle de construction de la réalité et d'appréhension de l'information par les individus et les groupes. *Études de communication. Langages, information, médiations, 35*, 31–46.

Migué, J.-L., & Bélanger G. (1974). Toward a general theory of managerial discretion. *Public Choice, 17*(1), 27–47.

Mintzberg, H. (1973). *The nature of managerial work*. Harper & Row.

Mintzberg, H. (1993). *Structure in fives: Designing effective organizations*. Prentice-Hall.

Morris, P. W. G., Crawford, L., Hodgson, D., Shepherd, M. M., & Thomas, J. (2006). Exploring the role of formal bodies of knowledge in defining a profession-The case of project management. *International Journal of Project Management, 24*, 710–721.

Naveh, E. (2007). Formality and discretion in successful R&D projects. *Journal of Operations Management, 25*, 110–125.

Office of the Commissioner of Official Languages (2010). *A golden opportunity: Vancouver 2010. Final report on the Olympic and Paralympic games*. Cat. no.: SF31-106/201.

Paquet, Y. (2006). *Relation entre locus de contrôle, désir de contrôle et anxiété*. Masson.

Pinto, J. K. (2014). Project management, governance, and the normalization of deviance. *International Journal of Project Management, 32*, 376–387.

Rotter, J. B. (1971). Locus of control scale. *Psychology Today, 42*.

Saint-Macary, J., & Ika, L. A. (2015). Atypical perspectives on project management: moving beyond the rational, to the political and the psychosocial. *International Journal of Project Organisation and Management, 7*(3), 236–250.

Sakka, O., Barki, H., & Côté, L. (2013). Interactive and diagnostic uses of management control systems in I.S. projects: antecedents and their impact on performance. *Information & Management, 50*, 265–274.

Schmid, B., & Adams, J. (2008). Motivation in project management: The project manager's perspective. *Project Management Journal, 39*(2), 60–71.

Séguin-Bernard, F., & Chanlat, J. F. (1987). *L'analyse des organisations: Une anthologie sociologique. Tome II: Les composantes de l'organisation*. G. Morin.

Seiler, S., Bogdan, L., Malgorzata, P., & Pinazza, M. (2012). An integrated model of factors influencing project managers' motivation—Findings from a Swiss Survey. *International Journal of Project Management, 30*(1), 60–72.

Sun, X., Zhu, F., Sun, M, Müller, R., & Yu, M. (2020). Facilitating efficiency and flexibility ambidextrousness in project-based organizations: An exploratory study of organizational antecedents. *Project Management Journal, 5*(15), 556–572.

Vidaillet, B. (2009). *Le sens de l'action : Sociopsychologie de l'organisation.* Vuibert, 2009.

Vogelstein, F. (2013a). *Dogfight: How Apple and Google went to war and started a revolution.* Straus and Giroux.

Vogelstein, F. (2013b, 6 October). And then Steve said let there be an iPhone. New York Times. https://www.nytimes.com/2013/10/06/magazine/and-then-steve-said-let-there-be-an-iphone.html (accessed 29 April 2022).

Vogelstein, F. (2017, 28 June). Inside Apple's 6-month race to make the first iPhone a reality. Wired.com. https://www.wired.com/story/iphone-history-dogfight/ (accessed 29 April 2022).

Weber, M. (1921/1968). *Economy and society.* In G. Roth, & C. Wittich (Eds., Trans.) Bedminster Press.

Weick, K.E. (1969). *The social psychology of organizing.* Addison-Wesley.

Weick, K. E. (2001). *Making sense of the organization.* Blackwell Publishers.

Williamson, O.E. (1963). Managerial discretion and business behavior. *The American Economic Review, 53*(5), 1032–1057.

Wynn, C., Smith, L., & Killen, C. (2021). How power influences behavior in projects: A theory of planned behavior perspective. *Project Management Journal, 52*(6), 607–621.

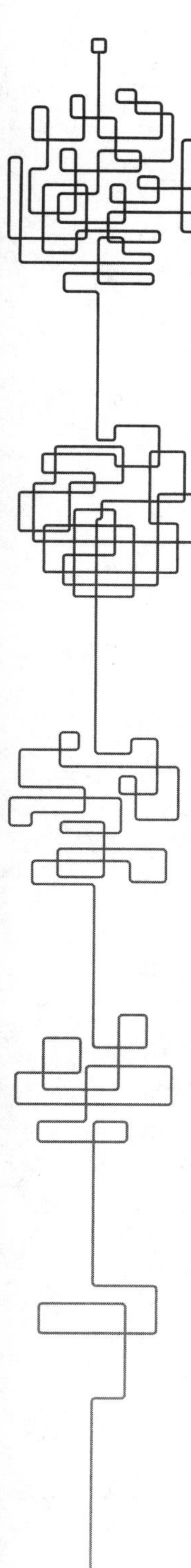

CHAPTER 9

PROJECT MANAGEMENT IN 3D

NOT ALL PROJECTS ARE CREATED EQUAL

"I suppose it is tempting, if the only tool you have is a hammer, to treat everything as if it were a nail."[1] *This phrase is on Nancy's mind as she contemplates the politics and the human aspects of projects. She expects these factors to play a role in the ExPlus project as well.*

From experience, Nancy Smart senses that the nature of this project and its organizational context are different from what she has previously faced. She is concerned that traditional techniques may not provide good results in this complex environment because of technical issues, external pressures, team management, hidden agendas, and divergent stakeholder objectives.

But she is also torn because she was not hired to play politics or pop psychologist. What is the "smart" thing to do? Without becoming paranoid and seeing political and psychosocial problems everywhere, Nancy can get a fuller sense of the situation by looking at the project's mandate, principals, and agents through a new lens.

NEAT AND EFFICIENT

The rational approach is the dominant framework in project management thinking and practice. The assumptions and parameters underpinning this approach are simple albeit demanding: the principals form a relatively homogeneous and stable block; they give a clearly stated formal mandate to the agents; and the goals of principals and agents are aligned and both groups are devoted to carrying out the tasks required.

The focus in this approach is to optimize the resources used in the project's execution. Given such stringent constraints, the project manager aims to meet the official objectives, but nothing more. For the same reasons, the agents are expected to work exclusively on the mandate, and the principals must stay united and consistent. Since the mandate serves as a reference document and the project plan as a road map, any significant deviation may lead to cost and time overruns or lower quality.

This reductionist approach results in a "well-managed" project that respects the well-known time, cost, and quality constraints. Beyond being a simple way of managing a project, it provides everyone with a common framework for perceiving and conceiving the project from beginning to end.

The rational approach has greatly simplified the management of projects by systematizing the process. It also works well in relatively stable project contexts where key elements can be broken down and reduced to unambiguous ones for management and control purposes.

However, this is not always possible. We will look at the contexts that give rise to "fuzzy" projects, in contrast to the contexts of neat projects that can produce clear, stable, and measurable mandates.

FUZZY BUT EFFECTIVE

Unlike neat projects, fuzzy projects are polymorphic and thus take substantially different forms. Fuzzy projects have one of these characteristics to a high degree, or several of them to lesser degrees:

1. A mandate that cannot be specified at the outset and is likely to evolve
2. A mandate that focuses more on results than on optimizing the use of resources
3. Several powerful principals who are actively involved and who have divergent expectations
4. Agents who have a personal interest in the project or enjoy a great deal of personal autonomy

An Uncertain Mandate

While the neat project has an explicit, circumscribed, and stable mandate, a distinguishing characteristic of a fuzzy project is that its mandate is ambiguous or likely to change significantly over time. The objectives in a fuzzy project are not very tangible, are often unstated, evolve with the circumstances, or may only be met long after the formal completion of the project.

Nancy was familiar with the moon landing in 1969, the first great achievement of the space program that President Kennedy had launched in 1961. But was she aware that this seemingly scientific endeavor took root in politically charged circumstances and was also expected to achieve nonscientific objectives? President Kennedy was narrowly elected in 1960, and a year later he was struggling to recover from a resounding failure dealing with the Cuban Bay of Pigs invasion. His Democratic party had lost seats in the House of Representatives, and the president was concerned about their chances in the forthcoming midterm congressional elections. The Americans were involved in a cold war against the

Soviets, who had seemingly pulled ahead in the great space race. The United States, the president, and his party were therefore in great need of a unifying project. But, what exactly? The seed for the moon mission took root in these circumstances.

Fuzzy projects are often borne out of uncertainty. For example, governments and businesses worldwide initiated a wide range of large-scale public and health-related projects during the COVID-19 pandemic and afterward. In particular, teleworking was used in public and private organizations with lasting effects. Like the US moon missions in the 1960s, these public and private projects generated cost overruns, along with significant economic, social, and technological results, including benefits that were not part of the project mandate and were unforeseen at the outset.

A Results-Focused Mandate

A mandate focused on optimizing results rather than on execution creates a puzzling situation. The most important expectations either are not well known or are hidden, which may complicate and hinder the execution of the project. Hence, the results can vary much more than with neat projects, and they may even lead to unintended consequences.

For example, projects aimed at increasing sales or reducing the spread of a disease may produce disappointing results or exceed expectations. Since these projects have high potential, some of the time, cost, and quality constraints must be tightened or relaxed to optimize results. In contrast, consider a project undertaken to make an older apartment complex fully wheelchair accessible. The principals are likely to aim for minimal compliance to the regulations if they think there is little to be gained by exceeding them. Contrary to the first example, such a neat project will most likely be managed under clear and strict constraints of time, cost, and quality.

Several Principals Actively Involved

Fuzziness is pervasive in multiorganizational projects, such as public-private partnership (PPP) projects where several principals have their say in decision-making. Other political or social projects, or those sponsored by principals with diverse interests, tend to place varied emphases on the constraints of time, cost, quality, and the types of project deliverables expected by different principals.

Autonomous Agents

These situations are common in cutting-edge projects that require a highly specialized team of experts, projects that bring together prominent or independent personalities, or projects that use volunteers as is the case for nonprofit organizations. Since volunteers are unpaid, the organization must allow them to "take their place"[2] by giving them a say. The unique characteristics of these projects mean that agents have a great deal of latitude to interpret and even negotiate the constraints surrounding the mandate. We also find a high degree of autonomy in committees or boards that have prestigious members.

As we show in the next sections, with any of the previous four characteristics that we discussed, fuzzy projects face uncertainty, not just risk (Gigerenzer, 2014; Knight, 1921) (see Box 9.1). With little formal consensus, fuzzy projects are fraught with sociopolitical complexity within the group of principals and the group of agents. Furthermore, these two groups may be socially distinct from one another (investors and scientists, for instance) (Geraldi, Maylor, & Williams, 2011; Maylor, Turner, & Murray-Webster, 2013) (see Box 9.2).

RISK: A CHALLENGE EVEN FOR NEAT PROJECTS

Neat projects, on the other hand, are those that originate from homogeneous and stable groups of principals, who give clear and precise mandates to teams of agents that are also homogeneous and stable. Such characteristics often lead project managers and principals to assume that their projects will evolve as planned since the time, cost, and quality parameters are well defined at the outset.

The project manager may be drawn into an "illusion of certainty" (Gigerenzer, 2014). At best, the risk parameters are presumed to be clear and measurable, making it possible to deal with "known unknowns" when forecasting future events. The manager can make probability calculations about future outcomes using trade-related concepts and tools. As a precaution, project risks are managed by attaching margins of error to the parameters—for example, a cost estimate of US$50,000 +/– a contingency of 10 percent.

Risk is a significant challenge, even for neat projects. For example, projects involving minor innovations (such as the latest Samsung and iPhone) or those in low-tech sectors or relatively stable markets are subject to risks that can derail them. In planning their implementation, the manager can use tools such as the Gantt chart and the Program Evaluation and Review Technique (PERT) graphs to optimize, in a risk context, the scheduling of the various project tasks by highlighting their interdependencies.

If the context can be mapped out in advance, the manager can also use the Critical Path Method (CPM) to define the critical path or the longest sequence of tasks required to complete the project within the planned timeframe. However, as mentioned in Chapter 6 on the rational approach, fuzzy projects (such as those with major innovations like the first iPhone) have high levels of complexity and uncertainty that may exceed the capabilities of traditional project management tools (Loch, 2017).

Uncertainty: A Major Challenge in Managing Fuzzy Projects

To deal with the complexity of a fuzzy project, the project manager must consider the mandate and the psychosocial and political factors that come into play as work progresses. In such instances, it is useful to consider many perspectives in viewing the project, and to use a dynamic approach to manage it.

Project management uses tools to deal with the risks that could hinder project implementation, even in instances when the time and scope cannot be accurately predicted. But the manager is less equipped to deal with some of the uncertainty that characterizes fuzzy projects. The uncertainty may come in the form of a vague mandate, which evolves as principals or agents change their views over time. The differences between risk and uncertainties are discussed in Box 9.1.

BOX 9.1

The Unknown: Risk and Uncertainty

It is essential to understand risk, a significant challenge in neat projects, and differentiate that factor from uncertainty, an even greater challenge in fuzzy projects.

The distinction we make between the risk found in neat projects and the uncertainty inherent to fuzzy projects stems from the works of University of Chicago economist Frank Knight (Knight, 1921) and a psychologist and director emeritus of the Max Planck Institute, Gerd Gigerenzer (Gigerenzer, 2014). Both highlight the difficulties practitioners encounter gathering knowledge and forecasting when faced with the complexity and vagaries of decision-making. They emphasize the paramount importance of the human factor in the contexts of risk and uncertainty. They also caution that in the face of uncertainty, calculation (even if probabilistic) is not enough to guide action. Beyond the knowledge and information available, intuition and "hunches" can help deliver successful projects.

The distinction between risk and uncertainty can help us distinguish the challenges encountered in traditional project management settings from those considered in this book. In a neat project, risk refers to a situation where all the relevant options, consequences, and associated probabilities can be known. A fuzzy project occurs in an uncertain context where the future is unknown and cannot be known.

If randomness can be measured with objective or subjective probability calculations, the project manager is dealing with risk. But if randomness cannot be measured, the project manager is dealing with uncertainty. In the face of risk, a reductionist management approach is appropriate. However, in the face of uncertainty, one should embrace uncertainty and not seek to reduce it. To that end, Gigerenzer (2014) suggests two categories of decision-making tools: probability calculations in a risk context and intuition and heuristics in an uncertainty context.

The project manager can mitigate risk by reducing its likelihood or its consequences. But this comes at a cost. To illustrate the point, consider how we manage the risk of having a car accident. We can reduce the occurrence of an accident by driving slowly, checking the brakes regularly, or cleaning the windshield. We can also reduce the consequences by wearing a seatbelt or having adequate insurance. Of course, if we decide not to drive at all, we avoid this type of risk altogether, but we forgo the benefits that come with driving. This withdrawal is akin to not going ahead with a project.

However, the project manager cannot do the same with regard to uncertainty, which is unpredictable and indeterminate, as Heisenberg's uncertainty principle shows. Generally, uncertainty is unforeseen because it is too unpredictable (a bird or a pebble hitting our windshield or, worse, hitting a deer) or poorly defined (a stressfull car ride).

It is customary to distinguish between the "known unknowns" that characterize risk (we are aware of the risk of having an accident, and we have statistics to guide us) and the "unknown unknowns" that characterize uncertainty (running into a bird or deer). This distinction between risk and uncertainty is one factor in ascertaining whether the project at hand is neat or fuzzy.

These "unknown unknowns" are hidden from the start, in the very definition of the parameters, and it would not be possible to calculate in advance their subsequent impact. At the outset, they bring into question the true nature of the mandate, the unspoken expectations of the principals, and the role that agents can actually play. By viewing the project in three dimensions (rational, political, and psychosocial) and involving both principals and agents, the manager can undertake a process of information gathering, assessment, and negotiation to identify and clarify the areas of uncertainty.

In addition to the risk/uncertainty distinction, it is important to gauge complexity,[3] a related and somewhat confusing concept. The project manager must also ascertain the level of sociopolitical complexity present in fuzzy projects, as explained in Box 9.2.

BOX 9.2

Divergence Among Stakeholders: Sociopolitical Complexity

Our views and emphasis on the sociopolitical complexity feature of fuzzy projects are based on the works of Geraldi et al. (2011) and Maylor et al. (2013). Geraldi et al. introduced the concept of sociopolitical complexity in project management. Subsequently Maylor et al. proposed three dimensions[4] of project complexity: structural, sociopolitical, and emergent or dynamic. More specifically:

- **Structural complexity** is intrinsic to the project and arises from the number, variety, and interaction among the various elements that make up the project deliverables and their completion.
- **Sociopolitical complexity** relates to the context of the project and the degree of divergence among the stakeholders' expectations.

- **Emergent complexity** relates to changing circumstances that influence the project's progress and dynamic changes in the project's structural and sociopolitical complexity profiles. It is, therefore, like risk or uncertainty.

Project managers attribute 80 percent of the challenge posed by complexity to structural and sociopolitical dimensions and 20 percent to emerging complexity (Maylor et al., 2013).

Neat and fuzzy projects may have high structural complexity, just as they may face different levels of risk or uncertainty, as noted in Box 9.1. In short, fuzzy projects differ from neat projects in that they are more uncertain or more complex, socially and politically. Fuzzy projects have multiple stakeholders with divergent or conflicting interests and changing expectations, while neat projects typically are characterized by a strong and stable consensus about their nature and their objectives.

Sociopolitical complexity is associated with the political and psychosocial dimensions of the project. First, there is divergence within the groups of principals and agents, and between these two groups. The complexity stems from principals who have divergent expectations of the project and from agents who do not agree on specific objectives or the means to achieve them, and who may exercise their personal latitude. While structural complexity may require technical ("hard") skills, sociopolitical complexity may require relational ("soft") skills, making it even more difficult to manage.

Several models exist to measure project complexity. An example is a tool developed by Maylor et al. (2013) that assesses—subjectively, but not arbitrarily—each dimension of project complexity on a "low-medium-high" scale (see Appendix 9.1).

Table 9.1 summarizes the different characteristics of neat and fuzzy projects. While fuzzy projects are fundamentally a quest, an experiment, or a discovery (Hirschman, 1967), neat projects are a deliberate leap into a planned future (Kreiner, 2020). As pointed out earlier, while neat projects evolve in a context of limited rationality, fuzzy projects exist in a broader context that encompasses the objective and subjective rationalities of principals and agents (Kreiner, 2020). Moreover, as discussed in Chapter 8, unlike neat projects whose managers may have limited autonomy, fuzzy projects require high autonomy from their agents (Hirschman, 1967).

TABLE 9.1 Distinguishing Characteristics of Neat and Fuzzy Projects

FEATURES	NEAT PROJECTS	FUZZY PROJECTS
Mandate	Clear, measurable, stable	Ambiguous, intangible, dynamic
Principals	Homogeneous and unified	Heterogeneous and diverse
Agents	Homogeneous and unified	Heterogeneous and autonomous
Risk/Uncertainty	Known risks: "known unknowns"	High uncertainties: "unknown unknowns"
Key Dimension of Complexity	Structural	Sociopolitical
Basic Nature of the Project	Deliberate leap into a planned future	Quest, experiment, or discovery
Performance Dimension	Efficiency	Effectiveness
Type of Rationality	Limited	Broad
Appropriate Management Approach	Rational	Political and/or psychosocial

We have underscored that the traditional rational approach performs best when the project is clearly defined and implemented in a stable or predictable environment. Typically, in such situations, the project has *one* principal (or a unified group of principals) and is executed by *one* cohesive team of agents. The manager and the team are free from political or psychosocial concerns that could impede the project's implementation.

Under these favorable conditions, there is minimal interference from exogenous variables, like tensions among team members or with external stakeholders. The project manager can take an efficient managerial approach and work on planning, organizing, directing, coordinating, and controlling the various stages of the project systematically and rationally.

RECOGNIZING FUZZY PROJECTS

How can Nancy Smart know that her project is relatively "neat," free of major political and social challenges? Her perception of the project's "reality" is inevitably tinted by her personality and training.

Focusing on the time, cost, and quality constraints allows the project manager to gather the appropriate data for project execution more quickly. But when speed is at a premium, precipitation creeps in. This is when the confirmation bias of the project manager can lead to the wrong determination of what is essential. This bias can mask relevant factors and consequently blur the assessments made by the project manager. The manager thus becomes shortsighted, losing the overall vision needed to succeed.

As we saw in Chapter 8, team members interpret and "create the reality" of the project entrusted to them. At best, this helps create a shared vision and commitment. But in the worst-case scenario, the project is run by shortsighted people (the agents) for shortsighted people (the principals). Such myopia is quite common, as was illustrated in earlier chapters. It is often a factor reported in surveys taken after project completion.

Project managers who rely solely on the rational method may not recognize elements that do not fit the models they know best. In the wrong organizational settings, they may be allowed to ignore these elements even when warning signals become apparent. Conversely, a good organizational setting that fosters healthy exchanges of viewpoints will prevent the pittfalls engendered by groupthink.

As a project manager, Nancy is no less or more prone than others to have biased perceptions. Clients, account managers, bankers, and those involved in the ExPlus project will also favor information confirming their opinions. "Seeing is believing" too often becomes "believing is seeing" in the realm of project management, as elsewhere in life. As we saw in past chapters, we cannot be immune to biases any more than we can be to optical illusions. However, if Nancy acknowledges the limitations of the rational approach, she can adopt a more comprehensive approach that considers the project's political and social dimensions. At the same time, she must avoid using a model that is more complex than necessary (see Box 9.3). The two questions are: How diversified are the principals who sponsor the project? How diversified are the agents who will implement it?

BOX 9.3

Occam's Razor or the Principle of Parsimony

Occam's razor is a heuristic attributed to fourteenth-century Franciscan philosopher William of Ockham. It suggests using the simplest explanation rather than considering hypotheses that are more complicated or too costly to verify. It is a call for simplicity, a principle of economy, and the law of parsimony. But, as Einstein suggested, "Everything should be made as simple as possible . . . *but not simpler*." Do not use something more complex unless you have to!

Based on the variety of the principals on the one hand, and that of the agents on the other, Figure 9.1 indicates the optimal approach for implementation. For ease of presentation, we describe four clear-cut schematic scenarios while recognizing that realistically many projects will be in mixed or intermediate situations.[5]

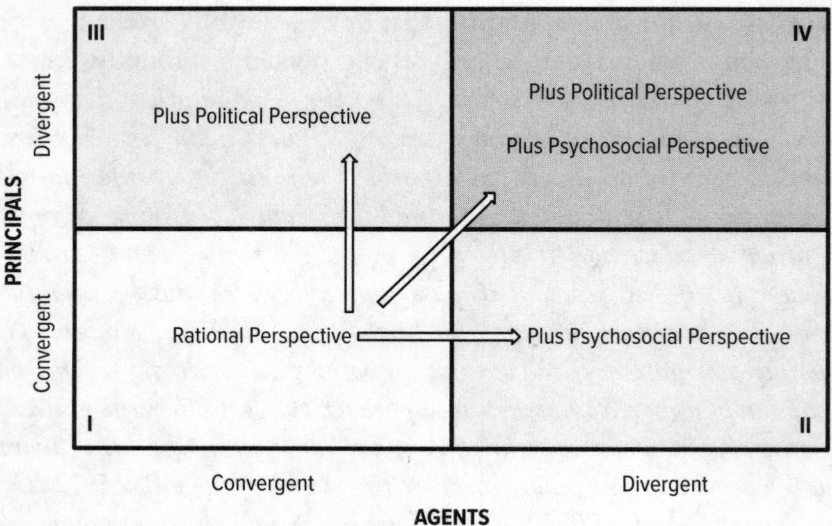

FIGURE 9.1 Guidelines for the best approach based on project complexity

From neat to fuzzy is a continuum, as illustrated in Figure 9.2.

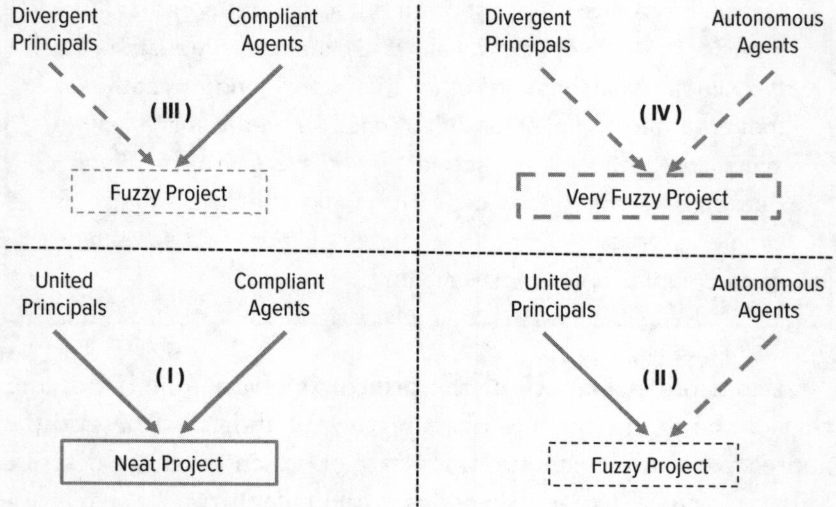

FIGURE 9.2 From neat to really fuzzy projects

Table 9.1 highlights the features that place Type I projects into the neat project category, which are managed primarily through the traditional rational approach. Type II, III, and IV projects fall into the fuzzy project category and should be managed using a multidimensional approach that includes political and psychosocial aspects. Table 9.2 highlights the type of complexity found in projects discussed in this book.

TABLE 9.2 Examples of Large and Small Projects of Various Levels of Complexity

	UNITED AGENTS	DIVERGENT AGENTS
Divergent Mandates	**Type III Scenario (Medium Complexity)** ■ First trip to the moon ■ Development of a common area in a condo complex	**Type IV Scenario (High Complexity)** ■ Columbus's first voyage to America or any Olympic Games ■ A startup company that found its own sponsor
Convergent Mandates	**Type I Scenario (Low Complexity)** ■ Regulatory compliance ■ Asphalting a driveway	**Type II Scenario (Medium Complexity)** ■ A project carried out by independent experts ■ A house remodeling involving different trades

Type I projects are those in which the principals have convergent preferences or stable expectations. In either case, the projects can be managed with the tools and resources at hand. Also, agents implementing Type 1 projects form a cohesive team where members tend to stick to the role assigned to them in the project charter or plan.

Organizations with strong upper management tend to commission Type 1 projects. What characterizes these organizations is that they have centralized planning and decision-making systems. They can be small and medium-size enterprises (SMEs), but they can also be public agencies or large firms with a highly bureaucratic structure. They can offer an improved product or service, or penetrate a new market with relative ease, because it is mandated by "the bosses."

The Type II scenario includes projects with a single principal or multiple principals who have converging expectations, like those of Type I projects. In contrast, however, Type II projects are implemented by agents with heterogeneous interests or perspectives and who also enjoy some latitude due to the intrinsic or extrinsic characteristics discussed in Chapter 8. This is often the case for projects undertaken by not-for-profit organizations, where the agents are volunteers who enjoy a high degree of economic or political autonomy in their work. A seemingly clear mandate may have led the project manager to believe it was a neat project. In such circumstances, the fuzziness becomes apparent only later, during the implementation stages.

Project team members can also include volunteer administrators who have more freedom to act than if they were paid, or supervised volunteers engaged for a fixed time in a well-defined project. Volunteers sometimes work alongside regular employees, giving rise to complex situations. Autonomous agents are sometimes intentionally selected to ensure the project's credibility. For example, prize selection jury members are often deliberately chosen for their reputation and independence.

The Type III scenario is characterized by several principals who have significantly different expectations of the mandate. In this case, the project's vagueness will quickly become apparent. This situation often occurs when several partner organizations (clients) work together on a project, as in interorganizational or public-private partnership (PPP) projects. However, the influence of several principals can be felt even if only one client organization is involved. This is often the case for professional bureaucracies (Mintzberg, 1993), which typically have autonomous departments. For instance, in a hospital, employees who work in one unit (like psychiatry) do not have much in common with those from other units (oncology). The latter agents may have similar concerns and views as those who work in competing organizations, but in the same field.

The planning system is decentralized in professional or large-scale organizations (such as a university or a firm in law, accounting, engineering, or computer science). The resulting strategy is fragmented because several administrative units have a say in the projects that are undertaken. As a result, what matters for some principals may not satisfy others. These situations are highly politicized, and the project may be pulled in all directions. The criteria for success are also complex—partly organizational, partly professional.

The Type IV scenario is the most complex since it involves multiple principals and several divergent agents. The decision-making system is decentralized, and the project implementation is subject to uncertainty from various sources that are difficult to predict. The project manager needs to pay attention to political and psychosocial aspects. Principals and agents have a significant influence on the project's major stages, starting with the mandate's initial formulation, which may change significantly over the course of the project.

This situation was illustrated with the Vancouver Olympic Games. This project had a dual challenge, so we analyzed its evolution using the political perspective and then the psychosocial perspective. Each perspective allowed us to better understand the phenomena that are generally obscured by the traditional rational approach.

A CIRCULAR APPROACH TO THE PROJECT LIFE CYCLE

In recent years, project management has evolved in practice and theory and has paid more attention to the complexity and uncertainty of projects. Instead of the limited rationality of the traditional approach that works for neat projects, managers use a broader rationality that considers the plurality of the parties' points of view. In this case, the predictive life cycle has given way to iterative and adaptive life cycles. "Agile" approaches, with their own publications, training, and software, illustrate this (see Chapter 6). Fuzzy projects are part of this dynamic, and both their number and diversity are growing, given their increasingly interorganizational nature. These projects are characterized by more ambiguous objectives, promises of ever-increasing benefits, and higher levels of complexity and uncertainty.

Their inherent sociopolitical complexity poses a particular challenge in the face of powerful principals and autonomous agents whose divergent interests are matched only by the intangible mandates entrusted to their managers. Indeed, successful management of a project is not a guarantee of the project's success in the eyes of principals and agents, whose quest for effectiveness is paramount. Consequently, projects must be managed differently, especially when they are fuzzy. It is not a question of abandoning the traditional rational approach, but of supplementing it with the political and psychosocial dimensions that positively leverage stakeholder interests. The first step is to review the life cycle.

The traditional predictive life cycle is rooted in engineering and construction projects, and it embodies this instrumental management approach. It envisions an orderly progression of the project from initiation, planning, and execution to closure. It does a good job capturing the project's "hard" aspects (such as schedules) but works less well for the "soft" aspects (such as stakeholder expectations). This rational approach helped build project management's professional foundation but has had limited success in dealing with soft aspects of projects (see Chapter 6).

Our proposed "circle of life" approach for managing fuzzy projects focuses instead on the interests of internal and external stakeholders. Broadly speaking, it is circular, not linear, and embraces uncertainty and change. It is structured around four phases with feedback loops (see Figure 9.3):

- **Do a premortem.**
- **Negotiate the mandate.**

- **Choose the appropriate management approach.**
- **Apply 3D project management principles.**

This interest-based "circle of life" is not sequential but iterative and adaptive in that the premortem and mandate negotiation may overlap and interfere with each other through feedback loops. The choice of the appropriate management approach and its deployment are also interrelated.

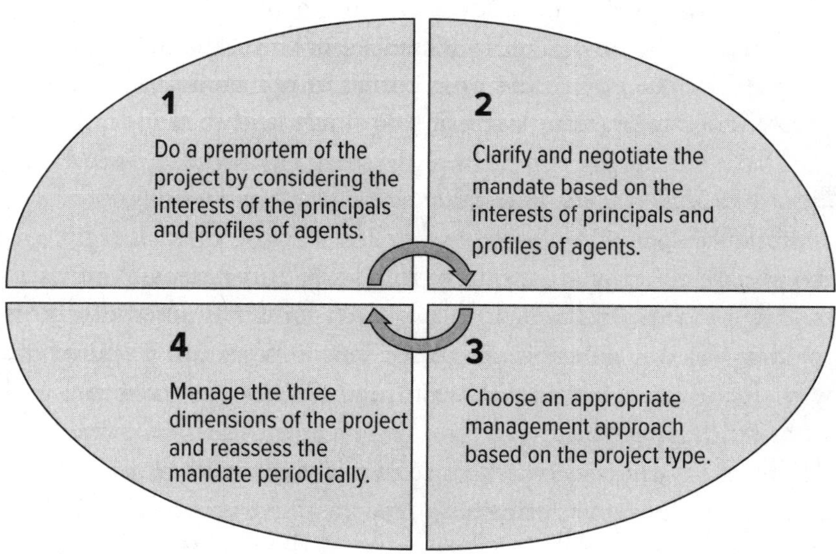

FIGURE 9.3 Managing fuzzy projects in 3D: A circle of life approach

HOW TO MANAGE A PROJECT IN 3D[6]

Do a Premortem

Surprisingly, though the project manager has incomplete knowledge at the start of the project, it is the safest and most fruitful time to ponder on how a project might unfold. The project team may collectively envision a future in which the project has failed, contrary to initial forecasts, and consider what went wrong. Looking "back from the future" makes it possible to understand and explain, rather than predict, problems. By doing a premortem, the project manager can generate creative and preemptive options to prepare for the future. To gain a clearer view of the project's political landscape and imagine a project that reflects the interests of all parties, the project manager must:

- Identify the principals and their interests.
- Identify the agents and determine their profiles.
- Assess the power and positioning of the principals.
- Assess the power and positioning of the agents.
- Generate options based on the above.

Identifying Stakeholders, Highlighting the Interests of Principals, and Profiling Agents

It is relatively easy to identify principals and agents inside and outside the organization. It is, however, harder to know: Who is for the project, against it, or on the fence? Who can stand in the way? In other words, where do principals and agents stand, and what do they want?

To these ends, the project manager can make practical and effective use of two approaches for identifying principals: the first is the Stakeholder Circle (Bourne & Walker, 2006) (see Figure 9.4), and the second is the Importance/Position Matrix (Mitchell, Agle, & Wood, 1997) (see Table 9.3). The project manager can supplement these approaches with informal techniques, such as relying on the intuition and "hunches" of agents. To avoid overlooking some stakeholders, the project manager and team can consider the rational, political, and psychosocial factors that impact projects. This is similar to scanning the environment of a project or a company with a PESTEL (political, economic, social, technological, ecological, and legal) analysis. As stakeholder expectations change, the project team may also periodically analyze their interpersonal relationships and social networks.

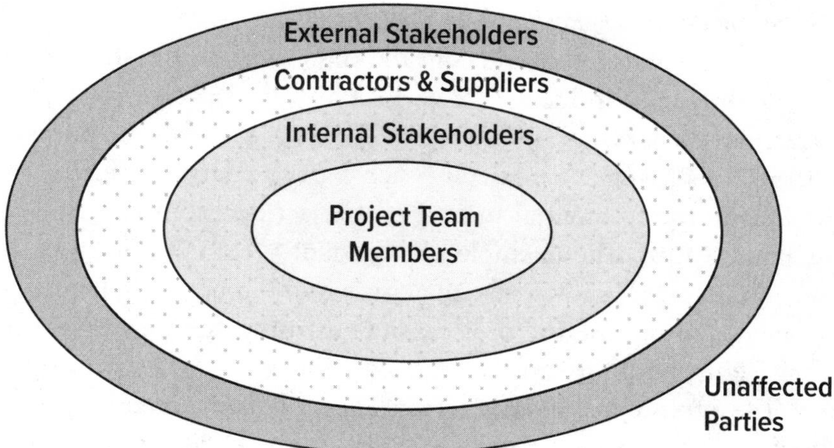

FIGURE 9.4 The project stakeholders circle
Source: Bourne & Walker (2006).

More concretely, the project team can draw up a list of stakeholders (both principals and agents), including all the people and organizations for or against the project (the technique of drafting a long list, from the inputs of participants, has been very effective in brainstorming). By combining the suggestions of many individuals, the project team can prepare the longest possible list to avoid unfortunate omissions. A single highly motivated and well-mobilized stakeholder can significantly contribute to the project's success or harm it. While identifying stakeholders may not involve lengthy discussions, understanding their interests will undoubtedly generate a lot of debate.

The manager should be careful not to reduce the proposed stakeholder placements to simple averages but instead, try to understand the reasons behind the different assessments made by various contributors. At this early stage of the process, the project manager should focus on generating divergence rather than convergence of opinions. These types of discussions will give the team a better understanding of the project's political context.

Assess the Power and Positioning of Stakeholders

The project manager should consider the strategies that stakeholders might use to influence the project and then prepare response strategies accordingly (Aaltonen, Kujala, Havela, & Savage, 2015). This involves visualizing each party's relative influence or analyzing their potential impact on project decisions (Bourne & Walker, 2006). The example of President Obama's library project in Chapter 7 shows that the citizens of Chicago used various strategies to oppose the project, such as using the media to give their claims visibility and legitimacy.

The project managers can also consider the strategies stakeholders are likely to use to oppose the project. Stakeholders must not be overlooked just because they have limited resources or inputs. While individually stakeholders might not be able to influence the project, they can form alliances and gain power and influence. While some parties will use direct strategies, others will use other means to influence the outcome.

Assessments of stakeholders' potential power and influence will spark much debate. The project manager should avoid simply averaging the rankings made by those who do the assessment. It is very instructive to understand the reasons for the different judgments about the power and influence of specific stakeholders. The importance of the stakeholder may be related to their position or function, or their personality or expertise, for example (French & Raven, 1959). The Ford Mustang project from Chapter 7 helps illustrate these points as it involved powerful principals and agents (see Table 9.3).

TABLE 9.3 Initial Mapping of the Stakeholder Power/Interest Relationship, from Iacocca's Perspective

POWER (Influence)

High

Board of Directors

Henry Ford II

Finance

Don Frey Marketing

Manufacturing

Low

Low

High

INTEREST

Source: Ika, Saint-Macary, & Bandé (2020).

Generate Options Based on the Interests of Principals and Agent Profiles

With a good understanding of the project's political landscape and especially the interests of the parties, the manager can generate project options accordingly. This inquiry could take the form of participatory workshops where principals and agents are heard, and where they learn from one another about the project, its mandate, and its implications. Ultimately, this collaborative and participatory approach will help clarify the mandate and gather experience and suggestions from one another.

An example of such an approach is the megaproject to renovate the Microsoft's Redmond campus (near Seattle, Washington). The multibillion-dollar project sought to redevelop 72 acres of Microsoft's headquarters by knocking down 13 buildings and erecting 17. It involved 70 different companies, including five teams of architects, a landscape architect, and three general contractors for its design and implementation, and it fostered a culture of engagement and collaboration. For example, every six weeks, 40 to 50 people, including suppliers (including competitors) and real estate team members, would meet for a review session of the design of each of the four big chunks of the project (Donovan, 2020).

Clarify and Negotiate the Mandate

Once the premortem is complete, the project manager can focus on assessing the project complexity, particularly its sociopolitical dimension. The premortem will also help clarify the mandate and understand the strategic, political, and psychosocial alignment. The manager will then be on firmer ground to explore project options and negotiate the mandate based on the interests of the principals and the profiles of the agents.

In order to measure project complexity, the manager may use a tool like the one proposed in Appendix 9.1. It provides information on how to assess the project's sociopolitical complexity on a "low-medium-high" scale. However, it does not distinguish between principals' interests or agent profiles. In all cases, Figure 9.1 proposes the best approach, based on low, medium, or high sociopolitical complexity.

Clarify the Mandate and Understand the Strategic, Political, and Psychosocial Alignment

Based on the premortem and the assessment of the project's complexity, especially the sociopolitical aspect, the project manager and team then must flesh out the needs (*Why this project?*) and understand the specific and strategic objectives (*What is the project for?*). The manager and team must also strive to understand the strategic, political, and psychosocial alignment to clarify the mandate.

Explore Project Options and Negotiate the Mandate Based on the Interests of Principals and Agent Profiles

Here, the project manager can do a summary analysis of the project options, considering the expectations of the principals and agents (e.g., simply inform and consult them, or involve them to minimize potential resistance to the project). To reconcile the parties' different interests, the project manager can implement a consultation and communication process, or even a pilot project if needed, to review the project concept and the mandate.

Project managers may face "the stakeholder dilemma"—negotiate upfront or deal with possible conflicts later (Freeman, 1984); no negotiation means no compromise that will satisfy all the parties. For this reason, a communication strategy and plan should be developed to ensure that the parties receive the right messages in the right format and at the right time. Communication media can include emails, informal conversations, formal meetings, and regular project reports (PMI, 2017).

Choose the Appropriate Project Management Approach

At this stage, the project manager must assess which type of project is at play, given the social and political context, and choose an appropriate approach. The manager will need to:

- Update the *mandate,* particularly if the objectives have changed.
- Reassess the project's *complexity,* especially if the stakeholders have changed.
- Identify the corresponding project *type.*
- Select the appropriate project management *approach* for the type of project.
- Gauge the advantages and disadvantages of the selected approach.

Table 9.4 contrasts the three approaches by highlighting their distinctive characteristics. Table 9.5 summarizes the advantages and disadvantages of each approach. While these approaches are presented in pure form in this chapter, in reality the actual cases will be a mix of situations. The manager can use a hybrid perspective and manage accordingly.

TABLE 9.4 Comparing the Rational, Political, and Psychosocial Approaches

	RATIONAL APPROACH: FOCUSED ON THE MANDATE	POLITICAL APPROACH: FOCUSED ON THE PRINCIPAL(S)	PSYCHOSOCIAL APPROACH: FOCUSED ON THE PROJECT TEAM
Initiation and Evolution of the Project	In vitro ("laboratory" project). The project is a stable and closed system that can be contracted and rationally managed in near isolation.	In situ (project conducted "in context"). The project is an open system, set and constantly negotiated by principals and other external stakeholders.	In vivo (a project carried out within a social group). The project is a social system, interpreted and managed by the agents, with their views and interests.
Strategic Objective of the Project	The objective is unique, explicit, known, and relatively stable.	There are many explicit and implicit objectives, reflecting the changing views of principals.	There are many objectives explicit and implicit, which evolve according to external and internal project contexts.
Project Main Terms of Reference	The project charter or project plan, serving as the contract.	The external stakeholders.	The members of the project team.
Main Challenge for the Project Manager	Rational management of the process; within time, cost, and quality requirements.	Arbitration between the different external forces.	Identifying and reconciling the interests of the team members.
Criteria for Project Success	Compliance with the constraints (time, cost, and quality) set in the project charter or plan.	Satisfaction of the expectations of the principals.	Subjective assessment of results by project team members.

Source: Adapted from Saint-Macary & Ika (2015).

TABLE 9.5 Advantages and Disadvantages of a 3D Approach

	RATIONAL APPROACH: MANDATE'S LENS	POLITICAL APPROACH: PRINCIPAL'S LENS	PSYCHOSOCIAL PERSPECTIVE: AGENT'S LENS
Disadvantages	Problem with blinders: risk of strategic or political failure.	Risk: Excessive analysis can lead to paralysis and inaction.	Risk of navel-gazing and paralysis due to self-analysis.
Advantages	Allows for internal project efficiency to be addressed.	Anticipates pitfalls. Reveals economies of scale between projects (within a program).	Considers internal dynamics. Allows for organizational learning, with long-term benefits.

Source: Adapted from Saint-Macary & Ika (2015).

Managing in 3D

Fuzzy projects are in a constant state of "becoming." The manager must monitor the project, periodically reevaluate the mandate and type of project, and—as captains do—navigate through its political context. Here are the activities that are required in this circular, nonlinear approach:

- Organize the project, bearing in mind the interests of the principals and agents.
- Implement the project by periodically reevaluating its mandate and what type of project it has become.
- Keep abreast of the political context of the project as it progresses.

Here we focus on how the manager can change the project's political context and thus mobilize, neutralize, co-opt, or bring stakeholders into play. Before engaging in political battles related to the project, the manager needs to know what type of political animal they are or want to become. In other words, is a manager politically aware and acting with integrity, or unaware and playing psychological games? An incompetent politician who cannot read the political landscape, or a naive politician who prefers to focus on project management's technical aspects? See Figure 9.5.

The project manager must avoid overkill when managing a project in 3D. On the one hand, the manager should not assume the role of the strategists of the parent organizations, as this would be the tail wagging the dog. On the other hand, the strategy cannot be implemented entirely through project management and its approach, given the high failure rate of projects.

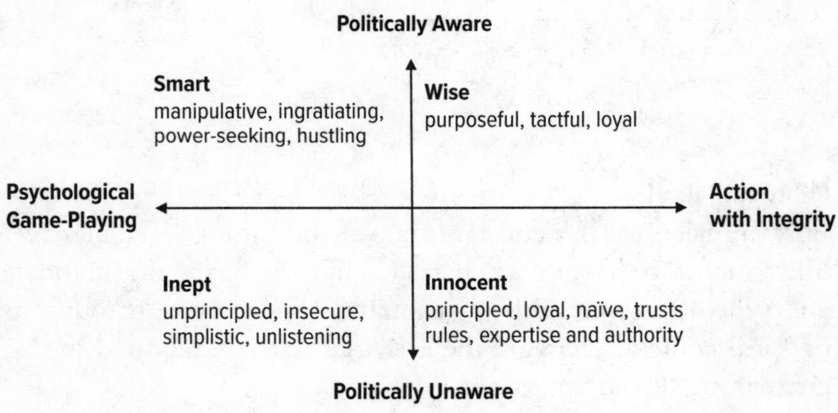

FIGURE 9.5 What type of political animal are you?
Sources: Adapted from Clayton (2017); Baddeley & James (1987).

The Ford Mustang example illustrates how Iacocca successfully changed the political context and neutralized or co-opted some of the stakeholders identified in Table 9.3. Iacocca expected resistance because he knew that the Mustang project was in competition with others, and that the allocated resources could have been used for other initiatives dear to Ford II. He was aware that under the guise of practical considerations such as cost, personal and political motivations were at play.

Iacocca also knew that such daring projects needed strong sociopolitical support. Because of this, he worked at overcoming his boss's misgivings about the Mustang and managed to make him an objective, albeit reluctant, ally. The fact that 22,000 Mustang cars were sold on the first day cemented their objective alliance. With such a roaring start, neither Henry Ford II nor the finance department could distance themselves from Iacocca.

Iacocca understood that organizations are made of moving parts. He was masterful in attracting new stakeholders. The articles he "leaked" to the press captured the attention of the board of directors, Ford dealers, the production department, and even the unions, all of whom began to express interest in the Mustang project. Gradually, the production department and the union became new stakeholders in favor of the project. Demand was so high that Ford built a second and then a third plant.

A project manager must pay particular attention to the positive or negative interests of stakeholders and the degree of influence or power they wield. Interest relates to the likelihood that the stakeholder will intervene and power to the potential impact the stakeholder could have on the project's progress and outcome. Project managers need to keep a close eye on these two dimensions and work to move stakeholders from the lower-left corner of the matrix to the upper-right corner (see Figure 9.6).

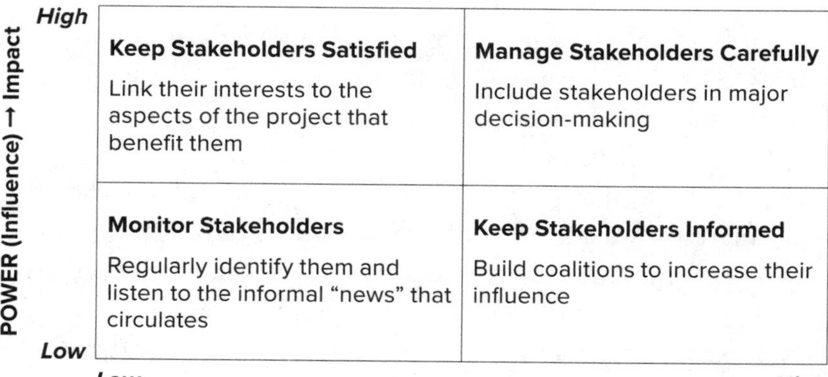

FIGURE 9.6 Communication and Stakeholder Engagement Strategies Based on the Power/Interest Relationship

Sources: Ika et al. (2020); PMI (2017).

In this way, Iacocca was able to stoke the growing interest of the board of directors in the project and succeeded in circumscribing Henry Ford II's field of action to some extent by mobilizing the press. He also piqued the interest of young potential Mustang buyers, spurring Ford dealerships to emerge as a new group of stakeholders (see Figure 9.7).

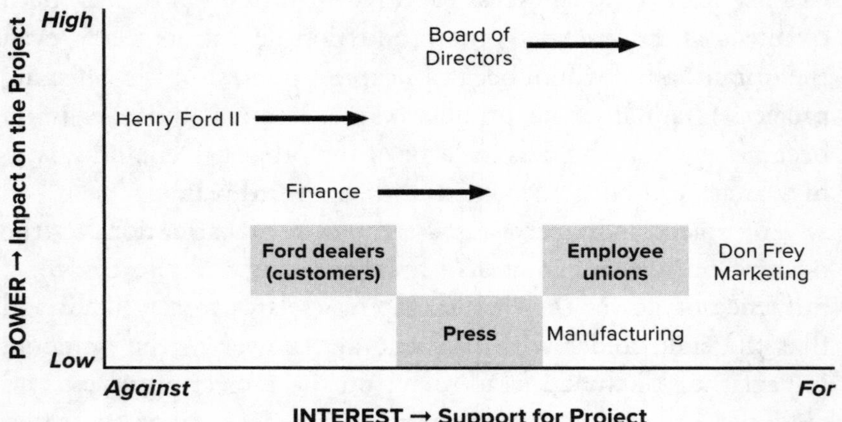

FIGURE 9.7 Remapping the Political Landscape: Adding Stakeholders and Altering Their Positions

Source: Ika et al. (2020).

Project managers must engage stakeholders throughout the project's life. They must include them, evaluate them, listen to them, and consider their power at all times.

In win-win negotiations, it is important to distinguish between the formal position taken by the stakeholders and their real interests. Stakeholders can then work together to find innovative and mutually beneficial options (Fisher, Ury, & Patton, 2011). For example, Henry Ford II's personal stance against the Mustang was at odds with his interests as a shareholder, CEO, and chairman of the board. The commercial success of the Mustang, combined with Iacocca's public association with it, led Henry Ford II to moderate his opposition to the project.

By promoting a win-win approach, the project manager can, over time, establish a climate of mutual understanding that solidifies alliances, facilitates communication, and shortens the duration of negotiations. Then, the parties are more likely to share knowledge and support the project. This will enable the manager to make decisions more quickly, reduce transaction costs related to monitoring and control, and avoid time and cost overruns (Pinto, Slevin, & English, 2009). The project manager can also benefit from the fact that projects and their stakeholders are interdependent to varying degrees. Furthermore, the contributions of stakeholders are likely to be both financial and nonfinancial in nature, as are the benefits they expect.

Trust is not binary, but something that evolves. The objective of the project team should be to build and nurture mutual understanding, and some degree of trust. The Presidential Library project is a telling example, as it suggests a breach of trust between the former president and his supporters. President Obama was asked for written commitments from local activists on things such as local hiring and contracts for minority firms, but he refused to sign a community benefits agreement (CBA), claiming that his foundation was a nonprofit organization and not a real estate developer. Trust cannot be claimed; it needs to be earned. And it is difficult to restore once lost.

Table 9.6 proposes 10 questions that a manager should consider in managing a project in 3D. It also provides some recommendations to facilitate rallying principals and agents.

TABLE 9.6 Ten Questions About Stakeholders in a Fuzzy Project

QUESTIONS	SUB-QUESTIONS	RECOMMENDATIONS
Who are the principals and what do they want? ***Who are the agents and what do they want?***	Which formal approaches can help identify and assess stakeholders?	The Stakeholder Circle and the Importance/Position Matrix are useful if updated periodically. Rely on the experience of team members and the formal stakeholders identified.
	Are relationships formal or informal?	Beyond stakeholders, pay special attention to informal stakeholders who are most likely to oppose the project.
	Have the dynamic aspects of the stakeholders and their interactions been taken into account?	Stakeholders evolve as the project progresses. Monitor their interactions. A social network analysis can help in this regard.
What powers and influence do the principals have and how do they exercise them? ***What powers and influence do agents have and how do they exercise them?***	Do some stakeholders control key resources the project needs?	If yes: Expect them to directly influence the project.
		If no: Anticipate the alliances they may forge with resource holders and the implications for the project.
	Do we have response strategies for dealing with the influence of key stakeholders?	Response strategies must be individualized, based on the influence and interest of each stakeholder.
Why is the project needed: What is the purpose/objective?	What justifies this project? Why do this project?	The business case and the project charter can help clarify the need for the project. See if the project starts from a problem to be solved or an opportunity to be seized.
	What are the objectives of this project? What are its benefits?	The business case, the project charter, or results-based management (RBM) can help identify the specific and strategic objectives and impacts of the project.

(*continued*)

TABLE 9.6 *(continued)*

QUESTIONS	SUB-QUESTIONS	RECOMMENDATIONS
Does the project align well with the organization's strategy, and the expectations of principals and agents?	To what extent does the project align with the organization's strategy?	If yes: This validation is complete.
		If no: Draw up or review the project charter, articulating the specific and strategic objectives and the impact of the project.
	To what extent does the project consider the interests of the principals?	Discuss with the principals and try to understand their expectations before project implementation and reassess them periodically.
	To what extent does the project take into account agent profiles?	Analyze agent profiles in advance and re-evaluate them on an ongoing basis throughout the project.
What is the degree of sociopolitical complexity of the project (based on project type)?	What is the project's sociopolitical complexity on a "low, medium, high" scale?	Measure the project's complexity, particularly its sociopolitical complexity (see Appendix 9.1). Assess the convergence of interests among principals and the profiles of agents.
	What type of project does this level of complexity correspond to?	Figure 9.1 identifies the characteristics that fit the situation and can help guide the choice of Type I, II, III, and IV projects.
What is the appropriate project management approach?	What is the right management approach for the situation?	Select the appropriate management approach based on Table 9.4.
	What are the advantages and disadvantages of this approach?	Consider the advantages and disadvantages of the approach with the help of Table 9.5.

(continued)

TABLE 9.6 *(continued)*

QUESTIONS	SUB-QUESTIONS	RECOMMENDATIONS
How can the political context of the project be changed?	Which stakeholders will be moderately involved?	From a long-term perspective, give them the facts and consult them.
	Which stakeholders do we want to involve fully?	Listen to them, respect their values, adopt their language, and above all, allow them to participate in decision-making.
How do you win and rally the support of stakeholders?	How confident are we in the stakeholders?	Communicate regularly with stakeholders. Focus on their interests not the positions they take. Trust will build gradually.
	Do we have the confidence of the stakeholders?	

Source: Adapted from Ika et al. (2020).

CONCLUSION

Traditionally, project managers use established project management tools to carry out their mandate. This systematic, rational approach is well suited to dealing with traditional projects with clear, measurable, stable objectives and with principals and agents that form coherent and stable groups. Such "neat" projects can be set up and executed efficiently. But projects are increasingly being used to bring about changes in fields and circumstances that are "fuzzy." There, the rational approach often leads to failure. Compared to neat projects, fuzzy projects characteristically have broader and more ambiguous mandates because of intangible or changing objectives, principals with divergent interests, or agents with considerable latitude. In these cases, the political and psychosocial dimensions must be considered along with the rational approach. Managing fuzzy projects requires taking into account the complexity of their delivery context so that principals can be better served, and agents better utilized.

This chapter has sought to help managers identify the nonrational dimensions of fuzzy projects at the outset. The uncertainty inherent in such projects generates different risks from those encountered in neat projects. While considering these dimensions when drafting the mandate and engaging with agents and principals may be burdensome, it will ultimately benefit all parties. To manage a fuzzy project effectively and avoid complications, managers need complementary tools pertaining to the rational, political, and psychosocial dimensions. This multidimensional approach will give managers a more comprehensive view of the project and allow them to use their tools more judiciously. The chapter distills six takeaways for project managers and sponsors:

1. Project managers often use the rational, mandate-based approach to deliver both neat and fuzzy projects. While this efficiency-oriented approach is appropriate for neat projects with clear and unchanging objectives and coherent and stable groups of principals and agents, it has its limits with fuzzy projects that require an effectiveness-oriented approach, as they hold intangible and changing goals and involve powerful, divergent principals and agents.
2. While risk ("known unknown") is a challenge even for neat projects, uncertainty ("unknown unknown") presents a major challenge for fuzzy projects. Indeed, the mandate and the interests of principals and agents are not only vague, but they also change over time. Managers must avoid falling into an "illusion of certainty" in believing that the calculation of probabilities, which is effective in the context of risk, can be sufficient in dealing with uncertainty. When the future is unknown, in addition to relevant information, managers may also rely on intuition and "hunches" to deliver fuzzy projects.
3. The project manager should assess the sociopolitical complexity that characterizes fuzzy projects—that is, the

degree of divergence between the interests of the groups of principals and agents. Such sociopolitical complexity tends to be relatively high for fuzzy projects because the principals may have divergent expectations of the project, and the agents may have personal agendas that do not align with the project's objectives.

4. Since neat projects are "deliberate leaps into a planned future," they have clear, measurable, and unchanging mandates; relatively homogeneous and unified principals; and rather homogeneous and cohesive agents. They also usually confront risk and sometimes structural complexity, and they are efficiency-oriented by essence; thus, they only require limited rationality and a rational management approach. In contrast, fuzzy projects are largely the opposite.
5. A circle of life approach—iterative and adaptive—may be more appropriate for the life cycle of fuzzy projects. It includes four circular phases with feedback loops: premortem, negotiation of the mandate, selection of the appropriate project management approach, and managing projects in 3D.
6. Sociopolitical complexity is generally low for neat projects but medium-to-high for fuzzy projects. By contrasting the political perspective of the principals with the psychosocial view of the agents, the project manager must distinguish among four basic scenarios. Type I, where a low complexity inherent with convergent principals and agents prevails and the rational approach is appropriate; Type II, which features a medium complexity due to rather divergent agents and requires a psychosocial approach; Type III, with equally medium complexity but this time divergent principals, requires a political perspective; and Type IV features high complexity—that is, divergent principals and agents–hence the importance of combining political and psychosocial perspectives.

"Know Thyself," Socrates advised. Project managers who know what kind of political animal they are enjoy a significant advantage. They are in a better position to assess the advantages and disadvantages of the rational, political, and psychosocial approaches. They also know in what context and how to adopt hybrid approaches that combine two or three of these approaches.

REFERENCES

Aaltonen, K., Kujala, J., Havela, L., & Savage, G. (2015). Stakeholder dynamics during the project front end: The case of nuclear waste repository projects. *Project Management Journal, 46*(6), 15–41.

Baddeley, S., & James, K. (1987). Owl, fox, donkey or sheep: Political skills for managers. *Management Education and Development, 18*(1), 3–19.

Clayton, M. (2017). The game of projects. How to win at project politics. https://onlinepmcourses.com/project-politics/.

Donovan, K. (2020, 6 March). Getting everyone to pull in the same direction on a mega-project. LinkedIn.com. Getting Everyone to Pull in the Same Direction on a Mega-Project | LinkedIn (accessed 2 September, 2020).

Fisher, R., Ury, W. L., & Patton, B. (2011). *Getting to yes: Negotiating agreement without giving in*. Penguin.

Freeman, R. E. (1984). *Strategic management: A stakeholder approach*. Pitman.

French, J. R., & Raven, B. (1959). The bases of social power. In D. Cartwright (Ed.), *Studies in social power* (pp. 150–167). Institute for Social Research.

Geraldi, J., Maylor, H., & Williams, T. (2011). Now, let's make it really complex (complicated): A systematic review of the complexities of projects. *International Journal of Operations and Production Management, 31*(9), 966–990.

Gigerenzer, G. (2014). *Risk savvy: How to make good decisions*. Penguin.

Hirschman, A. O. (1967). *Development projects observed*. Brookings Institution.

Ika, L. A. (2009). Project success as a topic of project management journals. *Project Management Journal, 40*(4), 6–19.

Ika, L., Saint-Macary, J., & Bandé, A. (2020). Mobilizing stakeholders for project success. *PM World Journal, 9*(8), August. Available online at https://pmworldlibrary.net/wp-content/uploads/2020/07/pmwj96-Aug2020-Ika-Saint-Macary-Bande-mobilizing-stakeholders-for-project-success.pdf.

Ika, L., Couillard, J., & Garon, S. (2021). Coping with project complexity: The complexity based project management framework. *PM World Journal, 10*(5), 1–22.

Knight, F. H. (1921). *Risk, uncertainty and profit*. Houghton Mifflin.

Kreiner, K. (2020). Conflicting notions of a project: The battle between Albert O. Hirschman and Bent Flyvbjerg. *Project Management Journal, 51*(4), 400–410.

Loch, C. H. (2017). Creativity and risk taking aren't rational: Behavioral operations in MOT. *Production and Operations Management, 26*(4), 591–604.

Maslow, A. H. (1966). *The psychology of science: A reconnaissance*. Unknown Publisher.

Maylor, H., Turner, N., & Murray-Webster, N. (2013). How hard can it be? Actively managing complexity in technology projects. *Research Technology Management, 56*(4), 45–51.

Mintzberg, H. (1993). *Structure in fives: Designing effective organizations*. Prentice-Hall.

Mitchell, R. K., Agle, B. R., & Wood, D. J. (1997). Toward a theory of stakeholder identification and salience: Defining the principle of who and what really counts. *Academy of Management Review, 22*(4), 853–886.

Pinto, J. K., Slevin, D. P., & English, B. (2009). Trust in projects: An empirical assessment of owner/contractor relationships. *International Journal of Project Management, 27*(6), 638–648.

Project Management Institute (PMI). (2017). A Guide to the Project Management Body of Knowledge (PMBOK Guide) (6th ed.). PMI.

Saint-Macary, J., & Ika, L. A. (2015). Atypical perspectives on project management: moving beyond the rational, to the political and the psychosocial. *International Journal of Project Organisation and Management, 7*(3), 236–250.

Snowden, D. J., & Boone, M. E. (2007). A leader's framework for decision-making. *Harvard Business Review, 85*(11), 68.

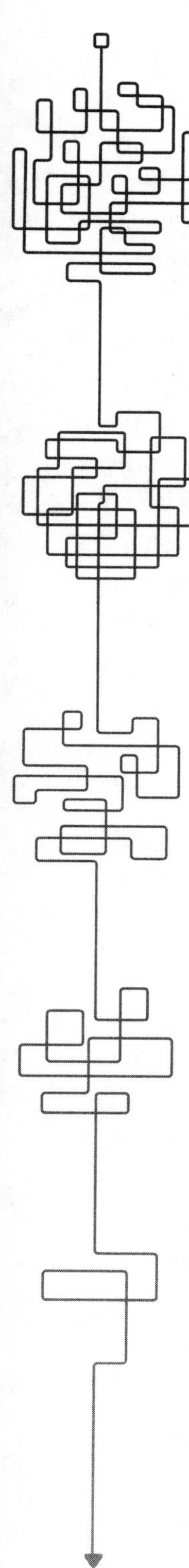

CHAPTER 10

CONCLUSION

The secret of change is to focus all of your energy not on fighting the old, but on building the new.

—Socrates

WHEN THINGS GET FUZZY

Over the past decades, projects have proliferated in the world of organizations, and in a variety of sectors, driven by globalization, the acceleration of technological progress, and shorter product life cycles. They have become the preferred means for implementing and changing organizational strategies (Joffre, Aurégan, Chédotel, & Tellier, 2006; Shenhar & Dvir, 2007), resulting in "projectification" of organizations and of society itself (Lundin et al., 2015).

In this process, the project itself has become a paradox. While project management as a theory and practice has gained mometum, all too often, the project itself stalls and may derail the strategy of the sponsoring organization. Delays, cost overruns, and benefit shortfalls in major projects frequently make headlines. Projects and strategies fail during their execution—which is considered their graveyard—embarrassing strategists and disappointing principals, agents, end users, and many other stakeholders.

Since failure is an unwanted outcome, no one assumes responsibility for it. Everyone passes the buck by blaming others, upstream or downstream. Executives claim that their idea was good but not understood, project sponsors that their excellent design was poorly implemented, and project managers will tell anyone who will listen that their execution of the plan was exemplary . . . given what they had to work with.

Notwithstanding these well-publicized failures, project management, which promises efficiency and effectiveness, has come a long way since its formalization in the 1940s. As we discussed in Chapter 4, it has moved from an instrumental approach in the 1950s–1980s where tools were dominant, to the eclectic and contingent approaches in the 1980s–1990s with increased interest in people, to today's more strategic and ecological approaches where the end impacts of projects matter the most (Geraldi & Söderlund, 2018; Morris, 2013).

Nonetheless, the rational approach that gave so much credibility to project management with its "best practices" continues to prevail for most projects. Before acting, one must carefully think almost about everything, planning the whole project in detail before implementing it (Kreiner, 2020).

This approach has worked very well in many industries, like construction, where such projects are common. With clear, precise, and stable mandates, neat projects can be implemented in a context of manageable risks. Principals and agents each form relatively cohesive and stable blocks. Furthermore, the relationship between the two groups is framed by a consensual contract.

However, though project management is good at delivering within the constraints of time, cost, and quality of neat projects, it does not deal well with the complexity and uncertainty of "fuzzy" projects. These are characterized by results-focused mandates that extend over long periods, that are ambiguous from the start or change over time. They may also have powerful principals with divergent expectations, or they are managed by agents with highly varied profiles or who are very autonomous. Consequently, projects that have many of these characteristics are conducted in a context characterized by high levels of uncertainty and socio-political complexity (Gigerenzer, 2014; Maylor & Turner, 2017).

In contrast to neat projects, fuzzy projects require a broader approach that accommodates the subjective rationalities of the principals and agents, not just the project's objective rationality (Kreiner, 2020). The examples discussed in this book—including new product development projects by Apple and Motorola, the Vancouver Olympics, voyages of exploration, and organizational changes—illustrate this new genre of projects with fuzzy characteristics.

Our conception and use of the term "fuzzy project" is rooted in the early findings of Albert Hirschman, one of the founders of project management, who examined a variety of projects funded by the World Bank in Europe, Africa, and Asia in the 1960s. While these projects were expected to be implemented through the straightforward, rational application of well-known techniques, Hirschman observed the regular occurrence of side effects and repercussions that were well outside the scope of what was planned. But, rather than being of marginal benefits, the "intangible and fuzzy outputs of these various projects" he observed "turn out, a bit surprisingly, to be inputs essential to the realization of the project's principal effect and purpose" (Hirschman, 1967). Thus, he came to see each project arising from "the varied interplay between the structural characteristics of projects, on the one hand, and the social and political environment, on the other."

To recap in our own words: We often start out with a plan that is overly rational and optimistic. During implementation, obstacles emerge that are well outside what we had planned. Yet we were able to deal with it and much of it turns out to serve the initial purpose of our project. Nancy Smart, and many of us, can relate to such scenarios in our professional and personal lives.

These observations are in line with a vast body of research and confirmed by the practical experience of project sponsors and managers. Practitioners and researchers agree that an increasing number of projects cannot be reasonably circumscribed within the rational and economic boundaries of traditional project management, and that political and social considerations are essential to understanding the behavior of projects that are more complex.

We proffer that the rational approach, with its standardized cookie-cutter methods, is not adequate for many projects, and that it is wholly inadequate for fuzzy projects. A substantial body of research has shown that the rational approach too often sacrifices effectiveness at the altar of efficiency. More than just being an "ugly word," efficiency then becomes harmful to the organization and the environment. Mintzberg's words to that effect are edifying (1989):

> The call to "be efficient" is the call to calculate, where calculation means economizing, means treating social costs as externalities, and means allowing economic benefits to push out social ones. At the limit, efficiency emerges as one pillar of an ideology that worships economic goals, sometimes with immoral consequences.

A single-minded quest for efficiency is like putting on blinders and is counterproductive when dealing with the complexity of fuzzy projects, which requires the project manager to take a broad perspective. The term "implementation," generally understood as a roll-out, underestimates the complexity inherent to carrying out endeavors that are beset by unknowns and a high degree of uncertainty. More likely, project implementation means "a long voyage of discovery in the most varied domains, from technology to politics" (Hirschman, 1967).

In the sociopolitical and uncertain context of fuzzy projects, the project manager's obsession with efficiency over effectiveness leads to what sociologists call "anomia of success" (Cohen, 1972), in which groups of people are disoriented because they lack common values and goals. This societal ill robs the project of its meaning, purpose, community spirit, or contribution to society

(Kreiner, 2014); this loss of meaning affects principals and agents alike. For lack of a common definition and assessment of success, project sponsors and managers are led astray, without a compass.

When projects are not neat, project managers who confine themselves to a rational approach often fail to meet the expectations of the principals and agents. In more complex situations, project managers need to take stock of the other dimensions of the project: one political—focused on the expectations of the principals—and the other psychosocial—focused on the interests of the agents.

As noted in Chapter 9, the life cycle of a neat project, with its orderly path of initiation, closure, planning, and execution, has often proven inadequate. By contrast, our approach to the project life cycle is different because it considers that the deployment of a project is an organic, not a mechanistic process. How the project will evolve, fail, or succeed cannot be ascertained based on the original state of affairs, within a predictable range of variation.

A better approach to dealing with the challenges the project will face is to invest more time and effort upstream. Such early effort will prove to be beneficial downstream, providing more flexibility at the execution and delivery phases (see Figure 10.1). In project management, the term "life cycle" was borrowed from biology but has been used mechanically. In contrast, we submit that the life cycle of fuzzy projects should be seen as organic, adaptive, and driven by human interactions within the project and considering its external environment. As such it is circular and iterative, allowing for adjustments and learning midstream as complexity and uncertainty arise.

How we see the project life cycle determines how we manage it, what actions we take and when we take them. At times, the project is likely to depart from what we had imagined. What matters is to not deviate from our purpose. In our approach, we keep our aim on the goal, not just on getting back on track. This requires improving our readiness to deal with the unexpected, not just our ability to make predictions. This will be illustrated later in this chapter, when we discuss the advisory committee set up by President Kennedy during the Cuban Missile Crisis. Since the way we assess progress is circular, not linear, our approach to dealing with these challenges is iterative, not sequential.

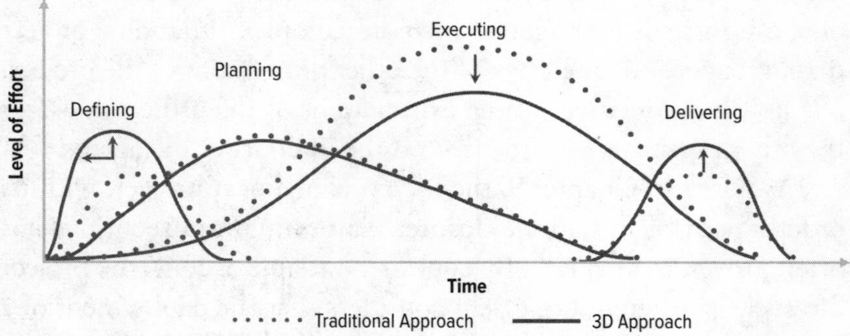

FIGURE 10.1 Effect of a 3D approach on the project life cycle

These key elements of this organic life cycle will allow project managers to consider the changing interests of stakeholders: premortem, which considers the political landscape; clarification and negotiation of the mandate in an inclusive manner, to reflect the interests of principals and agents; choice of an appropriate management approach, based on the degree of divergence between principals and agents; and the management of the project in three dimensions, where the political context is modified to deliver a project that will satisfy these stakeholders. Project managers must make the most of the changing and dynamic project environment, counteract threats, seize opportunities they encounter during implementation to fulfill the mandate, and meet the expectations of principals and agents.

Nancy Smart's project management training focused on the rational approach with its impressive toolbox. Despite this training, Nancy feels ill-equipped to deal with the human factor in fuzzy projects. She could draw inspiration from two metaphors. The first is that of the fox and the hedgehog by the English philosopher

Isaiah Berlin (1953) (see Chapter 1). We suggest that she may also learn from the chameleon with its ability to change itself and adapt to its environment, as seen by the African author Amadou Hampaté Bâ (1998) (see Box 10.1).

BOX 10.1

The Chameleon Is a Great Teacher: Observe and Learn

1. When the chameleon decides on a direction, it does not turn its head. *Have an objective and stick to it.*
2. The chameleon turns its eyes, not its head, looking up and down to find out what is happening around. *You are not alone. There is a whole world around you.*
3. When it gets to a new place, the chameleon blends in. This behavior is not hypocrisy; it is prudence and respect for others. *Do not fight. Seek mutual understanding. If we exist, so do others.*
4. The chameleon walks with care, swaying back and forth on two feet at a time, using its tail as an anchor. *So "proceed with care." Test and retest. Hurry slowly.*
5. When it sees prey, the chameleon does not pounce on it. Instead, it extends its tongue and reels it in slowly, ready to retract its tongue to avoid harm. *Small things can matter.*

So . . . If you want to create a work of lasting significance, be patient, be good, be easy to get along with, be humane.

Excerpts translated and adapted from Amadou Hampaté Bâ (1998).

Like the chameleon, Nancy will focus on the specific objective of her project and its benefits. In addition to reading her mandate, she will "read" the context in which she is operating. She is not alone in the project, so she will try to understand others—that is, her immediate collaborators, the agents who have profiles and expectations that differ from her own, and the principals who have influence and divergent interests. Like the chameleon, Nancy may need to take on the color of a changing context, including the internal and external stakeholders. She will grasp the ambiguity of the different levels of objectives in the mandate and the uncertainty and sociopolitical complexity surrounding it.

Armed with this understanding of the project's complexity and uncertainty, the project manager must adopt a chameleon-like attitude toward political, psychosocial, and other threats, and seize opportunities as they arise without rushing, making the most of the context surrounding the project. To deliver the project's medium- and long-term benefits, the project manager must be sensitive to the human aspects of the project. Since projects are unique, by definition, it is not surprising that managing them by applying a generic, highly standardized methodology—regardless of circumstances—often leads to failure. The results we reported speak volumes. To help us adopt more appropriate methodologies, we should start by painting a more realistic and nuanced picture of the nature of each project and its context. Specifically, this means triangulating the project from the outset along three dimensions—rational, psychosocial, and political—rather than confining ourselves to the first. Since the importance of each of the three dimensions can be measured, a tailored methodology can be designed to manage any given project.

By viewing the project as a whole, appropriate and adapted methods can be deployed "à la carte and progressively" instead of being triggered "ready-made and automatically." To obtain better results, we need to clarify the specific nature of the project and adapt implementation methods depending on whether it is a relatively neat project, a somewhat blurred project, or a fuzzy project.

Perceiving and managing a project in 3D, therefore, calls into question the practice of applying the strictly rational approach in all circumstances. However, it is important to remember that this traditional approach is based on solid foundations and offers certain advantages that should be preserved. Without "throwing the baby out with the bathwater," we want to better equip our project management toolbox and use it more wisely. To achieve better results, we need to broaden our vision and make better use of the rational approach by incorporating, in an appropriate manner, the contribution of the psychosocial and political approaches.

FOCUS ON PLANNING, NOT THE PLAN

In traditional project management, the starting point is the mandate given to the project manager and written into the project charter. However, in organizations, decisions are made long before they are written down or announced publicly. In the overall approach to managing fuzzy projects, much importance is placed on the information gathered during the initial planning, well before the formal announcement and mandate. This early phase in the project gestation is full of soft information that emerges during formal and informal meetings. This information is often as important as the formal plan (see Chapter 6).

To better understand a project, we need to look before what is traditionally seen as its starting point—we need to "begin before the beginning." This means involving the project manager in the project formulation process as early as possible. The agents will better understand the project's political dimension and be adequately prepared to negotiate the first steps, increasing the chances of delivering it efficiently and effectively. These last two criteria, which we discussed in the book's introduction, are essential to successful project management.

Important benefits often result from including the project manager early in the process. For their part, senior executives and project sponsors will benefit from the project manager's input on implementation. The project manager will grasp some key nuances of the project that are not (or cannot) be formally documented in the formal mandate. Starting earlier than the traditional beginning will allow the principals to bring the achievable closer to the desirable, thus increasing the effectiveness and quality of the expected results and the project's contribution to the strategic goals of the organization. We will come back to this later.

The list of benefits goes on. In virtually every industry, one factor that often tops the list for successful project implementation is senior management support (Pinto & Slevin, 1989). This research also confirmed how important it is for senior management's commitment to the project to be real and well known. It is not enough to support the project and its managers discreetly—everyone must be aware of it. Moreover, involving people with a relevant technical background early in the design process will likely result in a more efficient and effective deployment and use of organizational resources (see Figure 10.1).

In the construction sector, this practice is known as *early contractor involvement,* because the chosen contractor is integrated into the project at an early stage. This was the case with the Fiona Stanley Hospital in Perth, one of the largest construction projects undertaken by the State of Western Australia, at a total cost of US$1.5 billion. This mega-hospital project of approximately 800 beds was delivered on time, within budget, and to the quality stipulated in the contract, despite changes to the scope sanctioned by the client (the government) that amounted to over US$22 million. The additions included introducing neonatal and obstetric services, a new operating room for heart and lung transplants, and the expansion of the emergency department.

The hospital's construction success was made possible by involving the contractor in the design and planning of the project. The design was carried out collaboratively with the help of a consortium of experts and other practitioners in the health sector, planners, architects, and interior designers. The contractor collaborated with the design team to produce a series of mock-ups for the clinical wards before construction to anticipate and address potential problems.

Of course, this early integration of the contractor was not enough to avoid all problems. But the early inclusion of the contractor ensured project *management* success, because it improved estimates and allowed the team to find practical and innovative solutions to the challenges posed by the project's complexity (Love & Ika, 2022).

It is not always possible to involve the project manager early on. Often, the incubation period during which the idea of the project is being kicked around informally can last months and even years. While it is usually possible to identify the date when the project is formally adopted, it is hard to know when the idea germinated or took shape through discussion (Allison & Graham, 1999). Furthermore, senior management often believes that it can make the desired changes as part of normal operations, and the idea of having to initiate a separate project only emerges gradually. In addition, many projects are awarded to external parties who were not present when the project was first discussed.

If the project manager cannot be included at the outset, efforts should be made to fill this gap. The project manager can gain a personal and intimate insight into the initial planning stage by having access to the names and profiles of the decision makers (they can be contacted), as well as to source files and documents that preceded the final version of the plan.

Another reality is that one manager often replaces another during the project. Two examples of megaprojects demonstrate this. First, the Boeing 787 Dreamliner megaproject: With the project well behind schedule and running substantially over budget, Boeing executives realized that they had made a serious mistake appointing a project manager whose expertise was in marketing. They needed a different skill set to get the Boeing 787 off the ground because they were using new materials to make this airplane, and they had to set up a supply chain unprecedented in the aviation industry. To correct this hiring mistake, Pat Shanahan took over as the Boeing project manager in 2007 due to his skills in supply chain management (*New York Times,* 2007).

Secondly, the Crossrail megaproject in the United Kingdom, which may ultimately cost US$30 billion offers a cautionary tale. The rail project has experienced significant delays. The main component of the project—the Elizabeth Line, which will cross the City of London from east to west—was scheduled to begin operation in 2022. In 2018, the British government offered an additional budget of nearly US$900 million to keep the project going. But it had one condition: project manager Simon Wright had to step down to let Mark Wild take over (*The Guardian,* 2018).

Any manager who takes over a project must ask critical questions once they come on board. Far from simply understanding what is in the project's mandate, any new manager must strive to understand why, by whom, and for whom the project was designed and who, intentionally or unintentionally, would benefit from it. Box 10.2 suggests 10 essential questions that the project manager should ask before implementing the newly assigned project.

BOX 10.2

Questions Every Project Manager Should Ask Before Project Execution

1. Who are the clients, sponsors, and owners?
2. Why do the project, and for what purpose?
3. Who is it for, and what is in it for them?
4. Can we do it?
5. Is there more than one way of doing it?
6. What can go wrong in the project?
7. How much will it cost?
8. How long will it take?
9. How do we know we are on the right path?
10. What will make it a success for all?

These questions reflect the importance of planning and the critical nature of the front-end phase, where the project takes conceptual shape and includes all activities from the time the idea was conceived to the investment decision (Williams & Samset, 2010). This is the upstream phase where designers assess needs (why this project and what is it for?), analyze feasibility (can it be done?), weigh options (are there multiple ways to do it?), consider risks (what can go wrong?), and outline project plans (timelines and costs). This phase often spans several years. Such a long time horizon inherent in many fuzzy projects is crucial to ensure the delivery of value for money and sustainability, and can make the difference between success and failure. For example, the original idea for the Crossrail project dates back to 1974, but construction did not begin until 2009, after several failed attempts by the UK government (Gil & Fu, 2022).

When managing in 3D, considerable importance should be given to *planning*, which is more important than the plan itself. Planning must be taken care of (not just the plan), because it is an essential learning exercise. Planning allows the project team to anticipate the future and sketch out time, cost, quality, and resource estimates. More importantly, it helps practitioners learn by monitoring and evaluating the project during implementation, which will improve performance in future projects.

Moreover, projects necessarily involve reallocating resources and making changes that benefit some individuals and groups but harm others—or they believe they have been harmed, rightly or wrongly (see Chapters 7 and 8). Looking at the other side of the coin is also enlightening. It helps identify stakeholders who were overlooked because they were not part of the decision-making process or were ignored because they were not deemed to be in a position to help or harm the project. Intentionally or unintentionally left out, they are not part of the process; many may be harmed by or adversely affected by a project or, on the contrary, benefit from it and be allies. These groups and individuals are stakeholders whose importance and role are crucial and should not be overlooked.

This back-to-basics approach of paying more attention to the design and planning phases of the project, preferably in real time or afterward, allows the project to begin with more foresight. It will also prove essential later, during the identification and categorization of fuzzy projects.

BEYOND DIAGNOSIS

Involving the project manager as early as possible in the design process or allowing the project manager to analyze the project's genesis retrospectively, gives the principals and agents a much earlier and clearer understanding of the project's full context. This proposal is not entirely new, as it is already standard practice to consider the technical requirements of the project and the interests of the members when putting together the project team. In the private and public sectors, it is also common practice to ensure that the principals are represented on the team. This practice is even standardized in the case of multiorganizational projects sponsored by several organizations, as is often the case in international development.

In line with the metaphor of the chameleon, we highlight a practice that is tacit and underutilized. Instead of serving as a mere form of control or covert oversight, the involvement of these representatives should be put to better use. The active participation of representatives of the project's principals and ultimate beneficiaries (end users) can contribute to the project's real, organizational, and social success. Being mindful of this underlying project reality will allow project managers to anticipate and manage the many contingencies that arise from the divergent interests of principals, agents, and beneficiaries on an ongoing basis. They will not be caught off guard, and thus continually make up for lost time after the fact (Sibony, Lovallo, & Powell, 2017).

It is never too late to involve principals and beneficiaries in the project. Neglecting them increases the risk of derailment. Three examples illustrate this point. First, consider the US federal government's HealthCare.gov website project, designed to provide access to health insurance for more than 27 million people (Obamacare). The US$2 billion-plus project suffered from the critical lack of involvement of a key stakeholder in its planning, namely the US chief technology officer (CTO) for the White House. This made it challenging to coordinate the technical and political aspects of the project (Lee & Brumer, 2017).

Second, a Google subsidiary's megaproject to build a smart city in Toronto, called Sidewalk Labs, was abandoned just three years after its announcement in 2017. In addition to unprecedented economic uncertainty caused by the COVID-19 pandemic, the project faced strong opposition from the Canadian Civil Liberties Association due to data privacy concerns (Reuters, 2020). This association should have been consulted before embarking on the project.

Third, Nintendo's Wii U project, also known as Project Cafe, is a cautionary tale for project developers who fail to involve end users. Delivered to market in 2012, the game console tallied just 13.5 million sales compared to 100 million for its predecessor, the Wii. The problem was the controller's ergonomic design, which made it unsuitable to use for games played continually for long hours. Evoking reasons of commercial secrecy, Nintendo did not involve gamers in the controller's design. In addition to gamers, video game developers were not happy either. Hence, there was a comparatively small number of games available compared to the PlayStation 4 and the Xbox One. All of this caused Nintendo's stock to fall (Stuart, 2017).

By contrast, let us consider two projects where the involvement of beneficiaries had a very positive impact. The Cityringen Metro (literally the "city ring") is a 17-station underground line that circles downtown Copenhagen. The project implemented a community relations strategy that included traditional newsletters, web, and traditional media press communications, along with more innovative initiatives like site tours, online video vignettes of the tours, stories from construction workers, emails, and up-to-the-minute SMS text message notifications of delays and unexpected events or other inconveniences. This stakeholder buy-in strategy paid off. The project team was able to survey citizens continuously throughout the project and increase their satisfaction with the construction. Residents near the subway line were 85–90 percent satisfied with having a subway station in their neighborhood and 70–75 percent satisfied with the information provided during construction (Winterburn, 2020).

A successful approach to effecting change was made in NBA basketball. In June 2021, the NBA terminated its long-standing partnership with Spalding and unveiled a new ball made by Wilson Sporting Goods. This ball is made of eight panels from the same leather and has the same characteristics as its predecessor. The NBA and its new partner learned from the failure the NBA had suffered 15 years earlier when Spalding tried to change the ball (see Chapter 3), by adding young NBA stars to the consulting staff while developing the new ball (NBA. com, 2021).

BE MINDFUL OF BIASES

The 3D approach incorporates the general tenets of behavioral strategy. Nobel laureate Kahneman's pioneering work on human biases has highlighted the limitations of individual and collective decision-making, hampered by many serious cognitive biases (Kahneman, 2011). By recognizing the limitations of human cognition, we can reject the mistaken assumption that the formulation of the strategy from which projects and programs are designed is essentially a rational process. Rather than subscribing to a prescriptive and ill-founded pseudo-rational approach, the 3D approach takes behavioral psychology into account and considers how decisions are made and implemented in the organizational context.

"To summarize: becoming aware of our biases [while making a decision] is impossible by definition; correcting them ourselves is impossible in practice; neutralizing their effects is all the more difficult since many biases reinforce each other; finally, wanting to renounce the heuristics of which our biases are the reverse side would do more harm than good" (Sibony, 2015, our translation). So, are we powerless against these biases? Individually, yes, just as we are regarding optical illusions (see Chapters 5 and 6). Even worse, these cognitive biases come into play during the decision-making process, unlike errors of calculation and judgment that occur before the decision is made. By then, it is too late: like an optical illusion, we cannot help but "perceive" what we know to be false, even though we are aware of it. Optimism bias is a good example, as highlighted in megaprojects by former Oxford professor Flyvbjerg (2014). If optimism bias is present at the individual level, it can certainly be present at the project level. However, there is a caveat: the time, cost, and benefit estimates for large-scale projects are made by teams of professionals (Love, Ika, Matthews, & Fang, 2022).

So, how can managers minimize the impact of these biases? By taking preventive measures (ex ante) instead of corrective measures (ex post). Using safeguards and other structuring mechanisms can contain the effect of these biases and take full advantage of the benefits of teamwork and collective decisions. For example, one can de-bias cost forecasts for large-scale projects with risk management tools such as reference class forecasting (RCF), which relies on statistics from similar past projects rather than the perspective of the proponents who tend to be overoptimistic (Flyvbjerg, 2014). Unfortunately, this tool alone has not been enough to prevent massive cost overruns in large-scale projects. A case in point is the Crossrail project, whose 2007 budget included a contingency fund of about US$7 billion to guard against optimism bias. It suffered significant cost overruns amounting to nearly US$3 billion as of 2009 (Gil and Fu, 2022); this is in addition to cost overruns of a couple of billion dollars during project implementation.

We must also consider the Einstellung bias, which leads to a fixation on one option, given our knowledge or experience, and thus prevents us from considering alternative options to solve a given problem. To counter the effect of this bias, one can adopt integrated project delivery (IPD), as is done in the United States with project alliances and using a mixed team of principals and agents. The idea is to give the team the cognitive space to evaluate each other's ideas and assumptions, and co-construct estimates based on best practices from previous projects. This benchmarking helps us establish reference classes for a group of projects on a multicriterion basis: size (cost, time), procurement, and project type. Governments can develop a benchmarking process to better assess project performance by linking best practices to the results obtained during the different phases of the project. To do this, we need to look at projects that succeed, not just those that fail. In other words, we need to evaluate what did and did not work to avoid a possible statistical bias, which is often referred to as "sampling on the dependent variable."

Regarding probabilities, it is not enough to simply ask: What are the chances that project X will exceed the budget? Rather, a more effective question about frequencies should be asked: How many projects of this type do you think have used best practices and have gone over budget, and do you expect this to happen? (Love et al., 2022).

STRUCTURING THE PROCESS

The Greek historian Herodotus (450 BC) describes a practice used by Persian soldiers to make decisions about a tricky or complex project.

> If the idea of taking action or adopting a solution occurs to them while they are drunk, the Persians discuss it and make a decision. But the next day, when they are sober, the master of the house where the discussion took place submits the decision to them for reconsideration. If they still agree, it is adopted; if not, it is abandoned. Conversely, any decision they make when sober is reconsidered when they are drunk (Herodotus).

This example is relevant in several ways. First, it highlights that managing in 3D does not mean suppressing creativity and emotions, quite the contrary. Indeed, enthusiasm and overoptimism—which lead entrepreneurs to take significant risks—are necessary to engage in bold and creative projects, not to mention addressing grand challenges or world-scale puzzles such as global poverty, climate change, and COVID-19. The example of the Persian soldiers suggests that we need to free ourselves from the tyranny of the "or"—which would lead us to choose emotion "or" reason—and adopt the genius of the "and" and thus take advantage of these two human traits (Collins & Porras, 2005; Ika, Pinto, Love, & Paché, 2022).

Herodotus's example also highlights the need for proven systems that allow us to usefully frame our spontaneity without constraining it. For instance, partygoers need to decide how to get home safely before consuming alcohol—not when leaving the bar, because their decisions will be unwise. Before is the best time for the partygoers to designate a driver who will refrain from drinking, or they can agree to take a cab or public transportation home. In the organizational setting, the decision-making process must also be separated from its content and set early on. In the same vein, the project manager should be included as early as possible before the decision process is too far advanced.

The importance of having a process in place to structure decision-making before a particular need arises has been highlighted in studies that have compared the quality of decisions made by the same group of people under different modes. Disappointed by his team's dismal handling of the Bay of Pigs in 1961, President Kennedy (who later said, "How could I have been so stupid?") tasked his brother, a close advisor and the attorney general, with a major overhaul of their decision-making system to deal with major crises that would inevitably occur in the future. Robert Kennedy proposed the establishment of ExComm,[1] a cell of 14 senior government and military officials that incorporated automatic systems of dissent and critical evaluation into its operation. Historians and political scientists agree that the Cuban Missile Crisis, which occurred a year later, was handled effectively and successfully by the ExComm group. Since then, that structure has become a model for many organizations in the private and public sectors.

Ten years later, Irving Janis, known for his work on "groupthink," argued that the decisions made in the Cuban missile crisis were relatively free of the perverse effects of "groupthink" that had marred discussions and led to disastrous decisions in the Bay of Pigs crisis (Janis, 1972). In the early 1970s, Allison and Graham (1999) also expressed this view in the second edition of *Essence of Decision*, on the missile crisis. What is striking is that after the great Bay of Pigs debacle, President Kennedy and virtually the same decision makers achieved better results under even more complex circumstances when dealing with the Cuban Missile Crisis. Given that individual human biases are strikingly unchanged by experience, the decision-making structure put in place in advance made the difference, not the decision makers themselves or their experience with the first crisis.

When setting up fuzzy projects, which are characterized by high complexity, special attention must be paid to the decision structure early on to curb the combined effect of cognitive biases and groupthink. Otherwise, projects are launched on a sort of "death march" and are doomed to failure before they even begin (Pinto, 2013).

The mistakes in the billion-dollar public-private partnership (PPP) project for the extension of Highway 427 in the Greater Toronto Area, in Canada, may have been avoided. The project selected the wrong contractor based on criteria set by the provincial government—namely, technical execution capabilities, experience, qualified personnel, and financial capacity to carry out a project of this magnitude. However, the weighting of the criteria was not adequately assessed, and the selection committee did not consider the importance of experience in managing large-scale projects. A simple check would have revealed that the selected contractor had been part of a consortium that failed to deliver similar projects in the past. Then, they could have hired a competing company with a proven track record of completing large-scale projects. In doing so, the partnership would have avoided subsequent legal disputes over the safety of the highway route (Lancaster, 2021).

We recommend incorporating proven practices into decision-making and project planning. Like ExComm, these systems should require the formulation of alternative options and opposing views. This can be done by appointing a devil's advocate, expanding and instituting dissent by assigning the role of advocates to different members on a rotating basis, requiring the expression of opposing views and the submission of alternative options, which are then systematically evaluated.

It would also be beneficial to institute the practice of conducting premortems. In this doomsday exercise, participants are asked to assume that the project has failed and imagine a disastrous ending. They then formulate plausible scenarios to explain why the worst happened. This low-cost exercise allows the team to express doubts and anticipate problems with the plan they need to implement.

Project managers must also institute methods and practices to stem the effects of cognitive biases and groupthink drift while designing and formulating their projects. These methods can be equally valuable for designing projects in a bar full of Persian soldiers, in a White House office, in a boardroom, or the basement of a small business. However, as the behavioralists point out, it is necessary to think ahead and use collective mechanisms to counteract the effect of individual cognitive biases. When well thought out and integrated into the project management process, these mechanisms can highlight areas of uncertainty and improve risk assessment. They lead to better assessments, a greater number of options, and more informed choices. Managers can thus increase project efficiency and effectiveness at every stage, from design to implementation.

EMBRACING COMPLEXITY

Fuzzy projects are characterized by high levels of complexity and uncertainty. When faced with strong winds, a ship's captain may change course but always needs to rely on the compass to get to the destination. Captains learn to remain vigilant and wisely change direction while staying keenly aware of the context. In the rough waters of complexity, they cannot do the same things as they usually would and expect different results. Doing so would be the very definition of madness, as Einstein is purported to have said! Indeed, complexity has consequences.

We must also carefully consider the assumptions underlying the estimates and the statements found in the best project charters. Beware of taking these assumptions for granted without evidence or accepting their accuracy without proof. This tendency is particularly risky in complex situations. The Google Glass project is interesting in this regard, because the project proponents did not adequately read the environment (in this case, the market) before launching the project.

With an unlimited budget, the Google Glass project was initiated to develop augmented reality eyeglasses. Heralded by *Time* magazine as one of the best inventions of that year, this project promised to make the internet accessible to people's eyes, literally. It did not deliver. Although celebrities like then Prince Charles, Oprah, Beyoncé, and others sported Google Glasses, purchased at US$1,500 a pair, the project was abandoned after two years of unsatisfactory sales. Among other things, Google's conjecture that people would be willing to wear cameras on their faces did not pass the reality check. It turned out that truck drivers, pilots, machine operators, police, security guards, and doctors would have benefited from the technology much more than the average person or celebrity (Nieto-Rodriguez, 2020).

Sometimes uncertainty manifests itself in changes in the environment in the aftermath of the project launch, which complicate or derail its implementation. These changes can be economic, social, political, or technological in nature. They can be internal, like when the Boeing and Crossrail projects replaced the project manager during execution. These changes can also be external, as was the case with the COVID-19 pandemic, the financial crisis of 2008, the September 11 attacks in 2001, or Google's Sidewalks Labs project, which ended due to the COVID-19 pandemic and the ensuing economic uncertainty.

Unexpected events often thwart fuzzy projects. Worldwide examples in the twenty-first century range from September 11, 2001, to COVID-19–related decisions that upset whole societies and specific projects. The security budget for the Olympic Games in Greece went from US$100 million to over US$2 billion after 9/11 (Georgakis & Nauright, 2012). The Tokyo Summer Games were postponed for a year due to the COVID-19 pandemic, and they were then held on a much smaller scale in 2021. The 2021 Beijing Games were held six months later under the cloud of a lingering pandemic. The Russian invasion of Ukraine in February 2022 could have seriously hampered these games as it happened within days of the closing ceremonies.

Could we have predicted such events and anticipated their impact on the projects and, more importantly, our societies?

Undoubtedly, the world had seen other pandemics before. There were clear and specific warnings regarding a pending "airborne pandemic" echoed by Presidents G. W. Bush (in 2005) and B. Obama (in 2014), and by Bill Gates (in 2015), who all made specific speeches that are posted on the internet. The unfortunate fact is that even when a potential change is foreseen, we often do nothing. The same can be said of issues of territorial wars among nations, climate change, and the proliferation of satellites in our planet's outer atmosphere.

Nancy Smart, who has worked on a few projects, knows how wrong experts can be when making predictions on specific matters and how gloomy scenarios are often ignored. She wonders then how we can best address the high complexity that plagues fuzzy projects.

We need to approach complexity differently in fuzzy projects. As we pointed out in the previous chapter, it is tempting to treat fuzzy projects like any other, and to think of their risks as "known unknowns." The tendency is to try to bring the fuzzy project back to the initial plan and push harder for its implementation, whatever the cost. Through the fog of complexity, we set sail with renewed resolve and end up on the reefs. In this context, this reductionist attitude toward complexity—which we call "understand-reduce-respond"—often comes to nothing. So, what can project managers do differently?

A more appropriate attitude toward complexity is to take an approach of "understand-embrace-adapt." We need to grasp the nature and source of the project's complexity and gauge its structural and sociopolitical dimensions. Then we can embrace complexity rather than try to reduce it. We also need to adapt to the changing circumstances of the project (see Box 10.3).

BOX 10.3

Reducing or Embracing Complexity?

Theoretical work in philosophy and in the management of complexity suggests two distinct approaches.

The first school of thought seeks to reduce complexity by following Descartes's decomposition rule, which analytically divides the complex problem to be solved into as many simple elements as necessary to explain it.

The second school of thought strives to embrace complexity and adopt a more "sophisticated" way of thinking that involves learning to live with complexity by adapting to changing circumstances.

These two theoretical postures for dealing with complexity are based on the work of philosopher Edgard Morin (2008) and organizational theorist Haridimos Tsoukas (2017). Both complexity thinkers agree that one must be sophisticated and not "simplify" one's thinking to meet the challenge of complexity. Complex problems require complex thinking. These two authors point out a contradiction between disjunctive thinking, which separates problems that are nevertheless related and ignores the context, and conjunctive thinking, which connects them and considers the context.

The dichotomy between these two rival schools of thought in a situation of complexity allows us to reconcile the distinction between risk and uncertainty that we made in Chapter 9. We need to move from the simple thinking, specific to the context of risk and the "known unknowns" that characterize it, to the complex thinking necessary in the context of uncertainty where the "unknown unknowns" prevail.

On a practical level, the opposing schools of thought on situations of complexity result in two contrasting attitudes for practitioners.

The first attitude consists of trying to understand the complex problem at hand, then trying to reduce its complexity, and finally answering it with a simple formula. We call this attitude "understand-reduce-respond."[2] For example, to counter cost overruns, Flyvbjerg (2014) suggests understanding them as a complex phenomenon caused by overoptimism. Then, he proposes reducing the complexity and responding to it with a simple formula for de-biasing forecasts: reference class forecasting (RCF), which he presents elsewhere as a "simplification, like any other forecast." The only thing left to do is to rely on the project plan to deliver it, come what may.

Alternatively, the second attitude tries to understand the complex phenomenon in question, embracing its complexity rather than trying in vain to reduce it, and finally adapting to the circumstances to cope with the complexity. We call this attitude: "understand-embrace-adapt."[3]

Thus, to deal with cost overruns in complex situations, one must first understand that they are typically due to two major causes: biases (e.g., overoptimism) and errors (e.g., faulty calculations). Instead of minimizing changes in project scope, it is better to embrace the complexity and adjust the plan (if necessary) to adapt to changing project circumstances (Ika, Love, & Pinto, 2022; Ika, Pinto, Love, & Paché, 2022). These changes are neither good nor bad in themselves but are necessary for cocreating and sharing the project's future value among stakeholders. These adjustments, therefore, become essential to achieve consensus among stakeholders in the context of collective action.

Echoing President Dwight Eisenhower's famous words, project sponsors and managers should consider that making a plan is nothing—changing it is everything (Dvir & Lechler, 2004). It does not matter if it is a strategic, governance, or project management plan. Project sponsors and managers cannot sit back and do nothing to address changes in the project environment—to do so is to risk failure. To increase the chances of success, they can use creativity to respond to the uncertainty by making changes in strategy, governance, scope, and plan during project execution. However, since these changes tend to affect multiple stakeholders with divergent expectations, the high sociopolitical complexity, combined with the high uncertainty of projects, remains a major challenge.

Consider the contrasting cases of the Aurora VA Hospital in the United States and the Philharmonic Hall in Paris, which were both subject to scope changes and notorious disputes among stakeholders. The first resulted in a significant project downsizing, and the second in an equally dramatic expansion.

The goal of the Aurora VA hospital project, a US$2 billion project delivered in 2018 ten years late, was to create a state-of-the-art facility in Colorado to treat 400,000 veterans with various disabilities (see Chapter 5). Due to substantial cost overruns, the US Congress ordered the project to abandon the US$20 million post-traumatic stress disorder (PTSD) treatment center. The dismal performance of the Aurora VA hospital project led to accusations of deliberate obfuscation by the Congressional Budget Office, which ultimately resulted in the transfer of responsibility for the project's completion to the Army Corps of Engineers and a legal battle between the hospital and its original contractors.

The Philharmonic Hall in Paris, one of the most magnificent concert halls in the world (capacity of 3,400 people), was inaugurated in 2015 and cost US$500 million, about twice its initial budget. This was due to the addition of office space, a corporate restaurant, and a cafe during the design stage, which resulted in significant cost blowouts. These cost blowouts gave rise to a media and legal battle. The battle between architect Jean Nouvel, winner of the most prestigious prize in architecture, and the project's sponsor, the Philharmonie de Paris, ended in 2021 with an out-of-court settlement highlighting the building's architectural success (Ika, Pinto, Love, & Paché, 2022).

Other large-scale projects are changing strategy or governance due to the sociopolitical complexity of collective action. Crossrail provides a striking illustration. After unsuccessful attempts to implement the project, the UK government's Department of Transport (DoT) joined forces with the Greater London Authority (GLA), responsible for public transport policy in London. To be able to carry on with the project, they set up a public agency, a joint venture called Crossrail Ltd. But early on, the two partners disagreed about the project's future value. The DoT favored a user-pay principle, while the GLA insisted that broader economic benefits, such as productivity gains, should be considered in the project's benefit-cost analysis. The two parties only agreed to build the 188-kilometer commuter train after the government changed its policy to accommodate GLA's demands.

The Crossrail developers also had to engage in lengthy and complex negotiations with other stakeholder groups, including end users and local authorities that were not part of the formal alliance and had differing expectations. The local authorities wanted a say in the locations of the train stations. Of particular note, these external stakeholders wanted bathrooms at Farrington station, the developers objected, arguing that adding bathrooms would be costly and pose safety challenges. A local politician got involved, and the dispute went all the way to the British Parliament. Faced with this escalation, the developers had to give in. This illustrates how the sociopolitical complexity that underlies collective action may give rise to stakeholder conflicts, stifle consensus, complicate the decision to take action, and lead to cost hikes in projects (Gil and Fu, 2022).

Nancy Smart is aware of the issues related to complexity and uncertainty in projects. She knows that being locked into the straitjacket of a project execution plan often leads to failure. But, she also saw how embracing complexity worked well in the mass vaccination against COVID-19, especially with the variants. But she still wonders how project managers can navigate complexity, specifically when and how they should adapt their implementation approach.

Nancy's questions on the subject of complexity bring to mind an intriguing speech given by Andrew Haldane, the president of the Bank of England. "Catching a Frisbee is difficult," he said, as part of what the *Wall Street Journal* called the "Speech of the Year":

> Doing so successfully requires the catcher to weigh a complex array of physical and atmospheric factors, among them wind speed and frisbee rotation. Were a physicist to write down frisbee-catching as an optimal control problem, they would need to understand and apply Newton's Law of Gravity. Yet despite this complexity, catching a frisbee is remarkably common. Casual empiricism reveals that it is not an activity only undertaken by those with a Doctorate in physics. It is a task that an average dog can master. Indeed some, such as border collies, are better at frisbee-catching than humans (Haldane, 2012).

Haldane argued that complex problems do not need complex solutions.

> Modern finance is complex, perhaps too complex. Regulation of modern finance is complex, almost certainly too complex. That configuration spells trouble. As you do not fight fire with fire, you do not fight complexity with complexity. Because complexity generates uncertainty, not risk. It requires a regulatory response grounded in simplicity, not complexity (Haldane, 2012).

These ideas work well when dealing with the complexity of fuzzy projects. In real, complex situations, it is often more appropriate to use simple heuristics, which can do better than sophisticated algorithms. Chapter 9 called for a broader approach that considers the stakeholders' expectations about the project and deploys the rational, political, and psychosocial approaches appropriately. In line with Haldane, we propose an ecological rationality lens, which refers to understanding the circumstances under which a project, or any decision made during its implementation, does or does not work (Ika, Love, & Pinto, 2022; Love et al., 2022). Box 10.4 clarifies the concepts of ecological rationality, intuition, heuristics, and the adaptive toolbox.

BOX 10.4

Ecological Rationality, Intuition, Heuristics, and the Adaptive Toolbox

We borrow the concept of ecological rationality from the German psychologist Gerd Gigerenzer. He based his work on research by Herbert Simon, political scientist and Nobel Prize winner, who had shown that logical rationality had limits in a decision-making context where time, knowledge, and our capacity for calculation are also limited. We cannot aim for the best solution so we settle for one that is satisficing. The human mind operates with bounded rationality when faced with an overwhelming and ever-changing information that must be collected and weighed when making decisions. The human mind has thus adapted to its environment (ecological rationality).

The notion of ecological rationality refers to a functional correspondence between human cognition and the environment in which humans operate, and to the idea that we can design environments that are conducive to the achievement of certain tasks. While logical rationality is based on logic and probability theory, ecological rationality is based on the adaptation of the human mind to its environment.

Thus, decisions must be adapted to the environment in which they are made. Just as we use a hammer to drive nails and a screwdriver for screws, the decision maker needs different mental tools depending on the context. Gigerenzer calls it an adaptive toolbox, a collection of rules learned over time that guide decisions whether unconscious or not. As needed, some tools can be used in an environment of risk, others in an environment characterized by uncertainty.

Decision makers can adequately turn to logic and probability theory in a risk environment. In this instance, optimization is not only possible but also effective. On the other hand, in an uncertain environment, it is impossible to know in advance all the alternatives, their probabilities, and their consequences. Thus, applying probability theory is futile, and optimization is an illusion.

In such circumstances, decision makers need to consider intuition and heuristics because they must solve problems quickly and frugally with incomplete knowledge. Heuristics can give better results than an optimization approach in such an environment. Derived from the Latin *intuitio* (sight, look), intuition is a judgment that appears quickly to our conscience, whose underlying reasons are not completely known to us but whose strength allows us to act.

Etymologically, the word "heuristic" comes from the ancient Greek *heuriskô* (I find). Heuristics are rules of thumb that facilitate decision-making in complex situations. This notion of heuristics has nothing to do with cognitive distortions that lead to decision-making biases. Fast and frugal heuristics lead to ecologically rational decisions—that is, decisions that fit the structure of the environment, even if they are not logically consistent.

Typically, heuristics are used unconsciously. In this manner, baseball players keep their eyes on a fly ball while running, and they adjust their speed by keeping their "gaze angle" constant until they catch it. But heuristics can be used consciously as well. Airplane pilots commonly use the gaze heuristic. In a daring feat, the pilots of US Airways Flight 1549 gazed at the tower of the next airport and ascertained that they could not reach it, with their engines stalled. They changed course and successfully landed by gliding the plane onto the Hudson River.

Three sets of rules can help develop fast and frugal heuristics in dealing with complexity: (1) *search rules* that specify where the search should go; (2) *stop rules* that specify when to stop searching for information; and (3) *decision rules* that specify how the information gathered will factor into the final decision.

Sources: Gigerenzer (2014); Ika, Love, & Pinto (2022); Love et al. (2022).

A heuristic, or rule of thumb, is ecologically rational insofar as it adapts to its environment. The title of Haldane's speech, "The Dog and the Frisbee," stems from one such simple rule, the gaze heuristic. Gaze heuristic refers to how a complex problem can be mastered—for example, catching a Frisbee in a natural and complex environment. The dog runs at a speed that maintains its gaze on the Frisbee at a roughly constant angle, ignoring all complex data. The logic is that less information means better decision-making (less is more). The dog focuses on a satisfactory solution (satisficing) and acts on it. For if dogs, like baseball players, could systematically predict the trajectory of the ball or Frisbee, there would be no need for heuristics (Gigerenzer, 2014).

Similarly, in fuzzy project management, if the rational approach and its tools could predict project success, there would be no need for other approaches. Today's project managers must become chameleon-like, intuitively and wisely using an adaptive toolbox of heuristics to deal with different degrees of complexity (Gigerenzer, 2014). With respect to this toolbox, one should apply the rational approach in some cases. In others, the political approach based on the interests of the principals should be used. A psychosocial approach that considers the agents' expectations should be implemented in others.

Experience has shown that the most experienced managers use intuition in fuzzy situations when faced with too much or too little data, when decision-making time is limited, or when the window of opportunity may close quickly. In these situations where there is no instruction manual, the intuitive skill of decision-making works well (Leybourne & Sadler-Smith, 2005). Since intuition often comes from years of experience, managers need practice to accumulate heuristics and consciously sharpen their intuition.

Box 10.5 highlights the singular experience of four leaders whose "madness" has led to resounding success for their organizations.

BOX 10.5

Four Leaders Whose Insights Paid Off

Adam Werbach was the president of the Sierra Club, a *nonprofit organization committed to protecting the environment,* when he became a consultant to Walmart. Fellow environmentalists called him a traitor and a sellout. But Werbach wanted to bring change from within. He succeeded by enabling 40 percent of Walmart employees to adopt sustainable practices.

In 1914, Henry Ford was facing declining demand for his cars and high employee turnover. So, he doubled employee wages. Had he lost his mind? Within a year, employee turnover reduced to one-twentieth, productivity nearly doubled, demand for Ford cars exploded, and Ford workers could afford to buy the cars they were making.

In the 1950s, Bill Allen was CEO of Boeing, a company focused on the defense industry. But Allen proposed that Boeing build their own commercial airplane to help the nascent civilian air travel take off. The board of directors backed up his gamble and spent US$16 million on the new 707 transcontinental airliner. His crazy idea transformed both Boeing and air travel.

Uber CEO Travis Kalanick faced severe resistance when he introduced demand-based pricing: let's charge more when demand is highest or service supply is lowest. Many considered that idea irrational and that customers would reject it.

They didn't. The practice has spread and been adopted by traditional companies like Disney.

Source: Adapted from Bonnell (2018).

THE EFFECTIVITY OF PROJECTS

We must go further if we wish to move beyond good project management and ensure the complete success of projects for key stakeholders. Complexity requires sophisticated thinking, so we need a deeper understanding of complexity to adequately manage and evaluate fuzzy projects. The Google Sidewalk Labs, Nintendo Wii U, Copenhagen Cityringen Metro, and London Crossrail projects highlight that there are other stakeholders external to the core project delivery team whose voices count, including end users, the public, and society at large.

To illustrate this further, let us look at an unfortunately common problem in First Nations populations in Canada and Australia, and Indigenous Americans in the United States. Imagine that the residents of a small remote community need a well to get drinking water. Initially, two project options are on the table. Option A would allow the project to be completed quickly and cheaply, right on the edge of the village. Option B would be to dig the well on a more remote site where they could go much deeper, 1,000 feet rather than 250, and ensure a higher water flow rate.

First, let us evaluate these two options from the perspective of the mandate. Option A would be more efficient, using standard success criteria, as it would cost less and be completed sooner. However, Option B would be more effective as it would yield more water for the villagers and thus better results for the principals. Similar trade-offs between effectiveness and efficiency criteria are found in any project, such as improving customer service or launching a new product. In all these cases, the selection, design, planning, and subsequent project evaluation are based on the efficiency and effectiveness criteria used in project management (Shenhar & Dvir, 2007). Choosing between the first and second well-digging options depends on the available means, funding, and selection process.

The project sponsors (see System 1a in Figure 10.2) are usually in charge of decision-making. For the well-digging project, they could include the different government levels involved (municipal, state, federal). Once a choice is made, a call for tenders can be issued. One bidder will then be awarded the mandate to implement the project (e.g., Systems 1b, 1c). If the well meets the time, cost, and quality criteria when it is completed—that is, the quality and flow rate of water specified in the tender—the project will be considered successful. Case closed. But do the criteria used to ascertain the project's success act as blinders, preventing us from distinguishing project *management* success from true *project* success? Indeed, the criteria can be shortsighted and fail to consider the concrete success of the project for the organizations and external stakeholders. Yet concerns about organizational and societal impacts are increasingly important (Gil & Fu, 2022; Ika & Pinto, 2022). To those ends, the 3D approach invites managers to consider the political and psychosocial aspects of projects and the organizations that sponsor or deliver them, beyond the confines of the project.

To take an even broader view of the well-digging project, we could bring together the villagers (as potential users) and the staff who will be involved in the project. These two groups are important stakeholders from the psychosocial and political perspectives of the project, and the planning process could bring them together—they should not be mere footnotes in a plan.

Together, villagers may put forth more desirable options (for the end users) that are considered feasible (by the staff of the sponsor and/or the delivery organizations). Thus, an Option C might be to dig the well close to the community center and the school, where it would be much more accessible to the villagers year-round. While Option C may cost a bit more, take longer, or have a flow rate somewhere between Options A and B, it would be more accessible and yield greater health benefits.

Alternative and additional forms of consultations are possible, such as public hearings and surveys, with their benefits and shortcomings. Such consultations may prolong the early phases of the project, but they will also shorten its implementation by ensuring more end-user buy-in as well as preempt future delays.

The project is a system (see System 2) whose outputs serve a larger, social system (System 4). In this case, the well is a construction project. This technical system supplies water that improves the lives of the village inhabitants, who are part of another system comprised of direct and indirect end users or beneficiaries (System 3). The well construction could be commissioned by an organization that would perform the task in-house or subcontract it to another organization (e.g., Systems 1b, 1c). These latter systems have socioeconomic objectives that confirm their social relevance and positioning in a larger system, namely, the social system (System 4).[4]

For the organizational systems (Systems 1a, b, c), the technical system is a means of achieving the higher goals efficiently and effectively. For the beneficiary system and the broader social system, the technical system is a way to satisfy their needs or solve social problems in a manner that is impactful and sustainable.

Considering the social and political aspects of the project, care must be taken to ensure stakeholder participation and to integrate end users of the well and project management specialists early in the formulation and evaluation of possible options. Other options will likely emerge (as was the case with Excomm or the Persian soldiers) because mechanisms for critical evaluation and even dissent from the proposed options on the table will have been incorporated (see Figure 10.2).

While not all members of the groups being consulted—villagers and project management specialists—will be personally involved in the well-digging project, their input is essential to

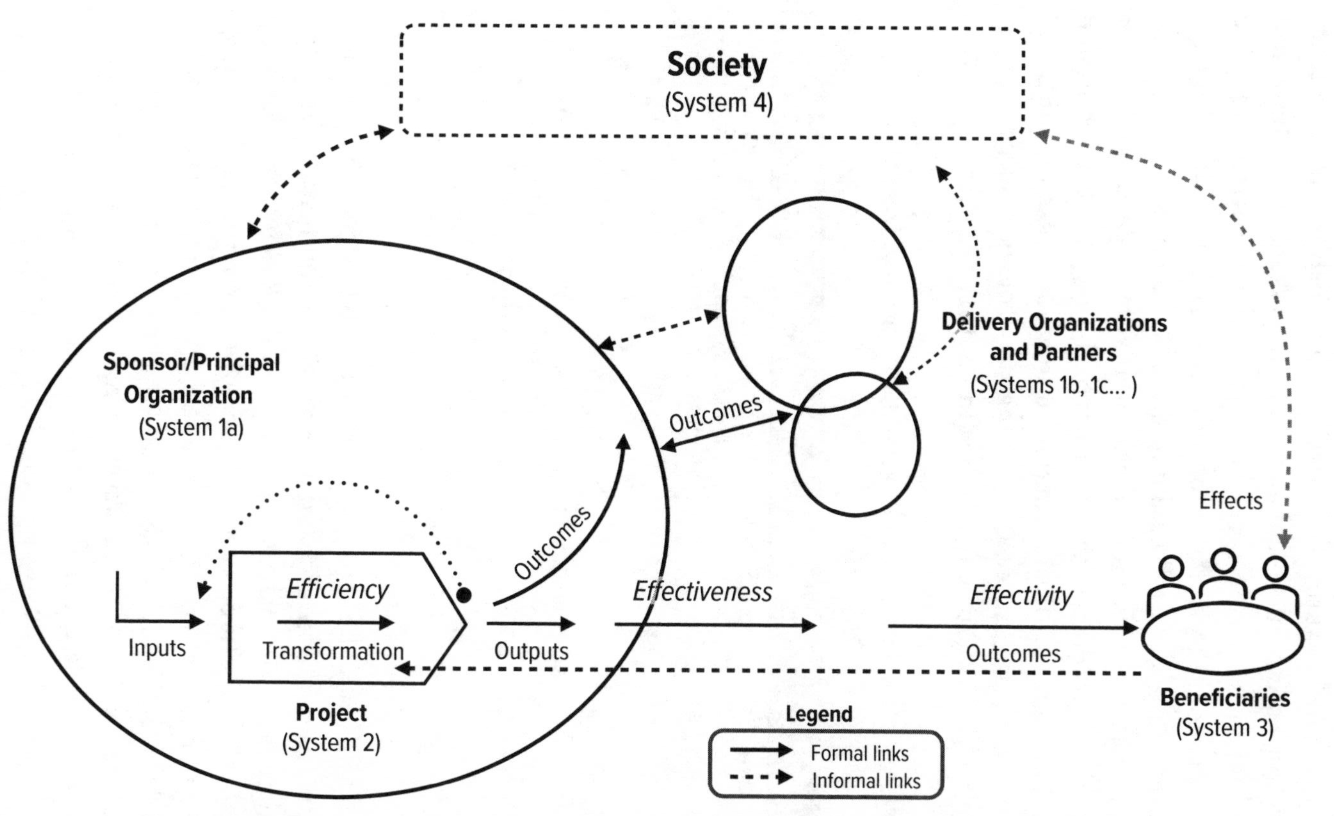

FIGURE 10.2 Project success across systems: efficiency, effectiveness, effectivity

ensure a better use of the well. Consequently, the effectivity of the project will be enhanced for all stakeholders, above and beyond internal efficiency and organizational effectiveness. The project should create value for these external stakeholders, as happened in the Crossrail case (Gil & Fu, 2022). It impacts specific aspects of their lives in one way or another. Effectivity makes it possible to reconcile the evaluation of the project in the short and medium term with the criterion of long-term sustainability, and gauge the actual success, including the ecological success, of the project (Ika & Pinto, 2022) (see Table 10.1).

TABLE 10.1 Characteristics of Project Efficiency, Effectiveness, and Effectivity

CRITERIA	PERFORMANCE MEASURES	LEVEL OF ANALYSIS	INFORMAL DEFINITION
Efficiency	Outputs ÷ Inputs	The project as a technical system (Inputs & Outputs)	Doing things right
Effectiveness	Outcomes	The project as an organizational system (Outcomes)	Doing the right things
Effectivity	Impacts	The project as an end-users/beneficiaries system and a social system (impacts)	Doing the best things for all

Efficiency (doing things right) can be assessed in the short term, using the project and its internal environment as the appropriate levels of analysis and evaluation. Effectiveness (doing the right things) can be assessed in the medium term, using the organization and project sponsors as the appropriate levels of analysis and evaluation. Effectivity (doing the best things for all) can only be assessed in the longer term, using beneficiaries or other social systems in the external environment as the appropriate levels of analysis and evaluation.

Breakthrough projects are typically conducted in basic research or space exploration. These projects can generate significant additional benefits beyond their initial objectives, even when they do not meet the prescribed constraints of time, cost, and quality.

White elephant projects as often reported by the press. Oddly, such projects may meet goals of efficiency and even of effectiveness (TCQ), yet they remain underutilized and too costly to maintain in the long run (see Figure 10.3).

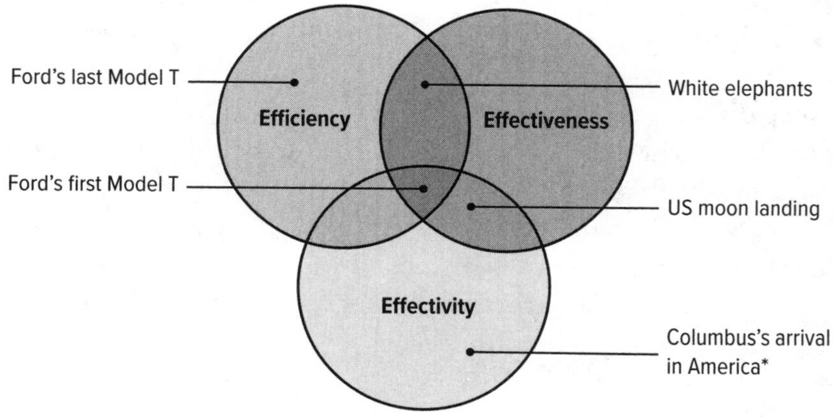

FIGURE 10.3 Expanded project evaluation criteria

These types of projects lead us to reexamine the perspective of stakeholders. As we pointed out in Chapters 7 and 8, we need to consider multiple perspectives and the impact of the project's results on the principals, agents, beneficiaries or end users, external stakeholders, and society as a whole. Perceptions of the project's value for individuals or shared value among stakeholders may differ from a so-called objective assessment of the project's efficiency and effectiveness. This presupposes a certain indeterminacy of project success (Kreiner, 2014; Ika, Love, & Pinto, 2022).

This more ecological approach broadens the scope of responsibility for the project and the work required in its implementation. But it helps to anticipate unforeseen obstacles that would prove costly. As a result, it is common to hold public hearings when a municipality or state wants to make zoning or policy changes that affect citizens' lives.

This approach also helps to highlight the benefits that would accrue from the project when a broader view is taken. The practice of holding public hearings is part of this, as we have noted. In the commercial sector, the launch of a new product can have immediate effects when it generates favorable expectations. For example, the successful launch of the first iPhone boosted the company's stock price the very next day. At times, the mere announcement that an organization is undertaking a project has similar effects on the value of its share and its perception in the eyes of the public. In the political arena, the simple act of announcing plans to deal with a pandemic or natural disaster has similar positive effects that would not have occurred if the plan had been handled behind the scenes.

THE SOPHISTICATED PROJECT MANAGER

In the successful book *Project Management: A Systems Approach to Planning, Scheduling, and Controlling*, published over a dozen times between 1979 and 2022, Kerzner (2022) suggested that "an ideal project manager would probably have doctorates in engineering, business, and psychology, experience in 10 different organizations in a variety of project office positions and be about 25 years old." Several authors and practitioners in the field have taken up this tongue-in-cheek definition that departs from a narrow perception and captures fully what is required in project management. Much more than the systematic design and implementation of a road map, Kerzner's definition emphasizes the importance of experience and human factors to better orchestrate the implementation of projects. Project managers are managers, of course, but also leaders and much more than technicians.

Managers must take a nuanced and personal view of the project implementation plan and execute it as a conductor would. But what kind of orchestra are they conducting? Is it a symphony orchestra where the musicians are grouped by instrument types and sit fanned out so that they can all see the conductor in the center? Or is it more like a jazz band?

The jazz metaphor can help us understand the context of complex projects (Joffre et al., 2006). Unlike neat projects, we submit that fuzzy projects are not conducted in the compartmentalized, standardized settings of symphony orchestras. Therefore, musicians are blended in various ways depending on the characteristics of the setting where they perform. Jazz conductors are not maestros. They do not direct the musicians to perform a piece according to their own personal reading of some music score. Instead, jazz conductors let the jazz musicians improvise and get new sounds from their instruments. Occasionally, some musicians will switch instruments unexpectedly. The conductor expects this because jazz musicians are not just trained performers—they are uniquely talented agents who have a lot of latitude.

Leading a jazz ensemble requires subtle listening skills and the ability to read the musical and visual cues between musicians. Above all, it involves being responsive to each audience, the main stakeholder who will decide on the quality of their musical performance. A jazz orchestra conductor coordinates, encourages, and promotes rather than dictates.

A fuzzy project manager must be many things at once: "a person of action," "a person of thought," and "a front person," as Gaddis (1959) wrote in the *Harvard Business Review*. In our view, they must be all those things and more. As a doer, the project manager must act to deliver the project's goods and services. As a thinker, the project manager must take on the role of a planner, which includes coordinating project activities and measuring how well the project aligns with the interests of the principals, agents, and end users or beneficiaries (proactive role). As a spokesperson, the project manager must continually sell and resell the project to stakeholders; negotiate and secure resources and management support; counter any resistance; and communicate, shape, and reshape policies, guidelines, and practices (champion role).

Project managers can skillfully use intuition and heuristics adapted to the project at hand (technical role). In the face of complexity, they can demonstrate the wisdom of the chameleon and adapt to the changing circumstances of the project (reactive role). Trusting their experience and skills, they can allow themselves to be creative and improvise like jazz bandleaders, finding pragmatic solutions to challenges that arise during the project (creative or innovative role). They can also practice shared leadership,[5] and rely with confidence on their own leadership and let others lead when needed (leadership role).

Nancy Smart has a big job on her hands. She is not only a manager but also a doer, thinker, and spokesperson, with roles that require her to be technical, proactive, reactive, creative, champion, and leader (see Bentahar & Ika, 2019). In a nutshell, fuzzy project manager Nancy is a jack-of-all-trades. Will she be up to the task? Yes! She's well-trained, caring, and . . . smart (of course).

CONCLUSION

This chapter presents the key lessons learned from our incursion into the world of organizational projects, which are often fuzzy and thus fraught with complexity and/or uncertainty.

The chapter suggests six takeaways for project managers and sponsors:

1. Know and understand the context: The manager must take on the color of the context, be cautious in dealing

with threats, and seize the opportunities that arise, and deal with things without rushing. To successfully deliver the project's medium- and long-term benefits, the manager needs to be patient, respectful, and sensitive to the human aspects of the project.

2. Focus on planning, not just the plan: Planning is a learning exercise. It allows us to anticipate the future and, above all, to learn through monitoring and evaluation to improve future project performance. We must "begin before the beginning" and thus involve the project manager in the project formulation process as early as possible. In this way, the project sponsor will benefit from the project manager's input on implementation, and the project manager will better understand the project specifics and nuances. This early integration and the sustained commitment of the principals will ensure organizational effectiveness, the quality of the expected results, and the contribution of the project to the strategic goals of the organization.
3. Structure the process of decision-making in advance: This helps to highlight areas of uncertainty, improve risk assessment, and counteract the combined effect of individual cognitive biases and groupthink. In addition, it better exploits the benefits of having a multiplicity of opinions and broader expertise when a diverse group of people is involved, by opposing options and opinions to be expressed. Doing premortems (by assuming that the project has failed and explaining why) allows the players to express doubts and methodically anticipate the course of future events.
4. Ask questions and listen: If unable to participate in the initial project definition, the project manager should read and get as much information as possible about the initial planning stage. This means having access to the names and profiles of the decision makers (who could be contacted) and to the source files and documents that preceded

the final version of the plan. A new project manager should ask critical questions before diving headlong into project implementation, striving to understand why, by whom, and for whom the project was designed and who intentionally or unintentionally might benefit from it.

5. Ensure the effectiveness and effectivity of the project: The design and evaluation of the success of fuzzy projects should be more sophisticated. The traditional criteria of time, cost, and quality capture the efficiency criterion of the project but obscure its temporal dimension and its raison d'être for the organization and external stakeholders such as end users or beneficiaries. However, the project is a way to achieve organizational objectives, satisfy the needs of beneficiaries, and solve social problems effectively. The project manager needs to be aware that the project is often part of a larger system. Therefore, it is crucial to understand the project's medium-term organizational and long-term social impacts on different stakeholders as they have different expectations.
6. Assume various roles: The project manager needs to be adept at planning and coordinating the project activities (proactive role). The project manager must carry out the project, repeatedly explain it to stakeholders, and shape and reshape the practices (champion role). The job also involves deploying the right logistics at the right time (technical role) and adapting to changing circumstances (reactive role). It also takes creativity and improvisation during the implementation (creative or innovative role). At different times, project managers must rely on their own leadership and that of others (leadership role).

Trying to reduce the complexity of a fuzzy project or forcing the implementation of a plan that has become obsolete will lead to failure. Instead, good project managers accept and even embrace complexity. Like the chameleon, they adjust to the changing circumstances of the project. They also develop an adaptive toolbox of heuristics and their intuitive ability to know which tools are appropriate for which context. *Adapting* will mean: navigating the project through threats and opportunities; giving the project team the latitude needed for innovative solutions; ensuring stakeholder buy-in; guiding, acting, being creative, and adjusting the project plan as necessary. In so doing, the project manager will demonstrate the leadership needed in a fuzzy project.

REFERENCES

Allison, G. T., & Graham, A. (1999). *Essence of decision.*

Associated Press (2007, October 17). 787 program chief replaced a Boeing. *New York Times.* https://www.nytimes.com/2007/10/17/business/17boeing.html.

Bâ, A. H. (1998). *Sur les traces d'Amkoullel.* Editions Actes Sud.

Berlin, I. (1953). *The hedgehog and the fox: An essay on Tolstoy's view on history.* Second Edition. Princeton University Press.

Bonnell, S. (2018). 4 leaders who won by following their instincts (despite being told they were crazy. Inc. https://www.inc.com/sunny-bonnell/how-to-follow-your-instincts-in-business-even-when-people-say-youre-crazy.html.

Cohen, H. (1972). The anomia of success and the anomia of failure: A study of similarities in opposites. *The British Journal of Sociology, 23,* 329–343.

Collins, J. C., & Porras, J. I. (2005). *Built to last: Successful habits of visionary companies.* Random House.

de Wit, A. (1988). Measurement of project success. *Project Management Journal, 6*(3), 164–170.

Dupré. J. (2021, Nov. 4). Does the skyscraper still have a future? https://www.bbc.com/news/world-us-canada-59139998.

Dvir D., & Lechler, T. (2004). Plans are nothing, changing plans is everything: the impact of changes on project success. *Research Policy, 33*(1), 1–15.

Flyvbjerg, B. (2014). What you should know about megaprojects and why: An overview. *Project Management Journa*l, *45(*2), 6–19.

Gaddis, P.O. (1959). The project manager. *Harvard Business Review, 37*(3), 89–97.

Georgakis, S., & Nauright, J. (2012). Creating the "Scarecrow": The 2004 Athens Olympic Games and the Greek Financial Crisis. The Center for the Study of Sport and Leisure in Society Working Paper #4. George Mason University.

Geraldi, J., & Söderlund, J. (2018). Project studies: What it is, where it is going. *International Journal of Project Management, 36*(1), 55–70.

Gigerenzer, G. (2014). *Risk savvy: How to make good decisions*. Penguin Books.

Gil, N., & Fu, Y. (2022). Megaproject performance, value creation, and value distribution: An organizational governance perspective. *Academy of Management Discoveries, 8*(2), 224–251.

Haldane A. C. (2012). The dog and the frisbee. Federal Reserve Bank of Kansas City 36th Economic Policy Symposium, August.

Hirschman, A. O. (1967). *Development projects observed*. Washington, DC: Brookings Institution.

Ika, L. A., & Pinto, J. K. (2022). The "re-meaning" of project success: Updating and recalibrating for a modern project management. *International Journal of Project Management, 40*(7), 835–848.

Ika, L. A., Love, P. E. D., & Pinto, J. (2021). Moving beyond the planning fallacy: The emergence of a new principle of project behavior. *IEEE Transactions on Engineering Management, 69*(6), 3310–3325.

Ika, L., Pinto, J. K., Love, P. E., & Paché, G. (2022). Bias versus error: why projects fall short. *Journal of Business Strategy*. https://doi.org/10.1108/JBS-11-2021-0190.

Janis, I. L. (1972). *Victims of groupthink*. Houghton Mifflin Company.

Kahneman, D. (2011). *Thinking, fast and slow*. Farrar, Straus and Giroux

Kerzner, H. (2022). *Project management: A systems approach to planning, scheduling, and controlling*. John Wiley & Sons.

Kreiner, K. (2014). Restoring project success as phenomenon. In R.A., Lundin, M. Hällgreen, Advancing research on projects and temporary organizations, Copenhagen Business School Press & Liber (pp. 21–40).

Kreiner, K. (2020). Conflicting notions of a project: The battle between Albert O. Hirschman and Bent Flyvbjerg. *Project Management Journal, 51*(4), 400–410.

Lancaster, J. (2021, April 29). Why you cannot drive on this new, $616M Toronto-area highway. CBC News. https://www.cbc.ca/news/canada/toronto/highway-427-extension-toronto-ontario-government-1.6005609.

Lee, G., & Brumer, L. (2017). Managing mission-critical government software projects: Lessons learned from the HealthCare.gov Project. 69–72. https://www.businessofgovernment.org/sites/default/files/Viewpoints%20Dr%20Gwanhoo%20LLe.pd.

Leybourne, S., & Sadler-Smith, E. (2005). The role of intuition and improvisation in project management. *International Journal of Project Management, 24*(6), 483–492.

Love, P. E. D., & Ika, L. A (2022). Making sense of hospital project (mis) performance: Over budget, late, time and time again—Why? And what can be done about it. *Engineering, 12*, 183–201.

Love, P.E.D., Ika, L. A., Matthews, J., & Fang, W. (2022). Risk and uncertainty in the cost contingency of transportation projects: Accommodating bias or heuristics, or both. *IEEE Transactions on Engineering Management.*

Love, P. E. D., Ika, L. A., Matthews, J., Li, X., & W. Fang (2021). A procurement policy-making pathway to future-proof large-scale transportation infrastructure assets. *Research in Transportation* Economics, *90*, 101069.

Lundin, R. A., Arvidson, N., Brady, T., Ekstedt, E., Midler, C., & Sydow, J. (2015). *Managing and working in project society: Institutional challenges of temporary organizations.* Cambridge University Press.

Maylor, H., & Turner, N. (2017). Understand, reduce, respond: Project complexity management theory and practice. *International Journal of Operations and Production Management, 37*(8), 1076–1093.

Mintzberg, H. (1989). *Mintzberg on management: Inside our strange world of organizations.* Simon and Schuster.

Morris, P. W. G. (2013). *Reconstructing project management.* John Wiley & Sons.

Müller, R., Sankaran, S., Drouin, N., Vaagaasar, A., Bekker, M. C., & Jain, K. (2018). A theory framework for balancing vertical and horizontal leadership in projects. *International Journal of Project Management, 36*(1), 83–94.

NBA.com (2021). Wilson reveals NBA official game ball in advance of 2021–22 NBA season. https://www.nba.com/news/wilson-nba-official-game-ball-unveil.

Nieto-Rodriguez, A. (2020, June 20). Notorious project failures—Google Glass: What lessons can we learn from noteworthy projects that failed or were delivered successfully? https://www.cio.com/article/3201886/notorious-project-failures-google-glass.html.

Pinto, J. K. (2013). Lies, damned lies, and project plans: recurring human errors that can ruin the project planning process. *Business Horizons, 56*, 643–653.

Pinto, J. K., & Slevin, D. P. (1989). Critical success factors in R&D projects. *Research in Technology Management, 32*(1), 31–35.

Shenhar, A., & Dvir, D. (2007). *Reinventing project management*. Harvard Business School Press.

Sibony, O. (2014). *Réapprendre à décider*. Débats Publics.

Sibony, O., Lovallo, D., & Powell, T. C. (2017). Behavioral strategy and the strategic decision architecture of the firm. *California Management Review, 59*(3), 5–21.

Stuart, K. S. (2017, 3 Feb.). RIP Wii U: Nintendo's glorious, quirky failure. *The Guardian*. https://www.theguardian.com/technology/2017/feb/03/rip-wii-u-nintendos-glorious-quirky-failure.

Topham, G. (2018, November 2). Crossrail boss steps down after project delays. *The Guardian*. https://www.theguardian.com/uk-news/2018/nov/02/crossrail-boss-steps-down-after-project-delays.

Warburton, M. (2020, May 7). Alphabet's Sidewalk Labs cancels Toronto's 'smart city' project. Reuters. https://www.reuters.com/article/us-canada-sidewalk-idUSKBN22J2FN.

Williams, T., & Samset, K. (2010). Issues in front-end decision-making on projects. *Project Management Journal, 41*(2), 38–49.

Winterburn, M. (2021, March 23). From Copenhagen to Toronto—Looking at a world-class transit example before Ontario Line construction begins. Metrolinx.com. https://blog.metrolinx.com/2021/03/23/from-copenhagen-to-the-toronto-looking-at-a-world-class-transit-example-before-ontario-line-construction-begins/

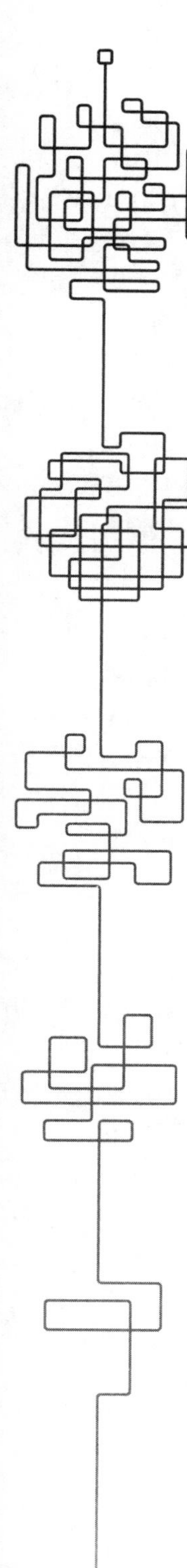

EPILOGUE

THEORETICAL AND EMPIRICAL BASES OF MANAGING PROJECTS IN 3D

This book was written by two authors, for good reasons. One approaches projects from the perspective of the overall strategy of organizations that initiate them, the other from the perspective of those who implement them. The common goal is to improve the way we think of and act on projects.

OUR RESEARCH

Managing Fuzzy Projects in 3D has a theoretical basis, but it is grounded in the real world of projects. It draws lessons from two decades of research on the delivery of projects. We collected data on more than 3,000 projects from around the world, the majority being projects that we characterized as "fuzzy."

We studied projects of varied types, sizes, and objectives. We analyzed data from hundreds of international economic and social infrastructure projects (Love, Ika, & Sing, 2022; Love, Sing, Ika, & Newton, 2019). We focused on projects that seek to contribute to meeting the challenge of sustainable and equitable poverty reduction and improved living standards in Latin America, Africa, and Asia (Ika, Söderlund, Munro, & Landoni, 2020). Our sample included neat projects with well-defined deliverables and objectives, like infrastructure, as well as those with fuzzy objectives, like capacity building and improving governance, that are more difficult to define and measure (e.g., Ika & Donnelly, 2017; Ika, 2018).

Dozens of interviews were conducted (e.g., Ika & Donnelly, 2017), along with hundreds of surveys among critical stakeholders, including project sponsors and managers (e.g., Ika, Diallo, & Thuillier, 2012; Ika, 2018). A database of over 2,800 World Bank–funded projects was also investigated. Finally, we analyzed relevant project reports and other published material (Ika & Saint-Macary, 2012). These projects, which on average cost about US$300 million and took six years to complete, were conducted in various sectors: health, education, governance, agriculture, infrastructure, and the environment (e.g., Ika & Feeny, 2022).

We noted the importance of the social and political aspects of organizations and projects while working in the banking sectors in the United States and in Canada. Later, our comparative studies of multinational engineering firms showed that the upper management of each firm had distinct social profiles and political connections. We found that managers act as a bridge between the internal and external environments of their organizations (Saint-Macary, 1994), which allowed their firms to win contracts, often beyond their fields of experience and technical expertise. Attending to the social dimensions of their environments was essential to the success of their projects, as was underscored by the former CEO of SNC-Lavalin, whom we quoted in Chapter 7.

WHY DO MANY FUZZY PROJECTS FAIL?

Our distress about the failure rate grew when looking into large international development projects, which are reputed to be inherently fuzzy, with unclear or unstable goals. Given their frequent underperformance, we sought to shed light on why they failed. We examined two large-scale projects: the Chad-Cameroon pipeline (US$4 billion) and the Medupi coal plant in South Africa (US$14 billion). This research helped identify contextual, managerial, and institutional problems that can hinder project success (Ika, 2012). This book examines these three problem areas.

Fuzzy Project Managers, Agents, and Sponsors Can Be at Odds

In the main, we found that the various stakeholders involved did not share common points of view. This was true for the sponsors overseeing the project on behalf of the funder (e.g., the World Bank) and the project managers implementing the project on behalf of the recipient country (e.g., Chad). To deepen our understanding of the perspectives of key project stakeholders and to shed more light on the managerial dimension of fuzzy projects, we conducted a quantitative study of about 100 large-scale projects in 26 countries in Africa. With an average budget of US$36 million and a duration of five years, these projects were carried out in 12 sectors, including health, education, governance, agriculture, infrastructure, and the environment (Ika, Diallo, & Thuillier, 2010). In these projects, we found that project managers were not typically involved in the front end and did more monitoring than planning. Generally, they were more concerned with the short-term success of projects and their visibility in the eyes of project sponsors. As a result, their priorities were different from those of the funder and recipient countries, which were more concerned with the long-term impact of the projects.

The fact that sponsors and managers have different perspectives creates a disconnect between strategy formulation and execution.

Focus often creates blinders. One group focuses on strategy formulation, neglecting execution, the other on execution, but losing sight of the underlying strategy. This finding was later confirmed in a literature review on the perception of strategy in project management in 33 scientific and professional articles, including publications in major project management journals (Ika & Saint-Macary, 2011).

The differences among the perspectives of principals, agents, and those reflected in the mandate form one of the premises of this book. This led us to develop an approach where project management is not treated as an isolated activity: it is seen as an essential cornerstone of the organization that should be positioned within the larger context of the strategy of the sponsors.

Fuzzy Projects Succumb to the "Planning Myth"

Prior research suggested that, from the point of view of project managers, project success may depend more on monitoring than planning (Ika et al., 2010). Intrigued by these findings, we conducted a more in-depth case study of the Chad-Cameroon oil pipeline project, which paradoxically turned out to be a project *management success* (delivered on time) but an international *development failure* (did not reduce poverty to the degree expected). This led us to identify what we refer to as "the planning myth"—that is, the generally accepted idea that the (project implementation) plan is sufficient to ensure both the ultimate success of the project and its management. Often, project managers have limited latitude since they are only involved in the implementation phase of the project (Ika & Saint-Macary, 2012). The concept of agent's latitude is explored extensively in this book to better understand the psychosocial dimension of projects.

Since one large organization, the World Bank, funded two-thirds of the projects in this sample, we decided to examine the perspective of their various project sponsors throughout the developing world. We conducted three quantitative studies on a database of nearly 180 projects, with an average budget of more than US$88 million and an average duration of four years in 12 sectors of activity (Ika, 2015, 2018; Ika, Diallo, & Thuillier, 2012). Since all these projects had the same core funder (the World Bank), we expected a certain coherence in the findings.

The results show that while the sponsors acknowledge the project managers' contribution, they perceive design and monitoring as the primary success factors (Ika et al., 2012). Sponsors use two dimensions to determine project success: *management success* and *business case success,* but the former does not necessarily lead to the latter (Ika, 2015). We concluded that a project can be assessed in the short term based on its management success (or failure), and in the long term on its business case success (or failure), leading to the four possible permutations (Ika, 2018) highlighted in Chapter 5. This short-term and long-term reading of project performance plays a significant role in our 3D approach.

Fuzzy Projects Can Be Structurally Complex

Many of the projects we studied are large infrastructural and transformational projects for their host countries. Yet, as shown in a qualitative and quantitative analysis of 30 large dam projects in Morocco with budgets ranging from US$1 million to US$95 million and duration of one to five years, the delivery of these projects was hampered by their structural complexity (Bentahar & Ika, 2020). For example, roller-compacted concrete dams (RCC), which require concrete with a low cement dosage and water content, tend to exhibit a high level of complexity at their construction phase due to the number and variety of project tasks, which are carried out by distinct project teams from different partnering organizations (Bentahar & Ika, 2020).

Fuzzy Projects Are Vulnerable to Biases and Errors

Our quantitative analysis of 85 transportation projects in Hong Kong, totaling US$14 billion, confirms that economic infrastructure projects often exceed their allocated budgets (Love, Sing, Ika, & Newton, 2019). This "behavior" of projects, or their tendency to deviate significantly between their planning and implementation (Ika, Love, & Pinto, 2022), is not limited to economic infrastructure projects. Indeed, a review of 47 social infrastructure projects (e.g., schools, hospitals, libraries) delivered in Hong Kong with a total value of US$6.5 billion (Love, Ika, & Sing, 2022) showed that many experience cost overruns.

Our research also revealed that international development projects (Ika, 2018) and infrastructure projects (Love et al., 2019, 2022) face the "planning fallacy" phenomenon but also its near opposite, the "hiding hand" (i.e., the theory that overly optimistic estimates of costs and benefits at the planning stage create impasses, which in turn motivate project implementers to find creative solutions). Once managers become aware of these human biases, mechanisms can be put into place to improve the chances of project success.

In the dataset of over 2,800 World Bank projects appraised between 1960 and 2019, we found that roughly 60 percent are prone to *optimism bias,* reducing the likelihood of success by up to 20 percent. This means that four-fifths of project underperformance may be explained by factors other than optimism bias, such as complexity and uncertainty (Ika & Feeny, 2022).

We came to understand that biases, such as the planning fallacy, coupled with errors such as scope changes, complexity, or uncertainty, take a toll on most projects (Ika, Love, & Pinto, 2022). This is what happened in high-profile social infrastructure cases like the VA Hospital in Aurora, Colorado (US), and the *Philharmonie de Paris* (France), whose significant cost overruns led to media and legal battles (Ika, Pinto, Love, & Paché, 2022). These insights helped us develop the ideas in Chapters 5 and 10.

Fuzzy Projects Have Vague Objectives and Sociopolitical Complexity

Delving further, we realized that structural complexity is not key to differentiating an international development project from other types, or an economic infrastructure project from a social infrastructure project. Rather, the key differentiating factors are the intangibility of their objectives and the sociopolitical complexity of their context, which includes the degree of divergence between their stakeholders (Ika, Love, & Pinto, 2022; Love et al., 2022).

While the literature typically focuses on the difference between hard and soft projects, the intangible characteristics of international development and social infrastructure projects are better suited to help us understand why they can have successful deliverables yet be deemed failures by key stakeholders. The Chad-Cameroon pipeline project illustrates this paradox.

We also studied four small-scale international development projects (with budgets of less than US$150,000) aimed at municipal government services in Vietnam (administrative reform), Ghana (handwashing), Indonesia (library services), and Sri Lanka (waste management). These public, organizational, and societal change projects had low structural complexity but high sociopolitical complexity (Ika & Donnelly, 2017). This research confirms that it is not the size, scope, or even the structural complexity that matters most when managing a fuzzy project. What matters much more are the intangible aspects, like social and political characteristics.

In another study, we compared two mainstream project management standards, one from the UK Association of Project Management (APM) and the other from the US Project Management Institute (PMI), to five management standards specific to international development projects (e.g., PM4NGOs). The findings are unequivocal. The international development standards emphasize considerations related to the socio-political complexity of projects, such as beneficiary participation, environmental impact, gender, unintended consequences, intangible objectives, evaluation techniques, and cross-cultural issues. However, the mainstream PMI and APM standards focus more on issues related to the structural complexity of projects, such as scoping and scheduling (Munro & Ika, 2020).

We came to realize that fuzzy projects may not fail if properly organized from the start. The insights regarding the sociopolitical complexity of projects played a crucial role in helping us conceptualize *Managing Fuzzy Projects in 3D*. Our research has shown that fuzzy projects may succeed when they have high levels of multi-stakeholder buy-in, collaboration, alignment, and adaptation (Ika & Donnelly, 2017). These insights informed our 3D project management approach by stressing the importance of strategic, political, and psychosocial project alignment. The findings also highlighted the dual challenge of coordination and collaboration required of any manager concerned with complete project success, notably managerial efficiency, project effectiveness, and effectivity of the results.

Securing stakeholders' buy-in and support is a priority. For instance, early consultation with end users will provide insights that will significantly improve planning and monitoring. Furthermore, users who have been consulted are more likely to buy into the project and support it throughout its implementation. To illustrate this point, we use two projects: the first Ford Mustang and the presidential library of President Obama. The first project overcame the odds thanks to astute stakeholder management by Iacocca, then marketing director at Ford. The second, seemingly more straightforward, was nearly derailed because of poor stakeholder assessment and engagement. These cases highlighted the importance of the political aspects of stakeholder management beyond merely rational considerations. The Ford case also demonstrated a successful stakeholder buy-in in project management (Ika, Saint-Macary & Bandé, 2020).

Using a 3D approach sheds light on decision-making in fuzzy projects. Our case study of a large-scale fuzzy project, the 2010 Vancouver Winter Olympics, offers a thorough illustration. We looked at the project through the rational lens of the mandate, the political lens of the principal, and the psychosocial lens of the agent. This three-dimensional approach allowed us to overcome the limitations of a rational and objective perspective of the organization that ignores political, psychosocial, and cultural tensions (Saint-Macary & Ika, 2015).

Collectively, our research findings were informative. They suggest a pressing need to address the complexities and uncertainties of fuzzy projects more adequately. Today's practitioners are hungry for answers as they are confronted with managing the characteristics inherent to fuzzy projects, fulfilling their project mandate, and satisfying both agents and principals.

While traditional project management offers best practice recipes that are effective under normal circumstances, it fails to deliver real, needed change in the fuzzy situations that practitioners increasingly face. Project *organizing* can help succeed more where *best practices* fall short. To this end, we have identified new ways of organizing projects that can contribute to their success, given the right fit. As we saw in Chapter 10, focusing on the initial organizing processes of the project early and on a sustained basis will lay a solid foundation for project managers to better anticipate, understand, and deal with unwelcome surprises down the road.

THEORETICAL BASIS OF THIS BOOK

Managing Fuzzy Projects in 3D will not, by itself, resolve the fundamental issues that have baffled practitioners as to why projects underperform or fail. But it will make us more savvy, able to anticipate issues and deal with the uncertainty that characterizes them. Lenses do not improve eyesight, but they do allow us to see more clearly through the fog of complexity. Our approach stands on the shoulders of the great researchers and thinkers in the field. At this crossroads in the evolution of project management and neighboring areas of theory and practice such as strategy and operations management, the new school of thought intends to contribute to "rethinking," "rebuilding," and even, if necessary, "reinventing" project management, as suggested by many authors

(Morris, 2013; Shenhar & Dvir, 2007; Winter, Smith, Morris, & Cicmil, 2006).

We believe—as does Gareth Morgan (1986)the author of *Images of Organization*, and Winter and Szczepanek (2009), who followed up with *Images of Projects*—that the project is polymorphic and takes on different forms over its lifetime as it is carried out within a unique and evolving context. This assumption poses unusual challenges for project management practitioners, as it means that there are various ways of viewing a project. Furthermore, a project cannot remain fixed (or frozen once and for all) and be envisioned only from one perspective. Not only can it be seen in different ways at any given time, but the same (top or project) manager may also see it in different ways over time.

We use the three perspectives to better grasp the project and its sociopolitical context, and to cope with the complexities and uncertainties of the project (Maylor, Turner, Murray-Webster, 2013). To this end, the book focuses on the rational, political, and psychosocial concerns together. The book draws on a few complementary theories to help guide managing projects in pluralistic contexts (Denis, Dompierre, Langley, & Rouleau, 2011), building on political analysis (March & Olsen, 1976), and the social psychology of organizations (Katz & Kahn, 1978; Weick, 1969). By using agency theory[2] (Jensen & Meckling, 1976) and stakeholder theory (Freeman, 1984), we contrast the perspectives of the mandate, principals, and team members. Then, considering the pluralistic nature of the contexts in which projects occur, we adopt an ecological rationality lens and stress the importance of an "adaptive toolbox" that would fit these underlying contexts or match the rational, political, and psychosocial dimensions. The essence of the theory of ecological rationality is that good project management approaches should match their context of application (Gigerenzer, 2014).

In closing, we would like to share some final thoughts with our project manager Nancy Smart. We hope that they will help her integrate this book's underpinnings with her own knowledge and wisdom, as an experienced practitioner.

A LETTER TO NANCY

Dear Nancy,

Congratulations to you for taking on the ExPlus project and your new employer for choosing you. It looks like a great match! And thanks for reading the early drafts of the book and for sharing your experiences and concerns, as you anticipate the challenges ahead.

The work that project managers like you perform has informed our thinking and approach. As fuzzy projects become more common, exchanges between researchers and practitioners are essential to advance project management knowledge and improve society at large. In the spirit of that partnership, let us tell you how we view our respective contributions to the field of project management.

As an experienced manager, you know that projects are not created equal. Neat projects can be methodically fine-tuned *in vitro* from one perspective. In contrast, fuzzy projects are rather organic and best managed *in vivo* and *in situ,* taking people and context into account and viewing things from many angles.

You hopefully noticed that our theoretical approach is grounded in the work and results achieved in projects, operations, and strategy-making. We kept in mind that "theory," derived from the Greek *theorein,* means "to look at" or "to observe." But it would be useless to observe and not act, just as it would be dangerous to act without thinking.

As we move forward in the twenty-first century, the specialized field of project management must continue to broaden its scope to include insights from other fields, or we risk creating an echo chamber of formulas and ready-made recipes. Our discipline needs to be grounded in economics, logic, and math, of course, but also in social and cognitive sciences, politics, and ecology—with even more perspectives to come, as projects grow into new areas.

Managers like you know intuitively, or learn the hard way, that every activity carried out in an organization, and every managerial decision made has economic, social, and technological aspects. This is because everything done in an organization requires people, resources, and know-how. Managing is complex, and this complexity makes it essential for us to understand the fundamentals of our work as we reexamine the interplay between people, resources, and know-how in new, fuzzy contexts.

In our common endeavor, we all face a major stumbling block: confirmation bias. This bias means we seek, interpret, and retain certain information while overlooking others. We need to make a conscious effort to view situations through different lenses and perspectives because, to a large extent, we only see what we look for. And what we look for is influenced by the paradigms we subscribe to, even unwittingly.

For a better understanding of organizations, we should view them as *instruments*—that is, tools used by owners, managers, employees, customers, and other stakeholders, each for their own benefit. You will come to appreciate their distinct expectations concerning the projects you oversee. This will allow you to assess every problem from their perspectives and enable you to face challenges wisely. This approach will ultimately improve how you manage the project and help you achieve better results for all.

We presented works in cognitive and behavioral sciences demonstrating that project managers are routinely led astray by biases of various types, akin to the optical illusions of all humans. In short, we don't really "see with our eyes" when dealing with unusual and complex situations. Instead, we "see with our brains" and *through* our eyes. So, please view our proposed techniques—such as premortem, ExComm committee, and the organic project life cycle—as corrective lenses. They improve our perceptions and the quality of our decisions, even if they do not change our eyesight and human cognitive processes.

What we can see is primarily a function of where we stand. So, strategists, project managers, sponsors, and customers are bound to view and assess projects quite differently. You will gain insight by putting yourself in their position when you negotiate and review the project mandate, during the premortem, and throughout the whole process of implementing the mandate. It will help you and your team to view the project from different angles and examine it in fuller 3D, beyond the constraints of the rational perspective.

The Vancouver Olympic Games case study taught us that more work should be done upfront, triangulating a project from multiple perspectives (the rational, psychosocial, and political), and that the project life cycle needed to be revisited. We must anticipate the unexpected, not scramble with delayed responses. The decisions that ensue are not isolated acts. They are commitments to action that become intertwined into streams of subsequent decisions within the organization (Langley, Mintzberg, Pitcher, Posada, & Saint-Macary, 1995). We concluded that decision-making should be "opened up" to decision makers at all levels of the organization. In project management, that means you, Nancy. As Mary Parker Follet (1942) noted long ago, decisions need not be "*made by the domination of one actor over another, or by a compromise between the two; they could also integrate their needs into a creative solution that gave more to both of them*"—a win-win solution so to speak.

Finally, we revisited familiar managerial themes like organizations, decision-making, and uncertainty from new perspectives to test and foster a multidimensional approach. We recommend that you use an ecologically rational perspective to help you better anticipate the circumstances under which a project management practice does or does not work. You will need an adaptive toolbox that that should be used according to the surrounding environment. Under complexity and uncertainty, heuristics or proven rules of thumb may help win success.

In closing, you Nancy—not us—are in the best position to know how to use the 3D approach *efficiently* and *effectively,* with the best impact for the organization's ecological system (i.e., with *effectivity*). Like any smart professional, you will adapt your techniques to the circumstances and context of your work. We look forward to seeing how you make out with the ExPlus project, and we wish you the best of luck! We also look forward to learning from you.

Yours truly,
Jan and Lavagnon

REFERENCES

Bentahar, O., & Ika, L. A. (2019). Matching the project manager's roles to project types: Evidence from large dam projects in Africa. *IEEE Transactions on Engineering Managemen*t, *67*(3), 830–845.

Denis, J.-L., Dompierre, G., Langley, A., & Rouleau, L. (2011). Escalating indecision: between reification and strategic ambiguity. *Organization Science, 22*, 225–244.

Follett, M. P. (1942). Constructive conflict. In H. C. Metcalf & L. Urwick (Eds.), *Dynamic administration: The collected papers of Mary Parker Follett*, New York: Harper and Row.

Freeman, J. (1984). *Strategic management: A stakeholder approach.* Pitman.

Gigerenzer, G. (2014). *Risk savvy: How to make good decisions.* Penguin Books.

Ika, L. A. (2012). Project management for development in Africa: Why projects are failing and what can be done about it. *Project Management Journal, 43*(4), 27–41.

Ika, L. A. (2015). Opening the black box of project management. Does project supervision influence project impact. *International Journal of Project Management, 33*, 1111–1123.

Ika, L. A. (2018). Beneficial or detrimental ignorance: The straw man Fallacy of Flyvbjerg's test of Hirschman's Hiding Hand. *World Development, 103*, 369–382.

Ika, L., & Feeny, S. (2022). Optimism Bias and World Bank Project Performance. *The Journal of Development Studies, 58*(12), 2604–2623..

Ika, L. A., & Saint-Macary, J. (June 1–4, 2011). Paradigm lost: The concept of strategy in project organizing. Proceedings of the 11th European Academy of Management Conference, Tallinn, Estonia.

Ika, L. A., & Saint-Macary, J. (2012). The project planning myth in international development. *International Journal of Managing Projects in Business, 5*(3), 420–439.

Ika, L. A., & Donnelly, J. (2017). Success conditions for international development capacity-building projects. *International Journal of Project Management, 35*(1), 44–63.

Ika, L. A., Diallo, A., & Thuillier, D. (2010). Project management in the international industry: The project coordinator's perspective. *International Journal of Managing Projects in Business, 3*(1), 61–93.

Ika, L., Diallo, A., & Thuillier, D. (2012). Critical success factors for World Bank projects: an empirical investigation. *International Journal of Project Management, 30*(1), 105–116.

Ika, L., Saint-Macary, J., & Bandé, A. (2020). Mobilizing stakeholders for project success. *PM World Journal, 9*(8).

Ika, L. A., Söderlund, J., Munro, L. T., & Landoni, P. (2020). Cross-learning between project management and international development: analysis and research agenda. *International Journal of Project Management, 38*(8), 548–558.

Ika, L., Love, P. E. D., & Pinto, J. K. (2022). Moving beyond the planning fallacy: The Emergence of a new principle of project behavior. *IEEE Transactions on Engineering Management, 69*(6), 3310–3325.

Ika, L., Pinto, J. K., Love, P. E. D., & Paché, G. (2022). Bias versus error: why projects fall short. *Journal of Business Strategy*. https://doi.org/10.1108/JBS-11-2021-0190.

Jensen, M., & Meckling, W. (1976). Theory of the firm: Managerial behaviour, agency cost, and ownership structure. *Journal of Financial Economics,* 305–360.

Katz, D., & Kahn, R. L. (1978). *Social psychology of organization*. Wiley.

Langley, A., Mintzberg, H., Pitcher, P., Posada, E., & Saint-Macary, J. (1995). Opening up decision-making: The view from the black stool. *Organization Science, 6*(3), 260–279.

Love, P.E.D., Sing, M.C.P., Ika, L.A., & Newton, S. (2019). The cost performance of transportation infrastructure projects: The fallacy of the Planning Fallacy account. *Transportation Research A: Policy and Practice, 122*, 1-20.

Love, P. E. D., Ika, L. A., & Sing, M. C. P. (2022). Does the planning fallacy prevail in social infrastructure projects? Empirical evidence and competing explanations. *IEEE Transactions on Engineering Management, 69*(6), 2588–2602.

March, J. G., & Olsen, J. P. (1976). *Ambiguity and choice in organizations.* Universitetsforlaget.

Morgan, G. (1986). *Images of organizations.* Sage.

Morris, P. W. G. (2013). *Reconstructing project management.* John Wiley & Sons.

Munro, L. T., & Ika, L. (2020). Guided by the beauty of our weapons: Comparing project management standards inside and outside international development. *Development in Practice, 30*(7), 934–952.

Saint-Macary, J. (1994) Dynamique sociale et stratégie d'entreprise : les cas de Monenco, SNC et Lavalin. *Gestion* (Winter).

Saint-Macary, J., & Ika, L. A. (2015). Atypical perspectives on project management: moving beyond the rational to the political and the psychosocial. *International Journal of Project Organisation and Management, 7*(3), 236–250.

Shenhar, A., & Dvir, D. (2007). *Reinventing project management.* Harvard Business School Press.

Weick, K. E. (1969). *Social psychology of organizing.* Addison-Wesley.

Winter, M., Smith, C., Morris, P., & Cicmil, S. (2006). Directions for future research in project management: The main finding of a UK government-funded research network. *International Journal of Project Management, 24,* 638–649.

Winter, M., & Szczepanek, T. (2009). *Images of projects.* Gower.

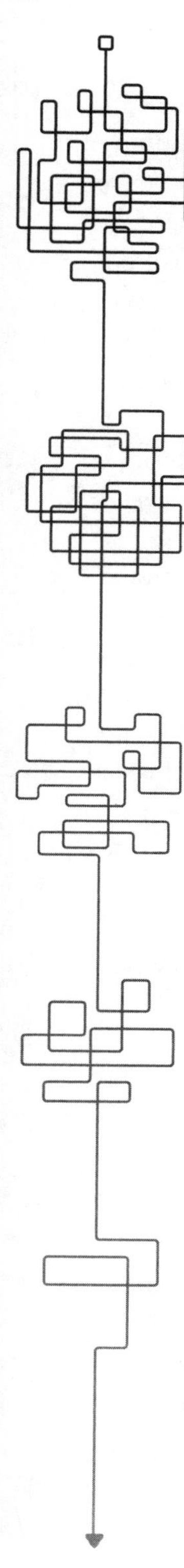

AFTERWORD

By Antonio Nieto-Rodriguez

MANAGING FUZZY PROJECTS IN 3D

I finished reading *Managing Fuzzy Projects in 3D* with great interest. This book offers an excellent deep dive into what Lavagnon and Jan aptly call "fuzzy projects." That is, projects that hold intangible, unclear, unstable goals or take place in sociopolitically complex contexts. I highly recommend *Managing Fuzzy Projects in 3D* as it is timely and extremely useful for today's project managers and sponsors.

JUST IN TIME

Projects change the world. Projects make impossible dreams possible.

The behavioral and social sciences endorse the idea that there are a few ways of working and collaborating that are particularly motivating and inspiring for people working on a project. These are that a project should have ambitious goals, a higher purpose, and a clear deadline. You have probably noticed that what people tend to remember most clearly from their entire careers is the projects they work on—often the successful ones, but also the failed ones.

According to recent research, the number of individuals working in project-based roles will increase from 66 million (in 2017) to 88 million (forecast 2027). The value of economic activity worldwide that is project oriented will grow from US$12 trillion (in 2013) to US$20 trillion (forecast 2027).[1] Those are millions of projects requiring millions of project managers per year. This is what I describe as the "project economy," a term I used in my 2018 book, *The Project Revolution, How to Succeed in a Project Driven World.*

This silent disruption is impacting not only organizations, but also the very nature of work and our entire professional lives. The traditional one-company career path of previous generations is now a distant memory. Today, people happily and fruitfully change jobs and employers a number of times during their careers. I believe that this trend will accelerate, and that professional careers will become a sequence of projects. Another notable trend related to this is the growth in self-employment—according to Quartz at Work, an HR consulting company, the number of Americans working for themselves could triple by 2020.[2] They will be, effectively, managing a portfolio of projects.

A GLOBAL REVOLUTION

The more you look, the more projects you will see. On my desk, I have a bushel of examples.

For instance, in December 2016, the US Senate unanimously approved the Program Management Improvement and Accountability Act (PMIAA),[3] which will enhance accountability and best practices in project and program management throughout the US federal government. The PMIAA will reform federal program management policy in four important ways:

- Creating a formal job series and career path for program and project managers in the federal government
- Developing a standards-based program and project management policy across the federal government
- Recognizing the essential role of executive sponsorship and engagement by designating a senior executive in federal agencies to be responsible for program and project management policy and strategy
- Sharing knowledge of successful approaches to program and project management through an interagency council on program and project management

In the United Kingdom, on January 6, 2017, the Association for Project Management was awarded a Royal Charter.[4] The charter recognizes the project management profession, rewards the association that champions its cause, and provides opportunities for those who practice its disciplines. The receipt of a Royal Charter marks a significant achievement in the evolution of project management and will have positive implications for those who make, and seek to make, a career in this field.

The Richards Group is the largest independently owned ad agency in the United States, with billings of US$1.28 billion, revenue of US$170 million, and more than 650 employees. Stan Richards, its founder and CEO, removed almost all of its management layers and job titles, leaving only that of project manager.[5]

In another example, in 2016, Nike was looking to fill a vacancy at its European headquarters. The job description was corporate strategy & development manager for the European, Middle East, & Africa (EMEA) Region. Such a job would traditionally entail strategic planning, market analysis, and competitive intelligence competencies. To my surprise, instead the job was described as "project management." This meant that Nike was looking for someone who could implement transversal and strategic projects for its strategy function. This was a clear shift of focus and culture: from planning and day-to-day activities to implementation and projects. Nike is not alone—I have seen similar job descriptions for strategy functions at UPS, Amazon, and others.

IN THE PROJECT ECONOMY, WE ARE ALL PROJECT MANAGERS

For centuries, learning was achieved by memorizing hefty books and mountains of written material. Today, the leading educational systems, starting from early ages, apply the concept of teaching projects. Applying theories and experimenting through projects has proven to be a much better learning method, and will become the norm. *Managing Fuzzy Projects in 3D* is very well suited in this context.

Not so long ago, professional careers were made in only one organization. Throughout the twentieth century, most people worked for a single company. Today we are likely to work for several companies, and at some point, we will most probably become self-employed, working primarily on projects. This sort of career is best approached as a set of projects in which we apply the lessons we have learned from previous jobs, companies, and industries while developing ourselves for our next career move, often not known in advance.

The emergence of projects as the economic engine of our times is silent but incredibly disruptive and powerful. Today every organization, public or private, operates in an environment subject to continual and sometimes disruptive levels of change. For example, political change can expose a business to new sources of competition. Markets may be open or closed. New game-changing regulations might be introduced without warning. There is, obviously, technological innovation, particularly associated with the internet and digital technology. To this can be added social shifts, with fluid customer attitudes to the environment, health, or social responsibility. Growing the business, boosting its profitability, or securing its continuation depends on anticipating, managing, and driving change, which in turn depends on initiating and successfully completing projects.

This extreme uncertainty generates a difficult operating environment for leaders and organizations. The yearly cycle that worked for almost a century no longer applies. The radically transformed circumstances call for new ways of working, more-agile operating models, and new forms of leadership. Organizational structures, processes, and systems need to be adapted, too, to ensure the sustainability of the organization and to take advantage of new opportunities brought by the deeply changeable world.

A USEFUL READING FOR PRACTITIONERS AND POLICYMAKERS

Lavagnon and Jan's book takes an innovative, three-dimensional view on managing fuzzy projects and is a timely resource, full of practical tools and real examples. Since it addresses many concerns you have undoubtedly felt, it will strengthen your knowledge and skills and help you thrive in a project-driven world. With three dimensions, not just one, this book offers a more balanced way to manage for success in the project economy.

One of the book's interesting ideas is that there is a difference between "project management" and "managing projects." The former takes the plan as the cornerstone of the delivery approach. In nearly ideal circumstances, it delivers quality projects on time and within budget. But in the face of complexity and uncertainty, it fails to meet the expectations of project sponsors, managers, team members, and end users. Managing in 3D is all about dealing with conflicting stakeholder expectations and the evolving context of project delivery.

We undertake projects to create value for organizations, project sponsors, and a host of internal and external stakeholders. Therefore, we need to differentiate traditional, "neat" projects from "fuzzy" projects. The former have clear, measurable, stable goals and are implemented by homogeneous teams. Conversely, fuzzy projects have unclear and evolving goals with multiple stakeholders, inside and outside the project. Think about COVID-19 vaccine development projects, mass vaccination rollouts, major infrastructure or climate-related projects. They all involve many levels of government, the public, and the scientific and business communities. Managing these projects means dealing with conflicting expectations.

I agree with Lavagnon and Jan: to manage fuzzy projects successfully we need to overcome the limitations of the rational approach (which only works well for neat projects). To this end, sponsors and managers must understand and openly acknowledge the political and social dimensions of fuzzy projects. I am happy to see that the book puts team members, sponsors, and end users at the heart of managing projects.

In this era of sustainable development, where meeting the triple bottom line of people, planet, and profit is becoming crucial, savvy project sponsors and managers will want to heed the insights this book provides into the sociopolitical complexity of fuzzy projects. This book is a must-read—perhaps, the world's premier book on managing fuzzy projects!

There are fewer "low-cost" ways of working more inclusive, impactful, motivating, and inspiring than being part of a project with an ambitious goal, a higher purpose, and a clear fixed deadline.

Antonio Nieto-Rodriguez

World Champion in Project Management | Thinkers50 & Top 30 Global Gurus | PMI Fellow & Past Chair | Professor | HBR Author of Project Management Handbook | Founder Strategy Implementation Institute | Founder Projects & Co | Director PMO | Marshall Goldsmith Executive Coach

APPENDICES

APPENDIX 3.1 Project Charter

1. **General Project Information**
   Specify the project name, ID, client organization, sponsor, name of the drafter of the document, and its version number.
2. **Stakeholders and Expectations**
   Identify key stakeholders, their positions and expectations.
3. **Overview of the Project**
   Provide a brief overview of the project.
4. **Organizational Context, Needs, and Objectives of the Project**
   Briefly present the organizational context of the project and its initiation; state the need as either a problem to be solved or an opportunity to be seized by the organization; and specify the strategic objective, the specific objective, and the planned benefits of the project.
5. **Project Description**
   Briefly present the project: scope (the amount of work required to complete it, what is part of the scope and what is not), deliverables (the products and services that the project must provide), and constraints (the boundary conditions that the project must stay within).

6. **Assumptions**
Specify the assumptions or statements that are taken for granted or made in absence of fact in the decision to charter the project.

7. **Milestones**
List the milestones, their due dates, and who is responsible for them.

8. **Key Human and Material Resources and Budget**
Briefly estimate the human and material resources needed, and establish the initial budget and source of funding for the project.

9. **Project Risks**
Provide statements of issues or things that may go wrong in the project.

10. **Governance and Organization**
Provide a graphic representation of the project's organizational structure and clarify the decision-making process: who will make the decisions and identify roles and responsibilities.

11. **Strategic Positioning and Adaptation of the Project**
Explain how the idea behind the project is aligned with the organization's strategy (strategic positioning); explain how the project will deliver benefits and value for end users, and why its deliverables are superior to existing products and services (competitive advantage or value); briefly describe how the project will be implemented, and articulate how it will stay aligned with the environment and adapted to changing circumstances (project implementation approach and strategic adaptation).

12. **Approval of the Charter**
Obtain signatures from appropriate authorities, including the project sponsor and project manager.

APPENDIX 3.2 Business Case

1. **General Project Information**
   Specify the project name, the intent of the business case (is it for approval? for information only?) and provide a brief overview of the project.

2. **Organizational Context**
   Provide a brief overview of the organization initiating the project: its strategic objectives; key activities, projects, and programs; main stakeholders; and human and financial resources capabilities.

3. **Justification for Undertaking the Project**
   Articulate the project needs (problem to solve or opportunity to seize), strategic objective, specific objective, and spin-offs.

4. **Project Description**
   Provide a scope statement, including what is in and what is out of scope for the project; specify its deliverables and constraints.

5. **Project Options Analysis and Concept**
   List the evaluation criteria and analyze options, including the status quo and their benefits, costs, and risks. Then select a concept (the best option) for the project.

6. **Strategic Alignment and Competitive Advantage/Value**
   Explain how the project will deliver benefits and value for end users, and why its deliverables are superior to existing products and services.

7. **Key Stakeholders and Expectations**
   Identify key stakeholders, their positions and expectations (to be specified, especially when the project does not include a project charter).

8. **Governance and Organization**

   Provide a graphic representation of the project's organizational structure and clarify the decision-making process: who will make the decisions, and identify roles and responsibilities (to be specified, especially when the project does not include a project charter).

9. **Implementation Approach and Strategic Adaptation**

   Briefly describe how the project will be done, and explain how it will stay aligned with the environment and adapted to changing circumstances (to be specified, especially when the project does not include a project charter).

10. **Approval of the Business Case**

    Obtain signatures from appropriate senior executives, including the project sponsor.

APPENDIX 3.3 Project Frame

1. **Project Name**
   Summarize the project objectives with an inspiring title.
2. **Objectives and Scope**
   Clearly articulate what we want to do and when.
3. **Costs and Benefits**
   Determine and analyze the project's short- and long-term costs and benefits.
4. **Milestones and Responsibilities for Implementation**
   Specify the work to be done and how to do it, and determine individual responsibilities.
5. **Progress Monitoring**
   Describe mechanisms for progress monitoring and reporting.
6. **Potential Problems and Risk Management**
   Anticipate what might go wrong in the project.

Source: Adapted from Lepsinger (2010).

APPENDIX 6.1 Key PM Professional Associations: Standards & Certifications

PROFESSIONAL ASSOCIATIONS	STANDARDS	CERTIFICATIONS
Project Management Institute (PMI), the largest project management association	*A Guide to the Project Management Body of Knowledge (PMBOK®)*	Project Management Professional (PMP® PMI)
International Project Management Association (IPMA), the oldest project management association	Individual Competence Baseline (ICB®)	Individual Competence Baseline (ICB® IPMA)
Association of Project Management (APM), "the only chartered body for the project profession"	Association of Project Management Body of Knowledge®	Project Management Qualification® APM
International Center for Complex Project Management (ICCPM), with its unique focus on navigating complexity	Complex Project Managers Competency Standards	Complex Project Management Competency
Project Management for Non-Governmental Organizations (PM4NGOs), dedicated to managing international development programs and projects within the NGO context	A Guide to the PMD Pro (Project Management for Development Professionals)	PMD Pro (Project Management for Development Professionals)
Project Management for Development (PM4DEV), an industry leader in managing international development programs and projects	Project Management for Development (PM4DEV)	Certified Development Project Manager® (CDPM)
Project Management Association of Japan (PMAJ), one of the most influential associations in Asia	Program & Project Management for Enterprise Innovation (P2M)	P2M
Axelos, a world-renowned provider of global best practice	Projects in Controlled Environments (PRINCE2®)	Projects in Controlled Environments (PRINCE2®)

APPENDIX 6.2 Project Management Periodicals

International Journal of Project Management (IJPM)
The #1 ranked journal; published in collaboration with the IPMA and APM

Project Management Journal (PMJ)
The #2 ranked journal; the research journal of the PMI

International Journal of Managing Projects in Business
The #3 ranked journal

International Journal of Project Organization and Management
Published since 2008

European Project Management Journal
Published by the Serbian Project Management Association

Project Leadership and Society
A sister open access journal of IJPM

Journal of Modern Project Management
A periodical published by Mundo Press since 2013

Project Management Research and Practice
A student-centric, open access journal

PM World Journal
A non-refereed online, professional, and knowledge-sharing publication

PM Network
A professional magazine published by the PMI

APPENDIX 6.3 Project Management Plan*

1. General Project Information
Specify the project name, ID, client organization, sponsor, name of the drafter of the document, and its version number.

2. Stakeholders and Expectations
Identify key stakeholders, their positions and expectations.

3. Overview of the Project
Provide a brief overview of the project.

4. Organizational Context, Needs, and Objectives of the Project
Briefly present the organizational context of the project and its initiation; state the need as either a problem to be solved or an opportunity to be seized by the organization; and specify the strategic objective, the specific objective, and the planned benefits of the project.

5. Project Description
Briefly present the project: scope (the amount of work required to complete it; what is part of the scope, and what is not), deliverables (the products and services that the project must provide), and constraints (the boundary conditions that the project must stay within).

6. Assumptions
Specify the assumptions or statements that are taken for granted or made in absence of fact in the decision to charter the project.

7. Milestones
List the milestones, their due dates, and who is responsible for them.

8. Key Human and Material Resources and Budget
Briefly estimate the human and material resources needed and establish the initial budget and source of funding for the project.

* The plan includes updates on steps #1 to #11 in the charter, and steps #12 to #14.

9. **Project Risks**
   Provide statements of issues or things that may go wrong in the project.

10. **Governance and Organization**
    Provide a graphic representation of the project's organizational structure and clarify the decision-making process: who will make the decisions, and identify roles and responsibilities.

11. **Strategic Positioning and Adaptation of the Project**
    Explain how the idea behind the project is aligned with the organization's strategy (strategic positioning); how the project will deliver benefits and value for end users, and why its deliverables are superior to existing products and services (competitive advantage or value); briefly describe how the project will be implemented; and articulate how it will stay aligned with the environment and adapted to changing circumstances (project implementation approach and strategic adaptation).

12. **Project Work Plan**
    Outline the work plan using a Gantt chart with activities, their start and end dates, milestones, and resources involved in each activity.

13. **Project Monitoring Measures**
    For project tracking purposes, specify how the project schedule, costs, and quality will be monitored; who will take the lead for reporting on the project; and how often this reporting should occur.

14. **Approval of the Plan**
    Obtain signatures from appropriate authorities, including the project sponsor and project manager.

APPENDIX 9.1 A Scale to Measure the Complexity of Fuzzy Projects

This tool, developed by Maylor et al. (2013), consists of binary statements (yes/no) that practitioners can use to assess the complexity of the project. The first 21 statements measure structural complexity, and the last 11 statements capture sociopolitical complexity. Changes in complexity situations described in Statements 1–32 provide information on emerging complexity.

Assessment of Structural Complexity

1. The vision and benefits of the project are clear.
2. Success measures for the work are defined jointly with the client.
3. The technology is familiar to us.
4. The commercial arrangements are familiar to us.
5. The scope can be well defined.
6. Acceptance criteria for quality and regulatory requirements can be well defined.
7. A schedule and resource plan can be well defined.
8. The supply chain is in place.
9. Lines of responsibility for tasks and deliverables can be defined.
10. Accurate, timely, and comprehensive data reporting is possible.
11. Existing management tools can support the work.
12. Sufficient people with the right skills are available.
13. Managers have adequate control of human resources (i.e., direct reporting).
14. Key people are wholly committed to the work.
15. Integration across multiple technical disciplines is not required.
16. The budget is sufficient for the task.
17. The budget is flexible.
18. The work will be carried out in a single country/time zone/language/currency.

19. The work is independent of other projects and business-as-usual operations.
20. The pace can be sustained and is achievable.
21. Resources (e.g., test facilities, equipment) will be available when needed.

Assessment of Sociopolitical Complexity

22. The work has clear sponsorship consistent with its importance.
23. The business case for the work is clear.
24. The goals for the project are aligned with the organization's strategy.
25. Your senior management supports the work.
26. Team members are motivated and function well as a team.
27. Managers are experienced in this kind of work.
28. The work involves no significant organizational/cultural change.
29. The work will be unaffected by significant organizational/cultural change.
30. The external stakeholders (i.e., not immediate team members) are aligned, supportive, and committed to the project and have sufficient time for the work.
31. The external stakeholders (i.e., not immediate team members) have a realistic, shared understanding of the implications of the work.
32. The core project team has the authority to make decisions.

The assessment of emerging complexity is judged by the extent to which the complexity situations inherent in Statements 1–32 remain stable or do not change. Therefore, each dimension of project complexity can be measured on a "low-medium-high" scale. Complexity is high on a dimension if most of the responses are negative or there are only a few complex situations of concern.

NOTES

CHAPTER 1

1. In reference to Icarus, a hero of Greek mythology who escaped from the labyrinth where he was imprisoned by constructing a pair of wings out of beeswax and feathers and flying away. Emboldened by his success, he ignored his father's warnings and flew higher and higher. He got too close to the sun, the wax melted, and his wings fell off. He fell into the sea, which became known as the Icarian Sea.
2. In the context of agency theory, the term "agent" is used in the etymological sense of "performer" and "actor."

CHAPTER 2

1. Characters of the famous British novel written by Daniel Defoe in 1719. It tells the fictional story of Robinson Crusoe, shipwrecked for nearly 30 years on a deserted Caribbean island. Alone for years, Robinson Crusoe manages to survive thanks to the natural resources of the island and the supplies recovered from the wreck of his ship. But one day, a group of warriors bring a prisoner to the island. Robinson frees him and saves him from a gruesome death. He names him Friday and makes him his servant. Together they hunt, raise livestock, and cultivate the land. An economy with one organization, fruitful and hierarchical, is thus born on the island.
2. https://financialpost.com/transportation/bombardiers-biggest-gamble-how-everything-went-so-wrong-with-the-cseries-dream.
3. https://montrealgazette.com/news/local-news/what-went-wrong-at-bombardier-everything.
4. https://www.reuters.com/article/us-bombardier-cseries-delays-idUSKBN1HI243.
5. https://www.whitehouse.gov/build-back-better/ (accessed 13 February 2022).

6. https://www.theguardian.com/cities/ng-interactive/2018/jul/30/what-china-belt-road-initiative-silk-road-explainer (accessed 10 July 2019).
7. https://www.reuters.com/world/india/india-targets-infrastructure-spending-growth-budget-2022-02-01/ (accessed 13 February 2022).

CHAPTER 3

1. The emphasis here is on clearly formulated strategies. But it is well known that a strategy can be successful even if it is not explicitly formulated. Indeed, as Bhide (2000) notes, 72 percent of the founders of Inc. 500 companies—the 500 fastest growing companies in the United States—did not have a formal and explicit strategic plan before they started.
2. For a succinct and revealing review of the reasons for failure, see Rivkin (2006).
3. https://simpleflying.com/united-airlines-ted-subsidiary/ (accessed 15 February 2022).
4. The Pygmalion effect is a psychological phenomenon in which high expectations lead to improved performance. In pedagogy, Rosenthal and Jacobson (1968) show that teacher expectations, whether positive or negative, impact their students' performance.
5. https://www.theguardian.com/technology/2019/sep/18/fairphone-3-review-ethical-phone (accessed 15 February, 2022).
6. https://www.irishtimes.com/business/technology/fairphone-4-eco-friendly-model-can-be-repaired-at-home-1.4754290 (accessed 15 February, 2022).
7. FIFA faced opposition from its players regarding the 2010 World Cup in South Africa regarding the ball—*Jabulani* (Zulu for "to be happy"). In response, FIFA took the bull by the horns and for over two years, they asked no less than 600 players from more than 30 professional clubs and 10 national teams to evaluate the ball.

CHAPTER 5

1. Although there are more statistics for large projects, research indicates that small projects also face difficulties and underperformance.
2. Roads have the lowest average cost overrun at about 24 percent, and dams the highest at about 96 percent, according to Flyvbjerg (2016). These statistics seem exaggerated to other researchers who have studied transportation projects. For example, one study finds an average cost overrun of 13 percent for various transportation projects (Love et al., 2019).

CHAPTER 6

1. We thank Jack Meredith, professor emeritus of Operations Management, USA for bringing this example to our attention.
2. The correct answer is 5 cents for the ball and \$1.05 for the bat = a total of \$1.10 and a difference of \$1.00.
3. *Formal rationality* is based on rules, laws, statutes, forms of regulation, and so on, operating in an impersonal way. *Substantive rationality*—favored by classical economics—takes into account personal values but assumes that the decision maker has *all the information necessary* to make the optimal decision. For their part, the proponents of *procedural rationality*, propose a more plausible decision-making process in which individuals are happy to settle for *satisficing*, nonoptimal solutions (Weber, 2021).

CHAPTER 7

1. This is an excerpt from the article by Ika, Saint-Macary, & Bandé (2020).
2. *Washington Times,* February 28, 2018, available at https://www.washingtontimes.com/news/2018/feb/28/obama-cheers-gentrification-as-plans-for-president/.
3. The opening paragraphs of the chapter, and the reflections that follow, draw on an article published by the authors (see Saint-Macary & Ika, 2015).
4. "Compromise" is about adapting to a goal or meaning different from the one you originally had (Sense 2003; Sense & Antoni, 2003).
5. "Influence" is the ability to obtain an outcome from others without exercising power over them (Sense, 2003; Sense & Antoni, 2003).
6. "Power" is the ability of an individual to exercise his or her will over others (Buchanan & Badham, 1999). Managers often derive their power from their position or title (in the organization's hierarchy), or from the status given to them by the nature, importance and visibility of the tasks assigned to them (Pinto, 2000).
7. For the purposes of this discussion, we borrow from the work of Saint-Macary and Ika (2015) regarding the Vancouver Olympics.
8. We use the word "explanation" in its general sense, i.e., a clarification or development intended to understand a phenomenon. Therefore, we do not assume any epistemological or methodological posture when we refer to "explanations." However, we believe that it would be appropriate to speak of "explanation" from a rational perspective, and "understanding" from a political and psychosocial perspective.

While the former focuses its attention on the project as an object (*mandate*), the latter two are essentially interested in the subjects who act (*principals* or *agents*) (Saint-Macary & Ika, 2015).

9. Georgian luge athlete Nodar Kumaritashvili.
10. *Calgary Herald,* Dec. 18, 2010.
11. "In case of divergence between the English and French texts, the French text shall prevail" (see Article 24 of the Olympic Charter).

CHAPTER 8

1. The image of the organization (or a project) as an instrument used by agents may surprise some, but it is not unprecedented. In fact, it is faithful to the etymology of the term "organization," which comes from the Latin and Greek words (*organum* and *organon*) that designate respectively an instrument or an organ of the body.
2. Joseph Heller told the story of a successful World War II pilot who no longer wanted to fly combat missions because he wanted to succeed so badly that he came to fiercely resist failure.
3. *Forbes,* 8 September 2021.
4. Mintzberg later introduced *the missionary organization and the political organization*, where the standardization of norms is the main coordination mechanism.
5. This section builds on an article published by the authors using the Vancouver Olympics case (see Saint-Macary & Ika, 2015).
6. "Premier 'rigged' contest for 2010 games CEO, backs inferior candidate" (Furlong & Mason. 2011).

CHAPTER 9

1. The hammer analogy is generally attributed to the famous American psychologist Abraham Maslow (Maslow, 1966).
2. We would like to thank our colleague Michel Paisible for stressing the importance of this characteristic of nonprofit organizations.
3. We take complexity to be a property of a project that consists of many varied parts with a multitude of existing and emerging interrelations, which make it difficult to understand, foresee and control its overall behavior. Or the degree to which managers understand the cause-and-effect relationships between the different parts of the project (Snowden & Boone, 2007; Ika et al., 2021).
4. We use the term "dimensions" to keep things simple, though it suggests we may be able to break down or reduce complexity into elements, which is not always the case. Otherwise, we would prefer the

term "manifestations" of complexity, which better suits the holistic and emergent character of complexity. We would like to thank Dr. Stephane Tywoniak for sharing this nuance with us.

5. The four basic scenarios are not meant to be exhaustive. To make projects come to fruition, agents may seek out principals (e.g., Christopher Columbus or any modern startup looking for sponsors) and principals may become agents through personal involvement (e.g., Steve Jobs in all of Apple's key projects) or through an intermediary (such as a politician). In so doing, these "agents-principals" or "principals-agents" act as both project sponsors and project managers.
6. In this section, we draw on the reflections on stakeholders and their buy-in set out in Ika et al. (2020).

CHAPTER 10

1. Executive Committee of the National Security Council
2. This is the title of the paper by researchers Maylor and Turner (2017).
3. We adopt this formula from Love, Ika, Matthews, Li, and Fang (2022).
4. All of these systems are part of an even larger society, the *social system,* which itself is part of a *global system*.
5. In the face of the complexity of the COVID-19 vaccination program, shared leadership made a difference. It took a combination of vertical leadership (e.g., at the government level) and horizontal leadership (within the vaccination teams in the field) to get it done (for more on vertical and horizontal leadership, read Müller et al., 2018).

AFTERWORD

1. *Project Management Job Growth and Talent Gap Report 2017–2027* (Project Management Institute, 2017), accessed 1 October 2018, https://www.pmi.org/-/media/pmi/documents/public/pdf/learning/job-growth-report.pdf?sc_lang_temp=en.
2. "The Number of Americans Working for Themselves could Triple by 2020" (Quartz at Work), last modified 21 February 2018, https://work.qz.com/1211533/the-number-of-americans-working-for-themselves-could-triple-by-2020.
3. "US Senate Unanimously Approves the Program Management Improvement and Accountability Act" (Project Management Institute), last modified 1 December 2016, https://www.pmi.org/about/press-media/press-releases/senate-program-management-act.

4. "APM Receives Its Royal Charter" (Association for Project Management), last modified 6 January 2017, https://www.apm.org.uk/news/apm-receives-its-royal-charter.
5. "Stan Richards's Unique Management Style" (Inc.), accessed 1 October 2018, https://www.inc.com/magazine/201111/stan-richards-unique-management-style.html.

INDEX

ABOUT THE AUTHORS

Lavagnon Ika is professor of project management and the founding director of the Major Projects Observatory at the Telfer School of Management at the University of Ottawa. A keynote speaker, he has taught project management around the world for the past 20 years. He has been a visiting professor at the Skema Business School in France, the Swinburne Business School in Australia, the Institute of Public Project and Cost Engineering of the Tianjin University of Technology in China, the African School of Economics in Benin, the CESAG Business School in Senegal, the World Bank in Washington, DC (as a World Bank Fellow), and the Gordon Institute of Business Science of the University of Pretoria, South Africa (as an Andrew Carnegie Fellow).

He has led many project management workshops in organizational settings and advised project managers and senior business leaders in his consulting work. His clients include public sector departments such as Global Affairs Canada, Transport Canada, Justice Canada, the World Bank, and the African Capacity Building Foundation (ACBF), as well as private businesses.

Professor Ika is an associate editor of the prestigious *International Journal of Project Management* and a member of the academic boards of renowned international project management associations such as the US-based Project Management Institute

(PMI) and the Europe-based International Project Management Association (IPMA).

He has published more than 50 research articles in the fields of project management, engineering management, transport, operations management, and international development. His writings have been critical in shaping project management research and education, notably on curbing cost overruns and benefit shortfalls, and tackling the grand challenges of climate change, pandemics, and global poverty. He has also been influential in managing and leading projects in Africa. He is a leading contributor to a handbook on projects that experience cost overruns and benefit shortfalls, to be published by Cambridge University Press (UK) in 2023.

Professor Ika's work has earned him three Emerald Publishing House Awards of Excellence (Best Reviewer Award in 2018, Outstanding Paper in 2017, and Highly Commended Paper Award in 2011), as well as three IPMA Global Awards of Excellence (Research Award in 2017 and 2022, and Contribution of a Young Researcher Award in 2012). He was awarded the Telfer Innovative Researcher Award in 2017 and the Telfer Established Researcher Award in 2021. His articles have also received praise from practitioners. Professor Ika can be contacted at ika@telfer.uottawa.ca

Jan Saint-Macary is professor of strategy and management at the Université du Québec (UQO), where he founded and directed two executive MBA programs. Born in Haiti, he holds a BA in Economics from Drew University, New Jersey, a Graduate Diploma in Management, an MBA, and a PhD from the Montreal joint program of McGill University, Concordia University, HEC, and UQAM. He was awarded merit scholarships at Drew University (USA), and Doctoral Excellence Awards from the Government of Canada, as well as an Alcan Scholarship for Excellence.

He began his career in international banking at First National State Bank in the United States, and held other managerial positions at the Royal Bank of Canada, before joining the academic world. Over the past 30 years, he has taught strategy and project management, and worked as a consultant in North America, China, Belgium, Poland, Lithuania, Ivory Coast, and the Caribbean. He has been a keynote speaker for the highest-ranking executives of the Desjardins Group, the National Bank of Canada, and the Laurentian Bank. He works pro bono for SMEs and is a board member of not-for-profit organizations in the field of culture, education, and reforestation, in the United States, Canada, and the Caribbean.

His research interests are in strategy, project management, decision-making, negotiation, and financial institutions. He has been a guest editor in a special edition of *Why do projects fail in Africa?* in the *Journal of African Business*. He has coauthoreda major publication with Henry Mintzberg, a world-leading expert on management; presided over the 1st International Project Management Congress at the Université du Québec; and coauthored a book with Benoit Bazoge on the strategy of financial institutions published and used by the Institute of Canadian Bankers. He can be reached at jan.saint-macary@uqo.ca.

He and his wife, Rebecca, live in Ottawa. Their two brilliant children are in Montreal and do not visit often enough.